Curzon in India

1. Achievement

DAVID DILKS

Curzon in India

1. Achievement

Rupert Hart-Davis LONDON 1969

© David Dilks 1969
First published 1969
Rupert Hart-Davis Ltd
3 Upper James Street
Golden Square, London W1
Printed in Great Britain
by Ebenezer Baylis and Son Ltd
The Trinity Press
Worcester and London
SBN: 246 63885 0

For My Parents

Contents

List of Illustrations

The frontispiece is reproduced by kind permission of the Gernsheim Collection, Humanities Research Center, The University of Texas at Austin; the visit to Cutch by kind permission of the National Army Museum; and all other illustrations by kind permission of the India Office Library.

Foreword

THESE TWO VOLUMES do not pretend to provide a comprehensive record of Lord Curzon's time in India. The mass of relevant material is now so huge that four or five books would be needed. Moreover, a number of monographs and studies which have appeared during the last few years, or which will shortly be published, cover particular aspects of the Viceroyalty. Mr Kenneth Rose's study of *The Young Curzon* is due from the press soon and Sir Philip Magnus is engaged on a biography. Dr John Lydgate's thesis on the question of Indian military administration will, I hope, be available in book form. I have felt free, therefore, to follow a rather episodic and selective treatment, concentrating on those issues which have interested me most; Curzon's methods of administration, his relations with the India Office, the Cabinet and the Monarch, the affairs of Persia, Afghanistan and Tibet, the rending quarrel with Kitchener.

The process of gathering material has extended over a period of some seven years. In that time I have contracted many debts; to Miss Agatha Ramm of Somerville College, who first awakened my interest in Curzon's Indian career, to Dr C. C. Davies, under whose genial and expert guidance the detailed studies began, to the Warden and Fellows of St Antony's College for providing agreeable and scholarly surroundings. For much forbearance and help I am grateful to the Librarians and staffs of the Royal Archives, the Royal Commonwealth Society, the India Office Library, the London Library, the British Museum, the Public Record Office, the London School of Economics, the National Library of Scotland, the University Libraries at Cambridge and Birmingham, the Library of Christ Church, Oxford.

Lady Alexandra Metcalfe, the late Sir Harold Nicolson, Sir Stanley Reed, the late Lord Halifax, Sir Philip Magnus, Lord Hailey and Mr Kenneth Rose have helped me with recollections and information about Lord Curzon. Lord Scarsdale, Mr and Mrs Julian Amery, Lord Lansdowne, Lord Salisbury, Mr and Mrs Murray Lawrence and Lord Rennell have allowed scrutiny of manuscripts in their possession and have offered their hospitality. To them all my warm thanks are due.

I acknowledge with gratitude the gracious permission of Her Majesty the Queen to make use of material from the Royal Archives at Windsor Castle. Unpublished Crown-copyright material in the India Office Library transcribed in this book appears by permission of the Secretary of State for Commonwealth affairs. Transcripts of Crown-copyright records held in the Public Record Office appear by permission of the Controller of Her Majesty's Stationery Office. For permission to use other copyright material I am indebted to Lord Scarsdale and the Kedleston Trustees, the Army Museums Ogilby Trust, the British Museum, the Earl of Selborne, the Marquess of Salisbury, Murray Lawrence, Esq., the Earl of Midleton, Earl Kitchener, Lord Ampthill, the Earl of Antrim, Dame Eileen Younghusband, and Lady Napier.

Principal Characters

AMPTHILL, Baron: Governor of Madras, 1899–1906; Viceroy, 1904.

ARNOLD-FORSTER, Rt Hon. H. O.: Parliamentary Secretary, Admiralty, 1900–3; Secretary of State for War, 1903–5.

BALFOUR, Rt Hon. A. J. (later Earl of Balfour): Chief Secretary for Ireland, 1887–9; Leader of the House, 1891–2, 1895–1905; Prime Minister, 1902–5.

BRODRICK, Hon. St John (later Earl of Midleton): Financial Secretary, War Office, 1886–1892; Under-Secretary of State for War, 1895–8, and for Foreign Affairs, 1898–1900; Secretary of State for War, 1900–3; and for India, 1903–5.

CLARKE, Sir George S. (later Baron Sydenham): Member of the War Office Reconstruction Committee, 1903–4; Secretary of the Defence Committee, 1904–1907; Governor of Bombay, 1907–1913.

COLLEN, Lt Gen. Sir E. H. H.: Military Member of the Viceroy's Council, 1886–1901.

CRANBORNE, Viscount (later 4th Marquess of Salisbury): Under-Secretary for Foreign Affairs, 1900–3; Lord Privy Seal, 1903–5.

CURZON, Rt Hon. G. N. (later Marquess Curzon): Under-Secretary for India, 1891–2; for Foreign Affairs, 1895–8; Viceroy, 1898–1905; Foreign Secretary, 1919–1924.

DANE, Sir Louis W.: Secretary to Government of India in the Foreign Dept., 1902–8; in charge of British mission to Kabul, 1904–5.

DAWKINS, Sir Clinton E.: Finance Member of the Viceroy's Council, 1899.

ELGIN, Earl of: Viceroy, 1894–9.

ELLES, Lt Gen. Sir Edmond R.: Adjutant-General, India, 1900–1; Military Member of the Viceroy's Council, 1901–5.

ESHER, Viscount: Permanent member, Defence Committee; chairman of the War Office Reconstruction Committee, 1903–4.

GODLEY, Sir A. (later Baron Kilbracken): Under-Secretary of State for India, 1883–1909.

HAMILTON, Rt Hon. Lord George: First Lord of the Admiralty, 1885–6,

HARDINGE, Rt Hon. Sir Arthur H.: 1886–92; Secretary of State for India, 1895–1903.
Minister at Teheran, 1900–5.

HARDINGE, Hon. Charles (later Baron Hardinge): Secretary of Embassy at St Petersburg, 1898–1903; Assistant Under-Secretary for Foreign Affairs, 1903–4; Ambassador at St Petersburg, 1904–5; Viceroy, 1910–16.

HAVELOCK, Sir Arthur E.: Governor of Madras, 1895–1900.

KITCHENER, Field-Marshal Lord (later Earl Kitchener): Sirdar, Egyptian Army, 1890–9; C.-in-C., South Africa, 1900–2, and India, 1902–9; Secretary of State for War, 1914–16.

KNOLLYS, Viscount: Private Secretary to the Prince of Wales, later King Edward VII, 1870–1910.

LAMINGTON, Baron: Governor of Bombay, 1903–7.

LANSDOWNE, Marquess of: Governor-General of Canada, 1883–8; Viceroy, 1888–93; Secretary of State for War, 1895–1900; Foreign Secretary, 1900–5.

LAWRENCE, Sir Walter R.: Private Secretary to Curzon, 1889–1903.

LOCKHART, Gen. Sir William: C.-in-C., India, 1898–1900.

MCDONNELL, Hon. Sir Schomberg: Principal Private Secretary to Salisbury, 1888–92, 1895–9, 1900–2.

MINTO, Earl of: Governor-General of Canada, 1898–1904; Viceroy, 1905–10.

NORTHCOTE, Baron: Governor of Bombay, 1899–1903.

PALMER, Gen. Sir Power: C.-in-C., India, 1900–2.

ROBERTS, Field Marshal Earl: C.-in-C., India, 1885–93, South Africa, 1899–1900; C.-in-C., British Army, 1901–4.

SALISBURY, Marquess of: Secretary of State for India, 1866–7, 1874–8, and for Foreign Affairs, 1878–1880, 1885–6, 1887–92, 1895–1900; Prime Minister, 1885–6, 1886–92, 1895–1902.

SANDHURST, Viscount: Governor of Bombay, 1895–9.

SELBORNE, Earl of: First Lord of the Admiralty, 1900–5; High Commissioner in South Africa, 1905–10.

SPRING-RICE, Rt Hon. Sir Cecil A.: Chargé d'Affaires at Teheran, 1900; First Secretary at St Petersburg, 1903–1904; Minister at Teheran, 1906–8.

YOUNGHUSBAND, Sir Francis E.: Resident at Indore, 1902–3; British Commissioner to Tibet, 1902–4.

Abbreviations used in Notes

FULL TITLES of books and articles, with place and date of publication, will be printed in the bibliography at the end of volume II, where the unpublished M.S. collections upon which I have drawn are also listed. Usually, letters and documents are to be found in the papers of those to whom they are addressed. The main exception is Curzon's Viceregal papers, amongst which are printed copies of most of his outgoing letters. I have not thought it worthwhile to cite the number of each file from which a document is taken, since the handlists are generally clear. For instance, Curzon's letters to and from Queen Victoria and King Edward VII are printed in Curzon Papers 135 and 136; Schomberg McDonnell's letters to him are in C.P.14. Where a document might not be readily located, I have given the file number.

It is not uncommon to find minor differences of wording between copies of the same telegram. In such instances, I have followed whichever version seemed most likely to be authentic; and I have occasionally standardised spelling or inserted punctuation marks. Square brackets enclose my interpolations.

The abbreviations used in the footnotes are:

A.P.   Ampthill papers.
A.F.P.   Arnold-Forster papers.
B.P.   Balfour papers.
A.C.P.   Austen Chamberlain papers.
J.C.P.   Joseph Chamberlain papers.
C.P.   Curzon papers.
C.P.2   Curzon papers (that part of the collection until recently held at Kedleston).
G.P.   Godley papers.
H.P.   Hamilton papers.
K.P.   Kitchener papers.
L.P.   Lansdowne papers.
M.P.   Midleton (Brodrick) papers.
R.P.   Roberts papers.
S.P.   Salisbury papers.
S.P.2   Salisbury papers held at Hatfield.

ONE

Apprenticeship

THE CURZONS have held the manor of Kedleston, near Derby, for the better part of nine hundred years. Their name seems to derive from Notre Dame de Curson, in Calvados; and like the Norman family de Courson, they have in their arms the popinjay. Domesday Book records a Curzon as holding Berkshire land in fee from the Earl of Derby. A deed of 1198, still in the family's possession, granted the manor, advowson and mill of Kedleston to Thomas Curzon.

The present hall at Kedleston was built two hundred years ago by the fifth baronet, Sir Nathaniel Curzon, created Baron Scarsdale in 1761. He seems to have been a determined gentleman of spacious tastes, for the existing house was but sixty years old. In its stead he erected what the first Marquess characteristically called 'a mansion not far removed from the dimensions of Windsor Castle'. James Paine completed the solid north front in 1761. Robert Adam, still a young man but then approaching the height of his powers, lavished all his sense of symmetry, passion for detail and free-ranging fancy upon the interior. Seemingly unhampered by vulgar considerations of expense, he also built the south front, the lovely bridge over the lake, the boat house and the orangery. Sir Nathaniel managed to have the turnpike deflected so that it should skirt, rather than bisect, the park. Every house in the village, which had lain inconveniently adjacent to the old hall, he demolished. The new Kedleston was intended to possess four wings, of which only two were completed. It stands in a rolling parkland with stately oaks, streams leading to a waterfall and lake.

Kedleston was soon inspected by Dr Johnson. 'It would do excellently well for a Town Hall' he said. On a second visit, with Boswell in the autumn of 1777, he pronounced rather less severely, though still grumbling at needless expense and the extravagance of the rich decoration. The building, he thought, consumed an amount of labour disproportionate to its utility. Boswell, charmed by the sight of the lake and the handsome barge, the grey stone of the building, with the church nestled at its side and the woods beyond, exclaimed 'One should think that the proprietor of all this *must* be happy.'

'Nay, Sir,' rejoined Johnson 'all this excludes but one evil—poverty.'

It was here that George Nathaniel, first Marquess Curzon of Kedleston, was born on 11 January 1859, eldest son of the Reverend Lord Scarsdale and his wife Blanche. Lord Scarsdale was an undistinguished country gentleman, devoted to his pastoral duties, who had come young into the title on the sudden death of his older brother. The education of his swiftly increasing family was conducted on lines exceptional even in the later nineteenth century. The elder children were confided to the sole care of a Miss Paraman. In her moments of sanity she behaved well enough. She eventually left her small worldly fortune to the eldest girl, Sophy; George Curzon acknowledged her skill as a teacher, corresponded with her faithfully and visited her during her final illness. But in their early childhood Miss Paraman figured as an ogre, forcing the children to own up to crimes they had not committed, then punishing them as self-condemned. For weeks on end they would be forbidden to speak to each other or to a living soul. Lord Scarsdale appears to have been so entirely detached from his children's upbringing that he did not realise their plight. Nor did his wife, whom George worshipped, but from afar. 'I suppose' he recorded, 'no children so well born or so well placed ever cried so much or so justly.'[1]

His experience at preparatory school was almost as unfortunate. There he was taught, and again well taught, by one James Dunbar, who, like Miss Paraman, had a penchant for sadistic punishment and frenzied outbursts of temper. It was at this school that George Curzon's academic promise revealed itself. He worked quickly, accurately and neatly in mathematics and the classics. With Dunbar also he maintained friendly relations for twenty years, until the former, imagining a slight where none was intended, broke off the acquaintance.

In 1872, at the age of thirteen, Curzon began at Eton a career of almost unbroken academic triumph. At first, he felt acutely his loneliness and his parents' lack of concern:

> Many thanks [he wrote pathetically] for your letter yesterday saying you couldn't come. I was very sorry as I was all alone and everybody else's people came.
>
> Your loving boy,
> George.

The curriculum at Eton had only just ceased to be entirely classical. Science did not obtrude itself at all; mathematics and modern languages seldom. The French master, asked in 1860 to define his position, replied memorably 'I suppose I am an *objet de luxe*'. George Curzon could not be called a model pupil, for he was self-willed, masterful and rebellious. His tutor, the Reverend Wolley Dod, he despised as weak and generally useless; but in Oscar Browning, later Fellow of Trinity College, Cambridge, he found for the first time sympathetic understanding allied with deep knowledge. Their association at Eton was a brief one, cut short in 1874 by Browning's virtual banishment from the school on suspicion of homosexuality. Though a classic by training, he had encouraged the teaching of modern history and had frowned upon excessive deference to athletic prowess. Curzon corresponded with Oscar Browning for the next fifty years, stood by him in an incident which made him an object of ridicule and said always how grateful he was to him for getting the ablest boys at Eton to read widely and think for themselves.[2]

Because it was forbidden, Curzon punctiliously attended Ascot races every year and kept a stock of champagne and claret in his room for wine parties. His work was invariably well done. Continuous academic success bred that confidence in which he had hitherto been lacking. George Curzon's record, indeed, had never been equalled by any boy at Eton. Prizes in Shakespearian studies, mathematics, Latin and Greek, ancient history, French and Italian followed each other unceasingly. It was here that his taste for formal declamation and for informal debate developed. When, in 1877, he won the prize for the best Latin oration, the Headmaster, Dr Hornby, announced the victory thus:

> The best declamation has been written by Foley, the second best by Mr Curzon. Unfortunately, in the greater part of what he has written Foley has been anticipated by Cicero. The prize therefore goes to Mr Curzon.

The last months at Eton passed in a glow of success and good fellowship. Curzon had already begun to move in a wider world. He had called on Mr Gladstone in London and persuaded him to address the Literary Society, to whom a majestic discourse on Homer was delivered. Gladstone accompanied Curzon to his room, upon the luxurious furnishings of which he commented somewhat sternly. His young host argued, without avail, that beautiful surroundings tend to elevate. Together they sought and found the spot where, fifty years before, W. E. Gladstone had carved his name in the stone of a wall, and the record of the debate in which, convinced by an opponent, he voted against his own motion and secured its defeat by one vote.

Curzon's departure from Eton was for him an occasion of heartfelt sadness. To the school he remained a devoted son and frequent visitor. It

had been, he recorded, a happy and glorious time, marred in the early
stages by the premature death of his mother but in the last years glittering
with promise.[3]

*   *   *   *

George Curzon was nearly twenty when he arrived at Balliol in the
Michaelmas Term of 1878. 'I do not know' he wrote 'that I build many
castles in the air for Oxford specially. My castles come later on in life and
perhaps have dim chances of realisation; but I recognise, at any rate, that
they cannot have any unless this Oxford time is spent in laying the foundations and preparing for the superstructure.'[4]

The Master of Balliol, Benjamin Jowett, like Oscar Browning deliberately sought out and trained up potential statesmen, diplomats and dons.
Lansdowne, Loreburn, Milner, Asquith and Arthur Godley had not long
departed from the college. St John Brodrick, Walter Lawrence, Rennell
Rodd, Clinton Dawkins, Cecil Spring-Rice, Arthur Hardinge, Louis
Mallet, Edward Grey, J. E. C. Welldon, J. W. Mackail and W. P. Ker
were among Curzon's contemporaries or near-contemporaries there.

Even in this coruscating company Curzon shone. He soon made his
mark in the Union, of which he became President. He revivified the
Canning Club and Oxford Conservatism. In 1880 he took a good First in
Honour Moderations. The testimony about Curzon's personal relations
with his contemporaries conflicts. The rhyme about 'a most superior
person', the phrase applied to Gladstone a half-century earlier, is notorious.
It appeared in a thousand newspaper paragraphs and haunted Curzon's
later career. In a delightful and nostalgic speech, made towards the end of
his life, Curzon said that he envied the guest, T. P. O'Connor, his sobriquet
'Tay Pay', 'more particularly when I contrast the lot of one who has
groaned for a lifetime under the cruel brand of an undergraduate's gibe'.[5]

Oscar Browning, with whom relations were restored as soon as might be,
visited his pupil at Balliol and found him simple, modest and popular.
Walter Lawrence, a faithful friend, coadjutor and confidant of later years,
wrote that Curzon at Balliol was already remarkable, but that in his
simplicity he did not realise it.[6] The curvature of the spine which afterwards caused him agonies was not yet more than a persistent discomfort,
and certainly not enough to curb his irrepressible high spirits. 'The Duke
of Marlborough,' he told Cecil Spring-Rice, 'had an Emu given him. It was
sent to Blenheim, and great interest was taken in the chances of its capacity
for procreation. Eventually it laid an egg. The Duke and Duchess were

absent from home. A telegram was sent to the latter by the agent to apprise her of the event, "Emu has laid an egg. In the absence of Your Grace, have put goose to sit on it".'

Well before he took Finals, Curzon's fame had spread beyond the confines of Oxford. Sir Winston Churchill remarks truly that he was at twenty-one notorious as The Coming Man.[7] 'It would astonish you and gratified me' wrote his intimate friend St John Brodrick, 'to know how well you are already thought of by leading men. It is a wonderful feat to achieve—to be wished for in the House—before you have left Oxford.'

The accumulation of offices in the societies and clubs, together with his fondness for good company and copious talk, cut heavily into Curzon's working time between Moderations and Greats. Perhaps if he had concentrated wholly on the Finals work he yet might have succeeded. As it was, he devoted a good deal of effort to competing in 1881 for the Chancellor's Latin verse prize and the Lothian prize, for which he submitted an essay of 216 closely written pages on John Sobieski, King of Poland. In both he was adjudged *proxime accessit*. A period of frantic work for Greats ensued. Curzon knew that he had begun a year too late, told his friends that he would willingly accept a Second, yet hoped against hope that his powers of concentrated study would pull him through. In the event, he misunderstood, probably from exhaustion, an important question on the Moral Philosophy paper and another in Logic. So he failed by a hairsbreadth to gain a First, cursed himself for not managing affairs better and determined to redeem his reputation.

Jowett said consolingly that the Second should be regarded as an accident, for a First would have been justified by industry and capacity. His Eton friend and hero Alfred Lyttelton wrote words full of understanding and good sense:

> Of course, you could have got the first class for certain if you had denied yourself the Union, the Canning, and those other literary, political and social enterprises which have earned you the name of the most famous Oxonian that in my knowledge of Oxford I can remember. After the annoyance and vexation have passed you will be able to think that you have a substantial consideration to show for your *academic* loss.[8]

* * * *

The subject set for the Lothian prize in 1883 was 'Justinian'. For a month before leaving on a tour of Egypt, Palestine and the Balkans George Curzon slaved at the British Museum. Those books of which he could get copies were packed and read on the journey. The essay he wrote in intervals of leisure on steamers, in his tent, or on camel-back. From *The Times* he learned in a café at Budapesth a few weeks later that he had won the prize. This was the first step on the road to a recovery of self-respect and confidence. Later in that year, after another bout of concentrated reading, he sat for and was awarded a Fellowship at All Souls. One more academic goal remained. In December, Curzon happened to see, busily at work in the Bodleian, an acquaintance who had taken a First and whom he imagined, wrongly, to be preparing an essay for the Arnold Prize. The subject was 'Sir Thomas More'. Quite undeterred by the fact that he knew nothing about Sir Thomas More, Curzon determined to compete.

For nearly four months he shut himself up in London and worked twelve or fourteen hours a day. The essays must be handed in by midnight on a Monday. On that evening Curzon took the train to Oxford, continuing to write until the last moment. As the clocks tolled twelve he knocked up the janitor at the Schools, apologising for the inconvenience on the grounds that this was the winning essay. A few weeks later the press announced that the Hon. G. N. Curzon had been awarded the Prize. No one had ever before won both the Arnold and Lothian prizes.

With this record, Curzon could doubtless have made a distinguished career as a don. However, he was not by temperament or instinct a gown-man. For some time he had spoken on Conservative platforms; and when Lord Salisbury succeeded Gladstone as Prime Minister in the summer of 1885 Curzon became his assistant Private Secretary. The main duty of the post was the collection of speech material, which had then to be laid orally before Salisbury at his house in Arlington Street. He listened with exquisite politeness and deference and encouraged his youthful adjutant, then twenty-six, to stand at the impending General Election, the first to be held under the extended franchise of the previous year. The fact that many constituency boundaries had just been redrawn added another large element of uncertainty to the outcome.

Curzon, duly adopted for South Derbyshire, fought energetically but in vain. None of the shopkeepers, he told St John Brodrick, dared profess Conservative sympathies. A valiant but foolhardy individual who spoke up for him in a tavern was promptly knocked down and put on the fire.[9] The Liberal coasted home comfortably by more than two thousand votes. Salisbury expressed regrets:

> For some reason or other the opinion of the miners seems to have set very strongly against us everywhere — and the new voters show that radicalism which it seems they have to get over like the distemper.[10]

On meeting Parliament in February, 1886, Salisbury resigned the Premiership and no longer needed Curzon's services. Exclusion from political life proved short-lived, however. A few months later he stood for the Southport division of Lancashire and wrested it from the sitting Liberal member after a vigorous campaign. Salisbury returned to power, this time for a spell of six years.

★   ★   ★   ★

Well before leaving Oxford, Curzon had begun to mix freely in London society. He made hosts of friends but was especially intimate with the four daughters of Sir Charles Tennant, Laura, Margot, Lucy and Charty. They wrote him affectionate, trusting, flirtatious letters, replete with *bons mots* about mutual friends and public affairs, interspersed with high-flown talk about the Perfectibility of Man. He replied with equal ardour and sparkle. The sisters found him sweet-tempered, affectionate and gay. Of them he knew best Margot and Laura, who married H. H. Asquith and Alfred Lyttelton respectively. It was Margot who quoted with glee and approval the saying of Blake, 'Prudence is a rich, ugly old maid wooed by incapacity' as a foreword to her autobiography. (This self-revelation shocked *The Times*, even in the palmy days of Lord Northcliffe.) Having endured the endless discourse of Sir Charles Dilke, she said 'If he were a horse, I should certainly not buy him.' On another occasion, Laura was accosted in a passage by the same Sir Charles: 'If you will kiss me, I will give you a signed photograph of myself.' She replied: 'It is awfully good of you, Sir Charles, but I would rather not, for what on earth should I do with the photograph?'

Rennell Rodd, who had first spoken to Curzon of Laura Tennant's intoxicating charm, called her Madonna. Nearly forty years after, Curzon reminded him of 'that angel of light ... none of us can ever forget her...'[11]

In the spring of 1886 she died after childbirth. St John Brodrick telegraphed the news to Curzon. Overwhelmed, he groped for a reason and found none:

> Blessed little soul. God send it be well with her. It must be so, and is so; but for him, St John, did any blow like this fall upon man before? And that Alfred, our cherished and beloved ideal, should be the sufferer: this is most amazing, most unutterably pathetic.
>
> How I need someone with whom to talk all about it. I would give anything for your company, even for an hour. As it is I am stunned and cannot grasp it. Write to me.[12]

Amongst the politicians, Curzon knew best St John Brodrick, Lord Salisbury and his nephew Arthur Balfour, who became in 1887 Secretary for Ireland amidst general derision, soon converted—according to taste—into admiration or hatred as he put down terrorism with courteous but implacable firmness. Until then, Balfour, who was to play a central rôle in the two supreme crises of Curzon's political life, had been known as an ornament of society, a Parliamentary associate of Lord Randolph Churchill and a thinker. Even John Morley, who had published in *The Fortnightly Review* extracts from Balfour's *A Defence of Philosophic Doubt*, confessed to the author that he could not understand a word of it.

The premature death, a dozen years earlier, of May Lyttelton had stifled in Balfour any desire for marriage. 'I hear you are going to wed Margot Tennant' said a friend. 'No,' he replied 'that is not so. I rather think of having a career of my own.'

Arthur James Balfour possessed intellectual and Parliamentary gifts of the first order, coupled with a charm so pervasive and an unpretentiousness so endearing that his social renown exceeded that of any other figure in English life. Curzon had been on friendly personal terms with him since Oxford days, met him much and relished to the full the quality of his repartee. When, at the end of a long and indifferently successful luncheon party, Mr Frank Harris stated as a fact: 'All the faults of the age come from Christianity and journalism,' Balfour replied instantly: 'Christianity, of course ... but why journalism?'

Soon after Curzon's election to Parliament Balfour proposed him for the Carlton Club, warning that although it was infested by the worst of the species bore political 'It must be accepted, like late hours and constituents, as a necessary, though disagreeable, accompaniment of a political career.'[13]

Two other aspects of Curzon's social life deserve notice here. The Crabbet Club brought together men who combined love of good talk with animal spirits. Among the select membership Harry Cust, George Wyndham, Bob Houghton (later Lord Crewe), George Curzon, Lord Elcho and Godfrey Webb were outstanding. The Club was designed, said Wyndham, to play lawn-tennis, the piano, the fool and other instruments of gaiety. Each year it foregathered for a week of games, conversation and competition in verse. The prize was a Georgian goblet, bearing the inscription "Crabbed age and youth cannot live together".

Over these joyous gatherings presided the host and genius of the Club, Wilfrid Scawen Blunt, clad in the garb of a sheikh and dispensing sharp observations about men and affairs. After dinner all sang lustily the Club song, set to *The Vicar of Bray*:

> The world would be a weary place
> If wise men had their way, Sir,
> And every tortoise won the race,
> And only fools might play, Sir,
> Against such doctrines we protest
> And vow to live and laugh our best,
> And so we say
> That, come what may
> Our life shall be a holiday.

The Club, the motto of which was *Mens insana in corpore sano*, had no political affiliations. In public life, Wilfrid Blunt stood for everything Curzon thought most mischievous; in private, they delighted in each other's wit and verbal facility. At Crabbet Curzon's brilliance as an after-dinner speaker found generous recognition, while his capacity for writing doggerel flowered freely. In one set of Crabbet verses he recommended to fellow-members a life of 'frank and systematic and premeditated sin'; another showed that he had already developed the habit of making fun of his own appearance:

> My looks are of that useful type—I say it with elation—
> That qualify me well for almost any situation—
> I've sometimes been mistaken for a parson, and at others
> Have recognised in butlers and in waiters long lost brothers.

The membership of the Crabbet Club was limited in number and confined to men. The Souls, that other but less cohesive group which Curzon adorned, had no definite organisation or purpose. They were, in the words of their high priest Balfour 'a spontaneous and natural growth, born of casual friendship and unpremeditated sympathy'. He once remarked that no history of the later Victorian age would be complete unless the influence of the Souls upon society were dispassionately recorded. Until they sprang into life, prominent politicians of opposite parties rarely, if ever, met socially.

The rhymes in which Curzon welcomed his Soulmates at two dinner parties provide the most authentic nominal roll of this Platonic Academy. Many of them had known each other from childhood. Some were also members of the Crabbet Club; all were distinguished for vivacity and intelligence. The Elchos, Pembrokes, Granbys, Staffords, Wenlocks, Ribblesdales and Brownlows represented aristocratic high society. St John Brodrick and his wife Lady Hilda, Alfred Lyttelton recently bereaved by the death of the beloved Laura, George and Lady Sibell Wyndham, Harry

Cust, Schomberg McDonnell, Edgar and Lady Helen Vincent, Harry and Daisy White typified the worlds of statecraft, literature, diplomacy and finance. Other politicians, like John Morley, Henry Asquith and R. B. Haldane, hovered on the fringes. The Souls' irreverent and gadfly attitude to the more turgid depths of German philosophy profoundly offended Haldane. He did not come often.[14]

Both Balfour and Curzon were distinguished stars in the Souls' constellation. Perhaps the former found his spiritual home among them more fully than Curzon ever could. Balfour's perfect manners, power of extracting the very best in conversation from all whom he met, his sensibility, knowledge of music, letters and philosophy fitted him exactly to inspire this esoteric company. Curzon excelled Balfour in readiness of speech and in warmth of affection, but cared far less for reflection, far more for the efficient despatch of serious business. Moreover, in that period of thirteen years which separated graduation from marriage, there was only one year, 1886, of which Curzon did not spend a substantial period abroad.

Brains and wit, rather than wealth or birth, provided the passport to the Souls' charmed circle. They were not bent upon reforming the world, and would have scoffed with elegant self-consciousness at any such notion. Edgar Vincent, whom Curzon was to appoint Ambassador in Berlin, looked back on a cosmopolitan experience of sixty years and could recall no social group their equal in interest and variety:

> Intellectual without being highbrow or pretentious; critical without envy; unprejudiced but not unprincipled; emancipated but not aggressive; literary but athletic, free from the narrowness of clique, yet bound together in reciprocal appreciation and affection. No society had less ostentation or pretence; none was more free from false standards, dull conventions and antiquated prejudices.[15]

They cared nothing for the cards and racing which characterised the smart set around the Prince of Wales. The Souls' games were of a different kind: 'Clumps' like an early edition of Twenty Questions but always with an abstraction as the object, and 'Styles', in which a piece of prose or poetry must be composed in the manner of a celebrated author. The title of this loose-knit group, supposed to derive from their passion for self-analysis, was alleged by critics to give a somewhat misleading impression of unearthly bliss. Lord Vansittart remarks that their conduct was more carnal than their name; Harry Cust, he adds brutally, 'bulged with sex and stories'. Even to Daisy Brooke, later Lady Warwick, convert to Socialism, mistress of the Prince of Wales and dear friend of Curzon, they were perhaps more pagan than soulful.[16]

The world in which the Souls moved was dealt a mortal blow by the First World War and has long since disappeared without trace. The politicians still had time to think, for Parliament did not normally sit for more than six months in the year. At Panshanger, Wilton, Taplow and other delightful country houses the Souls met often and talked much. The favourite haunt was Stanway, a perfect Gloucestershire manor house gazing across the vales of Severn and Avon to Malvern and the marches of Wales.

It was in this fashion and company that George Curzon spent most of his leisure between 1886 and 1895. He found in the Souls a satisfying combination of laughter and earnestness. Most of them were busy men following a career and were Curzon's seniors in age. He was distinguished from them, not by seriousness or the possession of ideals, but by the special, indeed unique, quality of his determination, staying-power and application. The fellow-devotees deemed most likely to rise high in Tory politics, George Wyndham, Harry Cust and Alfred Lyttelton, never quite fulfilled their promise. In these joyous times with the Souls and the Crabbet Club George Curzon contracted ties of deep affection and unfading memory. After his return from India in political defeat, ill-health and private sorrow, the springs no longer bubbled so freely and sometimes ran dry. But those who read Curzon's last tribute to George Wyndham will realise what the halcyon years had meant to him:

> They told me, Heraclitus, they told me you were dead
> They brought me bitter news to hear and bitter tears to shed.
> I wept as I remembered how often you and I
> Had tired the sun with talking and sent him down the sky.

The love of fun and good company was a part, and an integral part at that, of Curzon's life; but by his deliberate choice it was a definitely subordinate part.

*   *   *   *

It is recorded of Lord Milner that his zeal for the British Empire and for Imperial Federation was fired by a speech delivered one evening at the Oxford Union by George Parkin. Curzon's lifelong passion for Asia was quickened by a lecture given in 1877 to the Literary Society at Eton. Sir James Fitzjames Stephen spoke of an Empire in the East more populous, more amazing, more beneficent than that of Rome. 'Ever since that day' Curzon confessed 'the fascination and sacredness of India have grown upon me.' At Balliol, where he doubtless imbibed some of Jowett's long-standing interest in India and the Indian Civil Service, he said earnestly to Rennel Rodd:

> There has never been anything so great in the world's history as the British Empire, so great as an instrument for the good of humanity. We must devote all our energies and our lives to maintaining it.[17]

Bent already upon a political career, Curzon wisely rejected Oscar Browning's advice to travel mainly in Western Europe. That was too narrow a horizon, he replied, and the man who did not know the Near East and Asia was unfit for statesmanship. Since 1878 he had visited most countries of Western, Central and South Eastern Europe, Palestine, Egypt and North Africa. Rome his imagination peopled with the shades of Cato, Pompey and Caesar; Egypt with the Pharoahs, Palestine with the familiar figures of the Old Testament. By the time of his election as M.P. for Southport, a definite programme of Asiatic travel had taken shape. The main obstacle was lack of funds. Indeed, had not Southport Conservative Association reduced almost to nothing its financial demands, Curzon could not have stood for that constituency. To find his contribution of £50 in 1886 meant that an eagerly-anticipated holiday abroad had to be abandoned. 'I am' he told St John Brodrick, 'a veritable pauper.'[18] Backbench Members of Parliament then received no salary. Curzon had a small allowance from his father, but little hope of its increase, for there were nine surviving brothers and sisters and the splendours of Kedleston hardly fitted the resources of the estate.

Command of words provided the solution. Even at Oxford, Curzon had supplemented his income by writing. During the sessions of 1886 and 1887 he attended assiduously at Southport, delivered a notable maiden speech and worked away at articles for the reviews. In August, 1887, while Parliament was still sitting, his first journey round the world began. Of the early stages his companion was J. E. C. Welldon, later to be Bishop of Calcutta during Curzon's Viceroyalty, whom no less an authority than Jowett thought 'a very honest and able man with a long life before him, and if he is not too honest and open, not unlikely to be an Archbishop of Canterbury'.

They travelled through Eastern Canada to Niagara, Chicago, Salt Lake City and San Francisco; thence Curzon went on alone to Japan, China, Malaya, Ceylon and India. The journey of 31,500 miles took six months. At every stage he noted down his impressions of the scenery, the political prospects and the people, having already developed the methods which were within a few years to make him pre-eminent among English authorities on Asian politics. Each journey was preceded by careful scrutiny of all the available books and articles. A list of the beautiful or historic places was kept. Informed questions must be asked, photographs procured or taken. The traveller must always be ready to fall in with the ways of his host and to make all necessary mental adjustments to the unfamiliar conditions.

This journey served to confirm and deepen Curzon's burning conviction of the British Empire's value as a civilising agency. At Hong Kong he discovered with delight that the Chinese residents had subscribed two hundred and forty thousand dollars to celebrate the Queen's birthday. The festivities there he thought far more effective than those in London on Jubilee night.

> No Englishman can land in Hong Kong without feeling a thrill of pride for his nationality. Here is the furthermost link in that chain of fortresses which from Spain to China girdles half the globe.

Curzon was seeing British power in the Far East, built upon a trade still hardly challenged, in the last few years of primacy, before the rise of Japan and the intervention of Russia, Germany and France altered the balance. Later he was to witness this process at first hand, and having seen former days of British strength measured the decline and desired the more keenly to arrest it.

At Singapore the impressions gained in Hong Kong were intensified:

> The strength and omnipotence of England [he wrote to his father] everywhere in the East is amazing. No other country or people is to be compared with her; we control everything, and are liked as well as respected or feared.[19]

This first visit to India concluded with an excursion along the North-West Frontier. It whetted the appetite for travel in Central Asia, for the steady advance of Russia towards the Indian Empire was acknowledged on all sides to import a new factor into the international equation. Tsarist rule had rapidly extended southwards from Central Siberia beyond the Aral Sea and towards Afghan Turkestan. The independent khanates of Central Asia were successively swallowed up. Tashkent capitulated in 1865, Samarkand three years later. Khiva was taken in June, 1873, five months after Schouvaloff had promised Granville that nothing of the sort would happen. The Russian tentacle had thus reached out across a distance of more than a thousand miles. The indigenous wealth of the captured territories did not seem to be great.

Schouvaloff gave assurances that Russia would not take Merv, capital of the Tekke Turcomans, one of Tamerlane's four Imperial cities, a mere 250 miles from Herat. In 1884 Russia took Merv, announcing that the inhabitants had asked to be annexed. This explanation was not implicitly believed in London. In the following spring, the Russians defeated an Afghan army at Penjdeh. Even Mr Gladstone asked for an immediate credit of £11,000,000 to meet the threat. Russia's frontiers had spread out to Batoum and Kars, to the Oxus and the Pamirs. But what was her motive? Was it purely commercial; was she merely seeking prestige and glory; was she bent upon subjugating Afghanistan and threatening, even invading, India? All these solutions, and many permutations of them, found protagonists. Russian intentions could only be guessed at. During the crisis which culminated in the Berlin Congress of 1878, a memorandum of the Russian War Ministry noted that while India was the main concern of Great Britain, the Bosphorus was that of Russia. The Bosphorus was of value to the British as an avenue to Russia's southern shores, 'and the possibility of attacking India is important only as a means of winning concessions from Britain in the Straits question which is vital to us.'[20]

In the same year, 1877, the debating society of the Rev. Wolley Dod's house, under the presidency of G. N. Curzon, discussed the question: 'Are we justified in regarding with equanimity the advance of Russia towards our Indian frontier?' The President, say the minutes, spoke of Russia's ambitions and aggressive policy. He did not imagine that she would invade India; but 'a great question of diplomacy might arise in Europe in which the interests of England were opposed to those of Russia. It might then suit Russia to send out an army to watch our Indian frontier. In such a case as this England's right hand would obviously be tied back.'[21]

After the immediate crisis of 1878 had passed, Beaconsfield said that the Cabinet did not fear any invasion of India across the North-West frontier, for the Russian base was too remote, the communications too difficult and the terrain too forbidding. Five years afterwards, the Russian Foreign Minister explained privately to his Ambassador in London that there was no intention of menacing India. The Russian position in Turkestan was purely defensive: 'But it gives us a base for operations which if required can become an offensive one.'[22]

In the wake of the armies followed the railway. The Transcaspian line was carried to Merv and Bokhara, and then, by 1888, to Samarkand. Curzon left London early in September, travelled through St Petersburg and Moscow to Tiflis and Baku, then across the Caspian to Samarkand and even to Tashkent, where he stayed with the Russian Governor-General. Again the pen was made to pay for the journey. Sixteen articles of some

2,400 words apiece were written during eight weeks, and published in a syndicate of northern newspapers. Curzon judged that the Transcaspian railway served a common strategic and commercial motive. Russian trade in Asia was expanding at British expense. In Bokhara, which still enjoyed some degree of autonomy, British goods had long been sold, passing via India and Afghanistan. But in 1888 British manufactures were seen once only. 'Bokhara' Curzon noted, 'has in fact dropped like a ripe pear into Russia's lap.' In Afghanistan, as the Journal of the Finance Ministry revealed, Russian trade was growing rapidly, while the British and Indian share declined sharply. Northern Persia showed the same characteristics. In some regions, especially Khorasan, British merchandise was virtually excluded. Rail communication, 'the new and bloodless weapon of nations', was therefore being exploited to the full.

The strategic aspects preoccupied Curzon deeply. His view was substantially the same as that which he had expressed at the age of eighteen, with some allowance for the power of swift concentration conferred by the new railroads. Russia was not intending to invade India, but she understood the value of pressure on Great Britain there to produce complaisance elsewhere; Russian policy was vigorous and pushful; if allowed to proceed unchecked it would become a serious menace. The British had only themselves to blame if they shut their eyes to the facts of Asiatic politics or dithered feebly. Each Russian move was watched in Asia; and each should provoke a counter-move. In particular, Russia's desire eventually to obtain a warm water port on the Persian Gulf must be resisted. As for Russian rule over the vast new empire in Central Asia, it might achieve for the people there what British rule had done for India. If it were devoted to that object, and not to aggression, Great Britain should wish the Russians well. These were the themes of Curzon's articles and lectures and of the book he published on his return, *Russia in Central Asia*. It placed him, at the age of thirty, among the leading experts on Asiatic questions; while the articles increased his reputation as a publicist to the point where he could step up at one bound from *The Manchester Courier* to *The Times*.[23]

Having attended Parliament and completed his manuscript during the spring and summer of 1888, Curzon set off for Persia via Constantinople in September, armed with a contract to produce a dozen letters for *The Times* at £12 10s apiece.

I am grieved but not surprised [wrote Arthur Balfour], at your preference of Persia to Scotland. For my own part I should have thought that we had all had enough of the Shah for one year, but I know there is no use in preaching to you. Travelling is worse than drinking.[24]

The early parts of the journey did not go well. Curzon had stocked himself up on no mean scale with watches, snuff-boxes, cigarette cases and other gifts suitable for presentation to Persians. The Turkish customs, indifferent to his specially endorsed passport, tried to levy duty. He refused. The customs insisted. Curzon said that a Member of Parliament should be treated with more respect. 'A Member of Parliament?' said the official derisively. 'You? You are merely a commercial traveller in cheap jewellery.' Only the arrival of transport from the Embassy saved the day.

These travels in Persia took five months, during which some two thousand miles were covered on horseback along the stone-strewn tracks which passed for roads. Persia cast over Curzon a spell from which he never tried, or wished, to escape. The blend of splendour and squalor, dignity and decay, the ludicrously inflated vanity of the Persians, their hospitality and love of immoderation, appealed irresistibly. He recalled with delight the Persian saying that there is as much sin in a glass as in a flagon.

The Kajar dynasty, then supreme in Persia, had long been celebrated for self-indulgence and perfidy. It was the custom to dispense with enemies or rivals by the simple method of administering poison, and the words 'Kajar coffee' struck a chill through the Middle East. The ruler rejoiced in some nine titles of varying grandeur, including Pivot of the Universe and Shadow of Allah. The then Shah, Nasr-ed-din, had in 1873 visited Queen Victoria, who in a fit of generosity kissed him on the cheek and personally invested him with the Garter. The King of Kings was much surprised to observe the sentry at Windsor Castle actually pacing his beat instead of taking a quiet nap and to note the strength and armament of the volunteers, commanded by the Duke of Sutherland, who paraded before the Prince of Wales. 'Are you not afraid' said the Shah 'to allow a future subject to command so well-equipped an army? Of course, you know your own business, but if I were you' (he paused, pointed to the Duke with one hand and drew the other across his own throat) 'I think *that* might prove, in the long run, to be the wisest course.'[25]

This Knight of the Most Noble Order of the Garter was particularly expert in devising and practising the ultimate refinements of torture. One favoured method was to drill holes in the naked trunks of heretics and then to insert flaming brands until the victim slowly roasted to death. It was with justice that he offered to the new Tsar to inflict on Alexander II's murderers agonies which could not be surpassed anywhere in Asia.

Curzon interviewed the Shah, soon to be assassinated, questioned the Ministers, pestered the officials, toured the ruins, admired the temples and old towns. Corruption and graft were regarded not as a transgression but as the mainspring of society. Half the money allocated for this or that purpose by the government never reached its destination but stuck 'to every intervening pocket with which a professional ingenuity can bring it into transient contact.'

The Zill-es-Sultan, eldest son but not heir of the Shah, professed the warmest sentiments of undying attachment to England. Lord Salisbury's government was the best in the world; but the Zill averred, as a connoisseur of such matters, that Lord Randolph Churchill was rather troublesome and none too loyal. Curzon asked what they would do with Lord Randolph in Persia? The Zill, with masterly discretion, replied that a course of office might be expected to produce a steadying effect.[26]

The whole trip provided a gruelling test of physical and mental endurance. About one route which had been described as an excellent macadamised highway Curzon commented that were Macadam to be raised from the dead and dropped down on the Askabad-Meshed road, he would stand aghast at such a prostitution of his respectable name.

The stage of 550 miles from Meshed to Teheran was accomplished in nine days. Curzon's servant spoke only Persian, so the rides passed in silence: '4 a.m. till 5 p.m., vile horses, bad roads, weary body. But fortunately I was well all through.'[27]

The favourable reviews of *Russia in Central Asia* reached Curzon in Persia. The dozen articles with which he had contracted to supply *The Times* expanded to seventeen. They aroused much interest and approval. The next stage was clear; a full-scale work on Persia. No such book had appeared in English since the Crimean War. It would deal with the country's antiquities, geography, communications, politics, trade and prospects. On his return to London in the spring of 1890 intense work began at once. Some two or three hundred works in the main European languages were searched and recognised experts consulted by letter and interview. The Royal Geographical Society commissioned a detailed map. Statistics were collected. Soon the first tome took shape. 'Figures and facts' runs a characteristic passage, 'which are, in their very essence an insult to the Oriental imagination—are only arrived at in Persia after long and patient enquiry and by careful collation of the results of a number of independent investigations. . .'[28]

The author's desire to prove himself thorough and industrious emerges clearly in the insistence that he had personally scrutinised all the books in his bibliography. He worked as hard as he had done for the Arnold Prize, immured in rooms at Norwood but emerging in July to entertain the Souls to dinner at the Bachelor's Club. Each was greeted, as before, with a verse:

2

> A second time these friends are met
> Again the festal board is set,
> The envy of a world to whet.
>   Again 'tis George N. Curzon,
> The minstrel of a former time
> Who mounts his Pegasus of rhyme
> And claps his rusty spurs on.

The exertions of Persian travel and of authorship, attendance at West-minster and Southport, nearly caused a breakdown in health. Nevertheless, by the autumn of 1891 two massive volumes were in draft. At this juncture, Curzon gratefully accepted the post of Under-Secretary at the India Office. Since the Secretary of State was a peer, it offered opportunities in the Commons. Every aspect of work proved absorbing:

> The office interests me enormously, and the old boys there, who were authorities and swells before I was born, treat me with amazing affability. I believe they expected me to walk in and pull their noses, instead of which they meet with ingenuous deference and an almost virginal modesty.[29]

The Permanent Under-Secretary, Sir Arthur Godley, found his new colleague excellent, immersed in the work, most efficient in Parliament, agreeable and amusing. The post raised one serious difficulty, however, for Curzon's new book was on the point of publication. He had written with much youthful freedom, not to say impudence, about the grasping nature of Russian policy and the manifold failings of Nasr-ed-Din. It was agreed that Lord Salisbury should scrutinise these passages. To the strictures on Russia he did not demur; indeed, he said they might do good. He objected strongly, and as Curzon later recognised justly, to the chapter about the Shah and the palace.

The draft certainly criticised the Imperial character in a comprehensive manner, mentioning *inter alia* his 'petty economies and grudging gifts', the 'meagreness of the acknowledgments received in this country by those who so sumptuously entertained him', the £3,000,000 stowed in his vaults 'while his country lay impoverished', his total want of military knowledge and capacity, his enjoyment of a military parade 'much as a child enjoys a Punch and Judy show'. Acts of cruelty, torture and extortion were deline-ated in faithful detail; the Shah's principal spouse was said to spend most of her time at home in a ballet girl's dress and to resemble a melon in outline. The Prime Minister ruled that all this must be deleted, or at least bowdler-ised. Salisbury disposed with massive finality of Curzon's protestation that these strictures were factual:

...your plea in behalf of your utterances, that they are *true,* is quite inadmissible. That is precisely the circumstance that will make them intolerable to the Shah...

   It is not safe to humble the Shah with the truth and freedom which is permissible and salutary in the case of Mr Gladstone.[30]

The book was not intended to be a collection of travellers' tales but a political treatise which would influence the informed public. Turkestan, Afghanistan, Transcaspia and Persia, Curzon wrote, might to some breathe only a sense of remoteness and of moribund romance; but to him they were the pieces on a chessboard where a game for the dominion of the world was being played out. Great Britain's future, on this view, would not be decided in Europe, or upon the seas, or in the nascent Dominions:

> Without India the British Empire could not exist. The possession of India is the inalienable badge of sovereignty in the eastern hemisphere. Since India was known its masters have been lords of half the world.[31]

Persia and the Persian Question appeared during the spring of 1892, dedicated to those civil and military officers in India

> Whose hands uphold
> The noblest fabric yet reared
> By the genius of a conquering Nation

The work was hailed at once as a monument of diligent research. It has remained, as the author intended, a standard authority and has just been re-issued, seventy-five years after the original publication. It was by no means the best financial success of Curzon's literary career; but it did more than any of his other books to establish him as a traveller and political commentator. Almost all the reviewers wrote in generous praise, though one churlish individual said that Curzon seemed to think 'that he has discovered Persia, and that having discovered it, he now in some mysterious way owns it'.

★   ★   ★   ★

Lord Salisbury's government had lasted nearly six years. At the General Election of July, 1892, George Curzon increased his majority at Southport; but although the Conservatives and Liberal Unionists still outnumbered the Liberals, the Irish Members provided Mr Gladstone with a margin of forty. Lord Salisbury left office on 11 August; less than forty-eight hours later Curzon, with Cecil Spring-Rice, set off for his second journey round

the world. Again a satisfactory arrangement was made with *The Times*.
They travelled across the United States to Japan, Korea, China; then
Curzon went on alone to Tong King, Annam, Cochin China, Cambodia:
'visits to fading oriental courts; audiences with dragon-robed emperors
and kings; long hard rides all day; vile, sleepless, comfortless nights;
excursions by sea boat, river boat, on horse-back, pony-back and elephant-
back; in chairs, hammocks and palanquins.'[32]

At Seoul an interview was arranged with the President of the Korean
Foreign Office. Curzon was particularly warned, on account of Oriental
respect for age, not to admit his extreme youth. Since he looked even
younger than his thirty-three years, this presented some difficulties.

'How old are you?' was, as always in the East, the first question. 'Forty,'
said Curzon unblushingly. 'Dear me, you look very young for that. How
do you account for it?' 'By the fact that I have been travelling for a month
in the superb climate of His Majesty's dominions.'

The President, knowing that Curzon had been a Minister, enquired
what salary he had drawn. Curzon told him.

'I suppose you found *that* by far the most agreeable feature of office. But
no doubt the perquisites were very much larger.'

In Korea it was practically impossible for anyone to become a Minister
unless he were related to the Royal Family. The old man said that he
supposed Curzon to be closely related to the Queen of England.

'No, I am not.' A spasm of distaste passed across the President's face.
Curzon quickly added 'I am, however, as yet an unmarried man.' This
immediately restored him to favour.[33]

Curzon felt and measured the strength of the rising sun in the Pacific.
Since his previous visit to Japan, in 1887, her railways, industry, economic
and military strength and national pride had flourished. Count Ito said to
him that in the Northern Pacific the Japanese fleet was second only to that
of China and far more serviceable. 'It is largely by the offer of the alliance
of her Navy' Curzon commented 'that Japan hopes in the future to control
the balance of power in the Far East.'

Since Chinese vitality continued to wane, she would surely have to
surrender more territory. Japan seemed ill-disposed towards China. Great
Britain, if she saw her interests clearly, would try to bring them together
and show them the real enemy advancing from the north towards Manchuria. Chinese weakness and corruption must presage her defeat in any
war with a well-equipped enemy.[34] These conclusions were set down in
Problems of the Far East, published just as the Sino-Japanese war of 1894
broke out. The moment could hardly have been more opportune. In a few

days the first edition was sold out; the second and third editions were rapidly exhausted. By 1896, the book had reached a fourth edition and Japan had defeated China. In his revised preface, Curzon did not miss the opportunity of poking a little fun at those who had ridiculed his prophecies of 1894. A combination of the European powers, from which the British stood aloof, compelled Japan to surrender most of her territorial gains. She retained, however, a huge indemnity, largely devoted to the development of her forces.

'This latest volume,' wrote the faithful Brodrick, had put 'a finishing touch to the conviction that you are a master of Eastern affairs and raised your already high reputation to the pinnacle which endures.'[35]

That letter reached Curzon in a remote fastness of Northern India, just as he set off on the last and most exciting of his Asiatic journeys.

TWO

Viceroy

FIVE YEARS had elapsed since Curzon's journey along the newly-built Russian railway in Central Asia. That time had not been marked by any crisis comparable with the Afghan war of 1878–80 or the Penjdeh incident. It was a period of consolidation and occasional alarms. Of course, the new situation offered the Russian government, or its agents—for there was often a distinction between their policies—opportunities for advance or intrigue. The minutes of one conference excited the ridicule of Staal, Russian Ambassador in London, who was almost driven to admire the hardihood and impudence of the military. The latter argued that the Russian title to expand across the Pamirs rested upon arrangements made with the British in 1873 (in which the Pamirs were not even mentioned) and on the right of succession to the Khan of Khokand, who had never tried to move to the line of the Hindu Kush. It was asserted that the Pamirs were needed for commercial purposes. 'De petits mouvements militaires' were also envisaged.

The soldiers, Staal was informed from St Petersburg, wanted the passes of the Hindu Kush so that India might be menaced at a given moment. 'Ce serait' he replied 'trop ouvertement demander la clef de la maison du voisin pour la mettre dans la poche. Le jour où une pareille prétension serait émise, la Quadruple Alliance serait faite.'

Late in 1891, a Russian expedition under Colonel Yonoff in the Pamirs encountered two British officers, one of whom was Captain Francis Younghusband. Yonoff insisted on their departure, an action which left a bad taste in the mouth of the Cabinet and outraged Staal ('un abus de force absolument gratuit'). The Russian government gave assurances that it had no previous knowledge of the expulsion. This hardly improved the impression.[1]

Yonoff told Younghusband that he was annexing for Russia a large tract extending right down to the Indian watershed and including a good deal of Afghan and Chinese territory. Younghusband remarked that the

Russians were opening their mouths pretty wide, at which the Colonel laughed and said it was only a beginning. Salisbury entered a sharp protest, but when Younghusband arrived in London, he found that the Secretary of State for India took a very perfunctory interest. The Under-Secretary, however, engaged him in a long conversation, put penetrating questions, expressed views. No one else he had met, even in India, had known the subject so well. This was George Curzon in his first ministerial office, and this the first encounter of a friendship broken only by death.

Lord Rosebery, Foreign Secretary in the new government, began a negotiation. However, the Russians made no haste to settle, partly because of the intransigence of the War Ministry, partly because the British desiderata were judged excessive. The health of M. de Giers was by now so frail that he could not, literally speaking, stand up to the Minister of War. The military, so Staal was informed, wished above all to draw near to the Hindu Kush, coveting the passes with an eye to ('en vue de') war with England. This had apparently been the motive of the Russian expedition to the Pamirs. Officials of the Foreign Ministry seem to have done their best to curb these tendencies. M. de Staal, favouring a policy of entente, expressed his relief. The other line, he feared, would drive England steadily towards those elements in Europe hostile to Russia.[2]

Curzon felt that his programme of oriental travel would be sadly incomplete without a visit to these desolate and disputed regions of the Pamirs; and to Afghanistan, the importance of which had been so evidently enhanced by the spread of Russian power. The fact that the government of India at first forbade both journeys did not make them the less alluring.

In the Pamirs Curzon endured forty degrees of frost night after night, shot ovis poli at nearly 17,000 feet, crept along crumbling ledges above the ravines, marvelled at the majesty of pine, glacier, torrent and peak. The Oxus River he tracked to the true source, a feat for which the Royal Geographical Society awarded its Gold Medal. That distinction, he once said, afforded him far greater satisfaction than the attainment of ministerial office. The average day's march or ride covered some twenty one miles. Everywhere along the frontier the officers entertained him cheerfully. One night his host was Captain Townshend, later to be celebrated as the defender of Kut, who sang French songs to a banjo. On the walls of his mud dwelling were pinned 'somewhat daring coloured illustrations from Parisian journals of the lighter type'.

To Chitral Curzon was accompanied by Francis Younghusband. Twelve times during the first day rushing torrents had to be crossed. Glaciers ran to the edge of the water: 'As the evening sun shone from the glittering snow peaks behind them on to their splintered crests, and then stained crimson the jungle in the valley bottom, already reddening to the fall, I thought that I had rarely seen anything more sublime.'[3]

The Mehtar of Chitral had reached his position of eminence by a somewhat involved process of deposition and murder. He had dethroned an uncle, who had himself shot another nephew. That nephew had succeeded his father, murdered two fraternal rivals and then announced to the Viceroy that he had succeeded 'with the unanimous consent of his brothers'. Curzon and Younghusband were entertained at lunch by the current Mehtar in a garden-house, adorned by a photograph of Margot Tennant. A few weeks after, the Mehtar was himself shot dead at the instance of treacherous relatives. Though he could hardly have known it, his guest was very soon to play a leading rôle in determining the British Cabinet not to abandon Chitral.

By the late autumn it was time to leave for Kabul. Lord Lytton had called Afghanistan 'an earthen pipkin between two iron pots'; the Amir, Abdur Rahman Khan, spoke of a goat between two lions, or a grain of wheat between two millstones. In 1885, just at the moment of Penjdeh, he had met the Viceroy, Lord Dufferin, in a great Durbar at Rawalpindi, vowing that even if his whole country and property were destroyed he would never abate his friendship for the British. The circumstances of this encounter are said to have excited the derision of Bismarck. 'C'est Offenbach tout pur. Il ne manquait pas même le sabre de mon père.'[4]

The Durbar rang to protestations of goodwill, but in practice the relations between the government of India and their supposed ally were tempestuous. He objected violently to their policy on the frontier. When the engineers blasted a tunnel through the mountains to make possible a swifter rail communication with the frontier, and perhaps beyond, Abdur Rhaman was invited to attend the official opening. He enquired whether it was the custom of the English, when they bored a hole in a man's stomach, to ask the victim to watch the process?[5]

During his Transcaspian journey of 1888, Curzon had watched how the Russians concentrated troops to support a rebellion against the Amir's rule.[6] It was suppressed with such ferocity that the Viceroy, Lord Lansdowne, felt bound to remonstrate. Abdur Rahman was furious at this interference with his affairs, Lansdowne vexed at being compelled to treat deferentially 'a cantankerous and suspicious old savage'. In 1893, Sir Mortimer Durand negotiated at Kabul an agreement whereby the tribes in a defined area of the frontier might be brought under some form of control without Afghan interference. The annual subsidy paid to the Amir was increased by one half. This produced a brief period of relief. Durand found the Amir courteous and even comparatively straightforward. At their final meeting, he was asked to deliver gracious messages to Lord Dufferin and Lord Salisbury. Reminded that Mr Gladstone was now Prime Minister, the Amir snapped, 'I know that, but Lord Salisbury is my friend and you are to tell him that I offer up constant prayers for his long life and prosperity. [*Pause*] However, if you come across Gladstone, you may wish him well.'[7]

Invitations to Kabul were not always welcome. Sir Alfred Lyall's verse gives the reply of the Ghilzai chieftain to the Amir's bidding:

> High stands thy Cabul citadel, where many
>   Have room and rest;
> The Amirs give welcome entry, but they
>   Speed not a parting guest.
> Shall I ask for the Moolah, in Ghuzni, to
>   Whom all Afghans rise?
> He was bid last year to thy banqueting—
>   His soul is in Paradise.

However, Curzon was determined to ride into Kabul whatever the risk. He composed with infinite care a letter of some seven foolscap sheets. It dilated on the writer's affection for Afghanistan and regard for its ruler. The Amir's dominions were somewhat fancifully likened to a rich stone in the middle of a ring, His Highness' person to the sparkle in the heart of a diamond. This did the trick. Abdur Rahman sent an invitation. The objections of the Viceroy and his Council Curzon overbore by persistence. Thus by early November he was threading through the jaws of the Khyber, along the contorted track and amidst the Afridis, each with a rifle at the shoulder; beneath the fortress of Ali Musjid, clinging to a crag above the most perilous passage in the gorge; then into a green plain to the fortress at Lundi Kotal. Three years later it was to fall when the Khyber Rifles could no longer keep their own kinsmen at bay. Here Curzon stood on the very edge of the Queen-Empress' dominions, gazing at the grey hills and snowy peaks of Afghanistan.

He was met by the commander-in-chief of the Afghan army and an escort of cavalry. They moved by stages of some twenty four miles a day to Jelalabad. On the eighth day after leaving Peshawar Kabul was sighted. At a little distance the party halted while Curzon rigged himself out for the ceremonial entry. Since the uniform of a mere Under-Secretary had produced a mediocre impression at Seoul in 1892, he had sought round for something more resplendent. Visits to theatrical costumiers in London and Calcutta produced an assortment of stars and medals (many of them Russian or Japanese), enormous gold epaulettes and a magnificent pair of patent leather boots. A military friend lent spurs and a huge sword. Groaning beneath the weight of this outfit, the Amir's guest made an impressive ride into Kabul, through the narrow streets and mean houses to a fine suite of rooms in the Palace.

His attire was not thought odd. On the contrary, it created a sensation. The court tailor was summoned and told to note carefully some of the more scintillating features. Unfortunately, the Amir demanded to know what feat or victory each medal and badge indicated. 'To these inconvenient queries I could only return the most general and deprecatory replies.'[8]

The huts and houses of Kabul clustered on the edge of a plain; a mountain towered above and in the distance ran the sparkling snowline, at 24,000 feet, of the Hindu Kush. On the banks of the Kabul river stood the workshops maintained largely from the government of India's subsidy. Here were built modern weapons, Hotchkiss guns and Martini rifles, cartridges, swords, boots and bridles. Curzon was shown over the arsenal. He asked why the breech-loading rifles and quick-firing guns were not issued to the troops? Abdur Rahman replied that he dared not do it; any regiment so equipped would mutiny and he had had enough of that.[9]

The Amir Abdur Rahman Khan, eldest son of Dost Mohammed, was now fifty years old. He had been a cook, a blacksmith, a gardener, a viceroy and finally a sovereign. For a dozen years he had languished at Samarkand, prisoner of the Russians. Now he was 'the brains and eyes and ears of all Afghanistan'. Luckily, that portion of the British public which foamed with Mr Gladstone at the iniquities of Ottoman rule knew little enough about Afghanistan, where the Amir's methods made those of the Sultan look comparatively mild. It must be conceded that Abdur Rahman displayed much ingenuity in contriving punishments. In the early 1890's the Lataband pass was infested with robbers. When a few hangings failed to deter them, the Amir decided on a novelty. Atop a precipitous cliff, he placed a cage, fixed to a mast. Into it was thrust the next highwayman caught and there he died of hunger and thirst. Every wayfarer moving through the pass was encouraged by the skeleton in the cage to reflect upon the rewards of rectitude.

Normally, robbers were punished by simpler methods. A rope was knotted tightly above the wrist by the butcher, who would then amputate the hand with a sharp knife, plunging the stump into boiling oil. An official found guilty of rape was stripped of clothes in midwinter and placed in a hole. Water was then poured upon him. As he became an icicle the Amir remarked 'He will never be too hot again.' Other malefactors were blown from guns or smeared with petroleum and set alight. The more fortunate merely had their tongues nipped out, lips sewn together, noses cut off, eyes put out or limbs amputated. Abdur Rahman described to Curzon, without a trace of compunction, how he had blinded with quick-lime rebellious tribesmen. To the best of his recollection he had put to death about 120,000 of his subjects.[10]

This was the potentate to whose gracious presence Curzon was conveyed in a royal landau at 1 p.m. on 20 November. The Amir sat upon green satin quilts spread over a bedstead, for he was recovering from a severe illness. His legs and body were swathed in a lambswool garment, a silk shawl lined with foxskins thrown round the shoulders. A skull-cap of silver cloth surmounted a turban. The Amir's features were finer and more benign than his visitor had expected. In physique he was thickset, fabulously strong; in conversation quick-witted and adept, ready with aphorisms and loving his own jokes, to which the courtiers responded with the right degree of joviality.

Abdur Rahman spoke of Russian aggressiveness. 'I have 20,000 Afghan troops along our frontier with Russia' he said. 'This would rise to 60,000 in war.' Curzon's position in these conversations, of which there were six lasting about three hours each, was sometimes an uncomfortable one, for he could not say openly to the Amir what he thought: that the Afghans could not be trusted to build decent forts; that it was absurd for the British to be held responsible for his frontiers when every Englishman was banned from the country; that he had not been invited sooner to England because he was being vexatious and disloyal all along the frontier; and that if the British were to fight for Afghanistan and pay a large subsidy some tangible return must be given. However, Curzon did make the second point. The Amir replied

> England and Afghanistan are one house. Why not therefore have one outer wall? Why does the Indian government fortify its frontier against me, instead of fortifying my frontier against the Russians? They are spending their money on the wrong wall.

Curzon replied that if it were one house, all must be free to move around; 'and you cannot expect one section of the inmates to defend an outer wall of which they know little and which they are not permitted to see'.

To this the Amir does not seem to have responded. The discussions wandered over a wide variety of subjects. The Amir, clearly imagining the

British parliament and the British government to be the same thing, charged Curzon with a number of messages for it. He joked a good deal at the expense of a rather bibulous Englishman in his employ, Sir Salter Pyne, who said he had turned over a new leaf. 'Ah yes,' rejoined his master 'you were a twenty-bottle man. Now you are a fifteen-bottle man!' He laughed uproariously at his own wit. At the fourth interview Abdur Rahman pronounced the Russians to be the greatest liars in the world. Curzon asked whether the Persians did not make a respectable second? The Amir admitted it: 'The Persian lies are women's lies, delicate, deceitful, cunning. But the Russian lies are strong, defiant, inveterate, mountainous, masculine lies!'

Curzon asked how he had come to hate the Russians so?

The Amir replied that when he was the Russians' prisoner, he had secretly learned their language. Pretending to understand nothing, he would sit there mute: 'I have often heard them tell their true minds calling me a poor ignorant barbaric Afghan and laughing at what they proposed to do with me. I have bided my time and never forgiven them.'

The penultimate interview proved to be politically the most significant. The succession to Abdur Rahman, who had a number of sons by several wives, had always been in doubt. Since Afghanistan was by no means a homogeneous kingdom, a disputed succession might easily involve the British and Russians in war. Curzon asked innocently what was the rule in Mahommedan countries? Should the successor be the king's eldest son, or the sovereign's nominee, or the son of the mother of highest rank? The Amir said with emphasis and at length that everything pointed to the eldest son, and then congratulated Curzon on the skill with which he had extracted this declaration. Curzon judged, rightly, that Habibullah would succeed his father.

At their last talk, the Amir discoursed about marriage in Great Britain, Since there were more women than men, numbers of them must remain unmarried, a dismal fate. As a man could take only one wife, the country swarmed with 'children of God'. Indeed, the British colonies, Canada, Australia and New Zealand were maintained as places to which these children could be sent. It was all due to the damp climate. Living in perpetual water and mud, the British were like rice. The men were not strong and could not cope with four wives.

Curzon was convinced of the Amir's fidelity to the British connexion, but realised that he must sometimes exhibit an independence galling to officialdom. He would turn to British advice and arms in a crisis. For his part, Abdur Rahman thought his guest to be a very genial, hard-working, well-informed ambitious young man, and admired his capacity to worm out information. Having said farewell, Curzon returned to India via Kandahar. The four hundred miles to Chaman were covered in thirteen days. He returned to England via Somaliland and Egypt.[11]

★　　★　　★　　★

Curzon's Asiatic journeys had now come to an end. Often he had missed the pleasure of friends' company: 'my thoughts strain homewards over the long leagues, and I think of the delicious country house parties, the fun and talking and wild delight.'

But this was a passing mood. These travels of a dozen years had been a source of income and reputation and of much more besides. Every interview and scene, every item of expense had been noted down. The first journey round the world lasted 191 days and cost £1 15s. per day, the second, a fortnight longer, £1 14s. 10d. He had been stoned by Spaniards, shipwrecked off Dalmatia, nearly drowned off Annam; had climbed Etna to watch the sun's rays steal across the snows, had seen Kanchenjunga loom through the mists of morning; had delighted in the almond blossom, the apricots, mulberries and vines of northern India. The fascination of Eastern travel lay largely in its contrasts; the broad plains and towering ranges, the sweltering day and bitter night, the cities both imposing and squalid, the people hospitable and treacherous, noble and despicable, dignified and deceitful. Here were lands civilised when Europe was of no account, containing historic cities and monuments, springs of religious teaching and scientific discovery. Such memories brought comfort in later and less happy years. At the time, experience of Asia confirmed his deep admiration of the work the British were doing in India and his determination to take a directing part in it.

Nothing could cure Curzon of what Arthur Balfour called inveterate restlessness. Oriental civilisations, he wrote banteringly, were all very well in their way, and Curzon might be quite right to study their decaying splendours, but globe-trotting might soon be given up for the charm of friends' society? Lord Scarsdale was equally, though less eloquently, puzzled. 'Why don't you stop at home' he asked 'and be quiet, and look after the estate, and take an interest in the tenants, as I have done, instead of roaming about all over the world?'[12]

It was not that Curzon had turned his back on Kedleston, where his speeches, books and political career aroused little interest. Far from it; he loved the house, with its green-veined columns of alabaster, the domed saloon, painted ceilings, fine pictures and books. But there was time for that later. India had fired his imagination, his deep desire to serve, his love of the magnificent.

★   ★   ★   ★

Mary Victoria Leiter was the eldest daughter of Levi Leiter, an American businessman of Jewish origins and colossal wealth, chiefly garnered in wheat and real estate. When she met George Curzon in 1890, she was at twenty a scintillating star of Washington society, one of the most beautiful and cultivated women of her day. A young officer of the Indian Civil Service, catching sight of her for the first time, perceived in a flash why the Greeks had besieged Troy. Curzon had, years before, hoped to marry Lady Sibell Grosvenor, now George Wyndham's wife. At a later stage, in rivalry with George Moore, he seems to have courted an authoress.[13] He and Mary Leiter corresponded regularly, and with growing affection, from the time of their first meeting.

In the spring of 1893, they became secretly engaged. Only her parents knew, for Curzon was determined to complete his Asiatic wanderings and felt that no married man should face the dangers of the Pamirs and Afghanistan. She implored him, but in vain, to stay away from both. Those adventures safely accomplished, the engagement was announced. 'It was clever of you and extremely characteristic' wrote one of his friends, 'to get engaged to Miss Leiter at Washington from the top of the Pamirs; you must tell me how it was done.'[14]

The marriage, which took place at Washington in April, 1895, was a fount of deep, though tragically brief, happiness to them both. 'I always think' she wrote artlessly, 'that the sweet test of affection is not if you can live with a person but if you *cannot* live without him, and if you feel that when Mr X comes into a room, that the room is glowing with pink lights, and thrills are running up and down your back with pure joy, then it is all right. Don't give your heart away until you feel all this, which I feel when George appears...'[15]

Curzon wrote to tell Abdur Rahman of the marriage and sent a photograph of his bride. 'Thank God' the Amir replied ambiguously, 'she is according to your own choice. I also congratulate you, my honest friend, that although you have only married one wife, she is competent.'

The Amir had studied the photograph attentively. His knowledge of phrenology, upon which he prided himself, revealed Mrs Curzon to be 'very wise, a wellwisher of yours, and modest'. He trusted that his friend would be happy and satisfied with her always and that God would bless them with a goodly offspring. 'If she should at any time thrash you', he added, 'I am certain you will have done something to deserve it.'[16]

The Curzons returned to England in May, 1895. They were able to rent 4, Carlton House Terrace, for Levi Leiter had settled a very large sum on his daughter, and Curzon had become at a stroke a rich man. The Priory, Reigate, they took as a country retreat. Towards the end of June, Lord Rosebery's government resigned and Salisbury became Prime Minister for the third time. Having failed to persuade the Duke of Devonshire to take the Foreign Office he decided to combine it again with the post of Prime Minister and asked George Curzon to become his Under-Secretary and sole representative in the House of Commons. To a young Parliamentarian the terms of the invitation must have been flattering:

> You are more familiar with Eastern questions than any man on our side: and your ability and position in the House of Commons will enable you to fight a good battle for us, if your policy is attacked...I am sure there is no post in the Government, in which the foundations of your future fame can be more securely laid.

Curzon sent an immediate and grateful acceptance, asking boldly that his name might be considered for the Privy Council so that there should be no stigma in accepting an Under-Secretaryship for the second time. The request was superfluous, for the Prime Minister had already submitted Curzon's name to Queen Victoria for this exceptional honour, which no one of his age, holding a political office, had received within living memory.[17]

Sir Winston Churchill has observed that the House of Commons found something lacking in Mr Curzon, considered him a lightweight. No first-rate Parliamentarian, he states, 'with the advantage of being an ex-Minister and without any definite disqualification, could have failed to establish by 1895 a claim to Cabinet rank'.[18] This is unfair. Curzon had been an M.P. just under nine years. He was but thirty-six years old and had since his entry into Parliament spent the large bulk of his time travelling in distant countries or writing about them. His total ministerial experience consisted of seven and a half months at the India Office, while Lord Salisbury had now, for the first time, to provide places in the Cabinet not only for Conservative claimants but for Liberal Unionists, to whom five posts out of nineteen were allotted. No member of the Cabinet was anywhere near Curzon in age.

As Salisbury had said, there was no post in which the foundations of

fame could be laid more securely than in this Under-Secretaryship. The
strenuous spell of three years' work which Curzon now began under the
Prime Minister's immediate eye amply justified all his early promise and
brought him the highest office in the oversea service of the Crown.

*   *   *   *

To his nephew Balfour, Lord Salisbury seemed 'a glorious bohemian'.[19]
He cared little for honours, still less for those who sought them, nothing at
all for Society or fashion. Kind to a fault, he despised petty intrigue and
fussy colleagues, asserted his authority but rarely. On one occasion he was
refused admission to the casino at Monte Carlo, on the ground that his
attire was too scruffy. This amused him hugely. Asked for an opinion
about some utopian scheme he would reply, with Dr Johnson, 'I will wait
till I am a tiger.' Intensely practical and realistic, he possessed the merit,
extremely rare in British ministers, of acting upon disagreeable facts.
Unwarranted optimism, he remarked, was merely a display of moral
vanity masquerading as virtue. Publicity he disliked on personal, but even
more on public, grounds. When it was argued that he should not conceal
his diplomatic triumphs, Salisbury replied serenely 'To talk about success
only makes the next success more difficult.'

There was nothing dramatic, he once wrote, about the success of a
diplomatist, whose victories were composed of a series of microscopic
advantages; of a judicious suggestion here, an opportune civility there, a
wise concession at one moment and far-sighted persistence at another; of
sleepless tact, immovable calmness, unshakable patience. To say that
Salisbury was often aware of the connexion between diplomatic success
and armed strength would do him an injustice. It formed the staple of his
thinking on foreign affairs and he did not quickly forget his experience
of trying to do business at the Constantinople Conference without money
in his pocket or a sword in his hand.[20] Accordingly he had no time for the
English practice of ranting vainly about others' iniquities. Asked whether
the Cabinet had arrived at any decision about publicising atrocities in the
Congo, Salisbury rejoined:

> My impression is strongly against interference on our part. We shall not
> reform our neighbours' ways, by turning the philanthropic pack upon them.
> They have no weapon but their tongues: and the only result they will achieve
> will be to make the tyranny better hidden, and therefore more cruel.[21]

Salisbury recognised, perhaps too well, that the steady broadening of the franchise had taken out of the hands of particular Cabinets the determination of foreign policy at its highest level. It would be wrong and futile to contract alliances—that is, military commitments of indefinite duration in Europe—and invite others to depend on British help which the Cabinet of a later day might be unwilling or unable to give. Nor was it safe to embark on a military venture anywhere unless there were a strong probability of seeing it through before a new Cabinet overturned the policy. Twice, he wrote, Great Britain had tried to conquer Afghanistan and both times she had failed egregiously. On each occasion the policy was upset by a swing of the pendulum at home. It might be taken as an axiom that no act of foreign policy could succeed unless it could be completed within one beat of the pendulum.[22]

These factors imposed strict limits upon the range of action which the Foreign Secretary of a democratic state might legitimately permit himself. Exasperated, Salisbury had once said that English foreign policy 'is to float lazily downstream, occasionally putting out a diplomatic boat-hook to avoid collisions.' That did not mean that he thought it a good method or a reliable one; rather, he believed it the only honourable course. Salisbury looked with a sceptical eye upon experts and especially upon the pretensions of the service departments. 'I have a very limited enthusiasm about Kowloon. It will be such an opportunity for the War Office to spend money.'[23]

Curzon found Salisbury, for all his disdain of the orator's arts, a fascinating speaker. Whatever the occasion, he seemed to embody wisdom, to be uttering aloud the reflections which might just as naturally have occurred to him in the library at Hatfield. 'His massive head, bowed upon his chest, his precise and measured tones, his total absence of gesture, his grave but subtle irony, sustained the illusion.' The love of epigram made his private conversation a delight, caused Salisbury himself intense enjoyment and peeped forth in public even at those moments when he had sternly resolved that he must not commit an indiscretion.[24]

This was the figure who, after Gladstone's retirement, towered over English politics. Curzon, much the more ardent temperament, often disagreed with his chief in points of detail and occasionally in weightier matters. They shared a fondness for scrutiny of large-scale maps as the indispensable foundation of foreign policy; both liked to work in the minutest detail and to be self-reliant in decision. The Prime Minister generally attended to his own business, of which he had a surfeit, and left his colleagues to see to theirs. Sir Winston observes that he played a greater part than any other figure in gathering together the growing strength of the British Empire for the time of trial. His colleague Sir

Michael Hicks Beach said that 'all who worked with him felt that he was essentially a great man.'[25]

Curzon felt likewise. He hoped to have a share in the making, and not merely the enunciation, of British policy.[26] Quite apart from the unrivalled prestige of the Prime Minister, his methods of conducting business from Arlington Street or Hatfield, and his disinclination to depend for advice on officials of the Foreign Office, made it difficult for an Under-Secretary to influence decisions. It was not for some nine months that Salisbury realised, after Curzon's protest, that he was not receiving copies of certain private letters and telegrams. That was promptly put right; but as for notes of conversations with Ambassadors, which Curzon as the department's spokesman in the Commons needed to see, Salisbury explained that he frequently kept none. When he had been Foreign Secretary under Disraeli, he had made copious records, but had resolved never to do so again after the incoming Under-Secretary, Sir Charles Dilke, made 'an abominable use' of the facts which thus came into his hands:

> The knowledge that I abstain from it makes both Hatzfeldt and de Courcel speak more freely than they otherwise would do: and they tell me (and I have no ground for disbelieving them) that they on their side abstain to a great extent from formal reports. Whatever reports I send are of course accessible to you.[27]

* * * *

A detailed account of the foreign policy pursued by Salisbury's third Cabinet would be out of place here. All that is needful is a record of one or two incidents, symptomatic of the place Curzon made for himself in the government, together with an indication of the general conditions in which British policy had to be framed and executed.

It is usual to describe the latter years of the nineteenth century as a time of 'splendid isolation' on the part of Great Britain; to say that her statesmen consciously and successfully aimed at a 'balance of power'; that her strength at sea ensured a prolonged period of quiet, the 'pax Britannica'. None of these statements is of much value. The notion of a worldwide pax Britannica is absurd. On the contrary, the nineteenth century abounded in wars, large and small. Europe and the Balkans, the Americas, Africa, China, Japan, Central Asia, were repeatedly racked by fighting and bloodshed. That the campaigns were—by the somewhat enlarged standards of the twentieth century—conducted by comparatively small armies is another matter. Even then, the great European powers in the last decades of the century numbered their troops by the million. The British put half a million men into South Africa during the Boer War of 1899–1902; no mean effort, for the crucial fact of Great Britain's international position was that she had a minute army and a huge navy. Her commitments were, or at any rate had been, of a peculiar kind.

She had no territory to defend in the adjacent continent of Europe. Her interests there were of a negative kind; it was important that no European power should reduce the others to servitude and that the Low Countries and their ports should not fall into the hands of a first-class power. The obligation to defend Belgium was of an ambiguous nature, offering the opportunity of interpretation according to the convenience of the moment. Because the Channel was still a real barrier, home defence for the British rested upon the possession of a navy strong enough to meet likely opponents in combination, not upon the possession of an army on the European scale. The British, so it was held, would never stand for conscription. Alas for the British, others took a less lofty view. Memories of Cromwell and the dangers of large standing armies were supposed to agitate the people's mind. All this may have been true, or it may have been said by politicians of all parties as a shield against the unpleasantness and unpopularity of putting up the income tax and calling up the young. The result, as Bismarck observed, was that Great Britain had an army which the German police could arrest.

Several meanings may attach to the word 'isolation'. It may connote a large degree of political or economic detachment from other countries; it may mean physical remoteness; it may merely indicate the absence of military commitment. It is in this last sense that it is most usually employed to describe the British posture in foreign politics of the later nineteenth century. Nothing could be more misleading. 'Splendid isolation' implies a delightful degree of independence with the chance to decide, in the light of circumstances, the right course of action in each crisis. It implies under-commitment, or even freedom from commitment. But the British were in relation to their resources and physical position the most heavily committed power in the world. About a quarter of the earth's surface was British territory; none of those countries, with the single exception of India, could defend itself against a determined opponent; all had to be protected, in theory at least, by the power of a small island, thousands of miles distant, with a population of about forty million and lacking land power.

The real position of British Ministers, in short, was often the reverse of comfortable or secure. Most parts of the British Empire, it is true, were defensible by sea, though some frontiers, especially the Canadian boundary

with the United States, could scarcely be defended at all. The frontiers of
Natal and Cape Colony were vulnerable to invasion by the Boer republics,
as the events of 1899 showed. Moreover, the advance of Russia in Central
Asia bade fair to give the British Empire what it had so far lacked, a land
frontier with a first-class European power and therefore to rob it of the
freedom to equate a small army with security.

> We cannot reconcile ourselves to the truth, [wrote Salisbury in 1885], that if
> we will not provide cloth enough for the coat we want, we must cut down
> our coat to the cloth we have got.... Our people require to have it driven
> into their heads that if they will not submit to a conscription, they must submit
> to a corresponding limitation of their exploits.[28]

Since then, however, and largely under Salisbury's aegis, the British
had acquired huge territories in Africa. Some of them, lying far inland,
constituted a serious risk. The results of the effort to relieve Khartoum in
1884–5 were not, as he remarked, of the most brilliant character. 'England's
strength lies in her ships' he told the Queen some time later, 'and ships can
only operate on the seashore or the sea. England alone can do nothing to
remedy an inland tyranny. . .'[29]

Urged to act strongly during the Armenian massacres, Salisbury regretted
his inability to place the Royal Navy on the slopes of Mount Ararat,
rather as Mr Chamberlain observed in 1938 that British warships could not
be deployed on the Bohemian mountain-tops. Any balance of power at
which British statesmen were aiming was, therefore, related less often to
Europe than to the defence of a widely scattered Empire. The phrase
'balance of power' also carries a variety of meanings. When politicians talk
of the desirability of a balance of power, they generally mean the desirability of a balance favourable to their own country or alliance. Equally,
balance may mean a level balance, an equilibrium. When applied to British
policy in the nineteenth century, the phrase is usually taken to mean that
successive Cabinets deliberately threw their weight behind the weaker state
or combination; but although the system of alliances centred upon Germany
was clearly the strongest, Salisbury often acted with Bismarck, judging
Germany to be comparatively peaceful. When he entered in 1886 his first
long spell as Prime Minister, the Cabinet had reviewed anxiously the
possibility of war not with the Triple Alliance but with France and Russia.
This was six years before the formation of the Franco–Russian alliance,
but those powers, though they had not yet come together, possessed
interests which clashed with, or might cross, British interests in Africa and
Asia. Most important of all, they were great naval powers. The Triple
Alliance was not. Hence the massive programme of naval building set in

train by Salisbury's second Cabinet. The naval estimates increased by some sixty per cent in the decade 1886–96.

The 'splendid isolation' of the British Government did not mean, then, detachment from the affairs of the world or freedom from obligations which might have to be redeemed by force. It meant freedom from prior military commitment to any power or bloc in Europe, and even then with such exceptions as the obligations to Belgium and Portugal, and the Mediterranean agreements of 1887. Salisbury was no more willing than Gladstone to depart from that policy. Great Britain could not bring to a European alliance any great weight on land; she did not wish to be involved to the hilt in contests which were not of supreme moment to her; and her Ministers, unlike those of states differently governed, could not honourably or dependably promise aid which at the critical moment might be withheld. In all this reasoning there was much weight; but if it brought the British solid advantage the policy also carried serious drawbacks. Coupled with a military strength inadequate to any realistic appraisal of British needs, it proved almost fatal in 1914. Long before then, the Boer War had shown that a determined enemy could produce a virtual paralysis of British foreign policy. These extraordinary circumstances must have brought either reform or disaster much earlier but for skilful management and a large bestowal of good luck. They are central to the understanding of Curzon's period at the Foreign Office and, even more, of his years in India.

By the time with which we are dealing, 1895–8, the partition of Africa had been largely accomplished, though the struggles on the Niger and the Nile were yet to be resolved. The chronic weakness of the Ottoman Empire, of Persia, of Siam, of China offered new opportunities, however. It meant that British ascendancy was being challenged with new vigour. This process Curzon had seen for himself. He had realised that the rise of a new power in the Far East must radically alter the situation there. British policy had to be made in new and more perilous conditions. A few months after his arrival at the Foreign Office, he delivered at Derby a warning couched in terms very similar to those employed by Salisbury in the 'dying nations speech' of 1898. Curzon spoke of the uneasy symptoms:

> We hear the moan of sick nations on their couches and we witness the struggles of dying men. . . . This state of affairs is likely to develop rather than to diminish in the future.

As the empty spaces of the world filled up, as population and trade grew, so the points of contact and friction would increase. This condition the British would feel more and more acutely.

Where fifty years ago we had every liberty of movement to go where we chose, we have had within the last twenty years scarcely walking-room; where we had walking-room, now we have scarcely elbow-room; and now, where England has hardly elbow-room, she will very soon have hardly room to move.

Lord Salisbury's method was a pragmatic one, to solve individual issues by patient and reasonable negotiation, but to make no extended promises of co-operation or alliance. With the principle, though not always with its application, Curzon agreed. The abrogation of the Black Sea clauses of the Treaty of Paris, and Penjdeh, had shown what Russia might do when she was on good terms with Germany. Salisbury must try to ensure that those powers did not act in harmony against the British; that France and Russia, their recent alliance notwithstanding, did not support each other too firmly outside Europe; that British interests were defended without recourse to war. Well before the Congress of Berlin he had concluded that the Ottoman Empire was too far gone to be worthy of support. He regretted that the friendship of a growing power, Russia, had been sacrificed to the defence of a decaying one. The performances of the Emperor William during the latter half of 1895 did not inspire in Salisbury much confidence. That sovereign, he judged, had been trying to frighten London into joining the Triple Alliance. This course seemed impossible, since 'the English people would never consent to go to war for a cause in which England was not manifestly interested'.

Nor was Salisbury impressed with German warnings about the dangers of isolation, which he rated far less than the risk of being dragged into wars which did not concern Great Britain. There was not a sensible statesman in England, the Prime Minister told Queen Victoria, who was not anxious for a good understanding with Russia. The Czar, who visited England in 1896, explicitly disclaimed any unfriendly intentions towards India. Salisbury, like the Queen, was struck by Nicholas' friendly demeanour, and determined that all needless aggravations must be avoided.[30]

Since the Armenian massacres, Salisbury had given up any idea of intervening with Austria–Hungary to defend the Sultan against Russia. It might not be possible for England and Russia to return to their old relations, but that was the desired object. 'All we can do is to try to narrow the chasm that separates us. It is the best chance of something like an equilibrium in Europe.'[31]

Salisbury seems at this stage to have been thinking, in his attitude to Russia, rather of the Near East than of Central Asia. The whole Russian administration, he explained to Curzon, had dwelt for the last forty years in an atmosphere of intense Anglophobia, produced by Britain's Crimean policy. The Court of Russia was mildly pro-British, though very indolent:

> But if they last they can hardly fail, in so despotic a country, to affect the Administration.
>
> I should therefore very much deprecate any opposition to Russia which is gratuitous, or is motived [*sic*] only by resentment or impatience. If any object is to be gained by it I have no objection: but as a mere outlet to indignation or patriotic temper, it may do some harm and can do no good.[32]

Gortchakov, in order to indicate his submission to the Imperial whim, had compared himself to 'une éponge à laquelle la pression de la main de l'Empereur fait rendre le liquide dont elle est pénétrée'.[33] Curzon, who followed Russian affairs keenly, felt no doubt of the Czar's power but a good deal of his steadiness. Nor could he forget the long list of broken promises. When Salisbury, early in 1898, revived the possibility of an agreement with Russia, his Under-Secretary doubted whether it was feasible or whether, if it were made, Russia would loyally observe its terms.[34]

Curzon protested against allowing Russia to move beyond the mountains into the plains of Mesopotamia and up to Baghdad, where British influence and trade were predominant. Sooner or later, he argued, this would provide Russia with an excuse for getting down to the Persian Gulf, which it was surely British policy to prevent. Salisbury replied that Russia was very unlikely to recognise British preponderance in Asia Minor without modification: 'I fancy we are asking a great deal more than she means to recognise—and that the negotiation will come to nothing.'[35]

This proved to be the case, largely for reasons connected with China. Some six months before, in the summer of 1897, the Kaiser and the Czar had met. The German demand for Kiao-chow was accepted. After the murder of two missionaries German vessels took possession of the port in mid-November. Salisbury, having to balance out interests the world over, was not thinking in his approach to Russia merely of the general advantages of goodwill. The last stages of the Anglo–French antagonism in Africa were played out at this moment. While Kitchener's advance down the Nile valley to the reconquest of the Sudan was being prepared, Salisbury had felt the need not to antagonise the Russians. At the end of 1897 he explained to members of his family why he meant to let France have concessions in West Africa. The prime rule in negotiation, he said, is to select the key point. This he had long since done. It was to secure the Nile valley without quarrelling with France, a combination of objectives which it would require much skill to achieve. 'If you want to understand my policy at this moment in any part of the world—in Europe, Asia, Africa, or the South Seas—you will have constantly to remember that.'[36]

Shortly after the Germans took Kiao-chow, the Russian Government sent a squadron to 'spend the winter' at Port Arthur. Curzon understood at once what this step portended. He told Salisbury on 29 December that domination by Russia and Germany of the Gulf of Pechili, so close to Pekin, must harm British interests in China, which far outweighed those of any other country. Some step would have to be taken if the European powers were grouping themselves against the British in the Far East:

> We shall probably be driven sooner or later to act with Japan. Ten years hence she will be the greatest naval Power in those seas, and the European Powers who now ignore or flout her will be then competing for her alliance.

As an immediate step, the China squadron might be sent for the winter to Weihaiwei. This policy was not acceptable for the moment. Salisbury had to think of Kitchener moving towards Khartoum and the expedition of Major Marchand also making for the Nile. He thought that Britain did not carry the guns to fight France and Russia together.[37]

On 12 January, 1898, Sir N. O'Conor, the British Ambassador at St Petersburg, was informed by Mouravieff that the Russian fleet was wintering at Port Arthur as a temporary measure. That same day, Staal told Lord Salisbury that the presence of two British vessels at Port Arthur had produced a bad impression in Russia. The Prime Minister rejoined that the ships had a Treaty right to be there. Nevertheless, they would shortly move to another anchorage. A week afterwards, Mouravieff remarked to O'Conor that the presence of the British gunboats at Port Arthur had been deemed in Russia so unfriendly an act as to set afloat 'rumours of war'.

Suggestions for Anglo–Russian co-operation in China proved fruitless, chiefly because Li Hung Chang let the British Government know that a British loan, offered on exceptionally easy terms, had been rejected on account of Russian menaces. Salisbury thought this action 'hostile and insulting', the Russians' attitude insincere and their language ambiguous. Soon afterwards, Lamsdorff, deputising for Mouravieff, indicated clearly that at all costs Russia would hold Port Arthur and Talienwan. China then accepted an Anglo–German loan.[38]

Late in February the Chinese Government offered Britain the lease of Weihaiwei. Salisbury replied that Britain's present policy was to discourage the alienation of Chinese territory. It would be premature to discuss the lease unless the action of other powers materially altered the situation. A few days later, however, Salisbury left for a rest in the South of France. The Cabinet received information that if Britain did not step in at Weihaiwei, Germany would very probably do so.

By then Curzon had prepared a memorandum on the advantages of taking up the lease. Russia, he observed, was about to obtain what would practically be a Russian railway through Manchuria to Port Arthur. She would by the lease or cession (the last being Mouravieff's word) of Port Arthur obtain a commanding position in the Gulf of Pechili. It would become, whatever assurances were given, her naval base in the China Seas. Russia's already preponderant influence at Pekin must increase. If the British retired to the south, Russia would in the end probably control all the provinces to the north of the Hoang-lo. Moreover, Germany was also claiming large advantages in the north. If Britain wished to retain a stake at Pekin, she must take the third port in the north of China Sea, Weihaiwei. 'If we mean no one else to swallow the cherry, why not take it ourselves, instead of having a bite at it, and still leaving it on the plate to excite the appetites of others?'

Copies of this note were given in the first instance to six senior ministers. The initial reactions of all were unfavourable, while the naval experts thought occupation politically desirable but strategically doubtful. The question then came before the Cabinet again and was argued at several meetings, which Curzon attended. Balfour changed his view. Joseph Chamberlain wished to have no stake in the Gulf of Pechili but to retire south to the Yangtse basin. Hicks Beach too remained hostile throughout.[39]

Balfour spoke most seriously to Staal of the alteration in the Far Eastern balance caused by Russian acquisition of the strongest fortified place on the Chinese coast and close to Pekin. Staal judged that it was the capital and the thought of preponderant Russian influence there which haunted British minds. 'C'est exactement cela', noted the Czar.[40]

Moreover, there was British opinion to consider. Balfour wired to Salisbury that the Cabinet believed Weihaiwei must be obtained at all costs; 'any retrogression on our part in this matter would have the worst effect possible in this country.' Salisbury telegraphed his agreement.

A British fleet was despatched from Hong Kong to demand the lease of Weihaiwei. Under threat, it was granted, on the condition that the British would leave it when the Russians departed from the Liaotung peninsula. Salisbury justified the step on the ground that British public opinion, already irritated, might otherwise have mounted to a pitch which the Cabinet could hardly control. He expressed his satisfaction that Balfour and

Curzon had converted the Cabinet. Curzon surmised that Chamberlain had not wished to quarrel with the Russians because he disliked the French even more and thought Britain might soon be at war with them on the Niger.[41]

A good deal of the gilt was taken off the gingerbread by a pledge gratuitously given by Balfour that Weihaiwei would not be connected with the interior by rail. Curzon went to his room and asked why he had said this? Balfour replied that he had seen a map which showed a line of mountains immediately behind the harbour, so he had assumed that no railway could be made. This episode Curzon never forgot.[42] It was his first direct experience, though by no means the last, of the slipshod manner in which Balfour handled great affairs. Nonetheless, the lease of Weihaiwei was a triumph for Curzon. He had realised for the preceding three months what the Russians were going to do, had a policy and argued it so well that the hostile Cabinet were convinced.

Another great issue had served to show Curzon's abilities to a wider public. This concerned the frontiers of India. The Mehtar of Chitral, who had entertained Younghusband and Curzon beneath the gaze of Margot Tennant, was murdered on 1 January, 1895. The uncle whom the dead Mehtar had deposed gained the support of a contumacious chieftain and besieged the Chitral Fort for seven weeks. Two expeditions had to be despatched. They restored the situation. A younger brother of the late Mehtar was recognised. All this happened in the last months of Lord Rosebery's Premiership.

Salisbury's Cabinet had to decide whether to retain Chitral or withdraw. The Fort lay but eighty miles from the newly acquired Russian tracts in the Pamirs. Curzon advised the Cabinet that the Hindu Kush was India's true boundary, which no hostile influence must be allowed to overleap. To evacuate Chitral would leave a solitary gap in the most vulnerable section. The fact that St Petersburg was already protesting against British retention told its own tale. Retreat would allow the Amir an opportunity to march in or intrigue, would produce the worst effect elsewhere on the frontier. There was no need for permanent military occupation. The tribes must be treated fairly, and by judicious distribution of cash, the roads could be kept open by tribal levies, as in Beluchistan and elsewhere. Curzon knew before writing this paper that the Viceroy's Council had been unanimous in the same sense. Other high opinion thought differently. Indeed, a truly British battle was waged for three months in the columns of *The Times*.

However, the Cabinet promptly agreed with Curzon's proposals, which Salisbury supported. Chitral was to be held, British power maintained up to the crest of the Hindu Kush and the road from Peshawar maintained. The policy was adopted with complete success. Chitral remained calm, even in the frontier risings of 1897. As Curzon noted with satisfaction, all predictions of huge expense, large garrisons, revolt and rapine proved to be moonshine.[43]

For a short time comparative peace descended; but peace and the northern marches of India could hardly coexist for long. The staple industry of these regions was war. Each clan and family pursued blood feuds from generation to generation with unrelenting fanaticism, hereditary skill and ferocious cruelty. Flaying alive was one of the less rigorous methods of punishing captives. By gentleman's agreement, this energetic routine was interrupted each year at harvest time.[44]

In the summer of 1897, a Political Officer and three of his escort were murdered on the frontier. But for the expertise and bravery of a Sikh subadar, the whole force would have been slaughtered. Within a few weeks, the fortresses on the Khyber, Landi Kotal and Ali Musjid, had fallen. At intervals during the next weeks, the border spurted into flame here and there.[45] Practically the whole field force of the sub-continent had to be mobilised. The tribes lacked nothing as guerrilla fighters and they were playing at home. General Egerton marched around the Madda Khel country at the head of a fine force. Unfortunately, he could not find the Madda Khels. The Afridis were not excelled in marksmanship and agility even by the Gurkhas. Often the columns could not march more than five or six miles a day through gorges, along narrow ledges on which two pack animals could not pass, under constant sniping. Some of the regions to which they penetrated had been unseen by Europeans since the days of Alexander.

The outbreak of fanaticism, the more serious because wholly unexpected, threw the Swat valley into turmoil. An individual known as 'the mad fakir' sprang to fame as a worker of miracles. He now proposed to work a miracle of monstrous proportions by turning out all the British from the area in eight days by means of a *jehad,* a holy war. Zeal and fanaticism soon provided an army. Intense onslaughts were made upon the British positions, largely held by Indian troops. The fakir prudently withdrew. Slowly the tribes between the Swat valley and the Khyber were forced to submit. Had these excitable, gullible and brave frontiersmen arisen together, the Indian army might have been hard put to it. As it was, there was no shortage of disasters. In August the posts along the Samana ridge were assaulted by vastly superior numbers of Orakzais. Twenty-one Sikh sepoys held a little post upon which visual signalling between the two main forts depended.

At last the walls were breached. Every defender was killed and the corpses mutilated.

This was the most serious crisis which had confronted India since the Mutiny. Every detail Curzon followed from day to day. Since Bokhara had been enfolded within the Russian Empire, the Amir had some reason to conceive himself the leader of Sunni Moslems in Central Asia. But it hardly seemed likely that he had fomented the risings,[46] though he might well have winked at them. Nor was it likely that Constantinople was the source of inspiration, since it was only a crude and untutored form of Mohammedanism that prevailed amongst the mountain tribes. There had been no movement at Chitral itself, and the retention of that place did not seem to be the cause of the risings;

> What is called a forward policy [Curzon told Salisbury], is the only policy which the natives really understand or respect. But if they see it weakly carried out or imperfectly supported, they jump at the opportunity of striking one more blow for complete independence. I believe therefore that the real lesson of these risings is that we have been trying to guard an enormously extended and physically very difficult frontier with insufficient bodies of men. . .

Curzon's own visits to the frontier had convinced him that the influence of a few outstanding men counted for everything there:

> Frontier officers of experience and popularity, and with some knowledge of the native languages, are far more likely to keep a frontier quiet and to find out what the tribesmen are doing or contemplating than the most highly trained official sent down from Simla. . .[47]

This view seems to have coincided with the Prime Minister's. He thought that it had often been the mistake of the government of India to think only of Russia 'which at worst is a distant danger, and to ignore the danger from native discontent which lies at their feet'. Salisbury told the Queen that there had apparently been a lack of clear knowledge about what was impending and also a want of preparation. This opinion she passed on to the Viceroy, without revealing its source.[48]

The government of India determined upon a demonstration of military might. Indeed, they had little choice. Crops and villages were burned, wells stopped, dams breached, animals slaughtered. There was nothing new in this policy, except its scale. It was known among the cognoscenti as 'hit and scuttle' or 'butcher and beat it'. Curzon had thought that the Afridis' behaviour must be rewarded in a manner they would not forget. After that, they should be skilfully treated. They would then, he felt sure, be found loyal adherents and useful recruits.[49]

It was freely alleged that the tribes had revolted because of the retention of Chitral and the construction of the roads to the Fort. During the autumn many a platform rang to denunciations of the folly and depravity of Lord Salisbury's government. The opportunity was too good to miss. Early in December, Curzon derided to his constituents

> the speeches of gentlemen, many of them of the highest eminence, who until this outbreak could not have told you the name of a single tribe on the frontier, but who, having got up the question during the past three months, now enlarge with all the enthusiasm of new-made converts, and with all the majesty of second-hand information, upon Indian frontier policy. . .
>
> Mr Asquith says that the tribes considered the construction of the road to be a gross breach of faith. I do not know what special means Mr Asquith enjoys of ascertaining what are the views and the feelings of the men of Swat. (Laughter) In another speech he talked about the half-naked tribesmen of Swat, and if his knowledge of their feelings is to be measured by his acquaintance with their exterior, I can only say that it need not be treated with any very remarkable respect. . .[50]

Evidently the British and Indian governments had to find a more reliable method of conducting their frontier policy. Curzon had little doubt where the model should be found. During these widespread risings, Beluchistan had remained quiet. It had been pacified by Sir Robert Sandeman, with whom Curzon stayed at Quetta and often corresponded. Sandeman possessed firmness, tact, thoroughness and massive commonsense. His personality became a legend.[51]

The essence of Sandeman's policy had been constant travel and personal intercourse with the tribes and their chiefs, together with subsidies to them for undertaking militia duties. That was the policy recommended by Curzon in the speech he delivered on 15 February, 1898, just after Parliament reassembled. He poured scorn on charges of ill-faith, made fun of the contradictory speeches delivered by members of the Opposition, pointed out that the Liberal Party was not innocent of all connexion with interference in Chitral.

> I have never quite understood why a Liberal Government is to be at liberty to drive a road through a free and independent country and to slaughter the inhabitants who resist, while a Conservative Government is not to be allowed to maintain that road when once it is made.

The fact that Curzon had himself been to Chitral, had met and questioned all the officers there, gave him an obvious advantage of which he was not slow to avail himself. Describing the two easy passes of the Hindu Kush, both near Chitral, one leading into India, the other into Afghanistan, he paused to correct an assertion of Sir H. Fowler that the height of these passes was Alpine and denied that the Chitral policy had produced the frontier uprisings:

> The fact is, and nobody who knows anything of the tribes will deny it, that the Afridis and Orakzais care nothing whatever for, and know very little of, the people of Swat. There is next to no communication between the two, and if those tribesmen could hear these debates I believe they would have an even worse idea of our intelligence than they already have in a few unfortunate cases of our arms.

The Lawrence policy of aloofness from the mountain tribes was dead and could not be revived, the whole situation having been altered by the advance of Russia and the British obligations to Abdur Rahman. As for the future, the policy of pillage and retreat meant a confession of failure. Yet the tribes could not be left alone; without peaceful passage through their territory, commitments to Afghanistan could not be honoured. The secret was to find men who, like Sandeman, would know the languages, mingle with the tribes, display conciliation and courage: 'It is a question not of rifles and of cannon but of character and of all that character can do amid a community of free men.'[52]

This was a noteworthy performance. Some commentators judged Curzon's oration to have been the outstanding effort of the session. In knowledge, judgment and constructive capacity he had shown himself the equal of any contemporary and of most of his seniors; and the occasion happened to occur at a crucial moment. Curzon had long since established himself as an outstanding junior Minister. He explained lucidly a policy which was not always easy to defend. Questioners who took a special interest in the Uganda railway, Armenian massacres, slavery in Zanzibar, Crete, Persia, Siam and other tiresome subjects rarely caught him napping. Question-time became an eagerly-awaited occasion, for Curzon possessed much quickness of mind, allied with a taste for cutting language. He had by now shed a good deal of the manner which had caused Labouchère to complain of 'a divinity addressing black beetles'. *Punch* published a verse:

> The mystery of Isis
> A wonder to the wise is:
> Yet 'tis, though fraught
> With marvel, naught
> To—Curzon on a crisis.

*   *   *   *

Salisbury admired the skill with which Curzon steered his way through the shoals. 'Your speech was all that could be desired'; 'I thought your speech at Southport admirable.'[53] The Under-Secretary enjoyed the work, though the burden was murderous, but could not find in Westminster any substitute for the East. Moreover, and vitally important, his career in the House of Commons must in any event be broken on Lord Scarsdale's death.

It was in April, 1897, that Curzon first opened his mind to Salisbury. He wrote of his acquaintance with the leading men in India, with the frontier problems, and neighbouring states:

> I believe a very great work can be done in India by an English Viceroy who is young and active and intensely absorbed in his work…a good deal of energy and application would be wanted and—what very few men take to India—a great love of the country and pride in the imperial aspect of its possession.

Curzon asked his chief to believe that this ambition did not imply indifference to his duties at the Foreign Office, and that his main motive was not personal, but a desire while still 'in the heyday of life to do some strenuous work in a position of responsibility and in a case for which previous study and training have rendered me in some measure less unfit for the effort.'[54]

Salisbury replied that he was not surprised at the turn Curzon's thoughts had taken, 'in view of the Peerage to which you are destined—or doomed'. He made no promises, observing that it might not be in his power to make the appointment a year and a half thence. The tone of the letter was distinctly encouraging:

> If the idea which you mention should be realised, India will be very much the richer, and F.O. the poorer by the transaction. No one could say of such an appointment that it had put upon the roll of Indian Viceroys a name not fully worthy of those who have gone before.[55]

Twelve months later, after his Parliamentary reputation and political standing had grown, Curzon wrote to the Prime Minister again:

> It may be thought that I am too young—yet I am in my fortieth year; or too ardent—yet nothing considerable has ever been done without enthusiasm.
> …For 12 years I have worked and studied and thought, with a view—should the chance ever arise—to fitting myself for the position.

He again disclaimed personal ambition as the root of his keenness. Many friends said that it would be folly to go away for five years, resign a Parliamentary career:

I can truly say that my anxiety in the case arises from an honest and not ignoble desire to render some service to a cause which I have passionately at heart.[56]

Though Curzon did not know it, Salisbury had in January advised the Queen that there were two members of the government who would make a good Viceroy. The first was the Chancellor of the Exchequer, Sir Michael Hicks Beach, the other Mr Curzon:

He is a man, in many respects, of great ability, as well as of extraordinary industry and knowledge. Lord Salisbury has had an opportunity of observing him closely for two years and a half; and is of opinion that his character and powers have developed with official work. His only fault is occasional rashness of speech in the House of Commons; but [Lord Salisbury added characteristically] he would have no temptation to that error at Calcutta. He has now a strong *physique*.[57]

In May Salisbury ascertained from Sir William Lockhart, Commander-in-Chief-elect in India, that he would be pleased to serve under Curzon. This news was passed to the Queen, who commented that Lockhart's good opinion of Curzon carried great weight. Moreover, Curzon's friendly feelings towards the Amir, and his knowledge of Afghanistan, were most important:

But that is not all [Queen Victoria wrote to the Prime Minister on May 29th.] The future Viceroy must really shake himself more and more free from his red-tapist, narrow-minded Council and entourage. He must be more independent, must *hear for himself* what the *feelings* of the Natives really are, and do what he thinks right, and not be guided by the *snobbish* and vulgar overbearing and offensive behaviour of many of our Civil and Political Agents, if we are to go on peacefully and happily in India, and to be liked and beloved by high and low, as well as respected as we ought to be, and not trying to trample on the people and continually reminding them and make them feel that they are a conquered people. They must of course *feel* that we are masters, but it should be done kindly and not offensively, which alas! is so often the case. Would Mr Curzon feel and do this?[58]

Salisbury next consulted the Secretary of State for India. Lord George Hamilton fully admitted Curzon's claims, but mistrusted his judgment. He had enquired privately in the India Office, where the general answer was 'a regular Jingo, with Russia on the brain'. Lord George preferred Balfour of Burleigh, strong, cautious, and much more likely to keep the soldiers in order. If Curzon were chosen, the Cabinet should send out a despatch, clearly laying down a policy, so that he would be prevented from launching out into fanciful frontier schemes:

His powers are rhetorical rather than constructive and he loves a splash. I think our dangers in India are internal rather than external, and Curzon's mind will be concentrated on foreign affairs, where if he makes a mistake he will aggravate domestic as well as external complications.[59]

Salisbury nevertheless determined to appoint him. Receiving the satisfactory result of a medical examination, Salisbury informed Curzon that he intended to submit his name shortly to the Queen. He enclosed her letter, which she had particularly asked that Curzon should see. The sovereign's forceful injunctions met with her Prime Minister's complete approval: 'Paper—and "damned nigger"—are threatening our rule in India,' he wrote 'and unfortunately as we grow more contemptuous, the Indian natives of all races are becoming more conscious of it, and more sensitive.'

The Prime Minister told Curzon how sorry he would be to sever their official connexion and to lose his help in the Commons. The last passage of the letter revealed more than his unfailing courtesy:

I have to thank you most earnestly for the unremitting labour and brilliant ability with which you have conducted the business of the Foreign Office in critical times—and have defended it with so much success in Parliament.[60]

Curzon agreed that the newcomer to India must set an example to those who by long residence in the East in posts of power had become hardened, sometimes almost brutalised. He would try to control the sort of spirit which had caused a French writer to say of British rule, 'Ils sont justes mais ils ne sont pas bons', for he had been thrown so much in the company of Asiatic peoples that he hoped he had lost 'the insular race-arrogance of the Englishman'.[61]

No news of the appointment leaked out. It was announced on 11 August, to a chorus of congratulation. Curzon was thirty-nine, the youngest Viceroy ever appointed with the single exception of Dalhousie. Liberal opponents, in particular, sent kind messages; Labouchère, Morley, Asquith, Grey, who said that no Minister's work had been more respected and admired by the opposition, Harcourt, who begged as a personal favour that Curzon would not make war upon Russia in his lifetime, T. P. O'Connor, who wrote of his 'real genius' for the House of Commons. Even Lord Scarsdale was a little overwhelmed:

I begin to realise [he wrote] what a splendid position you have deservedly won. Congrats pour in from every quarter and the county generally are as proud of you as I, your Father, am, and more I cannot say.

The Times commented in a balancing way: 'We sincerely trust, for Mr
3

Curzon's sake and for that of the Empire, that Lord Salisbury's very interesting experiment will succeed.'

Novoe Vremya remarked, after a very full review of Curzon's career, that his appointment had in it little that was consoling to Russia. After the Czar's solemn call to universal peace, the paper disdained to argue again Russia's unwillingness to invade India; but she was interested in the development of 'commercial relations' with Persia and in the 'stability' of her Central Asian frontiers. Mr Curzon's acts in India must be followed with a keen eye. [62]

Curzon's appointment meant the severance of his connexion with the Crabbet Club, for the rules laid it down that any member accepting a place in the Cabinet, a viceroyalty (especially that of India) or an Archbishopric was required to resign, although he might hope to resume his privilege if his new public duties were subordinated to the higher interests of the Club.

> I trust this may be the case with you [wrote Wilfrid Scawen Blunt, the President], and that you may prove the best, the most frivolous (even remembering Lytton) and the last of our Viceroys...I notice that you have no single qualification but that of Crabbet Club membership fitting you for the high post you are called on to fill, and the appointment is a new tribute, and the most conspicuous the Club has yet obtained, to its inestimable merits as a nursery of irresponsible statesmen. . .

*   *   *   *

On his last visit to India, in 1894, Curzon had stood before Government House, which was modelled upon Kedleston. 'When I next see this' he vowed 'I shall see it as Viceroy; and I shall bring Walter Lawrence as my Secretary.'

Lawrence had been a friend at Balliol who had passed first in open competition for the Indian Civil Service and had then enjoyed a brilliant career. As settlement officer he had recast the economic life of Kashmir and had written about that enchanted country a book which Curzon admired. [63] He had left the ICS to become agent to the Duke of Bedford. Curzon, knowing his special qualities, persuaded him to go back as Private Secretary to the Viceroy. This was arranged. It had a good deal to do with the success of Curzon's early years. The Viceroyalty itself Curzon owed to his own organising ability, 'middle-class method' as he called it, mental capacity and physical endurance. In the House, he had had to fight his own way up and was a self-made man.

George Curzon was not born into the ruling circle, nor did he possess the habits of an aristocrat in the sense that Lord Lansdowne, for example, possessed them. Aloof detachment and a preference for understatement were not among Curzon's characteristics. He craved activity, decision, efficiency. Beneath the façade of haughtiness Baldwin rightly discerned an exquisite sensitivity. His powerful emotions, disciplined only by continual effort, never lay far from the surface. Religious orthodoxy he had abandoned at Oxford in favour of a loose theism. Implicit belief in an after-life and in the value of prayer he retained to the end.

Curzon's normal working day was one of some twelve or fourteen hours. Six or eight hours' toil constituted his idea of a complete rest. It was not merely that he worked long hours; plenty of men in high positions do that. Curzon had a capacious memory, coupled with extreme quickness of decision. The result was that he often accomplished in a day what would take another man a week. Much of his achievement sprang from an almost unbelievable fluency. Hesitation in the composition of a speech, a letter or a despatch was almost unknown to him. His powers as a speaker he consistently under-rated. The reading of Hansard leaves the impression of a first-class debater, answering impromptu the arguments just advanced and returning surely to the main theme. His set-piece orations, and especially those delivered on solemn or ceremonial occasions, were even better. Best of all were the after-dinner speeches, nostalgic and hilarious by turns, which he was sometimes prevailed upon to give. His private talk, especially with women, was entrancing. 'Through all his conversation' wrote Lady Brooke 'like sunlight dappling a wooded stream, gleamed the constant flash of his wit, and the ripple of laughter that seemed the more wonderful to me because I knew of his constant pain.'[64]

In these years, when there was already no hope of cure, Curzon would refer to his weak spine, without rancour, as a fact which must be accepted, much as he might have regarded blindness in one eye, or paralysis of a hand, as a handicap severe but not dominant. In unremitting work he sought and discovered emancipation not only from the physical pain but from the fear that he might be prevented from achieving what was in him to do. 'When you are sufficiently absorbed in a big problem, you can forget yourself, and in that forgetfulness comes release.'[65]

Curzon once said that he tried to lift everything he undertook to a plane above the normal, a desire rooted not only in a passion for excellence but in a resolve to prove that he had risen superior to the infirmities of the bodily shell. The least gullible of men in issues of high politics, Curzon nonetheless had much in him that was simple-minded, almost naive. His love of magniloquence and display, his fondness for risqué jokes and riotous good company, might seem to place him more securely in the eighteenth century than in his own time. At the core of his character, however, lay intense earnestness, an unfeigned belief in the value of Empire not so much as a source of wealth as of opportunity to serve. It was not that he thought Englishmen necessarily superior as a race to all others. Certainly he did not conceive Western European civilisation to hold any immanent superiority over that of other regions. But he was convinced that the British had shown exceptional qualities as a governing race, and exceptional capacity to work hard and honestly for others. He was in that sense an unrepentant imperialist.

'Imperialism' has now so many meanings that it is valueless except as a term of political abuse. Though Salisbury had asserted that the trade of a great commercial country like Britain could flourish only under the shadow of Empire, the economic motive for the acquisition of Empire in the late nineteenth century has been much over-stressed. The British were investing heavily and trading freely in regions which formed no part of their Empire; South America, the United States, China, Western Europe. The large bulk of the newly-acquired territories in Africa were of minimal economic value and were certainly not acquired solely for economic reasons. Strategy and prestige often played a larger role; and if imperialism is 'the objectless disposition on the part of a state to unlimited forcible expansion'[66] neither Curzon nor Milner nor Cromer was an imperialist. Had Disraeli or Gladstone or Salisbury so wished, the British could have had for the asking much larger areas of Africa than they took. The belief that Britain, in virtue of industrial primacy, exported much surplus capital to colonies which provided raw materials and rich markets is a poor explanation of her African expansion and no explanation at all of the kind of imperialism of which Curzon was a spokesman. To his mind, the African colonies were of infinitely less value in every sense than the Asian. Certainly no African territory began to compare with India. In the exercise of British power beyond the confines of Great Britain Curzon believed wholeheartedly. It was to his mind essential to the continued existence of Great Britain as a first-class power. The price had to be paid in effort, sometimes in danger. Anyway, Empire was there, a fact:

> We cannot deny our own progeny. We cannot disown our own handiwork. The voyages which our predecessors commenced we have to continue. We have to answer our helm, and it is an Imperial helm, down all the tides of Time.[67]

★   ★   ★   ★

'The cloud is black all round for England' wrote Curzon to Milner early in

1898. 'I say my rosary every morning' he replied—' "North West Frontier, China, Uganda, Sudan, West Africa".'[68] Some of those anxieties were assuaged, temporarily at least, before Curzon left for India. The troubles on the North West frontier died down. The West African negotiations, after many vicissitudes, were resolved in mid-June. Salisbury had not lost sight of his key point, the Nile. 'If you wish to come to terms,' he told Chamberlain, 'it would be prudent to do so before we take Khartoum. We shall get nothing out of the French Assembly after that event.'[69]

The Ambassador in Paris, Sir E. Monson, thought the new Foreign Minister, Delcassé, very combative. Russia, he believed, would probably support France in case of war with Great Britain. Even Salisbury, never given to undue alarm, feared a clash not only in the Nile Valley but perhaps in Europe.[70] Two months later, in mid-September, Kitchener and Marchand faced each other at Fashoda. Salisbury stood firm, saying that the Sudan was British by right of conquest. Delcassé urged that there should be no humiliation. 'Do not ask me for the impossible, do not drive me into a corner.' Should war break out, France would not stand alone. France would rather accept war than submit.[71] But the Cabinet, believing that Marchand's tiny force occupied an untenable position, made no move towards concession. Late in October, the fleet was placed on a war footing. A fortnight later, the Cabinet decided that the sum of £500,000 should be assigned immediately for the provision of quick-firing cannon, especially for the Channel fortresses.[72] Salisbury had realised that Russia did not intend fighting France's battles in Africa, where Russian interests were non-existent: 'a war now would be inconvenient to her. She wishes to stop it: but whether it is stopped by France yielding or England yielding, she does not care...'[73]

Soon afterwards, the French gave way. China, another of the beads which Lord Milner used to tell in his rosary, was in a much less satisfactory state. Chamberlain had concluded that without allies Great Britain was powerless to resist the ultimate control of China by Russia, and placed at a great disadvantage in negotiating with France. His solution was a treaty with Germany 'providing for reciprocal defence'. The Prime Minister agreed that 'a closer relation' with Germany would be most desirable; 'but can we get it?'[74] The overtures to Germany of that year, in which Chamberlain played a prominent part, produced no alliance. It is difficult to see how they could have done, for the British could not offer Germany an army which would compensate for the increased hostility of Russia and France, while Germany could not offer the British any substantial addition of naval power.

*   *   *   *

To celebrate the passing of a Soul, George and Mary Curzon were entertained, on the eve of their departure for India, by sixty-five friends at the Hotel Cecil. George Wyndham had produced an affectionate poem of congratulation, looking forward to a joyous homecoming. Curzon saw round him the friends

> of a tumultuous but absolutely unrepentant youth, the comrades of a more sober and orderly middle age – and when I return five years hence, what I hope may be the props and the solace of dull and declining years...
>
> Come and visit us in India...You shall see the Eastern sun gild the eternal crests of the Himalayas in the morning, and sink to rest behind the boundless Western plains...George Wyndham shall compose a sonnet in the groves of the Taj; and the lady, or ladies, who accompany him, shall respond in a manner appropriate to the occasion and the locality. Above all, we will give you an English welcome in an Indian home; and you shall realise that behind the starch of a purely superficial solemnity, there lurk the same incorrigible characteristics which you have alternately bewailed and pardoned here.[75]

From Brodrick Curzon received a long letter of farewell, containing a solemn plea for a less frantic tempo of work. He recalled their twenty-one years of intimacy:

> It has been one of the brightest elements in my life, to work with you and see you gaily flying the fences which I have laboriously climbed...
>
> You will never want a friend – nor have need of any assistance I could give – but no separation will ever make me feel that you or yours are altogether apart from one who has so long been
>
> Your affectionate Friend,
St John Brodrick.[76]

THREE

The Government of India

AFTER A FEW DAYS' consultation with the outgoing Viceroy, Lord Elgin, Curzon assumed the Viceroyalty on 3 January, 1899. As he took his seat in the Council Chamber at Calcutta, the warrant of appointment, signed by the Queen, was read:

> We do hereby give and grant unto you our Governor-General of India and your Council as the Governor-General of India in Council, the superintendence, direction and control of the whole civil and military government of all our territories and revenues in India...and we do hereby order and require all our servants, officers and soldiers in the East Indies...to conform, submit and yield due obedience unto you and your Council.

No more responsible position was open to a British citizen. The population of India, estimated at 206 millions in 1871, had reached almost 300 millions, one fifth of the human race. The total would have been a good deal higher but for the broad swath cut by famine, cholera and especially by plague, which is said to have killed eight million Indians between 1896 and 1905. About two thirds of the people were Hindus, subdivided into numerous castes, cut off from each other; sixty millions or so were Moslems, with smaller numbers of Parsees, Christians and Sikhs. Twelve major languages and some two hundred dialects were spoken. India equalled, in area and population, the whole of Europe, excluding Russia. The border running from the Bay of Bengal to the Pamirs measured 1,400 miles, and thence to Karachi another 1,200. The sea frontier round the southernmost tip at Cape Comorin was about 3,000 miles long, roughly the distance between London and New York. Every variety of climate and scene was met, from tropical humidity to the bracing bite of the Himalayas, from the wastes of Rajputana to the luxuriance of Kashmir. One tenth of the entire trade of the British Empire passed through the ports of India. She was the largest producer of food and raw material in the Empire, the largest buyer of British goods. By the end of Curzon's time, nearly £350 million of

British capital was invested there. Most of it, to India's material advantage, had been borrowed at three per cent or three and a half per cent. That sum represented between a sixth and a seventh of Great Britain's overseas investment.

The position of the Viceroy stood out sharp and distinct from that of any other servant of the Crown. He represented the throne, corresponded directly with the sovereign, took precedence in ceremonial even over the King's brother or heir, was the fountain of honour, master of the Orders of the Indian Empire and the Star of India. In these respects he fulfilled the functions of a regent; in others, those of a president or prime minister. He and his colleagues were responsible to no elected assembly in India, a position which brought its advantages in freedom of manœuvre and also its drawbacks, for a Secretary of State could defend and expound his policy from day to day in parliament, whereas the Viceroy must often suffer abuse which he could not contradict. 'That' wrote Curzon, 'is what one *feels* in foreign service.'[1] A Viceroy did not have expert advice so readily available as did the Prime Minister, nor the same number of colleagues amongst whom to share out the burdens of government. Dalhousie once said that a Governor-General was unlike any other Minister under heaven, the beginning, middle and end of all. He was the ultimate authority in every disputed point 'from a sea-wall at Tumlick to a plunge-bath at Peshawar.' To Curzon it seemed that the Viceroy was inevitably becoming more of a prime minister and less of a figurehead. He must have a policy and explain it:

> What people at home do not realise [he urged upon the unconvinced Godley] is that the Viceroy is no longer the Great Mogul throned in majesty and wrapped in silence. With the telegraph wire everywhere and with an active and enterprising press, he and he alone is the Government in its personal aspect; and from his lips the Indian people look to learn how and wherefore they are governed...[2]

This mixture of functions brought special problems. The Sovereign, unifying force in a fissiparous country, was represented not by a figure uplifted above political controversy but by a regent who was the active head of the government, carrying measures which might be much disliked, and appointed in accordance with the Conservative or Liberal character of the government in London. It was, Curzon found, a position of loneliness. 'What one longs for is help, solace, advice, the talk of friends. The Viceroy is too much above everybody to get it...'[3] Lady Curzon put it in more homely fashion:

The lot of a Viceroy is one of absolute aloofness and everyone is in mortal funk of the august being. Being a yankee I can't understand it but I manage to assume the necessary amount of awful respect for His X when we appear in public.'[4]

Five years, Curzon believed, was not nearly long enough for a man to leave a lasting mark. A Viceroy who came out, as most did, knowing nothing of the East, had barely learned his business before being wafted away. Yet to stay longer than six or seven years meant death to both Dalhousie and Canning. Since their time the business had multiplied out of all recognition: 'I think' he told Salisbury, 'that the work of the post is the most continuous in the world; for there are no holidays and the concentration of authority is greater than in any administration that I have seen...'[5]

Correspondence with the home government about Aden, Persia, Afghanistan, Central Asia, Tibet and Siam came before the Viceroy in his capacity as head of the Foreign Department, which dealt also with the tumultuous affairs of the frontier and with the chiefs. As political head of the administration, he received hundreds of petitions upon every conceivable subject; dealt constantly with military questions, many of which had a bearing on frontier affairs or the politics of India; corresponded regularly with the Governors, Lieutenants-Governor and Chief Commissioners, with the Sovereign, the Secretary of State and the Under-Secretary at the India Office. The Viceroy carried on all the ceremonial and social duties of a head of state, presided over the Council, saw his colleagues and the Secretary to each Department; in short, gave the administration its cohesion and direction.

★   ★   ★   ★

Separate from British India, there existed more than six hundred princely states, covering about one third of the continent and including a quarter of its population. It is well to remember that these were not governed in their internal affairs by the British but by Indians. At the principal courts was a Resident, whose advice might or might not be followed. Short of proven madness or the most sustained and gross misconduct, the chiefs could behave as they pleased. Some of the territories were vast, Hyderabad being almost half as large as France, Mysore nearly two thirds the size of England. Generally, but not invariably, the standard of their administration was below that of British India. The 'princes' of India were in fact a polyglot body, some rich as Croesus, others no more than petty landowners or squires. They occupied a curious and ambivalent position. None possessed the real attributes of sovereignty, the right to make treaties and raise armies; but their security against external attack or internal upheaval was guaranteed by the paramount power. In return, Curzon insisted that the princes must attend to their duties. Frequent trips to Europe, in which a number of them liked to indulge, he vowed to stop. India could not afford that the princes should become disinterested aliens in their own territories, nor could their subjects be expected to pay indefinitely for the gratification of irresponsible whims. Yet the chiefs' support might in a moment of crisis mean everything; even at normal times the presence of a body dependent on British goodwill meant much.

Curzon saw with alarm the decline in character of certain Indian princes. Some were little better than sots. Maharaja Holkar of Indore was described by the Resident there, Francis Younghusband, as a lunatic with lucid intervals. Patiala was no more than a jockey, Curzon told the Queen, and the Raja of Kapurthala only happy in Paris. The premier Sikh had 'secretly married the daughter of a disreputable European aeronaut, who was giving performances in his State.'[6]

Such situations presented any Viceroy with a most teasing dilemma. Many of the globe-trotting princes were treated as royalty in Europe, not least at Windsor and Balmoral. The maintenance of the Native States was held to be essential to the raj; yet some of the chiefs themselves seemed likely, by their indifference and extravagance, to bring the whole edifice down.

> The Indians [Curzon wrote to the King] will not tolerate a wide abyss between British administration and Native administration. They have a natural loyalty to their own Chiefs, and perhaps a natural preference for Native over British rule. But if the Native Chiefs are to become absentees, if they are to be infected with foreign tastes and vices, then in proportion as they have lost touch with the people, so will their people lose touch with them...[7]

It was one of the many minor anomalies of British dominion in India that while permission of the Viceroy must be sought by most princes wishing to travel abroad, those who came under the Presidencies, Bombay and Madras, approached the Governor. Curzon decided that in future they too must apply to the centre. The number of permissions granted would be reduced. Hamilton commented that although the princes were supposed to be among the most loyal adherents of British rule, their position had not been made very enviable.

> We are always trying to keep in the paths of virtue and morality a number of gentlemen who have no liking for such walks...I suppose we are com-

mitted to the schoolmaster's methods, and travelling in Europe unfits the Native Prince for the schoolboy's part, so I don't dissent from your wish as headmaster, to stop the exeats of your pupils. But it is a funny method of governing a big Empire.[8]

To this remark Curzon did not demur in the least. It was not only true but inevitable, 'for what are they but a set of unruly and ignorant and rather undisciplined schoolboys?' The princes, in their own interest, must pass through some kind of discipline, must be weaned 'even by a grandmotherly interference' from frivolity and dissipation. The policy of leaving them to go to ruin, as an object-lesson to their people, would be fatal. Why did their people need an object-lesson anyway? Already protests at extravagance and tyranny were being heard. British policy since the Mutiny had been to sustain the native states 'not so much in the interests of the Princes themselves, who are often quite undeserving of the compliment, as in the interests of the people, who are supposed to like the old traditions and dynasties and rule'.

If the standard of behaviour were not raised, and the British allowed the Native States to be governed by 'a horde of frivolous absentees who have lost the respect and affection of their own subjects', what would be the justification for the States at all? If the rulers' thrones were to be guaranteed, some degree of control there must be. 'Princes cannot afford, any more than Viceroys, to live exclusively in palaces ... they must be out and about, setting an example among their fellow creatures.'[9]

A circular was accordingly published, enjoining higher standards of application. It met a good deal of criticism in England. Lord George told the Queen that it must cause resentment and diminish the influence the Viceroy had been gaining with the princes by personal contact.[10] However, the Indian press, always sensitive where the princes were concerned, approved overwhelmingly. This was the negative part of a policy Curzon followed consistently. The principal chiefs were visited in their states and entertained at Calcutta in Warren Hastings' old house. Help was given in the improvement of their administrations. Curzon described them as his colleagues and partners, who must take up their part of the burden. The more devoted and earnest responded to this treatment, while others tolerated it for lack of an alternative. The chiefs' contributions to the fighting forces of the British Empire in 1900–2, and during the World Wars, were generous. Most of them remained faithful to the Crown and to the British connection.

★   ★   ★   ★

Leaving aside the princely states, India was divided into administrative units of varying size, each under an official of the ICS. Two exceptions, the Presidencies of Madras and Bombay, stood in a relation to the central government and to the India Office different from that of the other provinces. Hamilton admitted from the start that he had found the Governor, Lord Sandhurst, and the Bombay government, hopelessly uncommunicative. Hints, remonstrance and finally orders had failed to produce any reaction. Elgin had complained constantly but without effect. Thinking Sandhurst a stupid fellow (his main qualification seems to have been his relation to Lord Spencer) Lord George looked to Curzon's accession as a favourable moment to bring the government of Bombay more firmly into leading strings.[11] He warned that Bombay was almost isolated from Calcutta. Previous protests having produced no visible effect, he thought he must now use language of 'offensive frankness'. The jealousy of the Bombay government, which was permanent, and the inability of Sandhurst to realise his proper rôle, would be one of the new Viceroy's main difficulties: 'we must lay down clearly and sharply the subordination of Bombay'.[12]

This was easier said than done. After a few months Curzon was convinced that Sandhurst had broken down and was unfit for the post. Repeated appeals for information[13] produced general assurances of loyalty but no real answer. Madras was equally detached, though in a different manner. In more than fifteen months, Curzon heard not a word from the Governor, whom he had requested to write at frequent intervals. Periodically a case would come to the Viceroy in which the Governor wanted to do this or that; but with these occasional exceptions Curzon knew 'far less of what is going on in Madras than I do of what is passing in Egypt or France; and as for the supposed responsibility of the Viceroy, it has long ago vanished into thin air'.

Admittedly, Indian administration was in many ways over-centralised and plenty of petty affairs came up to the departments which should have been settled locally. The authority of the Viceroy and his Council, however, had almost disappeared, for there was little contact between the supreme and local governments. Madras and Bombay had become virtually separate and independent dominions. Even when Sir Arthur Havelock did break silence, it was only to let Curzon know that someone had covered Queen Victoria's statue at Madras with tar. Meanwhile serious riots were taking place in the Tinnevelley district, about which the Viceroy was left to get his information from the press.[14]

Curzon proposed that the enhanced status of the two Presidencies be reduced. Bombay and Madras had populations of about 19 and 35 millions respectively. Other provinces, though far larger, were administered by a member of the ICS as Lieutenant-Governor. The Governors of Bombay and Madras, appointed from home, ruled with a small Council, and, lacking expert knowledge of India, were apt to be prisoners of their secretariats. They also enjoyed the right of direct correspondence with the Secretary of State, permitted to no-one else except the Viceroy. This system, Curzon judged, entailed in practice the detachment of these two administrations, and the prevalence of chronic mistrust. He quoted the celebrated description 'They are subordinate, with a qualified privilege of insubordination'. The only justification for preserving Bombay and Madras for men from home was that the right candidates should be forthcoming. In practice, they very often were not and the point was reached when these posts had sometimes gone begging among second- or third-rate politicians.

Hamilton admitted that for administrative purposes the whole machine would work more effectively if Bombay and Madras were put on the footing of the other Governorships, and that in recent years England had sent out to Madras and Bombay Governors unfit to discharge their duties properly. All the same, Lord George did not want to introduce a system whereby all the principal posts in India became the preserve of the ICS and from which men bred in the parliamentary life of England would be excluded. Curzon remained unconvinced. Some day, he hoped, there would arise in England a government which, putting administrative efficiency above social prestige and rank, would sweep away 'these picturesque excrescences on the surface of the most specialised service in the world'.[15]

By far the most serious event of Curzon's first two years was the famine, the most devastating on record. Parts of the Bombay presidency were terribly afflicted. The response of the government there seemed inadequate, even when Sandhurst had been replaced by Lord Northcote. Curzon surmised, no doubt rightly, that most people would think the Viceroy of India to some degree accountable for mistakes of famine policy. Yet the system was in practice one of complete decentralisation. 'I am no more responsible for them than the man in the moon, and ... for some time past, in public and private I have done nothing but hammer away at Bombay.'[16] Notwithstanding this prolonged battle, Curzon judged after meeting the new Governor that the main fault lay with the secretariat. Northcote would soon get to grips, he hoped, though for the moment he hardly displayed the confidence needful in a Governor and seemed to suppress himself 'almost out of existence'. Havelock was due to leave shortly and

Curzon was not heartbroken at the prospect, for he could not bring himself to believe that the government of Madras had been treated harshly. He realised the difficulties created by his youthfulness and pursuit of a more efficient administration:

> Of course I disturb and annoy these old fogies, looking into everything, writing about everything, picking out the flaws, always urging promptitude and decision, always detecting and protesting against delay. How can they possibly like it? It is a new sensation, which no man above fifty could relish.

Curzon tried to make it up by showing keen interest in the aspirations and successes of the Governors: 'but still, from time to time, they must smart somewhat, and at the bottom of my heart I do not blame them for it.'[17]

A variety of complaints and hints had meanwhile reached Lord George Hamilton from Northcote and Havelock. Their burden was that Curzon was centralising unduly the work of Indian government, and behaving too brusquely towards subordinates. Hamilton warned the Viceroy, but with consummate grace:

> I hope and believe your term of office will be an epoch, a hinge upon which a new and more generous policy will revolve. But all reformers have difficulties to overcome and in India the opposition is more fierce and persistent than in any part of the Empire. Knowing the need of husbanding your strength, I want to reduce to a minimum preventible antagonism...

Curzon could manage men, Hamilton wrote, as easily as he could do most other things; but the tone of the letters from Madras and Bombay indicated that the Governors' attitude was not confined to themselves. Godley, to whom this letter was shown, minuted that it would 'produce at least an intention to amend. I doubt whether it, or anything, can do more'.

Hamilton took these portents so seriously that he even alerted the Prime Minister.[18] Soon afterwards, however, he received reassuring news from both Governors, Havelock expressing much pleasure at the tone of the Viceroy's recent letters. Northcote explained that Curzon had in personal conference settled various questions on which a difference of opinion had been more assumed than real. On the merits of some of the disputed matters, Lord George admitted that the government of India were very probably in the right and that the experiment of bringing in Havelock from the colonial service, a 'stickler for gubernatorial etiquette', had not been a success.[19]

Curzon did not take Lord George's warnings in any way amiss. As it happened, he had in both these instances a good case. He told Hamilton again that so long as those two Governors alone had the right to correspond direct with the Secretary of State, they would air their grievances to him, regard themselves as petty Viceroys and India as a triumvirate. This situation seemed to him indefensible. He explained carefully to Havelock that the attitude of the central authority towards the government of Madras was unchanged, and received a friendly reply. Curzon had judged that Havelock, though by nature disputatious, had a good deal of common sense. His system smacked unduly of remote control and dependence on paperwork,[20] whereas the new Governor, Lord Ampthill, devoted a good deal of time to personal interviews and travelling, and to bustling up the whole administration.

No one could have been more helpful or less fussy in diffusing goodwill and erasing bad feeling than Hamilton. The Governors of the Presidencies had always been prone to complain of the attitude adopted at Simla or Calcutta; and Hamilton knew that Curzon's relations with subordinates were apt to be choppy. Each week he wrote to Bombay and Madras. He never failed to point out the primacy of the central government in India. Occasionally he would sound a gentle warning. Madras, popularly supposed to be the benighted Presidency, haven of the lethargic, was proportionately sensitive. Within a few months of arriving, Ampthill had convinced himself that Curzon in particular and the Government of India in general had their knives into Madras. He complained angrily of the tone of a letter written to him by the Viceroy. Hamilton, Ampthill's cousin, took a different view and told him in a kindly way that the Madras Government were not blameless and that it was unwise to get into the bad books of the superior authority at Calcutta except for very good cause. He added that Curzon had more than once spoken favourably of Ampthill's work. Ampthill withdrew his letter; Curzon confessed that he had not intended to use wounding language; Hamilton remarked urbanely that those accustomed to use forcible terms in debate retain the language of parliamentary warfare in less stormy atmospheres. He assured Ampthill, quite rightly, that Curzon would not esteem him the less for fighting on behalf of the government of Madras.[21]

Curzon's character and career cannot be understood unless it is realised that he wrote and spoke in an unvarnished way, abhorring, as he once remarked, the diplomatic lie. He expected others to do likewise and to accept his method, an expectation by no means invariably fulfilled. Lord George, who knew all this, explained it to Ampthill:

The more I see of his work the greater is my admiration for his marvellous industry and very great powers. His manner, which is inherent, is at times, to those who do not understand him, somewhat overpowering, but he has this extraordinarily good and rare quality that, although he may use very plain language to others, he does not mind being treated in the same way, if the language used has a due regard to his official position.[22]

Five Governors of Bombay and Madras served under Curzon. His relations with them reflected, besides local jealousies, differences of age and standing. Havelock, for example, was fifteen years Curzon's senior and had occupied a number of governorships before Madras. Of Northcote, thirteen years his senior, Curzon came to hold a very high opinion. The two Governors holding office at the end of the Viceroyalty were both Curzon's juniors in age and experience. With them he worked cordially, despite some squalls. Both backed him staunchly in 1905.

★   ★   ★   ★

M. Stalin observed to Herr von Ribbentrop, just after they had signed the fateful pact on the night of 23 August, 1939, 'It is ridiculous that a few hundred Englishmen should dominate India.' It was indeed astonishing, even absurd, that a tiny British bureaucracy (about a thousand strong in Curzon's day in the top ranks of the Indian Civil Service) and a British element in the Indian Army of some 70,000, should rule a continent the size of Europe. So minute a force could certainly not hold down more than isolated pockets of armed rebellion, nor so small a bureaucracy direct the machine without Indian co-operation. For every white soldier, the Army contained two Indians. The Government of India employed in 1900 more than half a million men of whom no more than four thousand were Europeans. Indian graduates filled positions of growing importance in the provincial services and the highest posts in the princely states, but had only just begun to penetrate the uppermost ranks of the covenanted Indian Civil Service. The entrance examination, despite many protests, was still held in London and demanded in practice at least a year or two of British education.

The officer of the ICS was recruited on a largely academic and literary examination. He came to India with no practical knowledge of administration and was thrown at once into serious work, at a salary of £320. He would study the vernaculars of his province and learn the rudiments of his craft in a sub-division of perhaps 400 square miles: sitting as a magistrate to compose disputes or impose punishments; supervising elections in which a large number of participants, in their zeal for a democratic process, might be tempted to vote several times; disinfecting wells in time of plague or cholera; dealing with the multifarious business of the municipalities, lighting, sanitation, transport, slaughter-houses; assessing land revenues; travelling all over the subdivision in the 'cold weather'; enduring as best he might the mosquitoes, the heat and the sweat. From a subdivision he would in time take charge of a District, perhaps ten times greater in area. By now his concern would be mainly with the administration of justice at a higher level and with taxation. After twenty years' service, he could expect to be drawing £1,800. He might at the latter end of his service become a member of the Viceroy's Council and even Lieutenant-Governor or Chief Commissioner. He would retire on a pension of £1,000, largely financed by deductions from salary.

The ICS held then, and holds in retrospect, a unique position among the various civil administrations evolved by the British. In point of individual members' quality, its reputation is rivalled only by the services which in the earlier twentieth century revived Egypt and the Sudan. But the ICS had longer in which to work, struck deeper roots and became the least corrupt and most trusted administration so far set up by any of the modern imperial powers. It stood out in startling contrast with the other Asiatic bureaucracies. Nonetheless, Curzon found its procedures slow, its mental processes fossilised and its senior officials generally mediocre. Hamilton did not doubt that, even when every allowance was made for Curzon's standard of excellence, the general level of the ICS had fallen. The attractions of an Indian career did not seem to take there the exceptionally able men of whom there had been a continuous stream during the reign of the East India Company and the first twenty five years of rule by the Crown. He surmised that the spirit of adventure and enterprise which had induced men to go India in the earlier nineteenth century now found a wider scope in other, less well-developed parts of the British Empire than in the orderly and symmetrical systems of Indian Government.[23]

The keys of India, Curzon reflected, lay in the desk of every young British civilian in the country. By his character and conduct he contributed to the future maintenance or collapse of British dominion. If he were keen, with a high sense of duty, and liked the people, the British position would be secure for a century. If his qualities were other, the structure would fall down. Curzon noticed with real regret that the younger ranks of the ICS in general contained a dwindling number of the zealous and able, and an increasing number of the indifferent or slack. It was not so much enthusiasm for the work itself as interest in India that was diminishing.

> I regard it as true that the average young Englishman who has been for ten years in the country no longer has the affection for the people, or the love for India, that his fore-runner possessed in days gone by.

Improved communications drew men's hearts away from India to England, taught them to regard themselves as temporary exiles in a land of regrets. These tendencies Curzon had done his best to combat, though he feared that unless his successor were a man of considerable activity and strength of will, a sharp reaction would soon be felt. But he realised well enough that no man was indispensable and that the wisest thing he could do was to ground his reforms firmly and to secure the best appointments to the highest posts in the service.[24]

Walter Lawrence noted the difference even since 1895. Everywhere the officials were becoming deskbound and almost submerged beneath successive waves of paper. Fewer officials spoke Indian languages fluently. They were becoming aliens in the land. In the phrase of another official, whereas the District Officer had formerly driven the stage coach, he was now the manager of a branch railway. Recognising that his association with a remarkable man made him critical, Lawrence thought many of the high officials no more than average. What critics of the army deplored was equally to be found in the ICS. The 'Secretariat Octopus', steadily centralising and aggrandising, fastened its tentacles everywhere and lacked touch with District Officers, the real executive. These officials, 'the Simla gang', worked in close liaison with other Secretariat men who had become Lieutenants-Governor or Commissioners:

> They are the Augurs of India, who smile at one another when a Viceroy tries to introduce reforms, or a District Officer is bold enough to utter an idea new to Simla. It is an accursed system and is sapping the usefulness and individuality of the Civil Service.[25]

Instances of deliberate malfeasance among members of the ICS occurred very rarely, but in 1899 two bad cases of dereliction of duty came before the Viceroy's Council, involving a number of officials in Madras and Bengal. The punishments proposed seemed absurdly light. The Viceroy's Council were shocked to deal simultaneously with two scandals of this kind. 'They indicate a laxity of standard' Curzon noted, 'and a capability of positive wrong-doing on the part of British officials which I had thought impossible under our system, and they must necessarily excite some suspicion as to the general tone of local administration both in Madras and Bengal ... '26

It is right to add that although the opportunities were numerous, peculation in the ICS was virtually unknown.

★   ★   ★   ★

Government House at Calcutta, where the administration spent the first three months of each year, had been modelled upon Kedleston. It stood in some twenty-six acres of gardens, amidst which flying-foxes, parrakeets and jackals abounded. The building could scarcely be called convenient, for the kitchens lay at least two hundred yards distant from the dining rooms; but it was certainly dignified and historic. Some of the furnishings had been taken from a ship sent out by Napoleon and loaded with provisions for his future residence in India. Viceregal life ran upon lines of well-ordered tradition which the Queen had specially enjoined the Curzons to maintain. An entourage of nearly nine hundred included a fine bodyguard, thought to be better mounted and turned out than the Household Cavalry, and a band which played each evening after dinner. When the Viceroy drove about Calcutta in his barouche, a party of eighteen postilions, guards and outriders accompanied him. The Indian servants wore scarlet livery with the Viceroy's monogram embroidered in gold.

The Calcutta season, social pinnacle of the year, included a Drawing Room held by the Viceroy and his wife, two Levées for some eight hundred guests a piece, the State Ball, the State Dinner for about a hundred British officials, an Evening Party for distinguished Indians, a State Garden Party, dances every fortnight, an official dinner every Thursday and unofficial dinners on most other evenings. At all dinner parties when twenty four or more were present, the National Anthem was played. Even when no outside guests were present, the ladies must curtsey as the Sovereign's representative entered the dining-room. Sir Winston, several times his guest, records the geniality, candour and fullness of the Viceroy's talk. Curzon practised the habit of treating young men on absolutely equal terms in conversation, and Mr Churchill, charmed, enjoyed hugely the 'sprightly and none too merciful chaff' of Bishop Welldon, under whose guidance his erratic career at Harrow had only recently been pursued.27 Avalanches of visiting MPs and travellers descended upon Calcutta every year. All expected to be entertained by the Viceroy.

Various members of Lady Curzon's family availed themselves freely of Curzon's hospitality, abused him behind his back and chattered about the

affairs of Viceregal Lodge. Walter Lawrence, who knew all this, felt unable
to speak to Curzon about it. He heard also many tales of Lady Curzon's
growing unpopularity; but as he confided to his diary, they were painful
and valueless, for he could not tell the Viceroy or his wife. Trivial incidents
were magnified out of recognition. Apocryphal stories circulated widely,
losing nothing in the telling. Remarks made heedlessly at table reappeared
in startling guise. When Curzon entertained a curate and politely regretted
his impending departure from India, the curate announced that he had
been offered a Bishopric.[28]

The newspapers began to carry accounts of the manner in which the
Curzons behaved. The Viceroy was alleged to have kept troops waiting at
Karachi, where there were no troops; it was said that several members of
his staff had resigned because they were made to dance attendance upon his
mother-in-law, who was actually in Chicago: he and his wife were supposed
to go in to lunch alone, and not to allow their guests to come in until they
were seated, or in another instance were said not to lunch with their guests
at all. It was reported that the Military Secretary had resigned because he
could not tolerate having to stand behind Curzon's chair at meals. In fact,
the social customs of the household had not changed since Lord Lansdowne's day. These fabrications Curzon warmly denied to the King and to
Hamilton, who, learning that the gossip had reached Royal circles, sent
on Curzon's letter to the Palace. 'Qui s'excuse s'accuse' minuted the
Monarch ungraciously.[29]

As usual, Lord George knew how to handle the situation with the right
blend of sophistication and reassurance:

> your work has been too great, and is generally too well acknowledged, to be
> affected by this kind of malicious depreciation. As a reformer, you have made
> enemies, who will hit you unfairly, but their motives are understood, and their
> statements are discredited in advance. So pray dismiss all this backstairs gossip
> from your mind; no one cares for it, or believes in it, whilst your general ad-
> ministrative work and speeches are universally praised.[30]

Each Viceroy was given an outfit allowance of £3,500. Curzon found
that the cost of taking over carriages and horses from Elgin, and of buying
and transporting supplies for the first Calcutta season, amounted to nearly
£11,000. The adverse balance of £7,500 he never caught up. After tax, the
salary amounted to £16,700 p.a., from which the living and entertainment
expenses at Government House were paid. Separate funds for tours, the
band, pensions, furniture and the upkeep of the official residences brought
the total to £73,000, upon which sum the whole Viceroyalty was run. It
was soon clear that this meant considerable losses. Curzon, who kept the

accounts in huge ledgers, discovered that in the first eighteen months he was more than £8,000 out of pocket. Part of this deficit arose from his desire to entertain on a lavish scale, part from the lack of supervision. The French chef, with an official salary of £250 p.a., was detected in 'some peculations of a character that excites admiration even in the East'. Curzon estimated that he was making at least £1,500, and the chef left forthwith. The Viceroy's tents and carpets were requested for garden parties, his furniture for plays, his kitchen for meals. In 1900 a stranger asked for one of the horses so that he might gratify an ambition to ride in a steeplechase. At each ball or supper the vintage of the drink was closely scrutinised. After one of the first parties, Curzon was rather taken aback to discover the remaining guests stuffing their pockets with cigars and cigarettes, the bill for which in 1899 amounted to £307. In a single month, Government House served 3,500 meals to visitors and residents. 'The fact is' Curzon observed, 'that Government House ... and Viceregal Lodge ... are gigantic hotels and stores upon which everyone indents without payment.'[31]

Within reason, the excess of expense over pay was not of vital importance to Curzon. He had always expected to spend freely and his private contributions to Indian charities approached £2,000 a year; but for others it might be a different matter. In 1903 he proposed that after his departure the Viceroy's salary should be increased, because of the steep rise in the outgoings. Hamilton refused on the grounds that a Viceroy would normally enjoy a private income which he could save while in India and was not compelled to accept the appointment anyway. Moreover, certain colonial governorships were known to carry inadequate pay. Curzon protested warmly but without avail that there was no real analogy. The Viceroy was in India not merely to represent the Sovereign and to be the head of society, reading from a sham throne speeches prepared by other people, but to be the responsible head of one of the greatest administrations in the world. For that purpose the best brains and the highest character were needed: and it seemed mere sophistry to argue that these qualities had no cash value simply because the post was so distinguished that men would take it whether they could save on the salary or not. The State should pay when it wanted the best article.[32]

★　　★　　★　　★

Early in April, when the weather in Calcutta became uncomfortably hot, the government and court set out for the hills, a journey of nearly forty-eight hours. Simla was perched 6,500 feet above sea level. Some fifty miles off, the mightiest mountains of the Himalayas, clothed always with snow, sparkled in the clear air. Holm-oaks, rhododendron-trees, pines and deodars flourished. A mixture of races, Punjabis, Ladakis and Tibetans, thronged the streets.

Lady Curzon and the two children would retire to a cottage about seven miles off and nearly a thousand feet higher. Her husband, however, did not like the place, for strange birds whistled and hooted all night. One was called the coppersmith because it seemed never to cease hammering on some metal substance. Another was known as the brain-fever bird, either because its note resembled the name or, as Curzon suggested, because its incessant racket produced the complaint. He preferred to camp at Naldera, where he could work and eat out of doors. The River Sutlej wriggled like a silver snake in its valley far below. Through the pines the breeze brought sweet scents. In these agreeable surroundings much business was done. Servants with huge files strapped to their backs rode in and out of the camp. During the daytime, signallers sent messages to and from Simla by helio-graph and at night by flashing lamps. In this way, as Curzon told Lands-downe, if he and the Duke had a mild difference in the House of Lords, the fact was known within hours in the Himalayan fastness.

Simla itself Curzon detested for its inane frivolity and atmosphere of petty gossip and scandal. The solitude of the Viceroy's position was accentuated, for the company was mainly military and here came none of the visitors from England who enlivened the season at Calcutta.[33] The social life of the place seems to have consisted of a welter of dinner parties, amateur theatricals, polo matches, dog shows and gymkhanas. Most of this Curzon contrived to dodge. Walter Lawrence noticed that Simla had become more frivolous in the last decade. High officials unbent to play 'hunt the slipper'. Newspapers carried 'Letters from Simla' which repre-sented that all was play. 'As a matter of fact' remarked Lawrence 'for us Simla is all work.' 'It is the montony of the days that kills' wrote Curzon; 'it is like dining every day in the house-keeper's room with the butler and the lady's maid.'[34]

There were, of course, occasional lighter moments. Near Viceregal Lodge stood a small chapel. On one Sunday afternoon during the mon-soon, Curzon and his ADC attended the service. The only other person present was the chaplain, who, with dogged fidelity, waded through every line of the service. He then pulled from his pocket a well-worn sermon on Dives and Lazarus. Dives' circumstances of life, in the chaplain's version, proved to be very like those of the Viceroy. The chaplain admonished his congregation to reflect well on the sins of Dives and on his torments in hell, and then announced the concluding hymn which, since the ADC could not sing, he and Curzon intoned together:

> The rich man in his castle,
> The poor man at his gate,
> God made them, high or lowly,
> And ordered their estate.[35]

After the exodus from Simla in the early autumn, the Viceroy by tradition went on tour. Curzon followed and extended the custom, covering about ten thousand miles a year in all parts of the continent and rarely sleeping two consecutive nights in the same place. In this way he could bring the government into touch with the people, meet the princes, officials, judges and local leaders, taste the full variety of Indian life and scenery and see at first hand the practical effect of proposals which came before the government. For these travels a special train was provided, built for the Prince of Wales' visit in 1875 and, by Curzon's time, beginning to fall apart. It consisted of twelve massive coaches, cream and gold, always hauled by two steam engines. The Private and Military Secretaries, two doctors, various amanuenses and some eighty other staff were housed on board. Hot water for baths was taken on at prearranged points, where it had been boiled up in huge vats. A pilot engine ran ahead of the train and the whole length of the line was guarded by levies from each village in its vicinity.

It became evident from conversations during the tours that the strict discipline of the Indian Services often prevented local expertise from making itself heard, for men did not normally volunteer unsolicited opinions on large questions. Many estimates, especially those of the military, proved needlessly lavish. 'The pundits and pedants of the headquarters offices', as Curzon termed them, seem to have enjoyed a special fondness for the construction of redundant forts and roads. He used to amuse himself by seeing how far he could prune back the costs while securing the supposed object. His all-time record was a reduction from 106 to 6 lakhs of rupees. Such incidents increased his mistrust in the wisdom of his military advisers and encouraged 'the attitude of vigilant and suspicious criticism which I have adopted towards their proposals'.

The military were not the only sinners. The spring tour of 1900 took Curzon by way of the Brahmaputra to Assam. 'The Viceroy' he wrote to Queen Victoria, 'is in a railway train in a station in the midst of a primeval jungle, where there is no population, no cultivation, no traffic and no raison d'être for the railway whatsoever.'[36]

This hiatus between departure from Simla and assembly at Calcutta meant that for eight or ten weeks the government of India virtually disintegrated. Once the colder weather set in, troop movements became feasible. The frontier sprang to life. In 1901, when Curzon and his party were visiting Burma, a small punitive expedition against the Mahsud Waziris was proceeding. The Commander-in-Chief, the Military Member, the Secretary to the Military Department, the Adjutant General and the Military Department itself were in five different places in India. At one point Curzon was receiving telegrams from seven separate authorities, to whom, with but a small portion of the files, he could hardly return adequate answers. Eventually, by the rearrangement of itineraries, Viceroy and Military Member contrived to meet and unravel the tangle. A somewhat similar crisis occurred in the following year.

Curzon used to remark that for sheer hard labour nothing equalled these peregrinations. At each stopping-place petitions were presented and grievances aired. Each was carefully studied and answered. The Queen, seven thousand miles distant, followed every detail. Her advice to the Viceroy lacked nothing in trenchancy.

> She hopes . . . that he will be able to hear from the princes and, still more, other respectable native people what they have to say and ask for, and not let everything be only brought to him by officials, and not let himself be hedged in by *red tapeism*.

Sometimes the tours were chiefly notable for their splendour and picturesque scenes. It was the custom for the Viceroy to meet in durbar the leading lights of each district. Often they were highly educated Indian gentlemen. At other times, as on the frontier or in the Persian Gulf, they would be warriors or pirates. In the autumn tour of 1901 to Burma, the Chin chiefs gathered from great distances in their war-paint to make offerings of peacocks, spears and elephant tusks. Some wore on their heads the green feathers of the parrakeet, which denoted the taking of human life. At Lashio, one of the Shan chiefs thoughtfully presented a fine bear, which promptly sank its teeth into Curzon's thumb. He decreed that it should go forthwith to the zoo. At Rangoon, the centrepiece of the celebrations was the Viceregal progress on a huge raft round a lake. In the waters were reflected the twinklings of innumerable Chinese lanterns, hung in the trees which fringed the shore. At times of distress or ill-health, Curzon would solace himself by recalling the marvellous places he had seen, the buildings he had saved from ruin or, almost as bad, from the Public Works Department, and many evidences of efficient and devoted service to the government of India. Most of all he relished the hilarious and incongruous elements of Asiatic travel. When an official party proceeded in state to the gold field at Kolar, the old Cornishman in charge slapped Curzon on the knee, crying 'Sonny, I knew you'd ask a lot of damnfool questions' and handed over a typewritten sheet of answers. Curzon enjoyed that immensely.[37]

Forty of the leading chiefs Curzon visited between 1899 and 1905. Their hospitality was princely in every sense. Special camps, carefully fattened tigers, grand displays of polo or dancing, banquets—all was arranged on a sumptuous scale befitting the King-Emperor's representative. However, the chances of mishap were numerous. When, at Datia, Curzon was met by the Maharaja in the State landau, it careered off at a brisk pace towards the town and entered through two archways, each at right angles to the main gate. By some miracle the landau scraped through. It rushed down a steep slope, a horse slipped, the landau somersaulted and the Viceroy was thrown on top of the Maharaja in his glory.

The next call was at Orcha, the Maharaja of which had heard of the incident. Curzon began to recount the full story. 'At this stage' he exclaimed, 'I found myself in the melancholy position of sitting upon the head of His Highness the Maharaja of Datia in the ditch.' 'And a very proper position for Your Excellency to occupy' rejoined the Chief.[38]

Again, the official trip to the Portuguese enclave at Goa, which Curzon had long wished to see, did not lack its moments of humour. At the outset, the gunboat ran aground in full view of the expectant populace. Eventually Lord and Lady Curzon were placed in an open carriage. A band struck up, the bodyguard took their places, girls threw flowers from balconies and the Governor beamed amiably. The procession set off but did not seem to arrive anywhere. Not for sometime did it dawn on Curzon that, presumably to create an effect of grandeur, it was going round and round the same streets. At the banquet that night, it transpired that none of the Portuguese dignatories could speak a word of English; nor could any member of the British party speak Portuguese. However, Curzon scored a triumph by persuading a bilingual lady to translate the latter part of his speech and teach him the pronunciation. He then stood up and with the utmost aplomb praised in Portuguese the work of his hosts. The State Secretary, who had drunk and smoked unceasingly, proposed Curzon's health and then surpassed himself by shouting for three cheers 'heep, heep, hah!'[39]

On all these travels the welcome was invariably of the most generous. The whole population would turn out and cheer itself hoarse. Holidays would be proclaimed, festivals celebrated and fireworks let off. Everywhere the special Indian penchant for triumphal arches and signs was in evidence. Some, like

HAIL OVERWORKED VICEROY

KARACHI WANTS MORE CURZONS

he found touching: others, as at Trichinopoly, seemed less apposite:

WELCOME OUR FUTURE EMPEROR

Enquiry showed that this had been made long before, when the Duke of Clarence had been there. It was brought out of storage when required. On another occasion, Curzon read:

GOD BLESS OUR HORRABLE LOUT

This, it appeared, meant 'honourable lord'. Over a baker's shop at Delhi he found the legend:

RAM DAS. BAKER. EXCELLENT LOAFER

and above another establishment:

GREATCOATS. WORN BRITISH. DAMN CHEAP

At Jeypore a huge sign proclaimed, by a slight displacement:

A GAL A DAY

while an arch at Chittagong bore the inscription:

HE COMETH AS A BRIDEGROOM

CLAD IN THE GARMENT OF LOVE

'I did not dare' Curzon commented, 'institute any enquiries either as to the character of the raiment or the identity of the bride.'[40]

*   *   *   *

The Viceroy's Council had to decide questions of a kind which did not confront the Cabinet in London. In some respects India already possessed what would now be called a mixed economy. The government, unlike its counterpart in Great Britain, undertook much commercial and industrial activity; built and ran railways; controlled the sale of opium and salt; manufactured its own warlike stores and was by far the largest employer of labour. The Commander-in-Chief, the Military Member and the Legal Member were largely preoccupied with their own duties. Railway questions took almost all the time of the Public Works Member. This left only two men for work which in England would have been shared by half the Cabinet. The whole internal government of a continent came before them, while questions of frontier and foreign policy preoccupied the Viceroy in his capacity as head of the Foreign Department. Curzon and Hamilton believed that the Council in the first two years were not a strong body. The C-in-C, Lockhart, an attractive and gentle personality, lacked administrative capacity and died early in 1900. The Military Member, Sir E. Collen, was described by Curzon as 'an obsolete amiable old footler, the concentrated quintessence of a quarter of a century of official life'. The Law Member, Sir T. Raleigh of All Souls, did not stray much outside the business of his Department. Curzon's old Balliol friend, Clinton Dawkins, was one of the ablest public men of his day, businesslike and quick, but due to leave the Finance Department for a more lucrative career with J. P. Morgan. Nor could the Lieutenants-Governor be called a strong body, though Curzon detected some excellent men among the junior ranks of the ICS:

> What every one wants in India is stimulus, encouragement, example, incentive from headquarters. For twenty years they have had nothing but a respectable presidency...precedent has become a pure fetish and there is a shocking dearth of ideas...I shall want every minute of my five years if not more.

There seemed to be no doubt that Curzon had struck a patch of desperate mediocrity in the upper ranks of the ICS. Lord George agreed. He remarked that in six years as Secretary of State he had not been impressed with a single serving member of the ICS whom he had interviewed, with the exception of Sir Antony MacDonnell. Curzon also esteemed him highly, though as for any sign of humour or emotion 'you might as well tap the Marble Arch and expect it to flow with champagne. However, I forgive him everything for his capacity. It is such a godsend in this pigmy-ridden country to find a man who at least has mental stature.'[41]

Of the others, Fryer in Burma was lazy and played out, Mackworth Young in the Punjab touchy, Woodburn in Bengal high-minded but lacking strength of character. Only one Secretary to Government (a position corresponding in some respects to Permanent Under-Secretary in an English department) could draft decently, Curzon told Hamilton glumly in 1900. For the moment, he felt, he must conduct the government almost alone in almost all its branches, for sheer lack of men capable of doing the work at this level. As a comfort, he recalled the axiom of the Duke of Wellington that if a thing is to be done in a particular way, the only plan is to do it yourself.[42]

With real regret Curzon saw the departure in 1900 of his close friend and confidant, Clinton Dawkins. He suggested that Godley might succeed to the vital post of Finance Member, but in vain. Eventually the choice fell upon Sir Edward Law, whom Lord Cromer described as 'the most quarrelsome man in the world'. Curzon, who noted that frequent interviews with him were among the recognised terrors of Viceregal existence, listened patiently but found many of his proposals ill-conceived or unpractical. Law seems also to have been smitten now and again with extraordinary fancies. Quite early in his Indian career, he convinced himself that the wearing of the fez, a phenomenon which appeared to be increasing, connoted an insidious political propaganda organised by the Sultan. The whole machinery of the government lumbered into action. Questionnaires went to local governments and District Officers far and wide. Answers were collated. They proved beyond dispute that the fez was worn solely for convenience and had no political significance whatever.[43]

Extra pressure was bound to fall upon this tiny executive under a Viceroy who was not content merely to keep the machine running. Curzon was almost certainly right to judge that if the improvement of Indian administration were to depend on the initiative of local governments, it would never improve at all. In the first four and a half years, he noted, no valuable suggestion to this end had derived from them, except proposals of local significance. Reforms had come from the heart, not from the limbs. The ICS had 'neither originality nor ideas nor imagination'; the notion of reform sent a cold shiver down its spine. The advisers of the India Office, many of them retired provincial Governors, believed that the great changes of his Viceroyalty had been put forward over the heads of local governments. This was untrue, as Curzon warmly protested. The process had been not one of centralisation but of raising the standard all round. The fountain of initiative was the supreme government, usually in the shape of himself. The machine had in 1899 been in a state of 'lamentable inefficiency and dislocation'. Constant cries about over-centralisation merely obfuscated the issue:

> When therefore, [Curzon asked Hamilton] your greybeards crowd round you and whisper warnings in your ear about centralisation and so on, I wish you to take their protestations with a very considerable grain of salt, and politely to remind them that we are dealing with a state of affairs in which "superfluous lags the veteran on the stage".[44]

Walter Lawrence, who served Curzon as Private Secretary for nearly five years, played a rôle of high importance, not so much in determining policy as in smoothing the way for its execution. Curzon did not credit Lawrence with any special capacity for strong decision and, in any case, liked to read the files for himself; but he did pay tribute from the start to the value of Lawrence's knowledge, tact and affability. 'His main function is to pour in the daily oil ... there are an infinitude of persons to be pacified and smoothed, and this sort of work he has done admirably.'[45]

Lawrence had imagined that the life of the Viceroy's Private Secretary would be the most enviable in the world. He soon found out the fact; proximity to power meant unceasing worry and fatigue. For the young and unmarried the life was a pleasant one; for the others, often separated from wives or families, and generally holding the more responsible positions, it was hard and sad, as he saw reflected in the faces of those around him.[46] A large part of the Private Secretary's day was spent at interviews with members of the ICS or with leading Indians and European visitors. Fluency in Hindustani served Lawrence almost as well as his charm and urbanity. The irreverent knew him as 'Soapy Sam'. He and his master generally agreed in their judgment of individual character and of political questions. Curzon liked to have Lawrence at his side and would allow him to say what others would hardly dare to utter. For his part, Lawrence admired Curzon's capacity as a ruler, speaker and administrator. He felt cheered when the Viceroy wrote to Hamilton and Godley in terms of warm praise which amounted to a declaration of their partnership: 'It does not alter my feeling of devotion for him as a chief, but it intensifies my affection for him as an individual.'

Like many other Private Secretary, Lawrence had to listen to the complaints of those affected or aggrieved by his chief's decisions. On one occasion, after a spate of troubles, he described himself as 'a kind of spittoon and dumping ground for all these high officials. They have not the pluck to attack the big man, so they yap at his unfortunate P.S.'[47]

Curzon's speeches were almost always written out in advance but delivered without notes, for he could commit them to memory almost at a glance. He would hand over each sheet to Lawrence for criticism and if it were judged sound, the draft would be torn up. Lawrence recorded that he had never seen such power of work, such assiduity and such accuracy:

> The trouble was that he expected to find the same energy and application in others, and when I pleaded that long years in the Indian climate are apt to enervate even the most diligent, he would never accept my plea. He held that India and its problems must needs arouse enthusiasm in all officials, and that the man who was not full of an almost missionary zeal for the welfare of Indians would be better at home.[48]

Twice each day the Private Secretary took up files and correspondence, explaining the purport of the less complicated and settling them on the spot. More tangled issues would be left with the Viceroy. Curzon would often read papers in bed during the morning, and would not begin work with the secretaries until noon or later. Except on big occasions, he was habitually unpunctual. His mood varied with the surroundings, to which he was intensely responsive, and with his health. After one of the 'angry days', as

Curzon used to call them, he would ask Walter Lawrence what had gone wrong. 'Too much hubris.' 'I was born so, you cannot change me.'

For most of the time the weak spine gave little trouble. The Indian climate suited Curzon. He enjoyed better health there, particularly during the first five years, than in England, though suffering a good deal from a nagging pain, like toothache, in the right leg. The heat and humidity of India, however, slowly killed his wife. Even after three months, her appearance had changed visibly for the worse.[49] Knowing how acutely Curzon felt her absence, she determined to stay at his side. The summer of 1901 she did spend in England, but without enjoyment:

> My heart has stayed behind so completely that the void in my breast never stops aching. I miss you every second, and wish I had never come away. I never will again. Life is too short to spend any of it apart.[50]

From the start, Curzon was wholly absorbed in his task:

> The outside impulse is required to a degree that I had never deemed possible. We seem a long way from home, and the echo of the great world hums like the voice of a seashell in one's ears. But nevertheless the work is to be done: and in five years it will be strange if one does not effect some good thing.[51]

The Secretaries to Government in each Department saw Curzon once or twice each week. Colleagues always had access to him. Papers on the important questions circulated constantly to the Council, which met weekly at Simla and Calcutta. Curzon showed much patience and skill in holding his Council together. Only three dissenting minutes were sent to the Secretary of State in six and a half years, and none of them was of first class importance except the last, which entailed Curzon's eventual resignation. Had the machinery of Indian Government been more adequate to the size of the task, Viceroys would have been less heavily overworked; but the poor standard of draftsmanship, and the constant changes in the secretariats, meant an extra burden at the top of the pyramid. In 1903 the Foreign Department, the special concern of the Viceroy, consisted in its upper echelon of five men, two of whom were young. The first Secretary in that Department with whom Curzon worked was as Sir W. Cunningham, whom he found industrious and agreeable but so deficient in initiative as to be 'little more than a very superior clerk'. Of his successor, Sir Hugh Barnes, Curzon had a very high opinion, parting with him only because Burma needed some energy after the placid reign of Sir F. Fryer.[52]

*   *   *   *

These, in the broadest outline, were some of the circumstances in which a Viceroy did his work seventy years ago. Like other holders of the office, Curzon normally worked seven days a week, for it was only on a Sunday that the Viceroy could put in more than a few minutes' study without interruption. There was little opportunity for physical exercise, though at Calcutta a drive or a walk might sometimes be possible after lunch and at Simla there was golf. Those relaxations apart, the life of a Viceroy, or of a Governor, was one of unceasing labour. Curzon generally contrived to vary the programme every few weeks with a weekend's camp or a shooting expedition. Otherwise the work must provide its own stimulus. India had not a perfect autocracy but an untidy, idiosyncratic, illogical form of government, many of its arrangements owing more to history than to convenience or symmetry. A man of extreme quickness of apprehension and decision, retentive memory, courage in facing the opposition and inertia of a conservative hierarchy, might nevertheless achieve much. Those qualities Curzon possessed in exceptional measure. Without them he could not have placed the whole administration upon the anvil, or have laid down a coherent policy for the main branches of its activity. Government in India was not, at that time, kept up to the mark by informed opinion in Parliament or in the press. Rather, it tended to become a caste apart, self-sufficient and convinced of its own wisdom. To all the obvious difficulties of ruling so vast and heterogeneous a territory must be added the immeasurably delicate problems of race.

I sometimes wonder whether 100 years hence we shall still be ruling India. There is slowly growing up a sort of national feeling. As such it can never be wholly reconciled to an alien government. The forces and tendencies at work are on the whole fissiparous, not unifying; and I believe that a succession of two weak or rash Viceroys could bring the whole machine toppling down.

Unless the mass of Indians could be convinced that neither from their own people nor from any alternative foreign rulers could they obtain a more just or incorruptible rule, then British dominion was doomed. In other words, the strength of the British, the 'speck of foam upon a dark and unfathomable ocean', depended upon the inferiority in character and capacity of the available Indian leaders:

'It is often said' [Curzon wrote to Balfour in 1901], 'why not make some prominent Native a member of the Executive Council? The answer is that in the whole continent there is not one Indian fit for the post. You can see therefore how difficult it is to keep the natives loyal and contented at the same time that one absolutely refuses to hand over the keys of the citadel.'[53]

The notion that the woes of India could be met by placing one or two Indians in a perpetual minority amidst a Cabinet of Europeans, Curzon told Hamilton, 'suggested to me Sidney Smith's reply to the little girl whom he saw stroking the back of a tortoise, that you might as well expect to gratify the Dean and Chapter by tickling the dome of St Paul's'.[54]

FOUR

The India Office

THE INDIA and Colonial Offices were unique in Whitehall. They had no special area of competence, but managed all the affairs—fiscal, economic, political and strategic—of great empires. Each was a Treasury, a Foreign Office, a War Office, a Home Office and a Board of Trade rolled into one. Moreover, the Act of 1858, under the aegis of which the India Office functioned, placed the Secretary of State in Council in complete command of Indian revenues. The whole Cabinet, in theory at least, might desire a certain course; so might the Secretary of State and the staff of the Office; but if the India Council said no, that was that. Since India paid for the whole organisation, the Treasury had little control over its activities.

The retired officials of the ICS who mainly composed the Council met each week in a finely-proportioned small chamber, modelled upon the East India Company's Court Room, from which had been brought the carved chimneypiece, two doors and some of the furniture. Giants of Anglo-Indian history—Cornwallis, Wellesley, Dalhousie, Lawrence—gazed impassively from the walls upon these latter-day deliberations. Below their portraits ran rows of leather-bound volumes, their covers worked in gold. The secretary of State presided from a walnut armchair, formerly used by the Chairman of the Court of Directors and bearing upon a velvet panel the arms of the Company in silk and silver thread.

The post of permanent Under-Secretary, held for the whole of Curzon's Viceroyalty by Sir A. Godley, had a special significance. A Secretary of State might know next to nothing of the remote and mysterious continent with which he had to deal. Yet its customs must be treated with respect. The Mutiny was but forty years past. The population was vast, the British garrison relatively tiny. Arthur Godley's academic career had been even more distinguished than Curzon's. Much influenced by Jowett, he had espoused Liberalism before joining the staff of Mr Gladstone, for whom he conceived a respect bordering upon reverence. In 1883, still in his thirties, Godley was offered this position at the India Office, for which he possessed

4

no special knowledge or training. Incredible as it now seems, he had not
been to India, nor, apparently, did he experience any keen desire to visit
the continent over the destinies of which he exercised more continuous
influence than any other man of his time. Late in life, Godley recorded that
until about 1895, his work at the India Office was thoroughly interesting,
though never absorbing. For another couple of years it provided an invaluable and much-needed distraction, but from 1898 until his retirement
the duties had become 'though not irksome or disagreeable, pure taskwork
... my daily official round was never part of my real life'.

On the afternoon of Saturday, 9 October, 1909, Sir Arthur Godley,
later Lord Kilbracken, for more than quarter of a century head of the
department governing the largest dependency in the world, walked out of
its doors for good and never thought of its business again.[1]

It would be hard to conceive of a temperament less like Curzon's; the
one cautious, balancing, inclined to accept deficiencies or bow to obstacles
with a certain resignation; the other ardent, enthusiastic, restless, believing
that obstacles were meant to be surmounted and at a brisk pace. Much, of
course, they shared; devotion to Balliol, affection for Jowett, love of the
classics. Each thought highly of the other's mental powers. By the later
stages of Curzon's Viceroyalty, as the story will show, Godley had come to
feel deep mistrust of his method of governing India. They had from the
start disagreed on crucial issues of external policy, and, even more vital,
upon the proper relationship of India to other parts of the Empire and to the
government in London.

Godley and Curzon corresponded every fortnight or so, sometimes every
week, between the end of 1898 and the summer of 1905. The Viceroy does
not seem to have known how large a part Godley played in his downfall,
for he continued to the last to speak of him in terms of praise. More often
than not, their letters treated of points of detail, laced with some general
comment by Curzon on the governance of India or by Godley on the rights
of the Secretary of State or the decline of the British character. He found
and admired in Curzon a man who, in marked contrast with the majority
of British ministers, made the effort to look ahead. To read Godley's
letters is like sipping good dry sherry. Once he told the Viceroy that after
seventeen years in the public service, his politics were those of a Ministeria-
list 'apart from the natural tendency towards Conservatism which is as
much an incident of my time of life as baldness or defective vision'.[2]

Curzon used to remark, not unkindly, that he now knew what was
meant by 'a Godley, righteous and sober life'. In their exchanges he
gave as good as he got. Godley reproached him for not giving credit when

the India Office decided at the last moment not to order the construction of a certain railway line. Curzon replied, 'I am the last person to dispute the courteous and agreeable manner in which they desisted; but when a position is shown to be untenable, I am always less impressed with the grace with which it is abandoned than with the mistake originally committed in taking it up.'[3]

★   ★   ★   ★

Though the formal process of Indian government depended upon despatches and telegrams, much of the real business was done in private letters and messages. 'Do not spring your plans or proposals upon the Secretary of State' advised Godley. 'Let him know beforehand while things are shaping in your mind. Take him into your confidence in advance.'[4] This counsel Curzon followed faithfully. Every week for nearly five years he wrote to Hamilton a letter of candid comment upon the personalities and policies of India. Lord George responded in similar vein.

At Simla or Calcutta, the letter would normally be dictated. On tour, Curzon would write in longhand. The circumstances of composition must always be borne in mind. There was no time for the careful choice of language and the letters, freely quoted in this account, were not intended as State papers. Rather, they were practical aids to the transaction of business between men separated by many thousands of miles, unable to meet or speak by telephone. Each wrote with complete frankness, sometimes with indiscretion. Though Hamilton and Curzon disagreed on several issues of high importance, their co-operation was a fruitful one, facilitated by Lord George's perfect tact and good manners. With Brodrick, Hamilton's successor, relations were never quite the same. By the beginning of 1905, the weekly letters had assumed another character.

Hamilton did not blind himself to Curzon's failings. 'It is such a pity' he told Godley in 1900, 'when a man has such a rare power of work, ability and go that he should so rub up the people around him.' He feared in the following year that the Viceroy's ability, amounting almost to genius, had become 'warped by his growing sense of self-importance. I must try and see whether I cannot innoculate him with a little humility, but it is not easy to get through his very tough pachyderm.'[5] Usually, however, Lord George wrote in a different strain. With the single exception of Gladstone, he remarked, he had never met anyone with a comparable flow of language and ideas.[6] He understood instinctively Curzon's need for encouragement and approval. 'You are the most industrious mortal I know' he exclaimed,

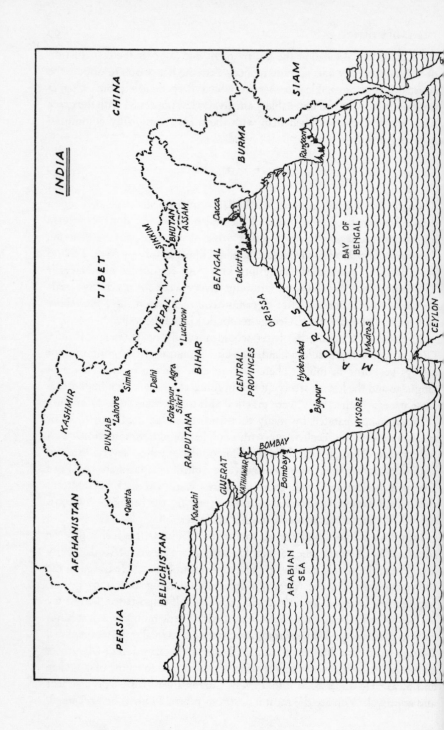

and again, 'I do admire your incomparable industry and assiduity, which I do not think I have ever seen equalled, considering how many questions of importance you have to deal with at the same time... '

Curzon's reforms, his vigour in practising patriarchal rather than bureaucratic methods, his practical but high-minded speeches and his courage in stamping out assaults upon Indians warmed Hamilton's heart. 'I am left' he reflected 'to discharge the functions of an old fogey, namely, to encourage and occasionally to put the drag on.'[7]

Curzon felt, and expressed, gratitude for such support. He asked that Hamilton should not, out of consideration, refrain from conveying bad news: 'I wish you would believe that I am not in the least degree annoyed or offended if I ask anything and you cannot give it. I am sufficiently reasonable to take the refusals and rebuffs along with the sweets of official life... '

When Curzon said that he felt ungrateful in disagreeing with Lord George, who had supported him against the views of the Foreign Office, the latter begged that nothing should interfere with the frankness of their exchanges.[8] Both continued to correspond, therefore, as if they were Cabinet colleagues discussing in complete privacy and freedom all the affairs of state.

In his capacity as the Queen's vice-gerent, Curzon wrote regularly to her about Indian affairs, generally avoiding purely political subjects. Almost every week the Queen replied in her own hand or telegraphed to the Viceroy, whose drive, thoroughness, desire to see for himself she admired. She followed with particular attention the lives of the princes and every development of the famine disaster in 1900. For the staid methods of officialdom she had no time: 'Red-tapeism is, alas! our great misfortune' she wrote 'and exists very strongly in the India Office.'[9]

When he reported that he had in the first months seen many of the Indian princes and nobles, she hoped he would also meet 'even ... the under-classes—respectable people.'
and again:

> The Queen Empress feels sure that if the Viceroy encourages them to speak openly to him, and lets them feel that he listens to what they have to say, *without* letting it *only* go through Anglo-Indian channels, then he will gain great influence over them.[10]

On 11 January, 1901, Queen Victoria dictated a last letter to him. Eleven days later she died. Though King Edward VII did not correspond quite so frequently with the Viceroy, he showed him much sympathy in most of the contentious issues of the coming five years. Periodically Curzon's friend Schomberg McDonnell, who was on close terms with the King, would send news of the Court. At Balmoral, in October 1901, he found the King in high spirits, 'very pleasant and very *reasonable* as he always is when he is out of London and beyond the reach of mendacious and mischievous men and women. He was full of your praises.'[11]

Of the King's entourage, Sir Dighton Probyn and the Private Secretary, Sir Francis Knollys, usually supported Curzon. They and the King showed themselves a good deal more solicitous and understanding of Curzon's position in 1905 than did Balfour and the Cabinet. McDonnell's letters leave the impression of impatience in Royal circles at dithering and of admiration for Curzon's efficiency and energy.[12]

Apart from this semi-official letter-writing, Curzon kept up an enormous private correspondence. Friends in some trouble or sorrow would always receive a kind and discerning letter; those with cause to celebrate could be sure of congratulation. Gifts were showered upon a growing tribe of god-children. From England came a good deal of gossip and many an entertaining story. Lord Salisbury, it appeared, had been compelled to give up lunching at the Athenaeum because his umbrella was invariably stolen. 'It's the Bishops', he said. General Tucker, asked by Winston Churchill for an opinion of his book on the frontier campaign, replied 'Well, I prefer Drama myself, but I quite feel no W.C. should be without it.' St John Brodrick reported that George Wyndham, exhilarated by his successes at the War Office, posed at dinner the question: 'Am I spoiled by all this adulation?' After debating with himself for an hour he concluded that 'People may say what they like but I am as good a fellow as ever I was.'[13]

With Balliol friends Curzon made special efforts to keep in touch. 'Do you know this translation of the old line', he asked Rennell Rodd, '*conticuere omnes intentique ora tenebant*? "They were all County Kerry men and kept whores in their tents." Distinctly good.'

Distinctly good.'[14]

*   *   *   *

The overwhelming majority of Indians depended upon agriculture, knew nothing of the Congress or of the government, subsisted on a knife-edge between indigence and a bare sufficiency. Successive generations of British Viceroys, officials and statesmen regarded themselves without hypocrisy as trustees for this inarticulate, illiterate mass. No one could be certain how the unique assemblage was kept together. 'Respect based on fear' said Lord

Roberts, 'remove the fear and the respect will soon disappear.'[15] In Salisbury's eyes, British rule depended first upon justice but in the last resort upon force, enormously enhanced by the reputation of invincibility.[16] Curzon and Hamilton would have agreed, though both laid emphasis on excellence of administration and the steady development of public works. More significant, how was the raj to be upheld in the next half-century or more?

India had a free and flourishing press. For how long would that be compatible with paternal government by foreigners? And what weight should be given to newspapers which but a small faction of the people could read, or to 'agitators' representing a minute minority? Curzon believed in the general loyalty of educated Indians to the British supremacy. He realised the hegemony which their education bestowed, the value of their knowledge, the usefulness of their service under the government of India and in the princely states. Yet, for the present at any rate, he did not find Indians fit for almost every post. In an emergency, the highly-placed Indian official tended to be unequal to the crisis and to abdicate responsibility, forfeiting the respect of Indian or European subordinates.[17]

Lord George, attributing British unpopularity chiefly to the angularity and rigidity of officialdom, approved Curzon's solicitude in receiving deputations, and judged the Congress to be a protest not so much against British rule as against a system which had substituted for the old-fashioned official 'a bureaucratic class ... who govern India with a code in one hand and a telegraph wire to the Governor in the other'.[18]

In the first few years of Curzon's Viceroyalty, the Congress appeared feeble. He assured one of its British sympathisers, Sir W. Wedderburn, that any reasonable expression of Indian opinion, even when opposed to his own view, was welcome:

> A minority ruling a vast majority ought, so far as is consistent with principle and duty, to endeavour to get public opinion on its side. This I aspire to do. But I have never thought myself that there was any special necessity in India for focusing so necessarily composite a public opinion or for trying to make it speak through a single megaphone. The noise comes forth as the voice of India. But if you go to the other end of the funnel, you find that it is nothing of the sort.

Curzon instanced the composition of the Congress of 1899. When the Lucknow members were taken away, very little remained and he refused to call it India.[19] At this stage, it must be remembered, the Congress had not adopted an attitude of undying hostility to British rule. It demanded reforms, many of which Curzon pushed through, and a larger Indian share in the upper ranks of the ICS. At the gatherings of 1900 and 1901, he was eulogised for energy, candour and fairness. Hamilton noted with pleasure the apparent decline in influence of the Brahmins, the most intelligent opponents of British rule. To this happy result Northcote at Bombay, and Curzon 'from his general sympathy with Native aspirations' had contributed largely. That the British should have grafted upon India ideas wholly alien to the instincts of the East Hamilton never ceased to deplore.[20] He feared that in fifty years' time, the adoption and extension of 'Western ideas of agitation and organisation' would bring real danger.[21]

Reflecting in his last year as Secretary of State upon the prospects of British rule, Lord George could not feel entirely sanguine. The spread of education, selection by competitive examination for the public service, a free press, the tightening grip of moneylenders, all were undermining the old foundation of British dominion, and 'substituting a shifting and un-stable quagmire of sham Radicalism and anti-English feeling such as can support no great system of alien and autocratic Government.'[22] Indian newspapers filled him with gloom. They were usually run, he told Ampthill in 1902, by men with a smattering of European education, imbued with ideals placed before them as the legitimate aspirations of the educated. These nostrums were eagerly swallowed, then applied without sense or intelligence. Governors and Viceroys formed the natural targets of news-papers seeking circulation by playing upon dissatisfaction. The usual cycle of the papers' relations to a Governor ran thus: hopeful cajolery, gratuitous advice, sharp criticism, violent attack. For the moment, Hamilton thought, the harm done by the newspapers was exiguous 'but what is going to happen fifty or a hundred years hence, when we have largely developed the number of people capable of reading the pernicious trash they disseminate, fills me with apprehension...'[23]

Curzon thought him too severe upon the native press (so-called to distinguish it from the Anglo-Indian papers). It was not universally hostile, though it always exaggerated; a man who was favoured became a god, one who was disliked a demon. Nonetheless, the press had given the clue to at least half the jobs and transgressions he had stamped out. Its hysteria and indifference to truth were a symptom, doubtless a grave one, of the thought and education of the community 'but one must not be too much disturbed by the mere froth ... it only floats on the surface, and I have little doubt that when my time comes to go, I shall find that deep and tranquil waters have all the while been running below'.[24]

Long since, in his book on Persia, Curzon had remarked that most

Asiatics would sooner be misgoverned by Asiatics than well governed by Europeans. 'Often when we think them backward and stupid, they think us meddlesome and absurd.'[25] The rulers of India were, then, pursuing objects which in the end proved incompatible. Curzon, wishing to make the British administration equitable and British dominion permanent, recognised that the 'advanced Natives' desired 'a larger control of the executive, for which they are as yet profoundly unfitted and which they will never get from me'.[26] The task of governing India, he knew, was becoming harder year by year. The doctrine of Empire, preached by the Viceroy and attractive to the princes, was regarded with a very questioning eye. If Empire was a partnership, why were Indians maltreated or proscribed in South Africa? Home governments, he wrote to Salisbury in 1903, had sacrificed Indian to home interests. English indifference and ignorance produced an effect. A stream of nonsense about the poverty and bleeding of India swelled feelings of discontent. It was not, Curzon thought, that India desired any alternative foreign rule. Rather, the articulate minority wanted a larger share in the administration, and to render the work of governing more difficult, or impossible, if it were not granted.

> The only way in which to meet and overcome these tactics is to rally round the Government all the more stable and loyal elements of the community: to pursue the path of unwavering justice: to redress, wherever they are found, a grievance here or an anomaly there: to make the government essential to the people by reason of its combined probity and vigour: to insist upon a juster and more generous recognition of India in the plans of British Governments and in the polity of the Empire; and to be perpetually building bridges over that racial chasm that yawns eternally in our midst, and which, if it becomes wider and there are no means of getting across it, will one day split the Empire asunder.[27]

★   ★   ★   ★

It was well said that British rulers of India, subordinate to a supreme but remote authority in London, resembled men bound to make their watches keep time in two longitudes at once. The Viceroy, wrote Godley, 'is, in many respects, an independent sovereign: but the essential fact is that he is the representative of H. M. Government in India, and the channel by means of which the views of the Government—and through them those of the House of Commons, who are our real masters—find their expression in the administration of India.'[28]

The House of Commons, however, seldom took a direct part. For practical purposes, it was the attitude of the Cabinet or of the India Council that counted. Godley conceived the Secretary of State in Council to play a rôle akin to that of the House of Lords, a restraining second Chamber.[29] Hamilton, Secretary of State for eight years, did not dispute that the system was 'double-headed and cumbrous', or that the quality of the Council declined sharply during his tenure. A body of that size, he remarked, could not discuss certain involved issues, whereas 'in the Cabinet my colleagues do not read their papers and so we get on'.[30] The business of the Office was divided among a number of departments and committees, providing ample scope for friction between the permanent officials and the members of Council. In virtue of his long tenure and dispassionate judgment, Godley acted as a catalyst in many disputes, but neither he nor any Secretary of State seems to have attempted a reform of the somewhat Gilbertian organisation.[31]

Curzon understood and accepted that the Council would not allow the government of India to do exactly as they pleased. His open statements that every branch of the administration needed overhaul could not be heard with unalloyed pleasure by men who had until recently been its senior executives, or by those still in charge:

> One cannot expect these old birds out here, whose feathers I stroke the wrong way, not to cackle home by post to the other old birds who have preceded them to the gilded aviary in Charles Street...to the smaller rebuffs — Pensions for Council, Governorships of Madras and Bombay, and so on — I am supremely indifferent. I would gladly pass them one of these bones a month to peck at and gnaw clean. All I want is to carry the big things, such as Frontier Policy, Education, Reform, Currency, Police, and so on, which will leave a lasting mark on the administration of the country: and for these I must trust to that quite invaluable Godley and to the Secretary of State.[32]

That trust was not misplaced, nor that hope disappointed. It is the fact that under the system, or despite it, Curzon's administration initiated a series of reforms unequalled in range or significance since the time of Dalhousie. In the first couple of years, some proposals to which Curzon and his colleagues had given much time, but which mattered comparatively little, were rejected by the Council in London. Godley did not attempt to defend all their decisions, some of which seem at a distance of time hardly explicable. 'I never saw' he wrote on one occasion in 1900, 'so large a number of men turning their backs upon themselves with such a complete absence of reason.'[33] When a project for compassionate allowances was twice put up and twice refused, Curzon commented that if the Viceroy, his Council, the Secretary of State and the Under-Secretary were all agreed upon a measure it seemed absurd that they should be defeated by a body of retired officials.[34] One Finance Member, exasperated beyond endurance by constant overruling from London, cried, 'I shall write my next despatch in my heart's blood.'

Not even Hamilton, for all his experience, could predict the Council's reactions. Sometimes he used a decision of the Cabinet to overbear their misgivings. About minor questions, he seems to have thought, the Council must be allowed to have its way. On the Viceregal estate at Simla, covering some 330 acres, no work could be undertaken without elaborate references to higher authority. Curzon proposed the appointment of a clerk of the works. The Council refused. 'Why', he asked, 'cannot the Finance Committee expend their virtuous energies upon something really big and problematic, like the Gold Reserve Fund, instead of dancing and stamping upon my poor little bantlings?'[35]

Curzon did not hide his annoyance that such a proposal, submitted after careful consideration, should be turned down. The second attempt proved successful; but henceforward the Viceroy's remarks about the Council's attitude became more pointed, even bitter. Godley had written a few weeks before of the absurd constitution of the Office, whereby members of the Council, unable to exercise their supremacy in great questions, compensated by making their authority felt in lesser ones. Most reputable firms in the City now refused to deal with the India Office, which haggled for the last penny in negotiation with railway companies. It was, Sir Arthur lamented, extremely difficult to induce the Council to take a broad view. Curzon, bent upon a large expansion of Indian railways, groaned at the delays and disorders. Even when decisions arrived, they seemed sometimes to reflect unduly the interests of certain companies.[36] The Finance Member confessed after a long investigation that he had been quite unable to discover the India Office's method of dealing with railway proposals.[37]

The fact that a policy was strongly advocated by the Viceroy, Lord George explained, did not produce upon the Council the effect which Curzon imagined; rather, it often hardened their collective heart:

> It may surprise you when I tell you that my influence here with individual Members of Council is always diminished if they think I am speaking from a brief supplied by you, or as your advocate.[38]

'I did not know' Curzon replied, 'that I was either so provocative or so formidable ... I really quite understand the position of men who, having trembled at the nod of the Viceroy for the greater part of their lives are eventually in a position where they can with impunity dance a hornpipe upon his prostrate frame... '[39] He came to believe that the India Council were more assertive and sensitive than they had earlier been. Conditions had altered, Hamilton answered, for in Elgin's time almost every reform originated at the India Office. 'His regime was one essentially of Indian bureaucracy.' On the other hand, Curzon had made many changes. Every branch of the administration felt his strong personality, and if the Council seemed hostile, it was chiefly because they feared it would be very hard to find a successor capable of shouldering the huge burden he would bequeath.[40] This was kindly and tactfully expressed. A few months earlier, however, Hamilton's Private Secretary had candidly admitted to Curzon that the Council, collectively and officially, did not look upon his administration with sympathy. This fact Ritchie attributed to their idea that the Viceroy should be run by the bigwigs of the ICS; the Councillors felt, uneasily and almost unconsciously, that Curzon's energy and originality exposed their own slavery to routine. Though the problems needed to be gripped, they disliked the action.[41] Walter Lawrence, on leave in England during the summer of 1902, heard somewhat similar stories. The old Anglo-Indians on the Council, 'defunct shades' as Lawrence called them, were reported to be antagonistic, though Ritchie and Godley expressed genuine admiration of Curzon's rule.[42] Almost womanlike in his gentleness, Hamilton 'seemed to have one idea impressed on his mind and that was that India was in good hands and that he had not much to say to it'. However, Godley unburdened himself freely. He thought the Council stronger than it should be. A Secretary of State could carry through any measure if he treated the Council judiciously and mastered the facts of the case. Lord George neglected both conditions.[43]

It happened that at this time the government of India were bringing forward proposals for a thorough reform of education and for an investigation of the police service, in which abuses flourished. Telegrams from London indicated a belief that the Viceroy habitually failed to consult the local governments.

> It is crediting me with the brains of a baby [he retorted] to imagine that, after three and a half years in India, I have not realised that Police administration and Police reforms are matters primarily, and indeed almost exclusively, affecting the Local Administrations; and that no enquiry or changes ought to take place without the entire concurrence and sympathy of those who will be so directly affected.[44]

Curzon had been looking back through his records and had built up a dossier of no fewer than twenty-two cases, of varying importance, in which his policy had been thwarted by the India Council. In most instances, he believed, the balance of right lay with India. Generally he had got his way, often after several attempts. Yet time was wasted, and the worry of the conflict or the sting of wounded pride were not forgotten. The Viceroy's task had to be performed in exile, amidst harassment, weariness, physical pain and opposition:

> If in addition to all these anxieties, against which I am capable of holding up my head, I have also to be perpetually nagged and impeded and misunderstood by the India Council at home, I say plainly that I would sooner give up the task...

The Council, he surmised, probably took some pleasure in thinking that they were exerting their authority and holding up a Viceroy whose administration was a tacit reproach to their own Indian careers.[45] The same mail brought Hamilton a secret note from Lady Curzon, who wrote of the misery of receiving almost daily proofs of suspicion and hostility. This attitude, unless abated, must drive her husband to resign.[46] Curzon said much the same in his next letter, protesting that he had not the least desire to override the local governments. 'I fear Curzon is breaking down' Hamilton minuted; 'his letter in its earlier part and his schedule of the Council's offences is almost childish'.[47]

He replied at length, pointing out that the Council had assented to most of Curzon's proposals. On two subjects, admittedly, the Secretary of State's own view had been traversed. In three important financial questions, Hamilton thought the India Council's opposition justified. He looked forward to a brilliant career for Curzon at home:

> But how would it be possible for any man to work in a Cabinet with colleagues, if he, on all occasions, were prepared to take and not to give? Chamberlain and Salisbury, since they have been in office, have been constantly overruled by the Cabinet, and they have accepted the over-ruling with a good grace... all that you have had to do has been in a few instances to slightly modify your own opinions...

Lord George wrote understandingly of the isolation and sometimes depressing surroundings which must attend a Viceroy. If the Council had imposed any check or restraint, it arose not from personal distrust but because they conceived that they could not 'in dealing with a man of your brilliancy and power, so forego their own responsibility as to assent to what you propose without full investigation and information'.

India, a country of 'almost archaic immobility', with a civil and military service intensely conservative, contained one fifth of the human race: 'are we not bound to see that in India we do not for the future recommit the fault of the past of moving too fast? ... I doubt if any Viceroy has ever been so fortunate in meeting with so little substantial opposition to his ideas and reforms.'[48]

But this explanation, Curzon felt, did not meet his point. He had objected not to the Council's powers, but to the temper of suspicion, even of hostility, in which they were exercised, and upon which both the Secretary of State and Godley had often commented. The parallel with Salisbury and Chamberlain seemed misconceived; the truer analogy would be Curzon's relations with his own colleagues in India, of whom he had no complaint and with whom he had not always prevailed. But what if Salisbury or Chamberlain gained the support of his colleagues and then had to submit his proposals for decision to a committee at Ottawa? Curzon refused to be convinced that the Council did not now interfere more frequently. Perhaps influenced by Lawrence's letters, he asked Hamilton to let it be seen that he did not approve needless worrying of the Viceroy.[49] For a while the disagreements died down.

Godley treated the complaint with low-spirited humour, remarking that English political machines always give every advantage to the man who says no. Having devised a constitution which made it really difficult to get anything done, the English worked it for all they were worth. He once described the Act of 1858 as one of the worst that ever passed Parliament; like Dr Johnson's leg of mutton, ill-designed, ill-drawn and ill-amended. It could be managed only 'by an elaborate system of shams, arrangements, acquiescences, and occasional illegalities: if everyone stood on his rights, the machine would come to a stop in twenty four hours'.[50]

The Council's power to override the Secretary of State, natural ally of the Viceroy, should be abolished. Godley reminded Curzon, very pertinently, of the difference between those who came under his personal influence and prestige in India and those seven thousand miles away who did not.[51] 'Two hours in the House of Commons' wrote Curzon, 'with a good speaker who knew his case would blow the whole thing into smithereens.' 'Of course it would' agreed Godley; but a bill to put it right would never pass the Commons, save with amendments worse than the disease. Like Hamilton, he did not want the Office's virtual independence of the Treasury to be infringed. After all, its constitution was no worse than the British constitution.[52]

Two other areas of potential disagreement between India and England deserve mention. 'My first duty' Curzon once told Godley, 'lies to my constituents and they are the people of India. I would sooner retire from my post than sacrifice their interests.'[53] When the Ambassador in Paris defended with 'pulpit mildness' the rights of Indians born in the island of Reunion, the Viceroy protested stiffly.[54] For the better treatment of Indians in Africa he waged a long battle. A request for Indian labour in German East Africa was refused. Curzon, who had been reading Mr Gandhi's contributions to *The Times of India*, returned a sharp negative when asked by the Governor of Natal to free Indian immigration thither from the legal restraints under which it took place. The Governor learned that the Indians were treated 'more or less on the level of aborigines with whom they have nothing in common but colour' and subjected to special treatment 'degrading and injurious to their self-respect'.[55] Brodrick's threat that the Cabinet might overrule India on this issue produced the first row in his official relations with Curzon.

Question of external and frontier policy brought forth innumerable complications. A rash move in Persia or Afghanistan, it was believed, might mean war with Russia. Apart from an occasional letter to the Prime Minister or Foreign Secretary, Curzon transacted all this business through the Secretary of State for India, although the decision usually rested with the Foreign Office or the Cabinet. The process was inevitably slow, often needlessly slow, and by the time all the authorities had been consulted, policy had often been reduced either to the lowest common denominator or to nothing. As Selborne once exclaimed, 'What an intolerable method of doing business! Indian Government, India Office, Minister at Teheran, Foreign Office, Cabinet Committee, Treasury, Cabinet! Bah! the Russians ought to walk round us each time.'[56]

★ ★ ★ ★

For the larger part of the Viceroyalty Indian subjects attracted so little notice that apart from the occasional question Hamilton had literally no work in the House. Dreading uninstructed parliamentary interference, Godley was glad; but Curzon deplored such indifference. He asked newspaper proprietors to devote more space to Indian affairs, reduced telegraph rates drastically and instituted press-rooms at Calcutta and Simla. The colonies received much attention, though their combined populations could comfortably have been put into a single Indian province. The words of their Prime Ministers, Curzon observed, were trumpeted round the world, while a Governor who ruled scores of millions in India remained wholly unknown. To Buckle, Editor of *The Times*, he remarked that there was certainly a fine commotion in England the minute anything went wrong; a frontier war, a hint of internal trouble. Then India became momentarily the pivot of Empire, relapsing quickly into the position of Queensland or Ceylon.

When troops from India took 8,000 Boer prisoners, nobody said so much as 'thank you'; when Natal and the Legations at Pekin were saved, it was thought part of the day's work:

> India sees the Indian Budget debated in a House of Commons consisting of six persons and she goes wild at the fancied insult. This Indian Empire can only be maintained by convincing the Native people of our interest in them, our regard for them, our pride in the undertaking. Any other country but Great Britain ... would advertise India in every household. We treat the whole thing as a commonplace accident.[57]

Sometimes he would relapse into depression at the indifference of those to whom he had a right to look for enthusiastic support; at the thought of having thrown up the chance of the Foreign Office; at malicious chatter in England.[58] Even the leading members of the Cabinet seemed to know little of India. 'It was eminently characteristic of the cultured ignorance of Arthur Balfour' Curzon reflected, 'to talk of Sindhia as "the Sindhia" throughout his speech.'[59] Separation from Mary intensified the loneliness of high place and the feeling of neglect.

> Grind, grind, grind, [he wrote to her], with never a word of encouragement: on, on, on, till the collar breaks and the poor beast stumbles and dies. I suppose it is all right and it doesn't matter. But sometimes, when I think of myself spending my heart's blood here and no one caring a little damn, the spirit goes out of me and I feel like giving in. You don't know—or perhaps you do—what my isolation has been this summer. I am crying now so that I can scarcely see the page.[60]

After disagreements with the Cabinet about Persia and Tibet, Curzon confided to Hamilton in the spring of 1903 that he sometimes worked on with a 'sublatent consciousness that I am wasting my life and my strength and that nobody really cares'.[61] Milner, losing patience, told the home government that he did not care twopence for the opinion of people six thousand miles away[62] and used to remark glumly that it is a hard task to keep a row of empty sacks upright. With his parliamentary training, Curzon never felt that hearty detestation of the British political system which came to dominate Milner's outlook; but both deplored the Imperial effects of the shifts and hesitations which characterised the latter stages of the long Conservative ascendancy.

Curzon tried, with a good deal of success, to treat the Viceroyalty as a trust above party politics, being buoyed up by the conviction that the governing of India was far and away the biggest thing that the British were doing anywhere. 'As long as we rule India we are the greatest power in the world. If we lose it we shall drop straight away to a third rate power.[63] He believed that early British departure must mean the disintegration of that elaborate structure, with a reversion to chaos. It seemed unthinkable, to Asquith and Morley as much as to Cromer and Curzon. What seemed equally unthinkable to Curzon was that the India Office or the Cabinet should still aspire to direct in detail, as distinct from superintend in general, the administration of India: 'You cannot treat the Government of 300,000,000 of people as though it were a subordinate department... '[64]

Alas for both sides, that is what the home government intended to do. The difference of view, however blurred in theory, proved in practice to be decisive.

FIVE

The Advance of the Glacier

CURZON ONCE DESCRIBED the government of Persia as 'little else than the arbitrary exercise of authority by a series of units in descending scale from the sovereign to the headman of a petty village.'[1] High posts were systematically sold; provincial authorities and the mullahs defied the administration; the Shah was grasping; the Grand Vizier, reputedly making between £70,000 and £100,000 a year, did not display much zeal for reform, and the Minister of Posts was in the habit of stealing any parcels that looked promising. Nevertheless, Sir Mortimer Durand, Minister at Teheran, did not take too glum a view of British prospects in Persia. The Russians, after all, were surrounded by populations of doubtful docility. Judicious moves on the Turcoman frontier could produce alarm from the Caspian to Merv. If the British Legation had money, it might do almost anything. As it was, the government should consider an announcement that if Russia moved in the north, Britain would move in the south.[2]

Following Persian affairs at the Foreign Office with minute care, Curzon agreed with that policy, feeling sure that Russia desired to reach the Gulf. Agreement with her about Persia seemed to be out of the question. 'We should get the kicks and Russia would pocket the halfpence.' This note, written in 1896, contains in embryo the policy Curzon pushed as Viceroy and eventually persuaded the home government to adopt. He observed in the same document that Persia, under that Shah whose foibles he had condemned so vigorously in 1892, was incurably rotten; any of his sons would, in all probability, be a charge for the worse.[3]

This was soon put to the test, for the old Shah, Nasr-ed-din, was assassinated. The second son, Muzaffer-ed-din, succeeded to the Peacock Throne, being preferred to his elder brother the Zill-es-Sultan. The latter does not seem to have felt undue tenderness towards his sovereign, for he would sometimes swing in a playful manner a sword which he had christened 'Muzaffer Kush' (slayer of Muzaffer). After living more than fifty years at Tabriz, often in penury, the Shah made amends on the grand scale, assisted by a flock of avaricious courtiers. 'It was' commented a later British Minister at Teheran, 'as though Henry V, on ascending the throne of England, had handed over to Falstaff and Poins the control of the national Exchequer... '⁴ The Shah seems to have lacked both the business capacity and the passion for cruelty of his father. Persia's debt soared within a few years, not least because of the Shah's fondness for toys, motors, jewels and those other less innocent recreations which caused him to be known in Parisian circles as 'Mauvaise-affaire-ed-din'. He did not fail to appreciate flattery. When a witty courtier turned out all the lights in the Palace, exclaiming 'Le "Chat" voit parfaitement bien la nuit', his delighted master awarded him on the spot a pension for life.

In 1897, the Grand Vizier fell temporarily from favour. The British Legation was reported to have played a large rôle, and Salisbury, fearing lest Durand had meddled unduly, warned that the Legation should not appear to take sides against the dismissed minister, who might resume office and bear resentment.⁵ During the following summer, the soldiery, restive for lack of pay, intimated that the Commander-in-Chief, should he show himself on the parade-ground, would be stripped and flogged. 'In any other country' remarked Durand, 'this would be disquieting, but it does not mean very much here.'⁶ The root question was whether the Imperial Bank of Persia, a British concern, could again shore up the administration, as it had done regularly since 1890.

By the end of June, the recall of the Grand Vizier, known as the Sadr-i-azam, was being pressed by the Russian Legation. Soon he was back in power, and evincing no goodwill towards the British. The Shah had already asked Durand for a loan of £2,000,000, while the Sadr-i-azam described how the troops and other employees were clamouring for arrears of pay.

> 'You may have seen' he said to Durand, 'when out riding or driving about Teheran the carcase of a horse or a mule with the dogs tearing at it, and at times turning to snarl at each other. That is Persia. The carcase is the State, and the dogs are the Ministers and others, all thinking only of the meat they can tear off for themselves, and snarling at each other as they tear...Yes, and I am one of them.'⁷

Salisbury, mistrustful as ever of Indian political officers, grumbled at Sir Mortimer's methods: 'he *will* imagine that he is an Indian Resident with 200,000 men behind him.'⁸ The Sadr-i-azam must not be pressed too hard, in case he should devote himself entirely to Russian interests.⁹ Early in 1899, by the seizure of £26,000 in newly-coined silver, he staved off a threatened outbreak by the troops. Durand judged that although Russian

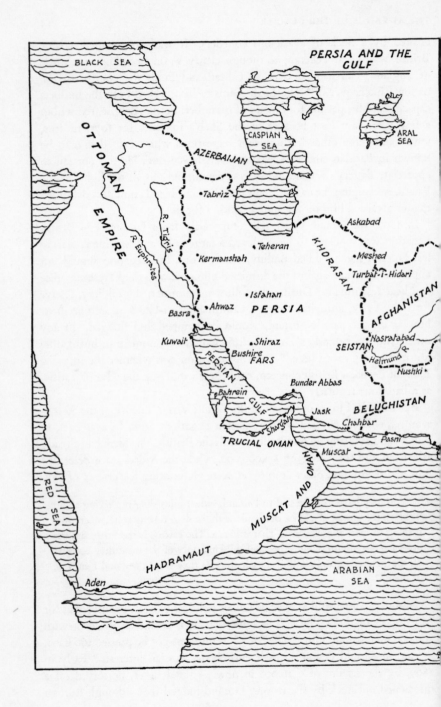

PERSIA AND THE GULF

BLACK SEA

OTTOMAN EMPIRE

CASPIAN SEA

ARAL SEA

AZERBAIJAN

• Tabriz

KHORASAN

Askabad

• Meshed

• Teheran

• Kermanshah

Turbat-i-Hidari

R. Euphrates

R. Tigris

AFGHANISTAN

• Isfahan

PERSIA

Basra •

• Ahwaz

• Nasratabad

Kuwait •

SEISTAN

• Shiraz

R. Helmund

PERSIAN

Bushire

FARS

Nushki *

Bahrein

GULF

Bunder Abbas

BELUCHISTAN

Jask

Sharjah

Chahbar

TRUCIAL OMAN

Pasni

Muscat

RED SEA

MUSCAT AND OMAN

HADRAMAUT

ARABIAN SEA

Aden

influence in the north, and even in Seistan, had grown rapidly since 1895, British political standing at Teheran had not declined. The death of the old Shah had not provoked the chaos, and therefore the Russian incursion, that had been expected, partly because of timely distribution of English money to the disaffected soldiers. The Shah, though weak, was not inclined to grovel to the Russians.[10]

★　★　★　★

In the nineteenth century Great Britain enjoyed undisputed paramountcy in the Persian Gulf. With most of the chiefs of the Arabian shore she had long maintained treaties. The Royal Navy had hampered piracy, slaving and gun-running, installed lighthouses and buoys, set up quarantine services and policed the waters. A very large percentage of the trade, and almost all the shipping, were British.

During the first weeks of Curzon's Viceroyalty, Kuwait was the focus of British activity in the Gulf. Sheikh Mubarak ibn Sabah, having seized the throne by murdering his brother and expelling other claimants, invited the British to declare his state a protectorate, which Salisbury at first felt inclined to do. Before leaving England, Curzon had agreed with the Prime Minister upon this step.[11] However, the British Ambassador at Constantinople advised that it might lead to complications with Russia and with Turkey, which possessed a somewhat nebulous suzerainty over Kuwait. A secret agreement with the Sheikh would be preferable. At this point, rumours of a Russian railway concession began to circulate, causing Salisbury to fear territorial claims. As Godley observed, 'We don't want Kuwait, but we don't want anyone else to have it.'[12]

Salisbury therefore decided to seek a most secret promise not to cede, lease, mortgage or otherwise alienate any part of the territory to the government or subject of another power without British consent. £5,000 sterling or even more would be available as a douceur. Curzon had hardly landed when he was asked whether he could put this through at once or whether the Admiralty should handle it?[13] He wired to the Resident at Bushire that this undertaking must be secured. A fortnight later, Col. Meade went quietly to Kuwait, adding to the terms, on his own authority, a proviso that the Sheikh should not receive the representative of any power without British consent. He was assured of British 'good offices'.

It was agreed that India could not undertake to send troops for the defence of Kuwait. Salisbury, though satisfied with the arrangement, did not want to give orders for naval action. If the Turks rapidly concentrated troops at different places on the Gulf, they might endanger Kuwait, but their methods were thought to be so dilatory that they were extremely unlikely to achieve this feat of organisation. For the moment, Col. Meade advised, there was little danger, since the hot weather was approaching. Some attempt might be made to seize Sheikh Mubarak's date harvest and the Turks would later try to put their claims on a more solid footing. Then Great Britain must intervene, but without declaring a protectorate. Curzon would have preferred a protectorate from the start, since the arrangement seemed to bring its obligations without its advantages.[14] However, a much more urgent issue had already arisen.

In the Napoleonic wars, the East India Company, anxious to thwart the French, had made a treaty with the Sultan of Muscat. Since 1873, the British had paid him an annual subsidy, contingent upon good behaviour. Their goodwill had helped to place Saiyid Faisal on the throne and in 1891 he had given a secret promise not to alienate any of his territory without British consent. Within a few years, however, the British position had been a good deal undermined, partly by the failure to support the Sultan against a rebellion and also through the activities of one Abdul Aziz, whom the British had ejected from Zanzibar. He became the confidant of the French vice-consul, M. Ottavi, and of the Sultan, who on two occasions in 1898 received with cordiality the commanders of French gunboats.[15]

Just as Curzon arrived at Calcutta, the government of India heard rumours that the Sultan had ceded to the French a port on the Muscat coast, for use as a coaling station. He admitted that he had promised to the French a place for storing coal, in a place as yet undecided. Major Fagan, the Political Agent, protested, as Curzon had ordered, but the Sultan remarked that if the British government objected they should settle matters with the French. Fagan telegraphed that the presence of a man of war at Muscat would be desirable.[16] Curzon was authorised to warn the Sultan that if his attitude continued unfriendly, his substantial British support would be withdrawn and might 'possibly take another direction'.[17]

There was no parallel, Curzon telegraphed to London, between a coaling station and the two small sheds at the side of Muscat harbour in which the British kept coal and from which fuel had always been supplied for the very rare visits of French warships. French trade at Muscat was insignificant and French merchant shipping virtually unknown. The lease therefore seemed to portend a desire to supplant the British as the dominant power.[18]

The Resident at Bushire, Col. Meade, had previously arranged to visit Muscat. Having made the secret agreement with the Sheikh of Kuwait, he arrived there to find instructions demanding the abrogation of the lease, the dismissal of Abdul Aziz and other minor satisfactions. The cession of the coaling station being known everywhere in Muscat, Meade felt that he must secure a public repudiation.[19] Meanwhile Salisbury had empowered Rear-Admiral Douglas to enforce Meade's demands. The Sultan had by now revoked the lease but had not answered the other points. Douglas disposed his ships in a threatening manner and the Sultan was summoned to the flagship. He found these events most helpful in guiding him to a decision. Having agreed to place himself in the British government's hands, he left the *Eclipse* to a salute of twenty one guns. In public durbar he announced the cancellation of the French agreement.[20]

Salisbury and Hamilton believed that Meade had outrun his instructions, at Kuwait and Muscat, more seriously than he had done; and that he had been wrong in telegraphing that the lease was to the French government. Before Curzon's correction reached him, Lord George wrote that Meade's proceedings had annoyed the Prime Minister and would probably confirm his tendency to attribute high-handedness to Indian politicals.[21] Having read the first batch of documents, Hamilton admitted that prompt action had been necessary to avoid a repetition of the performance in the Sudan. Salisbury, however, still clearing away the debris of Fashoda, had hopes of a settlement in the Nile Valley and spoke to Cambon more tenderly than Curzon wished about Muscat. It had just become known that the lease, of which Delcassé had recently denied all knowledge, had been signed nearly a year earlier. Hamilton minuted to Salisbury that the French demand had evidently been prompted by hostility to the British; but the Prime Minister wished to adopt Cambon's suggestion that the French should have a coaling station on the same terms as the British. The Treaty of 1862 applied equally to both countries; but 'the Residents are the most jingo, that is to say the most contemptuous of treaties, of all the Indian officials: and Curzon has fallen into their hands'.[22]

This observation did not do full justice to the facts. The secret agreement of 1891, made by Salisbury, was hardly compatible with perfect equality; and it expressly forbade the cession or lease of Muscat territory without British consent. The Sultan was still showing himself obstinate. Most Ministers favoured the threat of deposition. Salisbury refused. It looked as though another ultimatum, backed by threat of naval force, would be delivered; for, as Godley observed 'it is the privilege of an independent sovereign to be bombarded, not deposed'.[23]

The Foreign Office and India Office naturally regarded such affairs from different points of view, a divergence which widened when the whole field of relations with a European power was involved. Cambon and Delcassé had shown themselves conciliatory, yet Curzon could hardly fail to represent that having forced the Sultan to give way, the British could not, without loss of prestige, turn round and say 'you may do it after all, but it must be with our permission'.[24] The Prime Minister told Cambon that the action had been right in substance but regrettable in form. He wished it had been possible to tell the French in advance what was to be done and why. Delcassé, in the Chamber, interpreted this as a repudiation and an expression of profound regret. 'A most impudent travesty', said Hamilton.[25]

Curzon was depressed to discover that Salisbury had not asked why the French wanted a coaling station. Cambon had said that the coal was necessary for French commerce and men of war on their way to the East, but there was no commerce and French warships en route to the East did not pass by Muscat. With the Foreign Office, the Viceroy noted, it was all a question of treaty rights, with the government of India a question of motive. Nor was he appeased to learn from Godley that a coaling depot would merely be a hostage, to be seized in war. The same argument had been used when the Germans took Kiao-chow, but Britain did not nowadays go to war with France more than two or three times a century. In the interval the hostage became something much more substantial.[26]

Curzon believed that French and Russian policies in the Gulf were concerted in 'a systematic attempt to contest our position'. Russia had not a ship or a subject there; a coaling station could be of use to France only in Muscat harbour itself; and no compensation should be given for the revocation of the lease.[27] Conceding, rather surprisingly, that the present affair had so far gone off very well, Salisbury reminded him that London had other fish to fry. The French Chamber, which had still not ratified the Nile settlement, might flare up: 'if they try to give us trouble, they have more abundant opportunities of doing it than are likely to arise in the Persian Gulf. Both there and in Paris we have simply irrational people to deal with; and we must balance the disadvantages their unreason may cause.'

What was greatly wanted in such an Empire as the British, Salisbury remarked, was administrative altruism. 'While Meade was pluming his own feathers, it should have occurred to him that he was possibly ruffling ours.' He questioned Curzon's theory that Russia, longing for certain chestnuts, was using France to pull them out of the British grate. Perhaps with Russia's quiescence during the Fashoda crisis in mind, the Prime Minister argued that the Franco–Russian alliance now had meaning only against Germany, for Russia seemed bent upon ambitions which France could not easily help her to fulfil: the Siberian railway, an outlet in the

China Sea, the impending disruption of the Hapsburg Empire and the chance of making its Slav elements Russian, the hope of commanding the Straits. France had discovered that Russia did not wish to help her against England. Since the one contingency in which Russia would certainly be with her, a war between France and Germany, became less likely with every passing year, sympathy was visibly cooling:

> France has little interest in the banquet which Austria's disintegration is preparing. She is not invited. Her only interest in it is that it may give the German Emperor the means of purchasing Russian neutrality in the improbable case of trouble between him and France.
>
> I am disposed, therefore, to think that Russia's designs against England do not furnish so much as they did the key for deciphering the problems of modern politics: and that France sees no profit in acting as her instrument for that purpose...

It followed that Britain should not presume the hostility of the French government, though the ill-will of minor officials would persist. Even if hearty goodwill were not possible, a 'mutual temper of apathetic tolerance' might be cultivated between the two countries.[28] With this magisterial survey Curzon did not wholly agree. Doubtless the Franco–Russian alliance was losing something in cordiality; but so long as neither power had any other friend, was not each certain for selfish reasons to play the other's game? Whatever agreements Britain made with either, the policy of pin-pricks persisted. The Chinese agreement with Russia was followed by the demand for a railway to Pekin. The African agreement with France was accompanied by the plot at Muscat. 'Staal is always murmuring consolatory words about Afghanistan and Persia. Meanwhile his people are visibly nibbling at the one and biting hard at the other.'[29]

Meanwhile, the Muscat issue had not been settled. M. Cambon professed indignation at the delay. France, he said, had now agreed to a site at Bunder Jisseh, a place which, Fagan had reported, could easily be made impregnable. This was too much. Hamilton pointed out to the Prime Minister that if the French genuinely wanted a coaling-shed they would hardly select a place which had no traffic, accommodation or facilities. He recommended a proposal, endorsed by Curzon, to offer a part of the British site. Salisbury assented, telling Cambon that if the French claim to Bunder Jisseh were advanced officially the Sultan would be told that the British could not permit it. This served to anaesthetise the quarrel for some time.[30]

Both Meade and the Rear-Admiral had reported unfavourably on

Fagan's handling of the Sultan.[31] Curzon determined to place at Muscat the best officer he could find. His habit was to select for these vital ports not an obedient cypher but a man of fearless character. The choice fell upon Captain Percy Cox, who became one of the most celebrated and influential Englishmen in Arabia. At Simla Curzon talked long to him in this strain:

> Make the Sultan understand that every consideration of policy, of prudence, of past experience, of future hopes, compels him to be on our side—not necessarily against anyone else, but to recognise that his interests are bound up in loyalty to Great Britain.[32]

★   ★   ★   ★

Though Curzon was not receiving the secret material which would have revealed the full seriousness of the crisis in South Africa, he was alerted in July to the danger of war. Reversing its view, the War Office decided that no troops from India would be needed, but Hamilton declined to send the telegram.[33] In London, preparations had been hamstrung by a serious conflict of view between the War Office and the Cabinet, which had refused Lansdowne's request to secure extra transport. His colleagues found themselves in a dilemma painfully familiar to British statesmen. The soldiers wished to spend money at once in mobilising an Army Corps, while the Cabinet, on political grounds, felt able to do very little until the need became obvious to all. Premature mobilisation, it was believed, would be represented by the Opposition as an act of bullying aggression.[34]

By the end of August, Salisbury discerned no chink of light. 'I see before us' he told Lansdowne, 'the necessity for considerable military effort—and all for people whom we despise, and for territory which will bring no profit and no power to England.'[35]

Wyndham wrote enthusiastically about the War Office's ability to place 35,000 men at once in the field. Had he remembered to mention, Lord George wondered, that the first preliminary to producing these 35,000 would be to call out the reserves, who must then be clothed, accoutred and taught how to handle rifles which they had never seen before? The more he saw of the War Office, the more despondent Hamilton became. No one seemed to know how the team should pull together. A route would be confidently dismissed as impossible; a week later it had become the one by which an expedition should proceed.[36]

On 8 September, Chamberlain made a firm but conciliatory offer to Kruger. Simultaneously India was asked for reinforcements. The telegram reached Simla on 9 September. A week later the first troopships left. The speed and efficiency of this performance not only earned Curzon the good-will of the Cabinet but also contrasted vividly with British efforts. Lord George reported in the blackest terms on the state of the War Office, of which he doubtless heard a good deal from his brother-in-law, Lansdowne. The Commander-in-Chief, Wolseley, was said to be quite played out, and Sir Evelyn Wood half-cracked and wholly deaf. It appeared that the War Office was more of a danger to the British Army than to its enemies. Hamilton added an expression of his disgust at the invariable jealousy shown towards the Indian Army.[37] That letter reached Curzon just as the first batch of reinforcements arrived in South Africa. On the next day, 9 October, Kruger's ultimatum was issued. There followed the long series of British reverses and disasters. The prowess of the troops from India, who saved Natal, provided a lonely source of comfort in the next six months.

*　*　*　*

The events at Kuwait and Muscat provided a text for the homilies Curzon preached to Hamilton, Godley, Brodrick and Salisbury. The importance of the Persian question was not in doubt. As early as 1888 Salisbury had reflected that Persia could not long remain a cancelled quantity in the equation. 'If she cannot be counted on our side, she will be counted on the other—and whenever she is completely Russianised, she will be a more formidable base of operations than Turkistan.'[38] The intervening years had not provided a coherent policy. When Sir Frank Lascelles was at Teheran in 1893, his instructions were that if the Russians reached Isfahan they were to be stopped. He wrote to London to ask how? Rosebery sent to the India office to know what was their policy, but discovered that they did not have one.[39]

Curzon began from the premise, which could scarcely be denied, that the British position in Persia must decline unless a definite effort were made. He did not dispute Russia's overwhelming strategic superiority in the north, vastly reinforced by completion of the Transcaspian railway. Commanding the Caspian, she could dictate to Teheran; from Tiflis and Erivan, she could overrun Azerbaijan; the only useful troops in the capital were Cossacks under Russian officers. Fomentation or invention of frontier disorders would present no difficulty. Persia was in Russian eyes a power to be tolerated, even humoured, for a while, but certain to be partitioned. Nor did the northern part mark the limit of Russian ambitions, for the desire to secure a naval base for eastern operations meant either an attack on the Ottoman Empire or, more probably, penetration to the Gulf. Curzon did not in the least condemn such aspirations; but, as he observed, Englishmen were not compelled to look on the question from a Russian point of view. Rather, Persian integrity should be preserved as fully as possible and the centre and south must certainly be kept inviolate.[40]

These were the lines upon which Curzon argued with his superiors at home. Godley opined that Russia's 'natural expansion' to the northern part of the Gulf could not be prevented and should not, therefore, be opposed. Russian possession of a post in the Gulf would be disagreeable, but not vital so long as Britain retained command of the sea; if she lost such command, she would forfeit her dominion in India and her trade with the East.[41] But from the Indian point of view, the Viceroy answered, there was little to choose between a Russian port at the northern end and one in the south. Russia was no more entitled to Mesopotamia, Baghdad and a railway to Basra than to Khorassan, Seistan and a railway to Bunder Abbas:

> I will no more admit that an irresistible destiny is going to plant Russia in the Persian Gulf than at Kabul or Constantinople. South of a certain line in Asia her future is much more what we choose to make it than what she can make it herself.[42]

This last sentence contains the core of the disagreement between Curzon and his colleagues in London, a disagreement which continued to reverberate until, in 1903, they adopted what amounted to his policy. Lord George wrote in the same strain as Godley. Amidst general distress, corruption, and indigence, Persia's dissolution could not be long delayed; Russia would reach the Gulf; an irony of fate compelled the most enterprising and civilised nation in Europe to prop up rotten powers in the shape of Turkey, Persia, and China. Yet with Parliament and public perpetually influencing the trend of foreign policy, it became almost impossible to associate British fortunes permanently with such maladministration.[43]

As for asserting British rights where there was the power to make words good, wrote Godley, 'I believe I am in entire agreement with you, which is more than can be said of the Foreign Office.'[44] Brodrick, who had taken Curzon's place as Under-Secretary there, freely admitted that Britain had no policy in Persia or China. The Office knew that in Persia Russian railways were being projected and a Russian loan arranged, but Salisbury would do nothing beyond uttering a warning about the southern ports. His health was declining; Lady Salisbury was mortally ill; and they would disappear to Walmer or Hatfield, to the detriment of Foreign Office business.[45]

Brodrick did his best, with Balfour's help, to press a British subvention for Persia. Salisbury allowed Durand to propose a loan, to be advanced through the Imperial Bank and secured on the southern ports' customs, which would be placed under its control. This might lead, Brodrick hoped, to an embargo on Russian enterprise in the south; but 'as you know, Ld.S. wishes to shirk these things and now more than ever'.[46] When the Grand Vizier objected, Salisbury proposed a loan on the same customs but under a mutually acceptable commissioner. There would be no objection to a Russian advance, secured on the Caspian customs. This, said the Shah, would cut Persia in half. The Persian counter-proposal included the French, whom Salisbury refused to let in. Only bribery and fear, he told the Queen, moved the Persians: 'but we cannot bribe even if we had the money; and we have no soldiers in the Persian territory.'[47]

The Persians, meantime, had taken the most unusual course of complaining officially to Salisbury of Durand's unfriendly demeanour. Like Hamilton, Curzon dismissed this as a mere intrigue, guessing that the Grand Vizier had been for years a Russian tool, probably paid, but so clever and plausible that Durand was half-fooled.[48] Salisbury felt puzzled, for he did not believe that the Russians had yet offered a loan. Granted, they had a long land frontier with Persia; but there was the long littoral controlled by Great Britain. Russia had the best of the bargain, but not overwhelmingly. Was it that Russia interfered less in Persian affairs? Durand replied that on the contrary the Russians adopted a far more minatory tone. He did not deny that the Sadr-i-azam was much under Russian influence; but Russia had not yet won the day.[49]

Durand's position was an unenviable one. The Foreign Minister told him that England was rich. If Sir Mortimer really wished it, he could persuade his government to provide the cash which Persia needed above all things. Evidently he was no friend to Persia. Durand remarked that England had offered a million. 'But we want two million' answered the Foreign Minister with aplomb; 'can you expect us to be grateful for so little?' He hinted that Persia must look elsewhere.[50]

Meanwhile Curzon was framing a despatch. The pith of it was simple enough; that if Russia appeared in Eastern or Southern Persia, the cost of Indian defence must rise; if Russia reached the Gulf, the maritime protection of India must be expensively reshaped; and that the British should therefore thwart either development. Something more solid than Russia's assurances about Persian integrity must be found as a basis for policy. Friendly co-operation with her for the regeneration of Persia seemed, alas, unpractical, for Russia desired Persia's decay. It might be possible, as Durand and Brodrick had suggested, to try a division into spheres of influence; but since Teheran lay in the far north, Russian influence there, already dominant, would then become supreme. Anyway, the chances of acceptance were slim. In default of it, Persia should be told that further Russian encroachment meant a corresponding British move. Every un-obtrusive step to strengthen British influence should be taken. Curzon admitted in private that he intended to build up a position which would justify strong measures later.[51] This despatch could hardly have arrived in London at a less propitious moment, for the South African crisis super-vened.

Hamilton's early reactions served only to clarify the difference of view. Curzon's policy, as it seemed to him, assumed that force would be used in the last resort to uphold the British position in Persia; but had not the extension of Russian railways made a vast difference to relative strengths there and reduced British power to dominate the hinterland? Any tug-of-war on land must end to British disadvantage. The capitals of China, Turkey and Persia lay at the Russians' mercy and Hamilton had long wanted an agreement with them; 'but they are cute enough to know that time is on their side, and the influences behind them are increasing much more rapidly than the influences which are behind us; and therefore ... I think we must dismiss the idea as impracticable to contemplate, in certain eventualities in Persia, war with Russia.'

As for the Gulf, the railway would go there sooner or later. Had Britain the right or the power to stop it? Great Britain, he wrote on 2 November, 1899, had not a friend in Europe, being thought to resemble an octopus 'with gigantic feelers stretching out all over the habitable world, and constantly interrupting and preventing foreign nations from doing that which we in the past have done ourselves'.[52]

The Russians intimated plainly that while they did not wish to invade India or Afghanistan, yet if Britain chose to be obstructive, they must use their position in Central Asia. In that event, Lord George commented, France would probably combine with Russia. 'I think all my colleagues feel, as I certainly do, that this war makes self-evident that our Empire is in excess of our armaments, or even of our power to defend it in all parts of the world.'[53]

This case Curzon contested in principle and in detail. Britain's foreign policy, insofar as it existed, rested everywhere upon the assumption that force might be used. If she were always to recede before Russia, there seemed little point in taking up a position upon any issue, whether in Persia, Afghanistan, the Pamirs or the Yangste Valley, in any one of which places war might be necessary. Moreover, the public had been prepared to fight in 1885 over an unknown place called Penjdeh, hundreds of miles from the Indian frontier, and should be brought to realise that Russian advance beyond a given point in Persia or the Gulf meant danger and expense to India. Familiar with the topography of Persia, Curzon could not understand the references to easy or irresistible Russian advance. In fact, the northern third or so of Persia was separated from the rest by a vast desert. In such terrain railways and supplies cannot be conjured up. Moreover, as he pointed out, war was not in the least likely to result from his policy. Admittedly Russia could march on Herat; but she could do that any day. The Royal Navy could seize the Gulf ports, and Russia could do nothing about it. Lord George's belief that the situation had been entirely altered by the railways was simply countered; Russia had no railway within twelve hundred miles of the Gulf. British advantage there was as indisputable as Russia's at Kushk and Herat:

> And yet, while we have gone and pledged ourselves to fight over the latter, I am told not so much as to contemplate the possibility of war over the former. Nay, further, we are mildly to acquiesce in the bridging over the gap of 1,200 miles by a Russian railway, in order to destroy our solitary advantage, and to hand over to our enemies what we can still keep.

There was no difficulty about preventing a Russian line to the Gulf. If the Persians persisted, after warning, in allowing it, the projected terminus would be in British hands before the rails were laid. The Russians might fight, but it seemed very doubtful. Whatever they might gain at Herat or elsewhere, they would lose forever their access to the Gulf.[54]

*   *   *   *

The early weeks of the Boer War brought a bewildering tale of confusion and defeat, with which the machinery at home was sadly inadequate to cope. 'We Under-Secs.' wrote Brodrick, 'rather feel that such a critical situation as last week can't be dealt with by Ld.S (Hatfield), Joe (Birmingham), Arthur (Balmoral), Beach (Gloucestershire). However, we muddle along somehow.'[55]

Salisbury, whose wife had suffered a stroke earlier in the year, was desolated at her death in late November. From this time forward he hardly lived in London and seems to have become more markedly detached from his colleagues, not to say less competent to despatch his business. The speeches which he and Balfour delivered early in 1900 failed entirely to match the country's mood of resolution. Balfour, who had been told by

Selborne that the Cabinet must conduct the war in a less casual way,[56] pointed to the grave demerits of free institutions at times when the opinion of the community lags behind the needs of the case; while the Prime Minister reflected that the British constitution was not a good fighting organism 'when great Powers with enormous forces are looking at us with no gentle or kindly eye on every side'.[57]

Curzon watched these developments from afar with disquiet, not on account of India, which supported the war loyally and remained calm, but because the British position everywhere must suffer. Balfour's utterances, 'stamped with the familiar brand of eternal nonchalance', could cause him no surprise. Much more serious was the lack of prescience, and therefore of policy, not only in South Africa, but the world over.

> Lord Salisbury is an adept at handling the present ... But the future to him is anathema.
>
> Now an Empire cannot be run on these lines. We must take stock, must look ahead, must determine our minimum and our maximum and above all must have a line. It is easy to blame the W.O. here, the Exchequer there, or the Cabinet everywhere. It is the ingrained vice of modern British Statesmanship that is at fault...[58]

The Viceroy received by every mail letters bewailing the incompetence of the generals and the rudderless character of the government. Brodrick said simply that it was impossible to get vigorous consecutive action out of such a Cabinet under Salisbury, who brought up matters casually before colleagues conscious of being in the dark.[59] High society, including the Prime Minister's middle-aged secretary McDonnell, departed for the war. South Africa, Salisbury told him, had an admirable climate, except that there was so much lead in the atmosphere. After the arrival of more competent commanders, Roberts and Kitchener, the news of the war became less depressing.

The proceedings of the Cabinet, of which no minutes were kept, gained nothing in efficiency. Lord Salisbury, believing that it had resolved 'unanimously and rather energetically' against publication of some damaging despatches, was a good deal surprised to read them in his newspaper.[60] Amidst all this, Brodrick wrote faithfully to Curzon each week. His position at the Foreign Office, he confided, was an absurd one, with Balfour impotent and Salisbury immovable, using the war as a reason for putting aside all else.[61] Yet at least, as Salisbury had surmised from its beginning, the European powers had not combined. In late October, Count Mouravieff was alleged to have said that they must act together against the aggressiveness of the English. Salisbury was not much alarmed. He concluded an agreement with Germany about Samoa, which Brodrick thought to be chiefly justified because 'it squares Germany—very necessary just now ... The Emperor is our only makeweight for the moment ... A broken reed, you will say—but useful for the nonce. So long as Europe simply grumbles, no matter ... I have always hated the war (like you) and have been scoffed at for saying one Army Corps would not do it.'[62]

Hamilton reported to Curzon in a single sentence: 'Mouravieff has been buzzing about the different Foreign Offices of Europe and attempting to form a coalition against us: so far he has not succeeded.'[63]

In December, the Czar gave the most explicit assurances of goodwill, which the Prime Minister and Hamilton accepted as genuine.[64] Bulow let Balfour know that nothing would induce Germany to allow an alliance against Great Britain.[65] A month later, the Russian Ambassador is supposed to have suggested to the Emperor William such a combination. The Emperor refused to be seduced from neutrality, according to the German account; but the Russian record states that he offered a guarantee of quiet in Europe should the Czar ever be driven to direct his armies against India. Mouravieff coolly observed that 'the tendency of the German government to sow discord among other powers, and to urge upon them risky undertakings from which Germany would be the first to profit, is not new'.[66]

He seems to have decided by February that Russia could not alone put effective pressure on Britain either at the Straits or in Persia and Afghanistan. The Emperor William stated on 3 March that Russia had proposed a collective intervention to compel England to make peace. The British Cabinet, he remarked, would be 'unmitigated noodles' if they cared a farthing. Salisbury could not believe that Mouravieff's 'very inexplicable' proceedings represented the feelings of the Czar, and wondered whether such proposals had really been advanced?[67] Here his instinct was sound, for as we now know, the Russians had made no mention of enforcing peace.

The failure of these manœuvrings casts a good deal of light upon the international situation. Germany had excellent reasons for doing nothing effective against the British, since a serious British defeat would be a triumph for the enemies of the Treaty of Frankfurt. Genuine French acceptance of the severance of Alsace–Lorraine must precede European coalition in a matter of such vital moment. Such acceptance was unlikely to be forthcoming. Furthermore, the projected combination would not find it easy to prevail. The British had no territory to be taken in Europe; the Channel and the Fleet made invasion practically impossible, at least without prolonged and obvious preparation. Admittedly Britain had

5

plenty of territory in Africa which she might be hard put to it to defend against determined attack. In that continent, however, Russia had no interests and Germany possessed colonies which were permanent hostages to fortune and to British naval strength. Any nation fighting the British in Africa must wrest command of the sea from the strongest maritime power in the world. To put it at the lowest, that would be a hazardous operation, and it might well prove a disaster. Quite apart from their own suspicions and jealousies, the European powers had sixty capital reasons for minding their own business.

Continental opposition, then, took less perilous forms. Especially in France, British defeats were hailed with cries of malicious delight. The opportunity to take vicarious revenge for Fashoda, and to forget Dreyfus, could not be foregone. In the intervals of deriding British decreptitude, the journals surpassed themselves by publishing obscene cartoons of the Queen. When the French government conferred a decoration upon the most notorious offender, Salisbury ordered the British Ambassador to leave Paris.

$$\ast \quad \ast \quad \ast \quad \ast$$

In the autumn of 1899, the Shah's elder brother, the Zill-es-Sultan, warned Durand secretly that the government of Persia was entirely in Russia's hands. There was, he said, a written engagement to deliver Bunder Abbas within ten years. The exact nature of this compact was never known, though the British Legation later learned of an agreement whereby Russia might pass troops through Persia, perhaps to Herat or Chahbar.[68] Spring-Rice, recently appointed Durand's deputy at Teheran, thought like Curzon that the Russians wanted to maintain Persia's integrity, in the sense of desiring the whole lot as a nominally independent dependency. As he rendered their reasoning, 'Why should we marry the lady when we can have her without the ceremony?' The process could not be stopped by diplomacy. Russia wanted to use Persia as a route to the sea, with a permanent right of way.[69]

Balfour spoke to his uncle about Persia, but found him very difficult to move. 'I have not 200,000 men to oppose to Russia' and more to the same effect. The Under-Secretary, Brodrick, tried to tie him down on the question of consuls. 'I don't believe in strategic consuls.' 'You can't keep Russia out by consuls.' 'What interest have we in the Gulf if India didn't exist?' 'Why should not India pay?' 'India should pay for protecting her own commerce.' Presumably Salisbury had forgotten for the moment that

India was already bearing by far the larger financial burden in the Gulf and Persia. Brodrick and Sanderson fought Curzon's case. Part of the dialogue ran thus:

Brodrick: We have 'done' India pretty well.
Salisbury: Is thine eye evil because I am good?
Brodrick: You were Secretary for India and you know best. But the War Office always got the last farthing out of India.

Some minor parts of Curzon's proposals Salisbury accepted; but the principal points he would not tackle. 'The main difficulty here' explained Brodrick 'is everyone is lethargic about everything but the War—which is going hopelessly badly.'[70]

Very soon afterwards, on 30 January, 1900, the Russians announced a loan to Persia of £2,350,000 guaranteed on all the customs except those of Fars and the Gulf ports. In case of default, the Russian bank might establish control over these revenues. Persia would not conclude without its consent any fresh foreign loan until this were extinguished. The British Ambassador at St Petersburg was reduced to expressing his 'profound astonishment' at the negotiation of this loan without the exchange of view promised four months earlier. Mouravieff said he had left it all in the hands of M. Witte. The Cabinet concluded that Britain could make no effective protest.[71] Lord George regretted that Sir M. Hicks Beach, though an admirable Chancellor, lacked imagination and could never bring himself to consider 'that in Oriental countries it is necessary to take cognisance of the disposition of those in authority to make something out of any loan they may obtain'.[72]

Durand, Spring-Rice and Curzon were now at one in believing the Sadr-i-azam to be virtually a Russian puppet. He was reported to have kept the Shah in ignorance of the British offer of assistance. 'Everyone is afraid of coming near the Legation' wrote Spring-Rice, 'and even old friends are shy of us.'[73] Curzon reflected that if the British had made a loan on such terms, it would have been cancelled within twenty-four hours upon a threat to occupy Meshed or Tabriz. He would have liked to enter a formal protest and to try for a cancellation of the restriction of Persian freedom to borrow upon the security of customs within the British sphere of influence. Some compensation should be asked for; but 'as it is, we smile a sickly smile and invite the Shah to England, where he will be given the G.C.B., and feasted in the Guildhall as a dear good friend of our beloved country'.[74]

Salisbury merely reminded the Persians of two promises given earlier:

the customs of southern Persia must not be placed under foreign control and no southern railway concession must be given without British assent.[75]

We may now compare the British view of these developments with the opinions of Russian ministers. Count Mouravieff noted that if the English occupied any port or territory in the Gulf 'Russia will not idly watch such connivance by the Shah, but will take the necessary measures to restore her interests in Persia'.

For spheres of influence in Persia he had no use. It was contrary to Russia's traditional policy, would stimulate unfavourable developments at Teheran and would be valueless, for Northern Persia was already in Russian hands and inaccessible to foreigners. England's influence in the South was far from being exclusive; if she were given the official right to be in charge there, Russia would lose the chance of moving across the borders of the northern provinces.

The Foreign Minister preferred, therefore, to compete in the Gulf by encouraging Russian commerce and developing trade routes. The work of Russian railway surveyors in Persia, and the construction of lines in the Transcaucasus to link with a Persian system, must be pushed on. When Kuropatkin, the War Minister, noted that Russia could not keep the British out of the south without a direct agreement, Mouravieff commented that thanks to the Shah's commitments, Russia could now prepare all the strategic routes for approaching the Persian border and after that for penetrating the country. All this chimed closely with Curzon's assessment. The loan, Russia's Foreign Minister concluded, 'must serve as a weapon in our hands for fortifying our economic position and strengthening the political hold of Russia [over Persia] to the detriment of England'.[76]

The weekly dialogue on Persia between the Viceroy and the India Office continued. Hamilton felt that if the British insisted too stiffly on maintaining their influence there, a European alliance might result. Yet the events in South Africa had shown that invasion of India through any of the northern passes was 'a military impossibility' if the defending forces were properly equipped and handled. Access through Eastern Persia and Beluchistan would be easier and Russia must not be allowed to obtain a footing there. 'Your criticism is a just one that there is an inconsistency between my arguments and Salisbury's present action.' Time, he repeated, was on Russia's side in China, Persia and Asiatic Turkey. 'Her advance is like that of a glacier, slow but omnipotent.'[77]

The loan seemed to Godley 'something very much like practical annexation'. Outside political and official circles, however, no one appeared to be in the least troubled, no doubt on account of the war: 'It shows, I think, how hopeless it would be to get the Government, or the House of Commons, or (still more) the country to the pitch of being prepared to fight in order to keep Russia out of Persia.'[78]

The argument developed on familiar lines. Godley summarised his unchanged view by saying that, being dependent on 'that foolish and vacillating individual, the man in the street' Britain could not hold her own 'against Russia in a territory to which she can bring, with time, any number of men by land'. He added helplessly that though Curzon or someone else might for a year or two infuse a little vigour into Britain's Persian policy, it would soon relapse into sloth, followed by futile remonstrance: 'And you may be quite sure that I shall accept and loyally carry out, in my small sphere, the policy of Her Majesty's Government for the time being, if I can only make out what it is.'[79]

Early in May the Shah, now amply provided with funds, set off for a European tour. Curzon hoped that His Majesty would be told what was British policy; at the moment he was in ignorance of it, a misfortune shared by everyone else. The Shah, however, did not visit England, for Salisbury kept him away. When the Sadr-i-azam offered to come over, the Prime Minister merely remarked that he only wanted money and would not get it.[80] Curzon had already told Salisbury that the Russian loan was clearly 'a political *coup* of the first order', intended to carry Russian influence into a zone hitherto British. He had no objection to railways in Southern Persia if made by the British. He did not desire a British port in the Gulf, still less a Russian:

'I do not want to occupy a yard of Persian territory; but I want to prevent the occupation of certain parts of it by others. I do not think I am enunciating any new propositions... ' If this policy were now abandoned, India must become less secure, her financial burdens greater: 'Russia can already terrify us by moving a couple of battalions at Sheikh Junaid. She would paralyse us if she could simultaneously threaten from the Gulf.'[81]

This letter crossed in the mail the long-awaited reply, dated 6 July, to the despatch of the previous September. It reminded the government of India that the British base remained on the sea, whereas the Russians now had a safe stepping-stone for a fresh move. Already they could annex northern Persia without effective reply. In the Gulf, British supremacy went no longer uncontested. The challenge would grow, from the extension of railways to the sea and others' increasing trade. They could not, 'because their admission will infringe upon a monopoly which we have hitherto enjoyed,' be denied access to the ports. As for spheres of influence, Hamilton admitted that there was much to recommend an understanding with Russia; but if overtures were made to her, the Shah would probably be given the impression that the British desired immediate partition of Persia. The government therefore refused the proposal; nor would they make any fresh announcement at Teheran about their 'settled and declared policy in Southern Persia'. 'All vigilance' would be exercised in watching Persian affairs. Admittedly, conditions there might so alter as to compel a change in the methods of defending Indian interests.[82]

*　　*　　*　　*

By this time the affairs of Muscat had again come to the fore. The affair of the coalsheds droned on through 1899. After much haggling, during which Godley reported that the tradition of the Foreign Office favoured compromise or surrender,[83] an acceptable compromise was reached. Arms traffic in the Gulf had reached alarming proportions, for the French issued their protection to the subjects of the Sultan, who indulged in gun-running beneath the tri-colour. Some 35,000 rifles, with suitable quantities of ammunition, were suspected to be passing through Muscat each year.[84] Slavery also flourished, with French connivance. In the slave-market at Oman, Cox reported, demand had been good. Children fetched some 150 dollars, well-endowed girls double. Saiyid Faisal, with whom Cox was soon on close terms, issued an edict forbidding his subjects to accept French protection and then confiscated the French papers of slave-traders at Sur. M. Ottavi raged; M. Cambon protested; Lord Salisbury lamented the impudence of Indian officials, for the Sultan's zeal was supposed to spring from Indian inspiration. The French Ambassador, Clinton Dawkins wrote, had not been slow to appreciate the situation of Salisbury, who wanted only to bury the question.[85]

However, he did tell Cambon that the French claim to protect the subjects of another power was invalid and prevented suppression of slaving. It might be helpful if M. Ottavi were found suitable employment elsewhere.[86] As it happened, Curzon had nothing to do with the performance at Sur, nor had he made any offers to the Sultan.

'The situation of Cox triumphant, the Sultan malleable and Ottavi thwarted,' he wrote to Salisbury, 'is such a novel one that I am afraid the Foreign Office thought that I had played the prancing proconsul. I assure you that I have no desire to prance anywhere. All I want to do in Muscat is to get the dusky Arab, who presides over that place, on our side, and not in the French pocket. We shall do this all right, if you will back us up, and, above all, if you can succeed in removing that troublesome little Corsican Ottavi to some serener clime.'[87]

The Viceroy knew that the handling of these Persian affairs had irked Salisbury and given rise to charges of rashness. Yet in October, 1898, and on several later occasions, Salisbury himself had urged immediate construction of a Seistan railway; his first instructions had been to conclude a secret treaty at Kuwait, followed by authority to enforce an ultimatum at Muscat. Thereupon the Foreign Office waxed indignant at the admiral's threat to bombard. The Sultan of Muscat was desired to be in the British pocket, but the equal status of the French must not be touched. In short, the obvious consequences of orders were not foreseen. As for Salisbury, Curzon reflected, 'he will have a serious account to render at the bar of history, which does not forgive apathy because it rests upon experience, or cynicism because it is backed by character'.[88]

This judgement, Brodrick, replied, made insufficient allowance for the change in circumstances:

It is not only South Africa: we have had great difficulty in getting enough Ashanti troops and the situation in [the] Soudan is, in Cromer's opinion, more than shaky. You may say that inaction spells future trouble, but if you were here, I doubt if you would give France, Germany and Russia a chance of coming together on anything, even if that anything were Muscat, Kuwait, Bunder Abbas...

Brodrick admitted that he was oppressed by 'the sometimes needless inertia'; but Curzon's views rather perturbed Balfour and others 'as keen as yourself, because times are so difficult'.[89] In that case, retorted Curzon, Balfour must be easily put out, for India had recommended agreement with Russia, or, failing that, a warning that British interests must not be whittled away beyond a certain point. 'If that is Jingoism, I can only conclude that people's ideas have been changed by the war ... Forward views have, it seems to me, become a synonym for trying to look ahead: and there is not much place for that in our system.'[90]

In mid-August a French ship had anchored at Muscat, bringing a demand that the papers be returned to their owners. Fresh documents were given to slave-traders from Sur, in contravention of Cambon's promise. Warned by Cox, Curzon advised that Faisal should request a written statement of French claims. Ottavi overplayed his hand; Cox seized the chance to invite attention to the equal status established in 1862; the French could find no answer and withdrew. Curzon at once paid up the arrears of the Sultan's subsidy.[91]

Receiving from Hamilton another account of Salisbury's anxiety to give the French no pretext for a quarrel,[92] Curzon deplored such insistence upon the theoretical aspects of the situation at Muscat. Salisbury himself had breached the alleged equality in the secret treaty of 1891; it had been replaced by a quasi-protectorate, and M. Cambon's protestations were being taken much too literally: 'France is no more likely to fight with us about Muscat than we are to fight with Russia about Korea, whilst the perpetual deference to these manufactured French scruples in the case of Muscat is fraught with serious damage to our prestige in Indian waters.'[93]

But Salisbury rated the danger more seriously. A large part of the French population, though happily the smallest and weakest, seemed to him to want war. If Great Britain obviously strained the meaning of treaties, the middle party, under the influence of patriotic passion, might well join the war-cry, 'which will leave us in the dilemma of climbing down, or of going to war on a matter over which our own people will not support us at home ... as you are well aware, our character for hubris all over the Continent is a very bad one.' The Boer War had been a bad investment; but if it made the British nation realise that they could not have the moon every time they cried for it, the money might not be altogether wasted. To fight in the interior of Persia would swallow up twice or thrice as much income tax as the Transvaal. 'For, after all, you must divide victories by taxation if you wish to know in solid figures the real worth of Empire.'[94]

Curzon was not much moved. He expected France to help Russia in the Gulf, just as Russia helped France at Bangkok and Tangier. If Britain insisted on a coaling-station at Masampo, gave protection to Korean junks and blustered at Seoul, would Russia smile and acquiesce because she was acting in exercise of her equal rights? However, he knew that the Foreign Office thought the Indian government 'to be lacking in suavity, moderation and decorum: and to be rather philistine, if not forward, in its sentiments'.[95] Meanwhile M. Ottavi's performance became so outrageous that Hamilton had a gunboat sent to Muscat and even Salisbury promised to tell Cambon France was not playing fair. This he duly did, but still with caution. 'The French Chamber is full of Krugers.' Russia, 'much more powerful and quite as unscrupulous', was less liable to a rush of blood to the head. As for Germany,

she is in mortal terror on account of that long undefended frontier of hers on the Russian side. She will therefore never stand by us against Russia: but is always rather inclined to curry favour with Russia by throwing us over. I have no wish to quarrel with her: but my faith in her is infinitesimal.

Hence the extreme inconvenience, to which India's agents did not seem to be alive, of a quarrel with France. Lord Salisbury, watching their ways in the Gulf, experienced sensations similar to those of the owner of a large expanse of priceless china as he contemplated the antics of a highly muscular housemaid. Germany, Russia and France were bearing down upon the ports of the Gulf. The shore itself could be protected; but inland the only other force that would influence Persia was money. A competition in bribery would not be worth the outlay.[96]

Here, then, was a clear enough clash of view. Curzon did not believe that other powers were certain to overrun Southern Persia, or that France would fight over the Gulf, or that there was no hope of competing with Russia at Teheran. The government of India's rejoinder to the British despatch of July contradicted the assertion that Russia was already in a position 'to dominate and threaten almost the whole of Persia.' Nor had it been suggested that other powers be denied access to the Gulf. Railways built for military or political purposes, with termini which might become coaling-stations or naval bases, were another matter. Since Salisbury's reminder to the Persians, Russian engineers had travelled openly about Southern Persia and the Gulf. 'It is about as useless to come to me for hints about Persia' Curzon told Spring-Rice, 'as it would be to go to ex-President Kruger for a future constitution for the Transvaal.'[97]

SIX

Persia and the Gulf

THOUGH Lord George Hamilton warned Curzon often that the Boer War imposed a severe restraint upon British policy everywhere, he never concealed that other weaknesses played their part. The Foreign Office, he lamented in the summer of 1900, was in a hopeless state of flabbiness 'and I tell you frankly that I do not think you will get them to do anything either in connection with Persia or, so far as I can see, anywhere else. To let things drift seems now the accepted policy of that department, or at any rate of its Chief, and the misfortune is that time is not on our side, and the longer we drift, the worse position we find ourselves in.'[1]

Before this letter reached India, the Boxer rebellion had erupted in full force. Curzon could not understand why nothing had been done with Weihaiwei; but that was part of Britain's China policy, 'which has always been to me—and I believe to everybody else—a riddle insoluble by man.'[2] The senior Ministers in London had no more idea than the Viceroy what line they were supposed to be following. Salisbury was at last persuaded to ask Japan and Russia to send troops, but made no haste to set the detailed arrangements in train. Living now at Hatfield, he came to London only two or three days a week. On 29 June, Brodrick reported that the Cabinet at their last meeting had not discussed China, although an hour was spent in debating whether the Third Reading Clerk should be maintained in the Lords.

By early July, hope for the European Legations had been more or less abandoned. Salisbury, inaccessible and difficult to move, apparently regarded Pekin as predestined to Russia.[3]

India had promptly offered and sent troops which restored the situation eventually. But at home the malady remained. Though the weeks slipped by, Salisbury could not be induced to adopt or state a policy. The Chancellor, at his wits' end for money, objected to any large increase in the expeditionary force.[4] Seeming to believe that the Chinese crisis would burn itself out, Salisbury would do nothing 'except oppose any straight and practical line of action'. Lord George despaired at his 'steady declension in power and grip' and hated to write such criticisms: 'but unless I told you frankly what is going on, or rather what is not going on, you would be utterly unable to fathom or understand our embarrassed position: a Cabinet of twenty without a leader and four different heads of departments all with different ideas sending out orders to their respective officials in China. Fortunately our amorphous condition is not generally known... '[5]

Six weeks later, when the Prime Minister returned from holiday in France, the situation was no better. He found himself at loggerheads with a Cabinet committee which wanted to work with Germany at Pekin. The First Lord, Goschen, confessed to Curzon that he had no idea what policy Great Britain was following in China,[6] while Hamilton's letters implied that the composition of this 'most effete' Cabinet must soon change. Were it not for the regard felt for Salisbury by his colleagues, and their departmental efficiency, the whole concern must long ago have fallen apart. 'He won't press for a decision, he does not keep people to the point, and all sorts of irrelevant trivialities are discussed *ad nauseam* to the exclusion of affairs of real importance.'[7]

Shortly after this, the General Election of 1900 was fought. With a large majority, Salisbury set about the construction of his last Cabinet, in which there had not been a single alteration since June, 1895. His doctors urged that he should no longer combine the Premiership with the Foreign Office. The Queen, near the end of her life and devoted to him, felt some alarm at the prospect of his departure from the post he had so long distinguished, but Balfour advised that the double duties were too much.

Roberts, due to return shortly from South Africa, refused the War Office, whereupon Salisbury recommended Brodrick, who had long experience there as a junior Minister and had given 'ample proof of general ability and capacity', while working under the Prime Minister's eye at the Foreign Office. The Duke of Connaught, the Prince of Wales and the Queen herself demurred, but she soon relented.[8] Both Lansdowne and Balfour believed that the new man would show courage and determination in this most perilous of positions.[9] Salisbury offered it in realistic terms: 'You know the disadvantages of the post so well that I will not dilate on them.'

Brodrick found the army 'hopelessly disorganised and used up... ' and the arrears of work prodigious. He was determined upon large changes. 'No one', he predicted with accuracy, 'will be better hated in the War Office than I before two months are over.'[10]

Lansdowne, expecting to savour the seclusion of Bowood, found himself translated to the anxieties of Downing Street. At the Foreign Office his exquisite manners, perfect French and long experience of Imperial administration found a more congenial and tranquil field of exercise than at the War Office. His rôle in the conduct of policy was never restricted to those 'Foreign Office details' of which Balfour had written to the Queen. From Curzon's point of view, the change could not fail to be a welcome one. He knew Lansdowne tolerably well and respected him. The new Foreign Secretary, who had himself been Viceroy until 1894, might be expected to pay more attention to representations from India than his predecessor had done, and to score off the business more efficiently.

These hopes were not frustrated. Among Curzon's close friends, Selborne became First Lord of the Admiralty and Wyndham Chief Secretary for Ireland; Cranborne and Brodrick had also moved up the ladder; Balfour remained as Leader of the House of Commons, and Hamilton, to Curzon's relief, at the India Office. This reorganisation, then, had strengthened materially his personal links with the Cabinet, though not his agreement with their policy. Balfour regretted the decision to retain Beach at the Treasury, for he was unlikely to find with a good grace large sums for naval building and reorganisation of the army. Within a few months, quarrels developed within the Cabinet because he was always threatening resignation if more were asked for.[11]

The ministerial changes provoked a good deal of comment. Certainly the Cecils and their connections were well represented by Salisbury himself, his nephews Arthur and Gerald Balfour, his son at the Foreign Office, and his son-in-law at the Admiralty. The principles of the reshuffle, Asquith said unkindly, seemed to be to promote one's incapables and provide for one's family.

Mr Ritchie, the new Home Secretary, proposed at the first meeting of the Cabinet a certain measure. 'I warn you', he said solemnly, 'that it will lead to a great deal of discussion and waste of time.' Salisbury, who had seemed to be asleep, opened his eyes. 'Isn't that just what we want?' he asked.[12] Reports which Curzon received in the early weeks of the Government's life did not indicate that its cohesion or drive had improved. The Cabinet's work, Brodrick wrote, was not well done, with the Prime Minister 'shocking bad in the chair'. After each meeting 'Arthur tears his hair and declares ... he will retire from public life.' Brodrick described the Prime Minister as 'epigrammatic and demoralizing to the last degree'. A few weeks later he was writing of some soreness in the House about the promotion of Salisbury's relations and Balfour's haphazard management.[13]

★   ★   ★   ★

Durand was now replaced at Teheran by Curzon's friend from Balliol and All Souls, Sir Arthur Hardinge. The Shah, asked for his agreement, merely said, 'I hope he will be less blustering and mischief-making than his predecessor.' Somewhat to Hardinge's surprise, the Prime Minister spoke strongly to him of British interests in Persia. Russian influence must be resisted south of a line running from Kermanshah to Seistan inclusive, and especially in all those places within reach of British naval power. Sir Arthur was to behave courteously towards the Shah and his Ministers, who had taken a strong dislike to Sir M. Durand. The only justification for this was that he had 'perhaps something of the *ethos* of the Indian Resident'. Salisbury thought that Russia would not march on Teheran, which would entail the risk of a British stroke in the Gulf. At least until she had finished the Siberian railway, and completed her task in Manchuria, Russia would not be disposed to exert on Persia any pressure which could not safely be resisted with British moral support.[14]

The departure of Salisbury from the Foreign Office prompted Curzon to try again for a more spirited defence of British interests in Persia. The position there, he told Lansdowne, was 'far worse than it has been at any time in the last fifteen years: and we have no glimmering of a policy'.[15] He delineated in detail the decline of British influence, which had led Spring-Rice to liken the situation of the Legation to that of a jellyfish in a whirlpool; the closing grip of Russia; the perambulant parties of railway engineers in the south, the subsidised steamers in the Gulf, the penetration of the Cossacks to Isfahan. What were the spheres of influence in Persia essential to India which had been mentioned in the home government's despatch of the previous summer? How were they to be protected? It would be wise to struggle only for the essential points:

> I have no desire to push our pretensions to the limits that were once possible, but are now obsolete. Let our programme be proportioned to our capacities. But even a modest programme would be better than none at all.[16]

Lansdowne's reply offered hope. He cared little for spheres of influence, which would keep the British out of the north but would not prevent Russian and other intrigues in the south. Russia must not be allowed a footing in the Gulf for naval or military purposes. The new Foreign Secretary warned Persia that no outside interference in Seistan would be tolerated, but refused to draw a line beyond which Russia's southward progress would be opposed.[17] Hamilton largely agreed, with the qualifications that the British hold on the Gulf must be maintained 'on the Indian side' and that no 'provocative or aggressive' line be followed at the other end of the Gulf. Russia should be opposed in Asia, but not to the extent of occupying positions which must be evacuated in time of crisis.[18]

By midsummer, the war was costing £1¼m. each week. The Boers avoided major actions, attacking isolated posts. Probably they numbered no more than 10,000 against their opponents' 250,000. Kitchener said he could not send men home; the Chancellor of the Exchequer protested that he could not continue for ever raising huge loans. Hamilton, who loved Salisbury and owed everything to him, admitted that he was not the man to tackle this critical situation. So the situation drifted on. Lord George wanted Curzon to understand 'how the heart and vitals of the British Empire are just now enfeebled, so that you may understand the absolute necessity of lying low for the present. It is largely because I am influenced by these considerations that I urge upon you in Persia and elsewhere a quiescent attitude.'[19]

A letter from Salisbury, written some three months later, indicated that the consequence of the Boer War weighed heavily upon his mind. After all the expense, he did not think Parliament would find the money for a Persian loan. India, he understood, would not make advances from her own resources:

> Under these conditions we may expect that sooner or later Teheran will fall under the virtual protectorate of Russia. I do not see that, except by bidding higher, we have any means of preventing that issue. The destiny of the south seems to me less clear, for we have the power of resistance if we care to use it. That Russia would be glad to go to Bunder Abbas, and Germany to Kuwait, I have no doubt: but they have hardly strength to do it.

When that crisis came, Salisbury surmised, British success would ultimately depend upon possession of that railway to Seistan to which he had long attached importance. Lansdowne was hostile; and again the financial difficulty arose. England was unlikely to contribute, and India, it was protested, could not bear the whole cost:

> In the last generation we did much what we liked in the East by force or threats, by squadrons and tall talk. But...the day of free, individual, coercive action is almost passed by. For some years to come Eastern advance must largely depend on payment and I fear that in that race England will seldom win.[20]

This letter was provoked by a renewed financial crisis in Persia, which raised afresh the vexed question of Britain's true position in the south and east. To Russia, Seistan had obvious potential value, separating the vast desert, the Dasht-i-Lut, from Afghanistan and Beluchistan. A future connection between the Transcaspian and the sea would probably run through Seistan, possession of which might make the Kandahar-Herat defensive line and the Helmund Valley untenable. This view, which Curzon held consistently from his first examination of the Persian problem, was shared by Lansdowne and Salisbury, and confirmed when Isvolsky said during the negotiation of 1906 that the military party in Russia would not wish to abandon so important a stratigical asset as Seistan without substantial compensation.[21]

British trade in Persia generally stagnated after 1899, being hampered by the absence of roads, multiplicity of tolls, corruption of officials and tricks of the tribes, whose principal industry was highway robbery. Often they merely murdered travellers for valuables, but more refined methods were sometimes employed. One English traveller, a Mr Gentleman, was stripped naked by a band of ruffians, who fired revolvers into the sand around his feet. This caused him to leap about a good deal, to the general delight. Eventually he was left to regain Shiraz, clad only in an old copy of *The Times*. In Seistan, however, British and Indian traders could count upon more favourable conditions. Determined to use every method of building up British influence there, Curzon began to develop the trade route from Nushki. Slowly it was made safe from robbers and wells were dug. In 1898–9 the trade to and from Quetta had been worth 7¼ lakhs. In 1899–1900, it almost doubled.[22] Already Curzon looked to the day when the British would lease part of the Helmund Valley, dam the river and recreate in Seistan the garden and granary to the former prosperity of which countless ruined cities bore witness. This province had suffered invasion by Genghis Khan, reported to have cast his captives into eighty cauldrons of boiling water, and of his descendant Tamerlaine. The latter-day Governor, the Hashmat-ul-Mulk (glory of the country) contented himself with less comprehensive punishments, though he did achieve some local fame in 1899 by blowing a miscreant from the mouth of a cannon. He showed himself well-desposed to the British, who helped to frustrate constant Russian attempts to secure his dismissal.

In fostering the trade, Curzon looked to the day when a Russian challenge might cause the British to take Kandahar and the Helmund Valley. He wanted to build up a clear British interest.[23] Like other parts of Persia, Seistan was frequently visited by Russian 'geologists' or lovers of wild life, who generally turned out to be soldiers or agents. One of these naturalists, M. Zaroodney, was understood to make a hobby of distributing rifles on the borders of Beluchistan.[24] Lansdowne's warning to Persia that no Russian interference with Seistan would be tolerated has already been recorded. A few weeks later, Arthur Hardinge spoke to the Sadr-i-Azam in person about Britain's growing commercial interests there. Soon Lansdowne was telling the Persians that Seistan 'must remain free from the intrusion of foreign authority in any shape'.[25] This represented a limited but definite success for Curzon's policy.

From the early months of Hardinge's time at Teheran, he disagreed with Curzon upon several points, relatively minor but fruitful of discord. The customs services were administrated by Belgian officials under M. Naus, who appeared to the Indian authorities to show undue partiality to Russian interests and to be habitually obstructive. Curzon believed that they played the Russian game and hoodwinked Hardinge.[26] Moreover, consuls and vice-consuls in the south, many of whom were employed by India, felt that the Legation at Teheran offered them little support, while the Minister complained of their overbearing manners and unhelpfulness. That India's representatives were not always models of discretion Curzon conceded. One of them, Major Chevenix-Trench, he described as 'a very curious creature, exceedingly vain, rather bombastic, and consumed with the idea, wherever he be, that the hub of the universe is not far distant.' But he was a first-rate Persian scholar, with ability and purpose; he had recovered the position in Seistan, where his work had been almost invaluable. Curzon said he got better service from such men, who had usually been sat upon, than from a dozen more demure personalities who never climbed out of the correct official rut.[27]

The Russian loan of 1900 was soon gobbled up, and the Imperial Bank had already advanced money to the limit allowed by its charter. In May, 1901, Curzon suggested that Britain make a loan, nominally through the Bank, on the security of the Seistan revenues.[28] Nothing was done. Two months later, the Shah rejected demands which would have turned Persia into a virtual Russian protectorate;[29] and in mid-September the Grand Vizier told Hardinge that the deficit was half a million sterling. The Shah, whose extravagance was largely responsible, ordered his hapless minister to raise a million forthwith. Russia advanced the first £100,000 a few days later. If Russia made Persia pay off her debt to the Imperial Bank, Hardinge telegraphed, she must acquire complete ascendancy.[30]

Pressure on the Treasury was such, said Lord George Hamilton, that their help was most doubtful. Might the Government of India find half a million?[31] No such loan had been made to a foreign power before and only a clear return to Indian interests could justify it. Curzon replied at once that the money would be lent if it could be secured on the Gulf customs and the revenues, or less desirably the customs, of Seistan. Persia must be told that no rival interests or concessions could be allowed in those regions, though there would be no question of protectorate or partition.[32]

Hamilton had for the moment forgotten that by the terms of the Russian loan of 1900 no other country could lend directly to Persia. The Political Committee at the India Office felt that the conditions laid down by Curzon, which Hardinge thought too stiff, could not be secured through a bank.[33] Curzon was vexed, but not surprised. Hardinge's attitude seemed needlessly pessimistic, for the help offered came on easier terms than any Russia could give. The Sadr-i-azam, Hardinge advised, would reject them. Having information that the Grand Vizier was in Russia's pay, the Viceroy expected it; but would the Shah enjoy being swallowed by Russia? At worst, there would be an opportunity for a clear definition of British interests.[34] The question of cash, Hardinge telegraphed, dominated the whole situation: 'Unless Persia can somehow be freed from exclusive financial dependence on Russia, continued effective defence by diplomatic methods of British interests in Seistan and Gulf appears almost impossible. In a few months, or even weeks, matters may have gone dangerously far... '[35]

In this dilemma Lansdowne tried to find a middle course between Curzon's terms and Hardinge's. The latter suggested that a small loan on easy terms might well lead to a later transaction on stiffer terms. Lansdowne wondered whether an Anglo–Russian loan, secured for the British on the Southern customs and for the Russians on the Northern, would not be the answer?[36] Salisbury replied that the situation seemed sufficiently hopeless. If money were not found, 'Russia will establish a practical protectorate and we can only by force save the Gulf ports from falling into it.' An approach to Russia would be futile: 'She will pretend to consider it—will waste time in colourable negotiations—and when she has arranged matters to her liking will decline any co-operation with us.'[37]

Curzon fumed at the absurdity of this situation. Hamilton telegraphed that the India Office would not lend to Persia. The next morning arrived the letter from Salisbury already cited, to the effect that money was the knot of England's Eastern difficulties and that India would not admit Persia to be mainly her interest. So in the same moment the Prime Minister was saying that Persia would be lost because India would not stump up, while the India Office said the money was there but must not be used. 'It would be a comedy if it were not so great a tragedy.'[38] Hamilton clearly felt no keenness to finance the Shah's peregrinations about Europe, where his last cure had been assisted by a number of pretty but greedy ladies. If Hardinge was right in believing that Persia would not grant Curzon's conditions, then an Indian loan would certainly not be justified; and a small advance would merely postpone, and probably aggravate, the difficulty.[39]

In Petersburg, Lamsdorff denied positively that any further Russian loan to Persia was on the tapis. Since Sir A. Hardinge had telegraphed that the loan was actually on the point of completion, even the Foreign Office concluded that Count Lamsdorff's statement had been a trifle wanting in frankness. Some of the money had indeed already arrived in Teheran. Curzon, at once amused and mortified by this time-honoured performance, marvelled again at the gullibility and innocence of the English who accepted these rebuffs and meekly said how good it would be to come to terms with the Russians, such excellent fellows, meaning so well.[40]

Without much confidence, Lansdowne proposed the joint loan,[41] of which Schomberg McDonnell predicted that Russia would 'merely fool us as she has always done by procrastinating until her financial plans are ready: then she will politely tell us that she does not want us or our co-operation. Lord Salisbury is fully alive to this...'[42]

The India Council took a less negative view than its Political Committee and agreed, after all, to go as far as half a million, virtually on Curzon's conditions but with the significant difference that the loan could not be made through the Imperial Bank. The Council did not wish to be exploited by the Foreign Office, or to admit Persia to be an 'Indian interest'.[43] Anyway, Witte turned down the notion of a joint loan, asking calmly why the British did not advance money through the Bank? Charles Hardinge thought that Lamsdorff had not shown Witte the terms. Both were revealed as liars.[44]

After Hardinge's first interview with Witte, Lansdowne seems to have imagined that Russia genuinely wanted an understanding about Persia. He soon discovered differently. On 5 December the Grand Vizier told Hardinge that Russia would not permit the British loan. Evasive replies met Lansdowne's pointed questions at Petersburg. Sir C. Scott handed in a memorandum. Lansdorff ignored it, while the Grand Vizier compared himself to a bankrupt tradesman who must ward off creditors by constant talk of 'a remittance on its way' or 'funds coming in from a tardy debtor'.[45] The Cabinet's insistence that the loan should come from the British Government, not through the Bank, had killed a promising opportunity. Hardinge believed that if the Bank had been used, the Russians would have known nothing until the transaction was over. He doubted, somewhat gratuitously, whether Curzon had any conception 'of the subservience of these people to Russia, since they have realised that the loan contract of 1900 makes them absolutely dependent upon her for money'.

In a contest of wealth, the rich power had lost, simply because its power rival was willing to risk some of its money.[46] A new Russian loan, of £1,000,000, was announced in the spring of 1902.

★ ★ ★ ★

'I am relieved beyond measure' wrote Brodrick from the War Office in October, 1901, at the quietude, however temporary, in Afghanistan. 'It could never find us in more difficulty unless we were at war with France.' A further 61,000 men 'of sorts' had been sent to South Africa. Hardly any troops remained at home; and the tussles with Hicks Beach continued. Nor was that the limit of the Cabinet's problems:

> We have had a semi-panic here – the result of long tension as to the war and of the apparent apathy of Lord Salisbury and A.J.B.
> The truth is the nation wants leading and hermitage will not do.

Salisbury, back from holiday, was due to visit the War Office. But Brodrick expected nothing beyond a few jokes: 'the position is absurd: No one troubles in the least as to what he says or thinks on anything but F.O.'[47]

Godley put the same point rather differently. The Government, he said, was suffering from some disease or complex of diseases which he would not diagnose. Since the unwieldy Cabinet had reassembled, that fact had made itself the more acutely felt. Such a malady spread downwards through the departments, so that all became conscious of disorganisation and discouragement.[48] The Prime Minister, Brodrick reported in later letters, was visibly failing and 'solely occupied with keeping us together till after the War – après cela le déluge'. The contest between the Chancellor and the Service Ministers had still not been resolved. Selborne refused to reduce his naval programme; Beach refused to finance it. The first Lord had written a memorandum proving that his scheme would eventually lead to annual estimates of £33m., not £43m. as the Chancellor asserted. Nonetheless, Lord Salisbury summoned Selborne and lectured him for daring to propose £43m. and to force Beach's hand. The Chancellor threatened resignation. 'Heaven knows how it will end.'[49] Curzon's view of the Government's weakness, partly derived from the press, had not changed. So few of them appeared to be in earnest. 'Nonchalance filters down from the top: and the general impression is one of casualness and a light heart...'[50]

★ ★ ★ ★

In 1899, the Anatolian Railway Company secured permission in principle to extend their line to Baghdad and the Persian Gulf. Salisbury's chief object in signing the agreement with Mubarak was to obtain control of that part of the Gulf believed to offer the only satisfactory terminus. The government in London could then prevent the construction of the line, or alternatively impose conditions agreeable to themselves. Once the secret treaty was made, Curzon favoured a clear statement to the Turks that they should not try to take Kuwait by force. Salisbury refused: 'There is no danger of surprise on the part of Turkey: therefore I see no object in giving them warning. If they come on, they would be turned off, warning or no warning.'[51]

This characteristic reaction scarcely met the point. In the Autumn of 1899, the Porte tried to appoint a harbour-master at Kuwait. Mubarak foiled this move by the simple expedient of refusing to let the harbour-master land and sending him smartly back to Basra. O'Conor, British Ambassador at Constantinople, learning that the military authorities favoured occupation of Kuwait, warned the Turks that any such step meant complications. By then the Boer War, with all its effects on British policy, had begun. Curzon moved cautiously; the Cabinet generally failed to move at all. He would have liked to tell Germany about British relations with Mubarak. To a railway debouching at Kuwait he had no objection, once an Anglo–German understanding were reached. He suggested, and Hamilton agreed, that the Sheikh should accept no proposal from the Germans without reference to India.[52] Mubarak, however, handled his German visitors admirably. With every refinement of oriental politeness he refused to allow a terminus. Lord Salisbury did not feel sanguine about preventing a German railway from going to Kuwait, saying to Brodrick, 'I want the dynamics, not the ethics, of the question. We have at home only the 8th division and we cannot afford to unite three powers against us.'[53]

Lord George wished to run Germany against Russia in Turkey and the Gulf. Chamberlain and Balfour favoured the encouragement of German ambitions in Asia Minor as a counterpoise to Russia in Persia, both powers to be told that no interference in the Gulf would be tolerated. Salisbury, however, declined to broach the Kuwait question with Germany. 'The Emperor is one of the long spoon potentates.'[54] Curzon felt little confidence in either policy, but for different reasons. He knew that Germany could not build the railway without financial help from London, of which fact full use should be made in negotiation, but thought it would be illusory to rely upon German support in the Gulf against Russia.[55] In the end a slightly modified version of Curzon's proposal was adopted. Baron von Marschall was told by O'Conor of the secret agreement and the Porte informed that no European power could be given special rights in Kuwait. The German government said that Britain would be consulted if and when it was decided to carry the railway to the Gulf.[56]

Curzon and the Cabinet were at one desiring that any railway coming south to the Gulf should be made only by agreement with the British. When the treaty of 1899 was signed, the Admiralty did not realise that other sites, close to Kuwait and of debatable ownership, would provide equally suitable termini. Moreover, the rather energetic methods by which Mubarak had secured the throne, and his fondness for armed excursions into Arabia, would embroil a protecting power at Kuwait in a blood feud, providing the Turks with every chance of inciting the Amir of Nejd to invade. By an unlucky chance, the Turkish Governor of Basra was also mixed up in the feud. As if this degree of confusion were insufficient, the Sheikh again requested a British protectorate; so did the Amir, on condition that he might overthrow the Sheikh. Curzon noted that Mubarak's request stemmed from fear of Nejd. Turkish protection meant a Turkish garrison at Kuwait; and since Britain now had the disadvantage without its benefits, an open protectorate would be the best course. Lansdowne and Salisbury demurred. Turkey was warned that an attack on Kuwait would be thwarted by force if necessary; but in a private letter Hamilton said that Britain could hardly make good even her claim at Kuwait if it were contested by Turkey.[57] This is a good instance of the paralysing effect induced by the long struggle in South Africa.

Admitting that there might be overwhelming international reasons against a protectorate, Curzon remarked that he had never known an occasion when the same argument was not brought forward to dissuade any definite step for the defence of British interests. Nor could it be morally wrong to protect the Sheikh at his request, if it had been morally right to sign the agreement of 1899, for that assumed his independence. Anyhow, these issues would be decided by expediency, not by legalities. One-sided application of British scruples did not seem much of a policy.

> I may say that I do not believe in the Sermon on the Mount in international politics. I do not believe in turning the other cheek to the smiter. It was the Sermon on the Mount that was responsible for the peace after Majuba Hill, and that has already cost our country about 170 millions sterling in South Africa. This is rather a heavy price to pay for the principles of abstract Christianity.[58]

The late summer of 1901 brought renewed reports that the Turks were massing troops for an assault on Kuwait. In August, the captain of a Turkish vessel was told that the disembarkation of soldiers would not be allowed. What would happen if the Turks came by land, no one knew. The status of the Sheikh seemed equally mysterious. In 1898 the Foreign Office denied any Turkish claim to sovereignty over Kuwait; in 1901 O'Conor averred that the Sheikh enjoyed territorial independence under the spiritual sovereignty of the Porte; on the next day Lansdowne said that Britain had never claimed the Sheikh to be territorially independent; soon afterwards Turkey's sovereignty was denied; a fortnight later the Foreign Office stated that Britain had been willing for thirty years to admit the suzerainty, if not the actual sovereignty, of the Turks over the territory extending from Basra to El Katif.[59] It was not apparent how, if this latter view were correct, Salisbury could have authorised in 1899 a protectorate or the secret treaty.

By the end of 1901, the British position was becoming a little clearer, in fact if not in theory. A Turkish gunboat arrived at Kuwait with a demand that Mubarak leave at once for Constantinople. He refused, on British advice. O'Conor told the Porte that if the Turkish government could not control their own officials, the British might not be able to uphold the *status quo*. Five British warships anchored at Kuwait. These proceedings created some stir. British behaviour, wrote the Emperor William to the Czar, set in strong relief 'the enormous advantage of an overwhelming fleet which rules the approaches from the sea to places that have no means of communication over land, but which we others cannot approach because our fleets are too weak, and without them our transport is at the mercy of the enemy'.

The incident showed how necessary was the Baghdad railway, which the Kaiser intended German capital to build. Had 'that most excellent Sultan' not been dawdling for years, the line might now have offered Russia the opportunity of sending a few regiments to Kuwait from Odessa and thus turning the tables on England.[60]

Turkey took military possession of a natural harbour at Um Kasr, which might provide an alternative terminus for the protected railway. The whole situation was becoming increasingly awkward for British ministers. Selborne did not want to locate warships permanently in this remote part of the Gulf, though without them Kuwait could not be defended; Lansdowne minuted that the agreement with Mubarak was no guarantee of the British position. The Turks would be told that while their suzerainty over Kuwait was recognised, any attempt to give it concrete expression would be opposed. A railway would be acceptable, so long as British capital received at least as large a share as that of any other power. A terminus on the Gulf was not begrudged: but 'we shall resist ... all attempts by other powers to obtain a foothold on its shores for naval or military purposes. This, I take it, is the "bed-rock" of our policy in the Gulf, and we shall pursue that policy not in virtue of ambiguous understandings with local chiefs, but as the predominant power in southern Persia and in the Gulf.'[61]

This was in Curzon's eyes an infinitely more decisive assertion of British interests. It contrasted strangely with assorted warnings received in the last few years. Mubarak, who had been reported earlier to be intriguing with Russia, was warned against actions which might emperil him with Nejd. Later in the year, an armed attack on Kuwait was frustrated by H.M.S. Lapwing.[62] Curzon never ceased to regret that the opportunity to declare a protectorate had been missed in 1899, for the obligations had in practice devolved upon Great Britain.

At the other end of the Gulf, Hamilton would have liked to help Cox more vigorously in Muscat, but the Boxer rebellion, and the fact that Britain had quarter of a million men locked up in South Africa, made the Foreign Office most reluctant to risk any controversy with the governments which had sent troops to China.[63] Cox had been authorised to tell the Sultan that he might uphold his jurisdiction over flag-holders in his own domain and territorial waters. The Foreign Office suddenly dissented, in June, 1901; at which Curzon expressed surprise, for Lansdowne had when Viceroy ruled in the contrary sense. Cambon claimed there was no evidence of slave-trading from Sur under the French flag, and when Cox produced chapter and verse, said he was anti-French. Lansdowne refuted the change, and reversed his position. Though France showed no desire to give way, the Portuguese helped to solve the difficulty. They learned that dhows from Muscat had landed slave-traders in Mozambique. The ships were sunk, the slaves liberated and some of the traders, among them French flag-holders, sentenced to penal servitude in Angola. M. Delcassé announced an enquiry.[64]

* * * *

In justice to Curzon, it must be understood that his complaints of indecision and blurred lines of communication did not relate solely to the buffer states. A number of other foreign questions, not in themselves warranting a place in any but the most detailed account, came regularly before him. One of them may be taken as illustrating the imperfections of the system. In the hinterland of Aden, a body of Boundary Commissioners were supposed to be delimiting the frontiers, in co-operation with the Turks.

Aden was, nominally at any rate, administered from Bombay, under the orders of the government of India, and commanded by an officer of the Indian Army. Within a short time, the whole matter lay in confusion, not least because an official in London had drawn the wrong line on the wrong map. Sometimes the India Office dealt directly with the Resident at Aden, who would in turn issue orders to the Commissioners. They were directed by the Foreign Office, since it was only at Constantinople that political pressure could be brought upon the Turks.

When documents reached the Viceroy, the views and orders of Hamilton, the Resident, the Commissioners and the Bombay government were inextricably entangled. By the summer of 1902, the home government had either to follow Curzon's policy or sacrifice the position at Aden. He asked Godley why they could not have trused him to see them through. 'You treat my advice as though it were that of an impertinent schoolboy. Had I tried my best or my worst, I could not have made the infernal muddle that has been made at home.'[65]

Curzon was already longing for the whole administration of Aden to pass into the hands of the Foreign Office. 'However, I suppose there is nothing to be done but to let the Government swim about in their own mud.'[66] His own proposal was simple enough. Troops would be landed at Aden. The Turkish forces would be told to evacuate all the villages in dispute. If they refused, the villages would be held and the demarcation completed without Turkish assistance. Two ingredients were lacking: troops at Aden and resolution in Downing Street. India could supply the one but not the other.[67] After this, the attitude in London stiffened, but not for long.

The Turks distributed balm at Constantinople while advancing in the hinterland of Aden. More than one ludicrous incident marked the exchanges. On the very day when the Foreign Secretary commended O'Conor's diplomacy, Turkish troops were firing on the Boundary Commissioniers. Lansdowne told his colleagues that he opposed all attempts to extend the Protectorate. He understood that the Viceroy wished to include all tribes on the Hadramaut coast. In fact, they had been included for years. Assuring Lansdowne that he did not wish to increase the Protectorate by a square foot, Curzon begged him to eliminate unreasonable suspicions of India's proposals, and to persist in the firmer line recently adopted. The Foreign Secretary sent, as usual, a temperate and friendly reply: he had no desire to impute vast Arabian ambitions to India, and the Foreign Office did not desire to thwart Indian proposals.[68]

O'Conor, mistrustful of the methods of the men at Aden, proposed that

Mr FitzMaurice of the Embassy should join the Commission. He proved, to Curzon's huge amusement, a real Balaam, blessing the Commissioners, adopting India's proposals and denouncing Turkish iniquities with Gladstonian fervour. This probably helped Curzon in January, 1903, when he again suggested that a little reality might be injected into the proceedings. British weakness, he wrote, had encouraged the Turks to advance absurd pretensions 'and a disregard for treaty obligations that they would not have dared to show to a power of the calibre of Corea or Siam.'[69]

Hamilton agreed that troops should shortly go to Aden. When, four months later, the delimitation was still dragging on, Curzon groaned at the humiliation to England of allowing herself to be bullied and humbugged by the emissaries of a power whose continued existence in Arabia depended upon her sufferance. The farce was costing hundreds of thousands of pounds, which if precedent were a guide, India would have to pay.[70] However, the Foreign Office changed sides again. In May, it was decided to conclude the treaties in Southern Arabia for which Curzon had asked nearly a year earlier.

★　　★　　★　　★

The spectacle of Great Britain without allies, detested all over Europe, and incapable of beating the Boers quickly, provoked reappraisals of her foreign policy; but the basis of a more secure position was not to be found easily. Agreement, let alone alliance, with France or Russia seemed remote, and the alternatives hardly more promising. Curzon remarked in 1900 that he placed no reliance on American sympathy, confined to the upper classes, or on German friendship, rooted in expediency rather than sentiment:

> I never spent five minutes in enquiring why we are unpopular. The answer is written in red ink on the map of the globe. Neither would I ever adopt Lord Salisbury's plan of throwing bones to keep the various dogs quiet (Madagascar, Tunis, Heligoland, Samoa, Siam). They devour your bone and then turn round and snarl for more. No, I would count everywhere on the individual hostility of all the great Powers but would endeavour so to arrange things that they were not united against me ... *I would be as strong in small things as in big.*
>
> This may be a counsel of perfection. But I should like to see the experiment tried.[71]

It was not that Curzon disapproved of sound bargains. On the contrary; what he disliked was a series of piecemeal and unrequited concessions. Hamilton agreed that these brought no benefit; but intense British unpopularity was becoming a real danger. Although the fleet remained very strong, its relative superiority was declining. If allies were needed, as he believed they were, he would like to join with Germany.[72] This was written just after the Kaiser's revelation of Mouravieff's supposed intrigues. A few months later, in September, 1900, the First Lord of the Admiralty noted that France and Russia might still be tackled together; 'but there is Germany, and the combination would be too strong for us.'[73] Though the date of Boer defeat receded steadily, an army far larger than any the British had previously sent abroad was maintained some seven thousand miles from base. While that state of affairs persisted, extreme caution became the watchword everywhere.

The Cabinet, Curzon believed, were applying too crude a criterion. Plenty of matters could be settled without recourse to arms. If Lord Lansdowne mentioned the planting of a Russian officer at Tashkurgan or the threat of French gunboats at Muscat, the Ambassadors would certainly not reply 'You cannot fight because you are tied up in South Africa'. Admittedly, only the Foreign Secretary knew the whole situation. The Viceroy had no regular means of appreciating it, for the print sent out from the Foreign Office often lacked vital papers and was anyway at least three weeks out of date. If, because, of the Empire's troubles, he failed to point out threats to Indian interests, the home government would be justified, when one of these issues turned septic, in blaming India for sloth or blindness.[74]

Isolated Britain, mused Hamilton, was an object of envy, with interests touching upon those of almost every other great power. The position in respect of Russia was not an easy one, with Scott, at St Petersburg, weak and Staal, in London, played out. Lamsdorff had difficulty in holding his own and in reconciling promises with the performance of Russian agents. If Britain joined the Triple Alliance, Lord George argued, her defence spending would be cut and the peace of Europe guaranteed.[75] Curzon disputed the equity of such a bargain. It would mean incessant surrender of commercial interests to Germany. 'What should we get from her in return? We do not want her army. Her navy is not sufficiently strong to be of much value. Austria can give us absolutely nothing and might entangle us in a fight over the Balkan Peninsula. Italy is too weak to be of any assistance.'

Further, would Parliament tolerate a sustained policy of European alliances?[76] Hamilton rejoined that Russia in her duel with the British had in France a partner who could be of the utmost help in war. That the Germans would behave towards a British ally as Russia had done to France he granted; but it did seem that an Anglo–German alliance would maintain

European peace. British expenditure on the forces had reached about £60m. a year and income tax was unlikely to fall below 1s. in the £. Even then, the military establishments looked inadequate.[77]

The dialogue continued fitfully for some time. Curzon consistently refused to see the merits of alliance with Germany. The Emperor William he thought flirtatious, excitable and ineradicably jealous of the English, wishing to keep what he had in Europe, which meant protection of the eastern and western flanks by good relations with Russia and France. German intentions seemed plain.

> She wants the hegemony of land and sea; and she wants Colonies for her surplus population and markets for her expanding trade. We more or less stand in the way of the realisation of all these ambitions but the first: and the spasmodic friendliness of the Kaiser is merely an attempt to gain by expediency what he cannot at present wrest by force.[78]

There remained another course, which did not figure in this correspondence. The Admiralty had realised that the two-powers standard could not be kept up everywhere. Since British commitments were worldwide, the Cabinet must either accept probable inferiority in the Far East and Caribbean, or find an ally. The First Lord dismissed the first alternative: We could not afford to see our Chinese trade disappear, or to see Hong Kong or Singapore fall, particularly not at a moment when a military struggle with Russia might be in progress on the confines of India.'

As the British Far Eastern fleet would soon be outnumbered more than two to one by those of the French and Russians the corollary was obvious: alliance with Japan.[79] Earlier in 1901, there had been some talk of an undertaking by England and Germany to support Japan against Russia, and of an Anglo–German agreement. Neither proved feasible. In the autumn the Cabinet agreed upon a simultaneous approach to Russia and Japan. This was at the time of the Persian financial negotiations. Lamsdorff rejected the notion of a joint loan, while Staal said he had never favoured the division of Persia into spheres of influence;[80] but with Japan the Foreign Secretary made better progress. He tried to extend the scope of the projected alliance beyond war originating in China or Korea. Japan refused. Lansdowne told the Ambassador that his colleagues felt Britain should receive Japanese help in a war with Russia and France over an Indian dispute. It availed nothing.[81]

The Anglo–Japanese alliance, committing each partner to war only if the other were fighting two powers, was signed in January, 1902. It did not carry all the disadvantages which would normally have attached to a European connection. It diminished the likelihood of British involvement in

a Far Eastern war, since the French were no more anxious to venture their
fleet for Russian interests in Asia than the Russians had been for French
interests in Africa. More significant for India, the alliance decreased the
risk of a Russian seizure of Herat, for an Anglo–Russian war would provide
Japan with the opportunity to take Korea and North-East Asia. It was not
intended as an incitement to war and at first Lansdowne did not think that it
made war more probable. A year to two later, however, he acknowledged
that the treaty inevitably made Japan feel that she might try conclusions
with Russia.[82] Even if Britain did have to fight under its terms she was
probably adding little weight to her previously unwritten commitments,
for she could hardly have stood by as France and Russia crushed Japan.

The new obligation would be fulfilled by sea power, would not entail
conscription and applied only to the other side of the world. No doubt
Salisbury was the more ready to acquiesce for these reasons. It did not mean
an increase in naval building; indeed, it allowed partial withdrawal of
ships from the Far East, as did the Hay–Pauncefote agreement from the
Caribbean. Dependable command of Eastern waters even opened
the distant prospect of reinforcing India from Australasia, or, should
the Mediterranean be closed, from home by way of Canada.

Although the Cabinet had tried to make the alliance cover India, Curzon
knew nothing of the negotiations until the result was announced. Having
long foreseen its value, he immediately sent Lansdowne warm congratulations on his 'most statesmanlike agreement'. 'The noodles seem to have had
a lucid interval' said the Kaiser.[83]

The possibility of alliance with Germany did not take on new life
Hamilton had to admit that her people's antipathy towards Britain constituted a real obstacle and Selborne, who had wondered in 1901 whether
it would not be the only alternative to an unbroken rise in the estimates
was insisting by April, 1902, upon the urgent definition of a proper naval
standard. He had not previously 'realised the intensity of the hatred of the
German nation to this country. I have consulted Lord Lansdowne and ...
he shares my sense of the importance of the question and my anxiety to
arrive at a fixed policy.' By the autumn, Selborne had concluded that the
German Navy was being carefully built up 'from the point of view of
war with us...'[84]

*   *   *   *

In another weighty despatch and memorandum, sent home in November
1901, Curzon analysed the nature and progress of Russian ambitions in

Persia. Had they been purely commercial, there would have been no cause for opposition; but they were not, and if Russia once obtained a port on the Gulf, France and Germany would enter. 'The disastrous contagion of Kiaochow' would be reproduced. A rail link to the Indian Ocean must mean the loss of Seistan.[85] Godley, accepting the premises, repeated that Russia could not be kept out of Persia by military force. He stated, indeed, that Russia could not be kept out of India either, so depleted was the Army there. Soon afterwards, Sanderson asked whether India could help with road-making in Southern Persia. He spoke impressively of the parting of the ways, but it turned out that the Foreign Office dared not ask Beach for a penny and proposed to find the whole sum (£10,000 over five years) from Secret Service funds. British interest in Persia, Godley observed, was confined to the official classes, most of whom, asked whether they cared to the tune of £5, would say 'no'. Sanderson emphasised that Persia was exclusively an Indian interest.[86]

It is not difficult to imagine Curzon's dismay as he read such letters. Once more he explained that a good deal of this argumentation was unreal. Nobody in India or in Russia was dreaming of sending a large military expedition into the trackless wilds of Persia. Anyone who cared to take out a map would discover that the Russians had no greater facilities for the conquest of central and southern Persia than the British for its defence. An examination of the terrain, especially that lying between Seistan and the sea, showed clearly what kind of a military venture it would be. Therefore Curzon judged that Russia was in the last degree unlikely to embark on any military march to the Gulf. So long as the Royal Navy retained command of the sea, the final consummation of Russian designs could be thwarted. Nor, by taking a stronger line, would the British commit themselves to the defence of a frontier on which troops could not be placed. Movement across a line would mean a *casus belli* at British discretion but not necessarily a contest on the spot, the situation that already applied on the Russo–Afghan frontier.[87]

This excursus produced little effect upon Lord George. Godley agreed that if British diplomacy were persistent and courageous, which he did not anticipate, military action would not be needed;[88] but Lansdowne's line was a more resolute one. Spurred on by the Viceroy, he prepared a despatch to Teheran. It was in substance and often in language a copy of Curzon's proposals. Russia was not to have a military or coaling station on the Gulf; to any such concession the British would reply with 'measures which, in view of their naval strength in those waters, would be attended with no serious difficulty'; should Persia encourage Russian political influence in

Southern Persia and Seistan, the British government might find it impossible 'to make the integrity and independence of Persia their first object as hitherto'.

After Russia vetoed the British loan in December, the despatch was approved by the Cabinet, despite Hamilton's misgivings. Hardinge conveyed it verbatim to the Grand Vizier, who lamented the Russian loan of 1900, the prodigality of the Shah and the rapacity of his acolytes. In the Shah's name, he assured the Minister that no part of Persia's sovereign rights or territory would be abandoned.[89]

Here was the material for a coherent policy. Lansdowne did not like to encourage Hardinge to buy up the mullahs, 'although I have not the slightest idea whether the clerical conscience is expensive or not'.[90] All the same, Sir Arthur more than held his own. The performance of the Russians in Seistan, where their counsel intimidated the Governor and worked hand in glove with the Belgian customs officials, persuaded even Hamilton that a firmer policy must now be followed to prevent strangulation of the developing trade route from Nushki.[91]

It should be added that this concern for Southern Persia had nothing to do with oil. Curzon, who had been a director of a company which spent a good deal of cash in a fruitless search for it, attached at this stage no importance to the D'Arcy syndicate's concession, eventually to become the Anglo–Iranian Oil Company.

*   *   *   *

The Shah, flush with Russian money, was about to visit Europe again. He was sure to expect the Garter, which Lansdowne thought impossible, for it was no longer being conferred upon non-Christian sovereigns. Hardinge pressed the point, remarking that appeals to Persian vanity provided almost as powerful a lever as corruption. The constant Russian refrain of Anglo–Indian superiority towards Asiatics must not be reinforced. King Edward said he would not confer the order, which swore the Knight to exterminate the heathen; Curzon preferred that it should be a reward for good behaviour.[92] The court and politicians, Hardinge found on reaching London, were most keen that the Shah should not come in August, for that would interfere with their grouse-shooting. Salisbury would make no definite date.

'Everybody in the highest quarters' wrote Hardinge, '(except perhaps Lord Lansdowne) regards Persia, and all connected with it, as an unmitigated bore, and ... it is useless to hope that any sacrifice, however small, will be made for the sale of our interests there. No wonder the Russians always beat us; they are in earnest and we are not.'

Curzon, deeply disappointed but not in the least surprised, replied 'I know well that the subject is voted a bore and myself a lunatic. It is heart-rending to see this trifling with an international concern of supreme importance... '[93]

It was arranged after all that the Shah should come for a short visit in August. Having intimated that it would be an insult to be lodged at Dorchester House, where the inferior Afghan Nasrullah Khan had stayed, he had to be put at Marlborough House. Lansdowne gave the Grand Vizier assurances of British support for Persian integrity, so long as other powers were not permitted to encroach in the South. If Persia needed money, Britain would try to provide it in a suitable manner.[94] King Edward, recovering from a serious illness, excused himself from the State Banquet. Unhappily, no one present seemed able to talk anyone else's language. The whole affair proceeded in a deathly silence, interrupted now and again by a interpreted conversation between the Shah and the Prince of Wales. Only the description of Mr Balfour's uniform as that of 'un frère ainé de la Trinité' provided comic relief.[95]

The burning question remained unsolved. The Shah tiresomely refused to understand why, if his father had received the Garter from Queen Victoria, he could not receive it from her son. He brusquely rejected gifts personally tendered by the King. In court circles it was even feared at one moment that if the King offered the Grand Cross of the Royal Victorian Order in lieu of the Garter, the Shah might retaliate with a miserable Grand Cross in brilliants of the Lion and the Sun.

Lansdowne, mistakenly believing the King to have agreed, said that a new class of knights would be created and ordered speedy production of special insignia, which he caused to be illustrated in coloured pictures for the King's benefit. These reached the monarch while he was cruising off the Welsh Coast. Annoyed by what he regarded as an attempt to force his hand, he hurled the whole thing, box, notes and pictures, through a port-hole, indicting a stiff letter to the Foreign Secretary.

If the Shah leaves this country in the sulks like a spoilt child because he cannot get what he wants, it cannot be helped.

Lord Lansdowne states that a determined effort should be made to strengthen our hold upon Persia. In this the King entirely concurs. But we should not have lost the hold which Russia now possesses if the Government of the day had kept their eyes open, and had had more competent representatives at Teheran.[96]

The Shah, therefore, was sent empty away. However, the visit did
occasion a clearer definition of British policy. Lansdowne ruled that
British representatives in Persia must not foment agitation against the
régime or distribute money secretly, although 'a moderate sum' might be
spent in 'establishing closer relations with the Church party'. If it came to
military action, Britain would advance not out of affection for the mullahs
but 'in order, if possible, to save Persia and, failing this, to secure ourselves
within our own "sphere of interest" '. Balfour agreed in principle: 'until
Russia moves we remain still; as soon as Russia moves in the North we
move in the South'. Though there had been much talk of unrest in Persia,
Balfour thought that the Russians would not invade, and felt doubtful
about an inland operation by British troops. Where would they come from?
And if war broke out, would Persia be the most suitable cockpit?[97] Curzon
welcomed these declarations, as well he might. He cared little for the idea
of a military occupation of Seistan, but thought Indian troops could get
there before the Russians. Then Britain would at least have a strong lever.

That the Shah's visit to England had been a failure could not be doubted.
The Prince of Wales' departure to shoot in Yorkshire on the fourth day
gave great offence, and the Persians, realising the situation in London,
noticed the contrast with their lavish treatment in Russia and Germany.[98]
Having spent a quarter of a million on motors and toys the Pivot of the
Universe had to borrow money from a trader at Baku in order to get back
to Teheran, where the Grand Vizier, by adroit tactics and the timely
distribution of some £3000 among leading lights of the spiritual world,
staved off a determined effort to oust him from office. Hardinge believed
him more strongly entrenched than ever. The Shah was still sore about his
treatment, the Russians openly contemptuous and exultant. 'They could
not have believed that we should have played their game so well for
them.'[100]

Meanwhile, the matter of the Garter continued to agitate the government in London. Lansdowne thought of resignation. The King believed
that even if the Garter were given, the Shah would not alter his attitude to
Great Britain but would only 'laugh in his sleeve'. Balfour had to hint at
the dissolution of the Cabinet before King Edward relented.[101] This
decision revived Hardinge's drooping spirits.

For the moment, the Russian grip appeared firmer than ever. The new
Persian tariff, favourable to Russian trade, and upon which the Grand
Vizier had promised discussions with the British, was immediately pushed
through. He approached the Russians secretly for a guarantee of Seistan and
Persian Beluchistan against Britain. They made no commitment, partly

George and Mary Curzon

The 3rd Marquess of Salisbury

Government House, Calcutta

A triumphal arch at Rangoon

Visit to the Rao of Cutch. Walter Laurence, Curzon's Private Secretary, is standing immediately behind him

The Hon. St John Brodrick   *Lord George Hamilton*

Caravan passing through the Khyber Pass

The Amir Abdur Rahman, with some of his family and courtiers

Ruins of Fatehpur Sikri

Mosque in the Fort, Lahore, restored by Curzon

The Durbar: state entry of Lord Kitchener

The Durbar: Lord Curzon saluting the guard of honour

because they appreciated the shakiness of the Grand Vizier's position, partly for lack of forces in that region.[102] An inter-departmental committee in London recommended that if Russia advanced into Persia, Britain should occupy Seistan, Kishm and Bunder Abbas, the War Office confessing that beyond the maintenance of colonial garrisons and reinforcement of India, the British Army was completely inadequate for any operation whatever.[103]

SEVEN

Afghanistan and Tibet

WRITING SHORTLY AFTER the Central Asian crisis of 1885, Curzon had not thought that the foreign policy of Russia was a consistent, inexorable progress towards India, but rather a hand-to-mouth affair, vacillating between timidity and bravado, profiting from others' mistakes. Much of Russia's fitful progress was owed to the gullibility of her English rivals, who swallowed time after time absurd assurances and then uttered futile cries of protest. Great Britain had therefore no right to complain of Russia's advance. Her presence in Central Asia was a menace to India, of which she would take advantage. Of course, no one in Russia, save a few theorists and a giddy subaltern here and there, dreamed of conquering India. The project was 'too preposterous to be entertained'. Quite apart from all obvious difficulties, the logistic objections would be overwhelming. But a Russian attack on the Indian frontier was another matter. It would be undertaken to keep the English busy in Asia and therefore quiescent at the Straits, to prevent a repetition of 1878. Thus the keys of Constantinople might be won on the banks of the Helmund. Even in 1878, the Russian mission to Sher Ali set out from Samarkand on the very first day of the Congress of Berlin. Before it reached Kabul, the Treaty had been signed; nonetheless, a secret agreement was made. By the end of the year, the British were at war with the Afghans, who were promptly deserted by their avowed protectors.[1]

The Russian Foreign Minister, Giers, had observed in 1883 that the possession of Central Asia gave Russia a basis of operations which might be offensive.[2] At the time of Penjdeh, however, he assured the British government officially that Russia cherished no aggressive designs upon Herat or any part of Afghanistan. Since a large number of similar promises had been broken with impunity, discussion about the defence of Afghanistan continued unabated, and indeed more anxiously. Twenty years afterwards, the Russian Foreign Minister, Isvolsky, admitted to King Edward VII that India had not lacked cause to be suspicious in the days of Alexander II and

III. The Russian government had failed to control their Generals and officials and had largely extended the frontier.[3]

If an attack on India or Afghanistan were attempted, Russia must either cross the Hindu Kush or go south from Herat or through Persia. Because of the lack of roads or even tracks, an advance on India from the North West must pass through or near Kabul or Kandahar. Athwart the first route lay the Hindu Kush, which had some accessible passes in that region; while Kandahar would be approached via Herat, Farah and the Helmund, flanking the Hindu Kush. In 1888 Salisbury had repeated the warning to Russia given by Gladstone three years before: Herat meant war.[4] It was by no means clear where the struggle would be fought out. Great Britain did not have the men, nor did the Baltic enjoy the climate, to allow the invasion of Russia in that quarter. Alliance with Turkey and attack through the Straits looked less and less feasible. In short, Russia seemed to be like some huge monster, safe from mortal wound. A tentacle might perhaps be hacked off, but no more. The British Empire, on the other hand, was vulnerable if any combination of powers, or spread of commitments, caused command of certain seas to pass into other hands. John Morley's opinion that it presented 'more vulnerable surface than any Empire the world ever saw'[5] was an exaggeration; but India remained tenable by a European sea power only so long as major invasion overland remained impossible. Hence the crucial importance of the buffer states and the special attention paid to their preservation by those like Curzon who had no doubt of Russia's desire to move still further south.

It had long been agreed that Russia must not be allowed to capture Kabul or Kandahar. If she took Herat, the British and Indian forces would probably occupy Kandahar, with or without the Amir's assent, placing outposts on the Helmund and closing the passes leading from the Kandahar–Kabul road to the Indus. If an advance to Kabul were ordered, Roberts, then Commander-in-Chief, insisted that 30,000 troops must be sent from England as a first instalment.[6] The Cabinet in London would not give an explicit promise, for the ability to send a sizeable force to India must depend upon British commitments elsewhere. Indian plans, it was laid down in 1892, must rest on the assumption that no reinforcements would be available. Roberts replied that to maintain an Indian Army on this basis would cripple the country financially. The prospect of allowing Russia to establish herself in Northern Afghanistan, a territory guaranteed by the British, would 'ruin our prestige as an Eastern power'. Lansdowne, the Viceroy, agreed.[7] The military planning of India was thus left in a confused and unsatisfactory state. Everyone knew that if a full-scale contest developed in

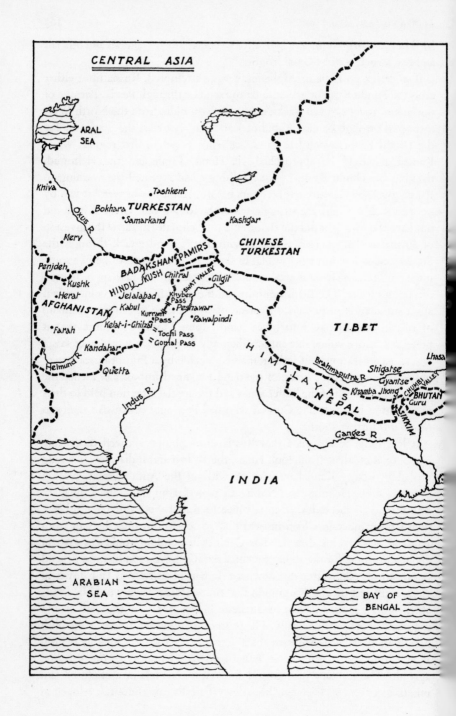

CENTRAL ASIA

ARAL
SEA

Khiva

OXUS R

Bokhara TURKESTAN
•Tashkent
•Samarkand   •Kashgar

Merv

CHINESE
TURKESTAN

Penjdeh
BADAKSHAN PAMIRS
Kushk   HINDU KUSH Chitral   Gilgit
Herat   Jelalabad SWAT VALLEY
AFGHANISTAN   Kabul Khyber
Farah   Kelat-i-Ghilzai Kurram Pass Peshawar
Pass   •Rawalpindi

TIBET

Kandahar   Tochi Pass
Helmund R.   Gomal Pass

Quetta

Indus R.

HIMALAYAS

Brahmaputra R.   Shigatse   Lhasa
Gyantse
Khamba Jhong   CHUMBI VALLEY BHUTAN
NEPAL   Guru   SIKKIM

Ganges R.

INDIA

ARABIAN
SEA

BAY OF
BENGAL

Afghanistan the Indian Army could not fight indefinitely without aid from home; yet there was no certainty that in the moment of crisis there would be troops available. The India Office observed in 1891 that with all the special problems in India—the possibility of another mutiny and of activity by Russian agents, the need to defend the ports and the perennial risks on the frontier—a Russian army even of 30,000 might be beyond the capacity of the Indian Army to repel.[8]

'Our principal and most dangerous enemy in Asia is undoubtedly England' reported the Russian Foreign Minister in April, 1895. 'Surely', commented the Czar.[9] All the same, he volunteered to Lord Salisbury in the following year the most solemn assurances. It would be absurd for Russia ever to try to take India; no sane Emperor could ever dream of it. That might well be true; but the sensitive place remained. As the Russian Ambassador, Staal, least bellicose of men, noted during the China crisis of March 1898, 'la Grande Bretagne, engagée simultanément sur plusieurs points du globe, doit compter tout particulièrement avec la Russie, qui peut la menacer du côté des Indes.'[10]

Hamilton, writing in the early weeks of the Boer War, observed that he did not believe Russia intended to invade India for the purpose of acquiring the country. British and Russian interests crossed in various parts of the world. Russia knew that India was Britain's most vulnerable point and had established herself in a position from which she could exert pressure. That capacity was much enhanced by the railway from Merv to Kushk post, within seventy miles of Herat. Witte, the Russian Finance Minister, told the British Ambassador at Petersburg, Sir N. O'Conor, that it had been built 'solely for strategic purposes'. However, he and Kuropatkin proposed that it should be joined to the Indian network through Afghanistan. Then no troops would be allowed to travel the line.[11] How this ban was to be enforced, and how the Amir's consent was to be obtained, they did not reveal. Traffic began to flow along the new lines just as Curzon arrived in India. The Russians at once informed the Governor of Herat, who passed the letter to Kabul. Abdur Rahman was in no doubt about the significance. It was, he wrote at once to Curzon, 'bad news which has doubled the grief I had in my heart ... they have done it in the name of commerce'.

Curzon did not dispute this view.[12] Thus began the long and turbulent official correspondence between the Viceroy and two Amirs. Abdur Rahman and Habibullah usually wrote to Curzon every two or three weeks. He would respond at similar intervals. Since his visit to the Amir four years earlier, Curzon had been recognised as a leading authority on Afghanistan and had garnered a good deal of recent information. He learned from the Amir's employee Sir S. Pyne in May, 1898, that a reign of terror prevailed. Abdur Rahman himself was loathed. Six horses saddled and laden with coin were kept always at the ready. He was supposed to have poisoned the Commander-in-Chief. A foolhardy individual who accused the Amir of depravity was seized and died after his tongue had been torn out by the roots.[13]

Abdur Rahman had written periodically to Curzon between 1895 and 1898. His letters were inscribed on thick paper, with gorgeous illuminations, and sent in a linen bag with a gold cord. In February 1898 he insisted that he was the staunch friend of the British government, despite the frontier troubles of 1897 and the officials of the Indian government. As for Curzon, 'I have always thought of you to be the best friend of mine in the world and you are at the head of all my friends.'[14] Once his 'best friend' had become Viceroy, however, the Amir lost no time in showing that affairs of state would be treated on the old footing. His letters reflected that love of disputatious argument and occasionally outrageous logic with which Curzon had long been familiar. Lord Lansdowne, whose opinion of the Amir had already been recorded, used to say that for all his ability he had the instincts of a pettifogging lawyer, loving to make at enormous length points of infinitesimal importance.[15] After setting out the details of frontier outrages, the imminent Russian peril, the lack of British support and the venality of petty officials, Abdur Rahman would generally conclude, 'Further, all is well.'

The basis of relations with Afghanistan had not changed. By an agreement of 1880, Afghan foreign relations were conducted through Great Britain. The Amir received a subsidy, originally granted in order to help pay his army and improve the defences, and increased by the agreement which Durand made at Kabul in 1893. The British had committed themselves to the protection of his territory, not for its intrinsic value nor because they could defend the whole of it, but because they were determined to avoid having a land frontier with a first-class power. The Amir allowed the government of India to maintain a Mohammedan agent at Kabul but made sure that he sent back very little of value. The military authorities knew practically nothing of the country. Whether Abdur Rahman could be relied upon to keep his engagements was a subject of dispute. Curzon generally took a view favourable to him; others thought differently. Early in 1899, the Emperor William told Sir F. Lascelles that he knew for a fact Russia had a treaty with Afghanistan, signed about a year before. Godley thought this quite likely, for the alleged date would coincide with the frontier troubles of 1897-8. Mouravieff denied it; and Hamilton, generally well disposed to Germany, said he had long since realised that when in difficulties she circulated some story about French or Russian designs.[16] The rumours did not altogether surprise the Viceroy. Some money might have changed hands and it was very possible that if the British threw over the Amir, Russia would take him up; but he did not believe that Abdur Rahman had given disloyal pledges or intended to substitute Russian for British influence. The Amir denied strenuously any agreement between himself and Russia, an assurance accepted by Curzon.[17]

In his first official letter to the Amir, Curzon reminded him, in response to an obscure observation about the lack of systematic arrangements with regard to Afghanistan, of the advice given by Lansdowne and Elgin that railways and telegraphs would be the most effective means of protecting the exposed frontier. At Kabul in 1894, Curzon had said that it was not safe to have no telegraphic wire between Herat and Kabul. He now disclaimed any desire to 'dictate to Your Highness or to interfere with Your Highness's free and uninterrupted management of the internal administration of your own dominions'.

Did the Amir wish the telegraph in his territory; did he wish the railway to stop at the Indian frontier? If so, he must not complain that British troops, when called for, came to his defence slowly.[18] Abdur Rahman replied that his remark about the want of systematic arrangements had referred to the need for breech-loading rifles and machine guns, with which the Afghans were capable of defending themselves. He wanted from the illustrious British government, therefore, money and arms, not troops, telegraphs or railways, which would be costly and superfluous. The people of Afghanistan had not the money for them and he had heard that every nation which had invoked others' help for such purposes had 'suffered much evil and sustained great losses'. He had told Curzon in 1894 that the people would consider such works a cause of ruin and 'would stealthily and mischievously cut the wires every night'.[19]

Curzon thought it pointless to defer unduly to Abdur Rahman, who knew perfectly well when he was imposing and would be the first to despise the British if they did not reply firmly. He did not expect to get anything out of the Amir in respect of railways or telegraphs; but the import of arms was becoming a serious matter.[20] Two days after the Amir's letter was written, the Commissioner of Peshawar telegraphed:

I think it right to bring to notice for information of Government that very large consignments of ammunition are going to Kabul. The following have just arrived: 2,000,000 cordite ·303 bore cartridges, 2¾ tons of Nordenfeldt and 9 tons Hotchkiss cartridges, the two last apparently unloaded cases. In the past four months Karachi customs have cleared, besides the above, 10 tons Martini-Henry and 9 tons Hotchkiss cartridge cases, besides several hundred thousand Lee-Metford and Mauser ball cartridges.

These startling figures cast a curious light upon Abdur Rahman's request for further stocks of guns and ammunition. Careful enquiries were set on foot. The Amir, it transpired, had been importing arms through India since 1882, with two intervals; the first when Lord Lansdowne imposed an embargo in 1892–3, and again during the frontier war of 1897. Moreover, the government of India had between 1880 and 1895 made the Amir a free present of huge stocks of arms. The agreement of 1893 laid down without qualification that the government of India would raise no objection to the Amir's purchase and import of munitions. Since then, massive orders had been placed. 'It appears to us' the government of India told Hamilton 'that Afghanistan is rapidly being coverted into one vast armed camp, equipped, by our aid and largely at our expense, with the latest implements of modern and scientific warfare.'

Admittedly, most of the arms were stored in arsenals where they would deteriorate, and most of the Amir's army would be untrained in their use. Nonetheless, they amounted to a formidable military danger; and while there was no reason to doubt the Amir's loyalty, Afghanistan was an unsettled country. It now seemed that Abdur Rahman recognised only one British obligation towards himself, namely, to furnish warlike stores in unlimited quantities. This view Curzon called 'novel and inadmissible'. He drafted a warning, friendly but unmistakable, correcting some points of fact and interpretation. The British government did not have, as Abdur Rahman asserted, an unqualified obligation to repel an external enemy attacking Afghanistan. The promise of 1880 said rather that if Afghanistan were the victim of unprovoked aggression, the Amir would be aided 'to such an extent and in such a manner as may appear to the British Government necessary', provided that he followed unreservedly British advice as to his foreign relations.[21]

Lockhart, the Commander-in-Chief, thought the Amir's attitude preposterous and noted that the Afghan infantry were daily becoming better equipped than the Indian with arms of precision. He favoured the immediate stoppage of the enormous imports of arms and the beginning of work on the railway from Peshawar towards Dakka. Curzon pointed out that these steps would involve the rupture without warning of pledges given to the Amir and would cause him to relapse into the state of mind in which he had sulked from 1891 to 1893. The Viceroy's draft was therefore sent to London with no substantial change. Salisbury, most anxious that

any war of words with the Amir should be curtailed, made a few altera-
tions, but did not touch the substance.[22] Accordingly, the Amir was told
that in case of invasion of Afghanistan the British government must judge
whether help would be given 'by money, by ammunition, by troops, by
all these together, or by any other means'.[23]

The government of India were to some degree in a cleft stick, and Abdur
Rahman knew it. It was desirable that Afghanistan should be strong, as a
deterrent and buffer; in which case, observed the Amir, all that was necessary
was that India should send along promptly arms and money. 'The rifles
and guns of the enemy' he observed gratuitously, 'cannot be silenced by
means of stones and sticks.' When Russia moved, Abdur Rahman planned
to incite the Mohammedan inhabitants of Turkestan. He did concede that
if, 'after a prolonged fight', his men should fail to turn back the invaders,
the help of British and Indian troops would be accepted as a matter of
course. The warning given by the British government against importation
of arms seemed to have produced no effect, for he requested rifles, machine
guns and ammunition for 280,000 men.[24]

Curzon believed, and it is plausible enough, that the Amir, enlightened
by the Tirah campaign and conscious of the enormous strength given by
the possession of some hundreds of thousands of modern weapons, had
revived in old age the idea of consolidating Afghanistan into an independent
military power. This was perhaps why he was always clamouring for more
arms and had come to boast for the first time about defending his country
without the aid of British troops. Certainly his activities on the frontier
gave an impression of independence. Curzon still did not think he would
cast in his lot with Russia, which would mean the loss of Herat. On the
other hand, the Russians might seize Herat and offer it back to the Amir for
an anti-British alliance. Then they might begin to experience the delights,
tasted by the British for nineteen years, of having Abdur Rahman as an
ally.[25]

★　　★　　★　　★

In his first years as Viceroy, Curzon had no more hope of firm support over
Afghanistan than over Persian affairs. The Foreign Office, he noted, displayed an altogether unnecessary degree of meekness and deference in
receiving protests from France and Russia about matters with which they
had nothing to do. In 1891, when Colonel Yonoff was swaggering about
the Pamirs, allegedly seeking ovis poli, there happened to be an Englishman who was genuinely shooting game on the Taghdumbash Pamir. He
built a low hut in which to cook food. Russia immediately protested

against the erection of this menacing fort. Now, eight years later, the
Russian government made another equally absurd charge. Curzon thought
it would save a good deal of trouble if a less credulous attitude were taken
up:

> We are about as likely to attack the Russians on the Pamirs as we are to
> organise a flotilla of balloons to make an attack upon Mars, and the Russians
> know this as well as we do. Whenever they are hard pressed for an argument,
> this is their invariable resource, and I think that they should be told plainly
> that we know what bunkum it is.[26]

Usually, Lord George Hamilton could be relied upon to explain carefully all the difficulties the Foreign Office was facing. Sometimes he would
allow himself a greater measure of frankness, confessing that the Office
lived from hand to mouth, with no clear policy or definite aims, except to
keep the peace. Salisbury's position and intellectual subtlety enabled him
to carry on this form of diplomacy with an authority and apparent success
that a lesser man could not attempt.[27]

Curzon's three years' experience as Under-Secretary had given him
exactly the same impression of the Foreign Office's proceedings: 'there are
no settled principles of policy in relation to any part of the world: and
everyone, from the exalted head down to the humblest clerk, sits there
anxiously waiting to see what will turn up next.'[28]

Salisbury, preoccupied with his French negotiations, then with his wife's
approaching death and the imminence of war in South Africa, was certainly
in no mood and probably in no position to protest with vigour at Russian
proceedings. Earlier in the year, during talks with the Russians about
China, he had observed that 'negotiating with them is like catching soaped
eels'.[29] He genuinely believed in the Russian threat in Central Asia and
especially in Eastern Persia, and the Russians made sure that the possibilities
did not escape notice in London. The War Minister, Kuropatkin, stated
that Russia intended to strengthen herself in Central Asia 'for defensive
purposes in that region and also for offensive operations in India, if necessity
should arise'. He added, however, that war with England would be most
unprofitable.[30] Doubtless these and similar statements contained a good
deal of deliberate bluff and some wishful thinking. The problem, for civilian
ministers, was to judge whether there was a residuum of fact or feasibility.
In so abstruse a question as the logistics of Russian advance over vast distances, ministers would naturally turn to their military advisers. In those
days, however, there existed no effective machinery for the co-ordination
of foreign policy and defence. The intelligence services of the War Office

were notoriously deficient. In any case, the Boer War overshadowed
everything else from October, 1899. Curzon would have liked to despatch
a stern reply to the Amir's letter of late September, but Hamilton and
Salisbury insisted that something smoother be sent. Curzon acquiesced
gracefully, realising how many troubles the Cabinet had to contend with.
On the limited plane of relations with Afghanistan, he regretted this
enforced failure to answer Abdur Rahman's intentional misrepresenta-
tion.[31] There seemed to be no sign of improvement in his attitude. When
the Viceroy complained of repeated Afghan outrages on the frontier, the
Amir retorted with ample proofs that the fault lay with the British.[32]

With the whole available force locked up in South Africa and suffering
almost daily defeats, and with the Indian Army depleted, it is no wonder
that the British looked on anxiously to see what use Russia would make of
the pressure point in Asia. Charles Hardinge, at St Petersburg, soon learned
through the indiscretion of one of the General Staff that the Russian garrison
at Kushk had been reinforced. The Foreign Office heard that much war
material had been sent to Central Asia. Sanderson, permanent head of the
Foreign Office, wondered why: 'I suppose it is merely to have it handy in
case of the death of the Emir or other opportunity for grabbing something.'[33]

Curzon did not take the news too seriously, believing that the Russians
could hardly go for Herat without some sort of pretext. Hardinge held the
same opinion, though, as he told the Foreign Office, the construction of
the entrenched camp at Kushk could only be intended 'to serve as a future
base of operations against us'. Sanderson replied that the Russians were
reported to have at Kushk sufficient material to extend the line to Herat.
He feared that the Russian Foreign Minister, Mouravieff, whose attempts
to form a European combination had just been reported, had every disposition to be mischievous. This seemed 'unaccountable at a moment when
Russia's obvious policy is to be friends with us'.[34] This was written on 22
November, 1899, when the Boer War had been in progress six weeks.
Why it should be Russia's obvious interest to show friendship to Great
Britain is not plain now; and at the time friendship was evidently some-
what remote from the mind of the autocrat who controlled Russian affairs.
The Czar wrote to his sister:

> My dear, you know I am not proud, but I *do like knowing that it rests solely
> with me* in the last resort to change the course of the war in Africa. The means is
> very simple—telegraph an order for the whole Turkestan army to mobilise
> and march to the frontier. That's all. The strongest fleets in the world can't
> prevent us from settling our scores with England precisely at her most vulner-

able point. But the time for this has not yet come; we are not sufficiently prepared for serious action, principally because Turkestan is not yet linked up with the interior of Russia by a through railway line.[35]

The rail link to which the Czar referred had already been under discussion for some time. On 2 January, 1899, the French military attaché at St Petersburg, after conversations with officers of the Russian General Staff, reported that if the railroad were built from Orenburg to Tashkent, Russia could place at Kushk 200,000 men. There were dreams of extending the line through Seistan to the Gulf. The General Staff had just been ordered to work out in detail a plan for concentration on the Afghan frontier. The Minister for War, General Kuropatkin, describing in detail the military movements he had ordered in Central Asia and elsewhere, spoke of placing in the event of war 100,000 men on the borders of Afghanistan. This number would later rise to 350,000, for 'la grande guerre des Indes'.[36] The Czar told the French Ambassador that Britain would show herself less arrogant everywhere once the line to Port Arthur and the link between Central Asia and the main railway system were built. This latter would be a strategic line, said Mouravieff. If some incident like Fashoda recurred, it would not suffice for Russia to be invulnerable on her 'Indian' frontier: 'il faudrait pouvoir faire, au besoin, une démonstration menaçante et avoir un bouton à presser au moment voulu.'[37]

The Russians may have feared lest the British at some stage launch an attack on their Central Asian lands, the inhabitants of which were not celebrated for docility.[38] If so, the fear was as fantastic as the calculation about the Orenburg–Tashkent railway was accurate. That line, completed in 1904, exercised a profound influence in the later stages of Curzon's viceroyalty. It might almost be said to have caused his downfall.

★ ★ ★ ★

Like the Viceroy's Council, Hamilton looked askance upon the accumulation of arms in Afghanistan. However, the reports of Russian reinforcements in Central Asia increased during the first three months of the Boer War. Those troops, as Lord George told Curzon in January, 1900, could be used only against territories in which the British had a special interest. This was hardly the moment to reduce the Amir's means of self-defence. 'We must be very watchful' wrote the Queen, 'and well prepared, and have plenty of artillery.' Abdur Rahman assured Curzon that so long as the British did not show indifference and carelessness, he would not fail in friendship. 'Afghanistan considers itself a partner of the illustrious Government in their weal and woe.'³⁹ A little later, early in February, the Amir wrote to India about the large Russian troop movements supposed to be taking place at Kushk. Mouravieff stated that beyond a routine movement of four battalions no such movements had taken place.⁴⁰ The Czar had already given the British the explicit assurances recorded earlier.

Like the Cabinet, the government of India was receiving many menacing rumours about a great Russian advance in Central Asia. Curzon placed much, but not implicit, reliance upon the solemn promises of the Czar. He wondered whether the despatch of a large force to Kushk was intended to prevent India from sending more reinforcements to South Africa, to preclude any interference in Russia's bold game or to scotch any possibility of an Anglo–Japanese alliance. It was impossible to feel secure. Curzon doubted whether, in the depleted state of the Indian Army, Kandahar could be taken and held, and was certain that an advance in force could not be made to Kabul and Jelalabad. He had seen a letter from Mr Frank Martin, at Kabul, to his brother at Calcutta, describing an interview with Abdur Rahman. The Amir had discussed the war in South Africa and the likelihood of a Russian invasion of Afghanistan, which he thought would be prevented by the danger of a Mohammedan rising throughout the Russian dominions. The Amir said he could not understand British suspicion of disloyalty. It must be due to the ignorant apprehensions of the British Parliament. He told Mr Martin to visit the public Turkish bath at Kabul in order to get a fair idea of the British Parliament. Mr Martin went at once to the bath, which he found

full of men, and the high dome overhead reverberated their calls for towels, soap and c., and their usual loud-voiced conversation, until the meaning of any individual words, and the words themselves, became lost in the confusion of sounds, and but added to the uproar.⁴¹

At this time, the Russian Foreign Minister was considering whether the Boer War should mean a change of policy. Mouravieff concluded that the situation did not justify extraordinary measures. The state of military preparedness in the Central Asian provinces should be kept up. This, he noted, always produced an impression on the British government. The work of Russian railway surveyors in Persia, and the construction of lines in the Transcaucasus to link the Russian and Persian systems, must be pushed on. The Orenburg–Tashkent line should be built. The comments of other Ministers are of interest. Witte warned that Russia's finances could not stand even extra measures of military preparedness in Turkestan. Kuropatkin saw that the most important task was to win control of the Bosphorus.

It was widely thought, commented Mouravieff, that England's failures in Africa would produce dangerous reactions on her position in India and Central Asia and that Russia should therefore take this moment to seize Herat, one of the most important points for a future attack on India. But so far no echoes of unrest had been heard in India or Afghanistan, despite the detailed reporting of the South African reverses. No doubt a stir would eventually be created; but that was not a sufficient reason for Russia to undertake 'the extremely complicated and risky conquest of an entire region'.

To take Herat would produce a bad impression throughout Central Asia, would cause alarm in Bokhara and bring on the open hostility of the Amir, whom the Russian government were just then attempting to impress with their peaceloving policy. Until now, the great obstacle had been the decision not to enter into direct relations with Afghanistan. Because of 'changed circumstances' that system had now become impossible. The Czar had told Staal that 'we no longer acknowledge the possibility of refraining from direct relations with the rulers of Afghanistan'. Mouravieff felt confident that by substituting a policy of friendship for one of conquest, Russia would achieve the predominant influence. In future she would be able to maintain representatives at Kabul, Herat and Mazar-i-Sharif.[42]

The Russian loan to Persia, of more than £2m., was announced at the end of January, 1900. A few days later, it became known that a Russian gunboat would shortly arrive at Bunder Abbas; and on 6 February M. Lessar called upon Lord Salisbury to make the communication about Afghanistan referred to in Mouravieff's notes. The time had come, said the Russian memorandum, to take a definite step to regularise the contacts between Russia and Afghanistan. For many years, Russia, out of friendly feelings for Great Britain, had foregone even non-political relations. She must now insist on the establishment of direct relations for frontier and trading questions, which would have 'aucun caractère politique'. Afghanistan would remain outside the Russian sphere of influence. Salisbury promised that India would be consulted, the Cabinet hoping that this procedure would enable Roberts to take Bloemfontein before a reply could come from Calcutta.[43] The military command in India began to consider mobilisation. A request from South Africa for a further batch of officers was refused and a conference under Curzon's chairmanship agreed upon the dispositions of the Indian army in the event of a Russian invasion of Afghanistan.[44] It was thought that the Russians would strike first at Herat, the fall of which might be expected promptly. Indian forces would, as a riposte, move to Kandahar and thence to the line of the Helmund, but could not be kept for long on the Jelalabad–Kabul or Kandahar–Helmund lines without reinforcements from England or an addition to the Indian Army.[45]

Curzon was only too pleased to play a waiting game about the Russian memorandum. First, the Russians must be made to show their hand; he assumed, correctly if Mouravieff's notes are a guide, that they wanted an agent at Kabul. Then the Amir's view must be consulted. For the moment, the government of India pointed out that the memorandum was not comprehensive. The Russian engagements of 1872 and 1873 to abstain from Afghan affairs, to which it referred, had been renewed nine times between 1874 and 1888, though Russia had by then become a neighbour of Afghanistan. If the new proposal meant a Russian agent at Kabul, it should be refused. However innocent the Russian intentions, a commercial agent would inevitably become a political envoy. In Asia, the demise of a ruler sometimes presaged an upheaval. 'At such crises commercial agents find it difficult to realise the limitations of their employment and are apt to blossom into a more ambitious and expansive activity.' An agent there would mean that:

> control of Afghan foreign relations, which is our sole *quid pro quo* for British subsidy and sacrifices, would disappear. The Amir would attribute the concession to our weakness, even if he welcomed it as placing him on equality with European powers and as providing him with an argument for Afghan Agents in St Petersburg and London. Finally, condominium at Kabul would produce the worst possible effect in India. Nor do the Russian reasons bear examination. There has been no growth of trade. The Amir stifles it on the Russian side even more than on ours.

Curzon doubted whether Abdur Rahman had yet accepted a Russian agent and on the whole believed in his continued loyalty. The Russian proposal might alternatively mean an agent at Herat, to communicate with the Afghan Governor there, in which event a British agent would also be required. Russia might be asked exactly how she proposed to obtain the purely non-political objects which she desired.[46] Before Lessar's memorandum reached India the Russian Political agent at Bokhara, M. Ignatieff, addressed to a trading agent of Abdur Rahman an official letter. It explained that certain troop movements in Transcaspia had attracted attention chiefly because they chanced to coincide with the continual reverses of England, 'which still continue, in her war with the little State of the Transvaal'. Ignatieff hoped that his letter might lead to direct friendly relations with Russia. Abdur Rahman complained to Curzon of these proceedings and sent him the letter, which contradicted in several respects the note of 6 February. At least this seemed to establish that no secret agreement had

been made between Russia and Afghanistan. But the tone indicated that
Abdur Rahman might perhaps be working up to a rupture with the British.
Equally, it might reflect no more than his normal degree of cussedness.
Curzon admitted that correspondence with the Amir was 'about as fruitless
an occupation as throwing pebbles into an ocean'.[47] Lord George agreed
with the government of India that the objections to a Russian agent at
Kabul were insuperable, whatever arrangements might be possible elsewhere. Believing that Afghanistan would eventually disintegrate, the west
falling to Russia and the east to India, the last thing he wanted was a Russian
presence at Kabul before the process began. An agent established in North
or West Afghanistan would, because the Russian garrisons were near, be a
person of much greater importance than any British officer who could be
put in the same places.

Salisbury agreed with the Indian view but decided to do nothing for the
moment, on account of South Africa.[48] The fact that Mouravieff had just
been found dead in his room provided a convenient pretext. Count
Lamsdorff, who succeeded him as Foreign Minister, was much preoccupied
with the troubles in China.

★   ★   ★   ★

Rumours of Russian movements of troops and stores did not abate for some
time. According to intelligence reaching India, military preparations were
being made on the Upper Oxus and in the Pamirs. The Indian authorities
judged that a main advance against either Herat or Afghan Turkestan
would be complemented by a simultaneous movement into Badakshan, or
upon the Hindu Kush. However, a British officer, sent to Central Asia to
find out how many troops had been moved, believed that the number was
about 4,000, which tallied with Mouravieff's statement. He reported that
the Russians did not intend to provoke an immediate quarrel in Afghanistan,
though they told him openly that they wanted Bunder Abbas.[49]

A little later, the British government received a document which had
passed, presumably through purchase or theft, into the hands of the
Embassy at Petersburg. It showed the orders issued by the General commanding in Turkestan and was of particular interest to the India Office,
which had not previously seen any document intimating that Russia might
aggress and march straight upon Herat without waiting for any act of
British hostility. How far this order represented official policy was unclear;
but it did appear, since the orders were dated in the spring, that there had
been serious proposals to provoke a quarrel in Central Asia at the blackest

period in South Africa.[50] Even at this distance of time, it is not easy to tell what Russian policy really amounted to. Probably the financial stringency mentioned by Witte, and the political arguments which appealed to Mouravieff, prevented more than a demonstration. Had the Orenburg–Tashkent railway been completed by 1900 the strategic situation would have been different. The Russian Foreign Ministry told their newly-appointed consul at Bombay in this same year, 1900:

> The fundamental meaning of India to us is that she represents Great Britain's most vulnerable point...on which one touch may perhaps easily induce Her Majesty's Government to alter its hostile policy towards us and to show the desired compliance on all those questions where...our interests may coincide.'[51]

The salient fact is that although India was in normal times Britain's 'most vulnerable point' the spectre of defeat in South Africa loomed more menacing than the prospect of trouble in Afghanistan. Between 1899 and 1902 the Indian Army was deliberately depleted. That was a real risk. As Hamilton was told in terms during the spring of 1900, the Indian Army simply could not cope for any extended period with the duty of defending Afghanistan. Russia could now pour into Afghanistan far more men far more swiftly than in 1885. But since India had not the money to pay for a large increase in the army, Curzon and his colleagues did not propose it. A committee under the Military Member, General Collen, recommended as Roberts had done that on mobilisation 30,000 men must be despatched from England. For a prolonged war, another 70,000 would be needed. This was an Imperial responsibility, Curzon argued. He pointed to the South African analogy. One ninth of the total British force serving in India, with some thousands of Indian followers, had at once been sent to a country in which Indians were scarcely interested, except insofar as 'they had quite recently been subjected to peculiar and invidious disabilities at the hands both of the Transvaal Government and of the Government of Natal'.

The Viceroy and his Council therefore invited the Cabinet formally to recognise the principle that war with Russia in Afghanistan would involve

> a strain which the Indian Army cannot possibly be expected to meet unaided, and which will demand the strenuous co-operation of Her Majesty's Government and of the military resources of the British Empire. And we further press, with a view to the formation of a systematic plan of Indian defence, that in the revision of the military system of Great Britain which will doubtless be undertaken in consequence of the present war, provision may be made for the requirements of India in the contemplated emergency, and that we may receive a clear and definite pronouncement as to the nature and extent of such assistance.

Hamilton refused to give an unconditional assurance. While all possible help would be sent, the future action of the British Government could not be pledged. Indian plans must therefore be based upon Indian resources. The government of India replied, in effect, that this was not feasible. So this debate, in essence a reproduction of the inconclusive exchanges of 1891-2, remained unresolved.[52] Salisbury described himself as greatly affected by the failure to build a military railway from Quetta to Seistan, or from Seistan to the sea. Though Curzon was exonerated from blame because of his financial difficulties, the omission might be embarrassing. The Prime Minister seems to have felt no doubt that Russia would advance; when she did so, the battle must be fought, if there were no railway, on the Indian border, by frontal attack on a mountain-chain held by the enemy: 'Occasionally the defence will fail for a time—and a spasm of sedition will start from one end of India to the other.'

But if a British force held Seistan, the Russians could not move eastwards without enormous effort. Though Salisbury did not believe that Russia was definitely bent on the conquest of India, he looked to the day when the Siberian railway would be complete. Then she would wish to control most of China: 'and if Afghanistan is unprotected she can force us to give way in China by advancing upon India. She won't try to conquer it. It will be enough for her if she can shatter our government and reduce India to anarchy...'[53]

Here was a factor of high importance, which preoccupied Curzon much. If Russia were allowed to move into Afghanistan, what would be the effect upon the people, or peoples, of India? That aspect alone provided a strong argument for advance, with or without reinforcements, into the nearer parts of Afghanistan.[54] During the explosion of 1897, Hamilton enquired of his experts what would happen if the Amir declared a *jehad*, a holy war, and put himself at the head? All agreed that the consequences might be most dangerous. They had grave doubts about the attitude of many Mohammedans in India.[55]

During the remaining year of Abdur Rahman's life, the relations between Afghanistan and the British government did not develop substantially. Both sides were content, for different reasons, to leave matters where they were. The Boer War dragged wearily along, absorbing British energies, soldiers and cash. The Amir plainly intended to have no railways or telegraphs, nor would he concert any common scheme of defence. He did not, towards the end of his life, draw the full subsidy of 18 lakhs p.a., but there was no sign of deliberate intrigue with Russia. Curzon, remembering the Amir's tales of his treatment by the Russians, and believing that though a cantankerous customer he was not a fool, felt confident of Afghanistan's fidelity to her obligations. What would happen on Abdur Rahman's death was another matter. Before leaving England in 1898, Curzon set down in a minute his conviction that Habibullah would succeed his father, who had said as much in open durbar at Kabul. Because of the Amir's inordinate suspicion and rather uneasy position, it would be best not to press him unduly for a declaration in favour of Habibullah. India should be prepared, at Habibullah's request, to move troops to Jelalabad as a gesture of support. Probably he would then ask for a mission to visit Kabul. If not, it must be proposed:

> Our engagements are personal to the reigning Amir. They will require to be revised, and, as I think, substantially modified in the case of his successor.

This policy was considered by Salisbury, Lansdowne, Hamilton and Balfour, and accepted as a basis for British action. Nearly three years afterwards, early in October, 1901, Abdur Rahman died. As Curzon had predicted, Habibullah's accession was marked by comparative calm, although from Kandahar and Kelat-i-Ghilzai came tribal voices prophesying war. No move to Jelalabad was needed. The Russians had made no attempt to produce a rival candidate and were fully occupied elsewhere. In this sense Manchuria and the Far East were to Russia what South Africa was to Britain. At the moment of the Amir's death, all the Russian regiments at Askabad, Merv and Kushk had been reduced to skeleton battalions. The British military attaché at St Petersburg estimated that the Russians had less than 8,000 men and only 24 guns available for action on the Afghan frontier. Charles Hardinge, generally well informed, thought that the Czar, Witte and Lamsdorff would all do their upmost to avoid complications in Central Asia at this time. Probably the Russians welcomed the commitments on the North-West frontier and in Afghanistan, which stretched British resources and reduced the likelihood of stiff opposition in the Far East.[56]

The new Amir wrote at once to Curzon, who sent a friendly reply. It happened that two million cartridges were reported from Peshawar to be awaiting despatch to the Amir. Curzon, long anxious for a revision of the agreements made with Abdur Rahman, thought that at the risk of offence, Habibullah should be told that the question of arms importation must be discussed before this consignment was released. Hamilton preferred to trust Habibullah for the moment, though agreeing that the importation of colossal quantities of arms should provide a peg for a negotiation.[57] Lord Lansdowne recalled that the threat to stop the import of arms was the one weapon which had brought the Amir to his knees, and Hamilton allowed Curzon to hint that a revision of the existing practice about arms importation might be made later.[58] Habibullah replied cordially to Curzon's letter, assuring him of feelings of friendship for the illustrious government, from whose agreement with the late Amir he would never swerve. This, as Curzon realised, indicated a belief that the old arrangements applied equally to the new ruler and seemed 'to foreshadow possible disappointment later on'. He did not wish to give the impression of courting Habibullah, who should be allowed to realise that he was dependent on the British.[59]

★   ★   ★   ★

An Asiatic agreement with Russia Curzon no longer believed to be feasible. The British stood across her advance to numerous goals, Constantinople, the Gulf, Herat, Korea, Pekin. In some of these ambitions Great Britain might prudently acquiesce, but to surrender in all would mean abandonment of the hegemony of Asia, for which Russia conceived herself to be fitted by temperament, history and tradition:

> It is a proud and a not ignoble aim, and is well worthy of the supreme moral and material efforts of a vigorous nation. But it is not to be satisfied by piecemeal concessions, neither is it capable of being gratified save at our expense... Each morsel but whets the appetite for more, and inflames the passion for a pan-Asiatic dominion...I have often pondered...whether we could not, by a friendly agreement with Russia, arrive at such a demarcation of our respective interests as would enable us to eschew rivalry and to cultivate an amicable co-operation, if not an actual alliance, in the future. At each stage I have found that in such an agreement the giving would be all on our side and the receiving on the other.

It seemed that the powers were closing in around India. Russia could take Northern Persia, and Afghanistan from Herat to the Oxus, at her whim. Kashgar and Chinese Turkestan seemed bound to fall. In Tibet, rumours of a Russian protectorate had already been heard. On the borders of Burma, British India encountered the French, wanting the whole of Siam. In a couple of decades or less, unless the ring-fence were strengthened, India might be conterminous with powers mainly inimical. In that event 'we shall not be able to move, to strike, to advance, in any part of the world where French or Russian interests are involved, because of the menace that will stand perpetually at our Indian doors'.[60]

Lansdowne agreed a few months later that an Asiatic agreement with Russia was impossible.[61] Indeed, her proceedings in Central Asia seemed to indicate a determination to increase her fighting capacity there. Although neither Curzon nor Lansdowne took too seriously the persistent reports of troop concentrations on the Afghan frontier, there were fortifications, stores, guns and soldiers at Sheikh Junaid, to which a railway had been made. A narrow-gauge line was being pushed on to the frontier, where rails were stacked for an extension to Herat. The Orenburg–Tashkent line was being built, with French encouragement. General Kuropatkin told the German Ambassador at St Petersburg that he intended to expedite its completion, and generally to strengthen the military position in Turkestan, so that a crushing blow might be struck in the event of complicatiosn with England. However, Charles Hardinge's examination of the Russian budget showed a distinct shortage of cash, welcome news at the Foreign Office.[62]

Early in February, 1902, Curzon wrote to Kabul that the British government wished the agreement of 1880 to continue and flourish. There had sometimes been misunderstandings which he wished to remove, so that a new agreement 'free from misconception' might be made. The Amir replied that there was no need for a discussion of the agreement, with which he was satisfied. Curzon, who felt no enthusiasm for a meeting on the basis, thought that Habibullah could in time be made to see that India, in return for an annual payment of 18 lakhs, was entitled to more friendly treatment.[63] Rumours of mutiny and disloyalty in Afghanistan were already reaching India. The British agent at Kabul reported on 12 February that six sepoys who had fled from a cantonment were brought to Kabul. Two were blown from a gun, two cast into a dark well and the others' eyes gouged out.[64] This information was doubtless reliable, though the agent, being kept virtually a prisoner, generally transmitted little news worth having. Abdur Rahman had confessed to Curzon in 1894 with immense pride that he personally concocted a good deal of the 'intelligence' reaching the agent.[65]

Curzon wrote a reply to the Amir's letter and submitted it to London. Hamilton and Lansdowne approved of it in general but told Curzon to revise his draft so that Habibullah would realise he was not sure to obtain all the concessions made to his father, especially the unlimited passage of arms and the continuance of the full subsidy. Hamilton and Salisbury had agreed that the old undertakings were personal to Abdur Rahman. New agreements were now indispensable.[66] The Viceroy's letter of 6 June therefore told Habibullah explicitly that he could not claim the subsidy or the guarantee of protection as of right. There was no desire to meddle with the internal affairs of Afghanistan, but the Russian advance had changed the circumstances since 1880. Would not a discussion in October be possible?[67] The Amir did not reply.

The vital question about the reinforcement of India in time of war remained unanswered for the moment, and indeed for the whole of Curzon's Viceroyalty. Estimates of the numbers Russia could put in the field were often alarming. The British Military Attaché in St Petersburg, for instance, calculated that Russia could in three months mobilise some 450,000 men for advance on India and in six months another 150,000 might be moved into the Caucasus. The Intelligence Department of the War Office concluded that the main line of advance would be through Seistan, with diversions towards Afghanistan and the Hindu Kush.[68] Lord Roberts, newly returned from South Africa to the post of Commander-in-Chief at home, had no more use for a waiting strategy now than he had when C-in-C in India. A Russian move, he advised, must be countered in Seistan and the southern part of Persia. A military railway from Quetta to Bunder Abbas, by way of Kandahar, would bring large advantages. Lansdowne, now Foreign Secretary, had wondered whether it would be possible on Abdur Rahman's death to run a line from Quetta to Seistan via Kandahar.[69] Neither explained how Afghan consent to such a railway would be obtained.

Hamilton corresponded a good deal with Curzon about these issues. Over the whole question hung the South African commitment, the gross defects which it had revealed in the machinery of the War Office and the training of the Army, and the admitted need for reform. He wrote simply, 'We have for some time past attempted to run the British Empire upon military establishments inadequate to its maintenance in times of difficulty.'

It was this factor that made the Cabinet most reluctant to move about Afghanistan and Tibet; for if war broke out with Russia, the Indian Army, unless heavily reinforced from home, could not hold the positions strategically and politically desirable.[70] The C-in-C in India thought that as many as 200,000 extra men might be needed to hurl back a Russian attack; whereas Lord Salisbury and his colleagues, at this stage, had to face the prospect that Russia would not challenge Great Britain in Afghanistan without being sure of French support. No reinforcements to India could be depended on, therefore, until the French fleet had been defeated. The Suez Canal might be temporarily blocked. Even the Cape route might not be safe. The War Office expressly warned that India must not rely on the despatch of a force. Nor could Afghan friendliness be assumed. Hamilton asked what the Government of India would do in the worst circumstances?[71] They replied that the policy of advancing still held good in general. The alternative of sitting still behind the frontier while Russia attacked Afghanistan would produce a 'disastrous impression' on the people of India and upon the Afghans. All the same, the goodwill of the Amir during a British advance could certainly not be assumed. More explicitly, Hamilton was told that if the British Government could guarantee to send 30,000 men at the outbreak of war, no increase in the Indian Army would be needed. Otherwise, some increase should be sanctioned; but the cost should be largely, if not wholly, borne by the Imperial Exchequer.[72]

This was not welcome reading in London. An inter-departmental committee judged in the autumn of 1901 that if the Indian Army had to advance into Afghanistan without reinforcements, the most it could do would be a forward movement to Jelalabad and Kandahar, and then only on condition of an increase of British forces in India. Otherwise the defensive operations must be confined to territory already under British control. This was a document of some importance. It marked the abandonment by the War Office, to the hearty relief of the Military Department, of the theory that a campaign in the Caucasus or Finland would help India in face of Russian attack. The only practical way to help India would be to send troops there, but the interval might be as much as nine or twelve months.[73]

The committee reported in favour of an increase of 18,500 in the British garrison in India. Curzon and his colleagues refused, saying that they had other things to do with their money. 5,000 troops might be added; but since they would be needed on account of admitted British inability to guarantee reinforcements, the Treasury in London should pay for them. It goes without saying that the home government had no intention of doing anything of the sort. So the garrison was not increased and the home government were not committed to the despatch of a stated number of troops.

★　　★　　★　　★

Lord Salisbury's decision to postpone discussion of direct relations between Russia and Afghanistan entailed a longer delay than Curzon and his colleagues had intended. The letter of M. Ignatieff, about which they had protested to London, was not brought to Lamsdorff's notice until January, 1901, nearly a year after it was written. The Foreign Minister said the letter was highly improper and could scarcely credit that Ignatieff had written it. He would enquire at once. However, nine months elapsed before he produced a memorandum justifying the letter by the memorandum given by Lessar to Salisbury on 6 February, 1900. In other words,

that note had not been an invitation to a discussion, but an intimation that
Russia's earlier pledges were no longer binding. When, a few days later,
Lansdowne said that he regarded Afghanistan's foreign relations as being
entirely under British control, Staal rejoined that some communication
between Russian and Afghan local authorities was essential. The Foreign
Secretary did not wish the Russians to think that he accepted their explanations, and told Lamsdorff in February, 1902, that arrangements for direct
communications on matters of local detail—into which category M.
Ignatieff's letter could hardly be said to fall—could be made only with
British consent. Russian proposals for the transaction of such business would
be considered 'in the most friendly spirit'. The only noteworthy feature of
the conversation was the fact that Lamsdorff appeared totally unaware
of the oft repeated and solemn assurances given by his predecessors. He had
earlier told Scott that there was no question of political relations with
Afghanistan or of hostility to British interests in that region. He also
confessed in private that one of his more serious embarrassments in conducting foreign affairs was the complete inability of the military party,
particularly in distant parts of the Empire, to take account of other powers'
interests.[74]

Lamsdorff showed no inclination to settle the question of frontier
relations. Two reminders were sent. Still no reply came. In November,
1902, the Russian government were told that the British government would
object to any change made without their consent and would regard it as a
breach of Russian assurances. During this further prolonged delay, many
stories of Russian attempts to establish contact with Afghanistan had gained
currency. The troops at Kushk and other places on the Afghan frontier had
produced no apparent effect. A little later, it had been alleged that a Russian
mission would go to Kabul. Curzon, disbelieving that Habibullah could be
such a fool as to encourage any such proposal, nonetheless felt a little uneasy
about Afghanistan. Accounts of activity in Transcaspia and of the concentration of guns at Kushk were persistent. He surmised that the Russians
were preparing carefully for a coup should occasion arise.[75] Charles
Hardinge, Scott's understudy at Petersburg, felt sure that Russian attempts
to get into communication with the Amir were being made. He thought
Scott had failed to impress on Lamsdorff the gravity of the complaint.[76]

By the third week of October, when Curzon and the Amir were supposed
to be hobnobbing at Peshawar, no reply had come from Kabul. The
Amir's agent in India, who seems to have had about as much influence as
the British agent at Kabul, assured the government of India that the delay
was due to the illness of the only munshi at Kabul who could translate into

literary Persian; but other reports spoke of the Amir as abandoning himself
to the delights of the harem. Discontent was said to be widespread.[77] A
dispute about water and the frontier had arisen between Persia and Afghanistan. Since the foreign relations of the Amir were in British hands, Curzon
proposed that a British officer should arbitrate. The Amir did not respond.
After two months, Curzon wrote again. The Amir replied on 15 October
but did not mention the arbitrator. Eventually Curzon simply said that he
had appointed Major McMahon and had told him to go forthwith to
Seistan. Habibullah then gave way.[78]

In a letter of 5 November, the British agent at Kabul wrote that the Amir,
according to reliable authority, had held a Durbar in mid-September with
a view to establishing trading relations with the Russians. Habibullah was
reported to have said that if the British government objected to European
arms and machines passing through India to Kabul it did not matter, for
there were other means. North and south made no difference. As for trade,
arrangements would be made with the Russian officials in Bokhara.[79]

This news and other reports from India caused Hamilton a good deal of
disquiet. Habibullah seemed to be gravitating towards Russia. Further
admonition, though justified and even necessary, might produce a result
which the Cabinet did not wish for.[80] He commented to the King that the
situation resembled ominously that which existed just before the Afghan
war of 1878, with the vital difference that Russia was now conterminous
with the whole northern frontier of Afghanistan.[81] Curzon, however, did
not take so serious a view. Admittedly, the Amir's behaviour justified the
gravest suspicion that he had delayed replying to Indian letters pending
communication with Russia. The Viceroy proposed to do nothing before
the Delhi Durbar in early January and to await a promised letter from the
Amir until then. If it did not come, or if it proved to be hostile, he would
wish to write to Habibullah, summarising recent unsatisfactory developments and requesting a definite basis for future relations. If the Amir
wanted those relations to continue, the two must meet and conclude an
arrangement. If he wanted a rupture, then at least Britain would be free
from her obligations towards Afghanistan and could do as she pleased for
the protection of her interests. The present agent at Kabul was hopelessly
incompetent and Curzon hoped to recall him in January, entrusting the
letter to a new agent.[82]

Intelligence received from Afghanistan in the late autumn of 1902,
pointing to a reign of terror and wanton cruelty on Habibullah's part, had
led both Hamilton and Curzon to conclude that an insurrection might
arise at any moment. The unpopularity and insecurity of Habibullah added

a new factor to the equation and affected closely Curzon's proposal for a meeting at Peshawar. If the many reports of his wobbly position were correct, it seemed unlikely that the Amir would take the risk of leaving Kabul. Moreover a personal arrangement with him seemed, in the light of this information, to be of little value, while the conclusion of an agreement with the British might accelerate his fall. Hamilton judged that a waiting rather than a forcing game was the right one.[83] The members of council at the India Office opposed any measure which might lead to a British invasion of Afghanistan, for they believed that whichever of the great powers crossed the frontier would be regarded thenceforward as the enemy of Afghanistan. All the advantages, so they thought, would be on the side of the power which stayed within its own border.[84]

On 9 December the Cabinet, for the first time in Hamilton's experience of nearly 17 years, began to discuss British relations with Afghanistan. The Secretary of State noted that except for Lansdowne and himself, there seemed to be no minister who knew what had occurred in the last few years and both were subjected to what he felt was an unfair cross-examination:

> the fact is that the reaction, after our recent outburst of war-like ardour, has already begun to operate, taxation is exceptionally high, trade is on the wane, distress is rife in our large towns, the weather is exceptionally cold, and all these circumstances in combination make the vast majority of the Cabinet look with apprehension and dislike on any movement or any action which is likely to produce war or disturbance in any part of the British Empire.

It was apparent that the negotiations with the Amir had failed, a fact on which various colleagues fastened. Some implied that the temporary stoppage of arms and the non-payment of the subsidy was a breach of faith. After the Cabinet the Prime Minister came to the India Office and spent two hours examining the Afghan problem so that he was now in partial possession of the main facts. Hamilton thought that Curzon should know of the general feeling at home; unless the Cabinet were absolutely compelled to move, there was a general disinclination to mobilise or do anything which would imply that forces were about to be sent beyond the frontier into Afghanistan. The Cabinet agreed with Curzon that the Amir's reply should be awaited until after the Durbar. But the result of addressing him as Curzon proposed might be to turn him altogether towards Russia and produce or accelerate a rupture. Ministers did not think that Habibullah was likely to agree to an interview if demanded in this way and did not wish to stake on that issue the whole of India's future relations with him. It was agreed that if Habibullah were shown to be unfriendly, and if he were seeking Russian support or alliance, British obligations towards him would cease forthwith.[85]

Balfour reported to the King that the policy pursued towards the Amir had for years been utterly unsatisfactory, though it was not easy to devise an alternative. The Cabinet were 'somewhat alarmed lest, by precipitate action, he [Curzon] should plunge us in diplomatic and, it may be, even military embarrassment'.[86] The Cabinet's fear of Curzon's proceedings may have owed something to a quarrel between him and them which had only just been resolved. What it is important to note at this stage is the extreme reluctance to run the least risk of complications with Russia. It was just twelve months since Balfour had written 'a quarrel with Russia anywhere, or about anything, means the invasion of India, and if England were without allies I doubt whether it would be possible for the French to resist joining in the fray. Our position would then be perilous... '[87]

The first part of the sentence betrays a lack of proportion. Even allowing for the fact that the Cabinet had never once discussed Afghanistan, Balfour should have realised that the invasion of India was an enormous, probably impossible, undertaking. It certainly could not be done without elaborate and expensive preparation. However, at this stage of his career, Balfour had devoted no attention to the question. In a memorandum for the Cabinet of 16 December, 1902, he described the situation as absurd, almost comic. The Amir did not seem to want the subsidy; his country was already gorged with arms and he could always get more. Quarrels between Russia and Afghanistan might arise. Balfour was inclined to think that Great Britain should withdraw, as courteously as possible, from any specific pledge to the Amir, and try by direct negotiation with Russia to uphold the *status quo*.[88] Evidently this paper reflected, to a large degree, the preconceptions of the Cabinet, which discussed Afghanistan again on 18 December. Lord George, in his account to Curzon, lamented the absence of the older men, Salisbury, Beach and Goschen. Their replacements had apparently criticised with some freedom the refusal to renew entirely and unconditionally the agreements made with Abdur Rahman. Hamilton had circulated papers, showing plainly that the majority's interpretation was wrong; and at this meeting of 18 December a more fair-minded attitude prevailed. He thought that he had succeeded in convincing the Cabinet that the agreements formerly in operation were very one-sided and placed the subsidising and protecting power in a position of undue risk, at times almost of humiliation. The difficulty of altering the agreements, even assuming that the Amir were agreeable, so as to give benefits corresponding to the obligations was now fully apparent:

the growing dislike, if not abhorrence, of any forward move, or of any action likely to entail military operations, is so strong that I really believe, if it was put to the vote, there would be a disposition to abandon all our present obligations, and to substitute nothing in their place except an attempt to come to an understanding with Russia.

Hamilton told Curzon that the only chance of obtaining the acquiescence of the Cabinet was to move most cautiously, to make no forward military movement and to do everything possible to re-establish a friendlier connection with Kabul.[89] For the moment, however, the crisis passed. The Amir, at long last, sent a letter to say that as soon as he was free from his most urgent affairs, he would visit Curzon. He acquiesced in Mac-Mahon's appointment as arbitrator. All the same, the proceedings at the two Cabinet meetings and the prevalent timidity must have given Curzon a good deal of food for thought. The King had been disturbed by the unsatisfactory state of the Afghan question and hoped that Curzon would stand no nonsense about the virtual imprisonment of the envoy at Kabul. He feared that the Foreign Office took the matter too easily, while Lord George seemed to think that since the agent was more or less a prisoner, it did not much matter whether he had been competent or not. Curzon replied that the least hint of action 'in fact, of doing anything but sit still and wait to see what turns up—throws them [the Cabinet] into agonies of apprehension, and brings down upon me a shower of telegrams'.

However, the Amir's latest letter seemed to show that he had not sided with Russia. His caution, Curzon guessed, was probably due to his precarious position at Kabul.[90] In St Petersburg, Scott was again told that Russia did not intend to establish political relations with Afghanistan. A prior understanding with Great Britain would be reached before a system of local contacts was established.[91] By mid-January, 1903, the situation was less clear. Lamsdorff said it would be incompatible with Russia's dignity to be bound for all time by engagements with another power limiting her legitimate intercourse with another country. He did not 'for the present' desire political relations. On 5 February, 1903, Sir C. Scott received a brusque note, indicating that Russia must be free to send agents into Afghanistan in future. This hardly seemed to square with Sir C. Scott's prognosis. He was, as Curzon minuted, known to be

very easily humbugged; and...there is commonly the most startling difference between Count Lamsdorff's confidential outpourings to him (as transmitted to London by the delighted Ambassador) and the official declarations from that Minister which follow a few days later.

Curzon thought the Russian memorandum was probably a piece of bravado, covering Russia's failure to establish relations with Habibullah.[92] It appeared that a fresh crisis in Anglo–Russian relations might break. But the situation was now different from that of 1900 in two crucial respects. The Boer War was over. The Anglo–Japanese alliance had been signed.

★　　★　　★　　★

The situation on the north-eastern frontier of India differed noticeably from that on the north-west. The innate fanaticism which made the north-west a perpetual menace was not found; and from most of Tibet India was separated by two British-protected states, Sikkim and Bhutan, and by an independent state, Nepal, sharing a border with Bengal and the United Provinces for more than five hundred miles. Of Tibet little was known. It was the most mysterious territory in the world, protected by the Himalayas and by vast glaciers, and tilting slightly southwards and westward. Tibet was perhaps the nearest earthly approach to a theocracy. It was nominally a part of the Chinese Empire.

After the Tibetans crossed into Sikkim in 1886, unavailing protests to China were made. Whatever the Chinese wished to do, they evidently lacked the power to enforce a policy on their feudatories. The Viceroy thereupon turned the Tibetans out by force. In 1890 and 1893, to keep up the appearances of Chinese suzerainty, agreements were made between Britain and China, defining the boundary between Sikkim and Tibet and providing for a trade-mart at Yatung, which lay in the Chumbi Valley on the fringe of Tibet proper, and to which Indian goods would have un-restricted access. The Tibetans took no notice of either agreement. Boundary pillars they quickly uprooted, the trade mart never opened; the grazing-grounds of Sikkim were soon invaded again. Futile remonstrances were sent to Pekin and to the Chinese representative, the Amban, at Lhasa. Since the Tibetans, who were estimated to number no more than five millions, kept all foreigners at bay, their activities seemed to be nothing more than a minor nuisance. Russia lay far away. That she would like to establish relations with the Dalai Lama at Lhasa, Curzon did not doubt.[93]

From the beginning of Curzon's term, he desired to make contact with Lhasa, but for commercial rather than political purposes. Clearly it was pointless to treat with the Tibetans through the agency of China: 'the whole thing is a farce, each party alternately parading and disavowing the other. If we could get at the Tibetans direct, and give them the land they covet, I believe we might get the trade facilities we desire...'

For the first time in many years, Tibet had a Dalai Lama who was of age, a civil as well as sacerdotal ruler, and who meant to make what he could of his independence. Curzon, inclined to credit reports that Russia and Tibet were in contact, meant to establish direct relations with the Dalai, by-passing 'that preposterous Amban', if a suitable envoy could be found.[94] According to Indian intelligence, the lamas in Tibet had discovered China's weakness and were being approached by Russia, for there seemed little doubt that Russian agents, and possibly even a man of Russian origin, had been at Lhasa.[95] This may have been Dorjieff, a Buriat Mongol monk who seems to have settled there for the first time in 1880. He distinguished himself in Buddhist studies, became an instructor of the young Dalai Lama and held much influence over him. He was reported at St Petersburg in 1898.

The first attempt to come to close quarters with the Tibetans was not a success. A Bhutanese emissary, Ugyen Khazi, sounded the Dalai Lama about his willingness to send a man for discussion of the frontier question. The Dalai replied that he would like to do so but did not dare for fear of the Amban. Curzon realised that they were running round again in the vicious circle, the Tibetans blaming the Amban for their own reluctance, the Amban blaming the Tibetans for his impotence.[96] Another effort was made, but proved abortive. A letter to the Dalai Lama, sent through the Governors of Western Tibet, assured him that the British government did not wish to interfere in the affairs of Tibet, drew his attention to the failure to observe the trade regulations and asked that an official be sent for talks. Early in 1901, this letter was returned unopened.

In the meantime, the Russian papers announced that the Czar Nicholas had received the Buriat monk Dorjieff as a member of a Tibetan mission. Curzon believed this to be a fraud, for he could scarcely credit that the lamas had so far overcome their 'incurable suspicion of all things European' as to send an open mission to Europe. There was no doubt that the Russians had been trying to penetrate into Tibet; but 'Tibet is, I think, much more likely in reality to look to us for protection than ... to Russia, and I cherish a secret hope that the communication which I am trying to open with the Dalai Lama may inaugurate some sort of relation between us.'[97]

In June, 1901, another letter, together with the unopened original, was sent to Lhasa through Ugyen Khazi, who was about to deliver there two elephants. It was couched in stiffer terms. It spoke of British forbearance and carried a warning that if no attempt to deal fairly were made, the government of India must reserve the right to enforce the Treaty of 1890. Curzon told the Secretary of State that if the British did nothing in Tibet,

Russia would be trying within ten years to establish a protectorate. That might not mean any military danger, at least for a long time

> but it would constitute a political danger; for the effect upon Nepal, Sikkim and Bhutan would be most unsettling, and might be positively dangerous. We cannot prevent Russia from acquiring the whole of Mongolia and of Chinese Turkestan...but I think that we both ought to stop, and can stop, a Russian protectorate over Tibet and the only way in which to stop it is by being in advance ourselves.

Curzon believed that this renewed effort to reach the Dalai would fail, for the Dalai's counsellors would not allow him to correspond with the British. Nothing could be done with the Tibetans until they were frightened; and if a refusal were met this time, Curzon proposed to push the Tibetans out of the British territory they had occupied since 1895. If they resisted, he would occupy the Chumbi Valley, just beyond. The Dalai would then probably offer to talk; and India would agree, so long as the talks took place at Lhasa:

> It is really the most grotesque and indefensible thing that, at a distance of little more than 200 miles from our frontier, this community of unarmed monks should set us perpetually at defiance; that we should have no means of knowing what is going on there; and that a Russian protectorate may, at no distant date, be declared without our having an inkling of what was passing.

All this, Curzon realised, must be a matter for the home government. The British interest was a negative one:

> Of course we do not want their country. It would be madness for us to cross the Himalayas and to occupy it. But it is important that no one else should seize it; and that it should be turned into a sort of buffer state between the Russian and Indian Empires. If Russia were to come down to the big mountains, she would at once begin intriguing with Nepal: and we should have a second Afghanistan on the north...Tibet itself, and not Nepal, must be the buffer that we endeavour to create.[98]

Hamilton was prepared, even at the worst times of the Boer War, for a stiffer policy in Seistan and Tibet than in Persia or the Gulf. Curzon's proposals about Tibet seemed to him, at first blush, somewhat aggressive; they might succeed, but if the Russian government had any connexion with Lhasa, a threat to invade Tibet might accelerate a Russian protectorate. Admittedly, if the Russians controlled Tibet, they would obtain in Nepal an influence which might be dangerous to Indian safety and fatal to the recruitment of Gurkhas. Then there was the Chinese government, whose suzerainty over Tibet was nominal; but an attack on a part of the Empire would be resented. Russia was pressing China to accept the Manchurian agreement and seemed to Hamilton to be bidding for the strongest possible position in the whole of Asia outside the Great Wall. For that reason, the Russians were unlikely to assume openly a protectorate over Tibet. Anyway, British military establishments were not equal to a sizeable expedition. If a force were locked up, the tribesmen on the north-west frontier might take advantage of the fact.

It was better, therefore, to begin negotiations with Tibet by explaining that no advantage was sought of her. Treaty rights must no longer be ignored. Closer relations were desired. Lord George thought it ridiculous that

> an unwarlike and unarmed population, dominated by monks, should for a century have kept us by discourtesy at arm's length, but the Tibetan hates foreigners with a truly Chinese hatred; and I should try to make that aversion to foreigners the foundation for negotiations for the purpose of assuring Tibet that, for reasons that must be obvious, our desire is by every means in our power to secure her independence.[99]

Though Count Lamsdorff dismissed stories in the Russian press which indicated that Dorjieff was charged with a diplomatic mission, he was received by the Czar, Lamsdorff and Witte. The contrast between this and Tibet's relations with India stood out clearly enough. Lamsdorff was told that the British government could not be indifferent to any disturbance of the *status quo* in Tibet, while Hamilton was informed officially by the government of India that the overtures now being made by Tibet to Russia, or more probably by Russia to Tibet 'lead us to think that before long our political concern in Tibet may be quickened, and that steps may require to be taken for the adequate safe-guarding of British interests upon a part of the frontier where they have never hitherto been impugned'.[100]

Shortly before this despatch was sent off, Curzon had at last realised that the relations between Tibet and Russia were rather more close than he had believed. So deficient was the intelligence system in Bengal that the two Tibetan missions which visited the Czar in 1900 and 1901 were not reported to the government of India. Although they had left Lhasa, crossed the British border and traversed India by rail, leaving from Indian ports, the Bengal government seem to have known nothing of their movements. As Curzon remarked, it would hardly have been thought credible that negotiations between Lhasa and St Petersburg could have been passing through British India itself.[101]

The chief minister of Nepal, who was deposed in the summer of 1901, had told the Viceroy that a wink from Simla would be enough to have the Gurkhas over the border into Tibet. But Curzon had no intention at this stage of using armed force unless Russia established a protectorate. The most he contemplated was a pacific mission, with a small escort, to Lhasa.[102] A reply to the letter just sent was awaited. In the autumn Ugyen Khazi returned from Lhasa with the letter, its seals still intact. The Dalai Lama, he said, had refused to accept it, on the ground that he was pledged not to correspond with foreign governments without consulting his Council and the Chinese Amban, and had denied any connexion with the Tibetan mission to Russia. This account Curzon disbelieved from the start, thinking that curiosity alone would have impelled the Dalai to discover whether he was being offered a tooth of the Buddha, a stableful of elephants or something else. He thought Ugyen Khazi a liar, probably a paid Tibetan spy; in the first of which suppositions he was almost certainly right, and in the second almost certainly wrong.[103]

Hamilton was therefore told that other means of entering into communication with Lhasa must be sought. A proposal of the Political Officer in Sikkim to occupy the Chumbi Valley was not adopted for the moment. Instead, Curzon and his colleagues proposed that the Tibetans should be turned out of the Sikkim territory which they had invaded and the frontier properly demarcated: 'Should they adopt an attitude of permanent hostility and of continued aggression across the border, it would be a matter for discussion whether we should not occupy the Chumbi Valley and hold it until the Tibetans had signified their willingness to come to terms, and to open negotiations at Lhasa...'

The despatch pointed out that the policy of complete isolation might not be difficult to understand from the Tibetans' point of view; but it was not compatible with proximity to British India, nor with the treaties into which China had entered on Tibet's behalf. The situation in which India and Tibet could not even exchange a letter could not in any case be lasting, and it should be ended as soon and as quietly as possible 'since there are factors in the case that might at a later date invest the breaking-down of these unnatural barriers with a wider and more serious significance'.

Hamilton agreed that Mr White should tour along the frontier, being careful not to stray across the border. The government of Nepal maintained at Lhasa a representative whose reports were often passed on to Curzon and which provided the main source of information about Tibet. He thought in the early spring of 1902 that the Dalai Lama had probably started negotiations with Russia.[104]

7

The main elements in the impending crisis were now starting to emerge. The home government had sanctioned a definite step, after many years, to enforce the treaties. Mr White proceeded to put up the boundary pillars and push the Tibetans out of Sikkim. The Chinese Amban asked what White and his party were doing. Curzon told him. During that same summer, whispers of an arrangement between Russia and China began to be heard. Sir E. Satow, British Minister at Pekin, reported a rumour that China might transfer to Russia her interests in Tibet in return for a promise to uphold the integrity of China. He believed that the Russian Minister had hinted that his country desired an agreement with China about Tibet.[105] Other accounts to the same effect circulated during that month. Eventually Satow was told by Lansdowne to warn the Chinese government against any such arrangement and to intimate that Britain must otherwise take steps to protect her interests by occupying such Chinese territory as might seem desirable.[106] The rumours were strongly denied by the Chinese government, who, Satow suspected, were concealing something. A member of the Amban's staff reported to Pekin intense Russian activity in Tibet.[107]

Late in 1902 the Russian government enquired in London about reports that British troops would go into Tibet to protect the construction of a railway there. 'What is rather unfair' lamented Sanderson to Charles Hardinge, 'is that they have no hesitation in asking us for assurances and explanations but when we ask for any they either ignore the request, or are grossly rude or tell us a downright and obvious lie. It is not fair dos.'[108]

Curzon would have laughed if he could have read that. As it was, he sent a tart reply to the Russian representation and noted that the familiar gambit generally presaged some unfriendly Russian proceeding. A few days later, the Political Officer in Sikkim reported a story that Russian troops from Manchuria would occupy Lhasa in the spring of 1903. Hardinge could find no confirmation of this at Petersburg, but in a despatch of 10 November he reported the alleged existence of a secret arrangement between Russia and Tibet. In return for non-interference with collections made among Russian Buddhists for the use of the Grand Lama, the Russians would be allowed to have a consular officer in Tibet. The strictest secrecy had been observed. So as not to offend the British, it had been decided not to send a consul but a secret agent for the furtherance of Russian aims. The agent, Hardinge understood, was now receiving his instructions in St Petersburg before proceeding to Tibet. This account, circumstantial and definite, coming from a man of whose abilities Curzon held a very high opinion, impressed him a good deal.[109] From all these reports the Viceroy believed that Russia and China had at least come to an understanding about Tibet. The recent action of White in turning out the Tibetans from Sikkim territory had given the authorities at Lhasa and Pekin something to think about; and for a time there had been talk of envoys and negotiations. Suddenly it all stopped. Curzon proposed that they should be allowed to procrastinate for some little time longer. Then, he suggested to Hamilton, the government of India should say that as the others clearly did not mean business it was proposed to send a mission to Lhasa to negotiate a new treaty. This would be a reversion to the policy of Lord Lansdowne, from which he had eventually desisted in deference to Chinese protest. The mission would conclude a treaty of friendship and trade with the Tibetan government and would be accompanied by a sufficient escort to ensure safety.[110]

Shortly after this, Sir E. Satow mentioned the rumours to Prince Ch'ing, who replied that he had asked the Russian Minister what they meant. The Minister said that Russia had no desire to encroach on Tibet, but seemed to acknowledge that the Buddhists in Russian territory had come to some sort of arrangement with their co-religionists in Tibet; with this the Russian government had nothing to do. Prince Ch'ing described the Tibetans as being very ignorant and difficult to control and the Chinese were considering how they might strengthen the lands of their Amban. Otherwise it was evident that the Tibetans would bring trouble on their country. He was uneasy at the independent tone they assumed, and appeared to know nothing about the Russian appointment of a secret agent.[111]

On Christmas Day, 1902, Curzon wrote for his colleagues a note pointing out that the situation was by now much more grave than it had been, though not yet desperate:

> Russia has concluded some sort of agreement with the Tibetan Government which will presently result in a Russian Envoy at Lhasa, and a little later in a Russian Protectorate. This is a challenge to our power and position wholly unprovoked, entirely unwarrantable, fraught in my opinion with the most serious danger, and demanding the most prompt and strenuous resistance. If we do nothing now—while all the cards are still in our hands—we shall deserve the worst that could befall us.[112]

EIGHT

The Army

AFTER SIX MONTHS' experience as Viceroy, Curzon said that he found it heart-breaking to discover dislocation in every joint of what he had fondly imagined to be an almost perfect machine.[1] That criticism extended to the army as well as to the civil service. Soon he began to scrutinise the proceedings of the military with extreme care, for estimates were frequently exceeded by as much as fifty per cent, superfluous forts were represented to be vital, military works were undertaken before sanction was given. The Viceroy's sharp comments, as he well knew, ruffled the Military Member of Council, General Sir E. Collen, 'a dear old boy, of courtly manner and a perfect gentleman', the incarnation of a quarter of a century's departmental life. He would come to the Viceroy and implore him not to be disrespectful to the system or to pass comments upon it which might be seen by others. In private, General Collen would groan about new brooms and parliamentary training, and wonder why what was good enough for Lord Dufferin was not good enough for Lord Curzon.[2]

In the Military Department, Curzon told Brodrick, there flourished

> red tape and officialdom of the most rampant kind: great jealousy and squabbling between that Department…and the Army Headquarters: an utterly vicious system of departmental finance…the hand of the Government of India recklessly forced by the military authorities, and, following their example, by every petty colonel and captain along the frontier. I come down heavily on all the cases as I detect them; and am not greatly loved by the soldiers in consequence. Had I the time and knowledge I would reform the whole system. I may get some distance with it before I have done.[3]

By custom, though not of right, the Commander-in-Chief sat in the Viceroy's Council. He presided over a separate staff at Army Headquarters and was responsible in effect for the testing and use of the men and material supplied by the Military Department. These departments seemed to Curzon, in his first few months at any rate, to be united by an appalling loquacity on paper and in conspiring to gloss over a good deal of jobbery.[4] The two soldiers on the Council did not by any means invariably agree with each other, however. In July 1899, Curzon acknowledged to another correspondent

> a good deal of latent suspicion and even friction between the Military Department and the Army headquarters, much as there used to be at home while the Duke of Cambridge sat enthroned at the Horseguards shaking his fist at the Secretary of State in Pall Mall. As long as the two Departments remain separate here (and it will need some strong military reformer – for I fear I have no time – to amalgamate them) I can conceive that a good deal of trouble and soreness would arise if the Military Member alone were admitted to Council and the Commander in Chief excluded.[5]

Curzon adhered only to a part of this early opinion. The presence of both C-in-C and Military Member on the Council he supported to the end of his term; the desire to amalgamate Army HQ and the Military Department he soon abandoned. Indeed, refusal to unite them in effect caused his resignation six years later. As to this, it is fair to add that Curzon found Elles a more satisfactory Military Member than Collen, and Kitchener more greedy of power than Lockhart or Palmer.

Hamilton agreed that both officers should remain members of the Council. At the Admiralty, where he had been First Lord for six and a half years, the division of duties was clear; whereas the jumbling of administrative and executive work in the War Office lay at the root of the troubles. The C-in-C at home, he believed, was hopelessly overworked, but in India both military theory and practice were represented at the highest level and the one officer acted to some degree as a check upon the other.[6]

Curzon felt in his first year that owing to a series of rather masterful Cs-in-C, the Military Department had ceased to perform some of its proper function as a board of audit. Officers in outlying regions had acquired the habit of regarding a provisional allotment of money as definite sanction. The Political Officer at Gilgit, for example, engaged labourers and began work on a road to Chitral, while the government of India were solemnly discussing whether such a road was desirable. The contract was cancelled and the workmen dismissed.[7]

In short, Curzon found the outlook and ability of the leading soldiers profoundly disappointing: 'Few of them read or study. Military science as such seems to be beyond them. A battle is in their eyes only a game of football. What is the good of heroism when you are being picked off by an enemy three miles away? You want science.'

On a later occasion he asked St John Brodrick, then Secretary of State for War, whether he did not find soldiers very irresponsible? 'They love a job as a German loves a shut railway carriage and a frowst. I have a few good men. But the majority fill me with despair: and as for a military Committee I would as soon remit a question of state to a meeting of Eton masters.'[8]

*   *   *   *

On 2 April, 1899, some twenty men of the West Kent Regiment, stationed at Rangoon, raped in open daylight an elderly Burmese. Not until June did the first rumours reach Curzon, and then only through a newspaper. The C-in-C, Sir W. Lockhart, had heard nothing, and the Lieutenant-Governor of Burma volunteered no report. Lord George Hamilton had also seen press reports. He telegraphed to India several times, asking, without prompting from Curzon, that if the regiment showed a desire to shield the culprits, the Viceroy and C-in-C should inflict a punishment which would mark indignation and disgust.[9]

Curzon was equally determined that nothing should impede a rigorous investigation. The reports, when eventually received, cast an unpleasant light on the sloth, incapacity and sympathy with crime of the military and civil authorities. Lockhart proposed, and his colleagues agreed, a series of dismissals and reprimands. In accordance with Hamilton's suggestion, the regiment was moved to the most unpleasant billet available, Aden. The Government of Burma were told privately what was thought of their failure to grip the issue, and Curzon insisted on the publication of a statement, which he wrote, condemning the negligence and apathy shown:

> It is for the soldiers of Her Majesty's forces in India to uphold the honourable traditions of the uniform which they wear, and, in the irksome and sometimes uncongenial conditions of service in a distant land, to practise that discipline which is their duty as soldiers, and the self-restraint which is incumbent upon them as men.[10]

The Viceroy felt that in the later stages of this episode he hardly received the support to which he was entitled, either from Lockhart and Collen or from the civilians on the Council, with the exception of the Law Member, Sir T. Raleigh. Curzon argued that the government had an overwhelming moral duty to express their view, adding that he would willingly take the whole responsibility since it would fall upon him anyway.[11] In that judgment he was certainly correct. To act against the West Kent Regiment, which was not smart or socially well-connected, required courage, but not in the same degree as some of Curzon's later exposures of brutality. Nevertheless, this was the beginning of the ill-feeling between him and the bulk of the Army which endured throughout the Viceroyalty and long after.

Within a few months, Hamilton was writing of an inclination in the War Office to think the Rangoon case had been magnified. Friends of the officers were bringing influence to bear at home for a revision of the sentences. Lord George promised and gave Curzon his warm support. In virtue of the sovereign's position as head of the Army, such matters always came to royal notice. Even in November 1902, the King, while acquitting Curzon of undue interference with military matters, thought his measures against the West Kents 'rather too drastic and sweeping'; to which Hamilton rejoined that the offence had been one of 'shocking bestiality' and the offenders without doubt protected by the regiment.[12]

Enquiries in the departments had already revealed an increasing number of collisions between Europeans and Indians. The coolies who pulled punkahs, fans, in the barracks, were specially liable to attack. Early in 1900, a private of the Royal Scots Fusiliers battered a punkah-coolie to death with a dumb-bell and, after unnecessary delay, was brought to trial and acquitted. Curzon asked that electric fans be provided in every barracks and for publicity to be given to the stiff punishment eventually imposed. Officers and soldiers must learn that no evasion, slackness or miscarriage of justice in the early stages would prevent retribution. 'Punishment by itself is not a sufficient deterrent, unless known; publicity given to punishment is.'[13]

A week or two later, juries acquitted soldiers who had caused the deaths of two Indians by careless shooting. Curzon believed that such incidents, followed by travesties of justice, were seriously weakening the foundations of British rule. He even speculated upon an eventual 'explosion that may culminate in another Mutiny'. Such cases, he wrote to Hamilton,

> eat into my very soul. That such gross outrages should occur in the first place in a country under British rule; and then that everybody, commanding officers, officials, juries, departments, should conspire to screen the guilty is, in my judgment, a black and permanent blot on the British name. I mean, so far as one man can do it, to efface this stain while I am here...'

That policy inevitably meant unpopularity with the Army. However, he resolved that the abuse must be faced and the soldiers frightened into 'conduct more becoming Christians and gentlemen'.[14] Other instances of death and injury during shooting expeditions caused the Viceroy to summon a committee, for whom he wrote a minute. He admitted that Indians, knowing their rights would be upheld by the courts, had in some areas become more assertive. Initiative in insolence sometimes lay there; trumped-up cases were not unknown. But the feeling, where it did exist, had largely been created by the British. The general inclination was still towards defence. British soldiers must not be deprived of legitimate recreation; but it must be enjoyed under rules more strictly applied. If the regulations were persistently broken, then shooting passes would have to be withdrawn:

> the conduct of a small number of soldiers may sensibly affect the position of all Englishmen, and the attitude of all natives in this country...the natural position of a British soldier should be that of a source of protection and not of alarm to the people...'

A revised code was proposed by the committee and immediately accepted.[15] Curzon noted resignedly that he was being denounced by British soldiers throughout India, and by hundreds of pudding-headed subalterns, for lowering the prestige of the ruling race.[16] He found among the officers nothing but 'tacit discouragement and sublatent antagonism'. The whole Army was banded tightly together throughout India. If, in the course of a shooting expedition, an Indian got killed 'their attitude is that of a very fast bowler at cricket whom I once met, and who, having killed a man by the ball jumping up and striking him on the temple, said to me, "Why did the d——d fool get his head in the way?" '[17]

It came to be believed that Curzon regarded soldiers as an inferior breed, dedicated to jobbery and willing to hush up malpractice. These stories bit deep.[18] Some of the Anglo–Indian newspapers, and especially *The Pioneer*, did their best week after week to create bad blood between him and the Indian Army. Walter Lawrence, aware of the bitter conviction of victimisation, yet sympathising with his master's indignation, tried to dissuade him from so strong a line:

> It is impossible to have an exactly equal law for Natives and Europeans. Juries will not convict and it is very dangerous to embark on any crusade however noble which raises the 'social question'. I do not like the significant comments of natives and the native press in which my chief is compared to Lord Ripon.

These fracas, Lawrence observed, had been happening for donkey's years. After many talks they agreed to differ upon this one subject. 'What is the use,' asked Curzon, depressed, 'of my wearing myself out to prove to India that I mean to hold the balance fair between the two races if all my work is to be rendered futile by these collisions?' Lawrence answered that

the work for India was not in the least impaired by a scuffle between a
bewildered soldier and a benighted peasant. Thereafter all papers on this
subject went direct to the Viceroy. In the summer of 1901 Lawrence spoke
to him about the Army's opposition, but without producing any visible
effect.[19]

★   ★   ★   ★

Count Bülow had anticipated that the possibility of a South African war
would make the British more malleable and certainly more careful in
dealing with Russia. Even if war broke out, the British Government would
be 'very unwilling to denude India, owing to the distrust of Russia so
deeply rooted in England'.[20]

This forecast, plausible and sensible as it was, proved false. Under
Curzon, India sent abroad troops on an unprecedented scale, paving the
way for the vital Indian contributions to the victories of 1918 and 1945.
India had provided most of the troops for the Ethiopian campaign of 1869;
at the height of the crisis in 1878 Beaconsfield had reinforced Malta from
India. These movements opened up new vistas:

> We don't want to fight
> But, by jingo, if we do,
> We'll stay at home and sing our songs
> And send the mild Hindoo.[21]

The immediate and efficient response of India in September, 1899, saved
Natal and was thankfully accepted by the Cabinet. Those soldiers were
British, with Indian followers. When Curzon volunteered a powerful
Indian contingent in December, Hamilton refused, on the grounds that the
Dutch in Natal and Cape Colony, already simmering, would probably
unite with the Boers if coloured troops were used.[22] A few weeks later,
Roberts said he would like an Indian prince on his staff. By then, Lord
George had even come to apprehend international reactions. 'My own
strong opinion' he advised Salisbury, 'is that if we in any way employ
coloured men to fight against the Boers we may combine the European
powers against us in a forcible and material combination.'[23]

The Queen deplored the disagreement in the Cabinet on this issue.
Salisbury replied that he much regretted his complete failure 'to persuade
people of influence in this country and in India of the danger which they
run by not paying sufficient attention to the feelings of Indians, especially
of the Indian Princes. It is a grave error, for which some day this country

will pay dear.' The Prime Minister feared that if, as the Queen asked, he 'put his foot down' in a matter where the great majority of the Cabinet and all the leading officials of the India and War Offices were hostile, the government would break up. Curzon's reaction was much the same as the Queen's; but for the moment there was nothing to be done. India remained entirely calm, despite detailed reporting of each folly and reverse. When Roberts, whose long career there had made him a legend, won a series of victories in February, 1900, the people covered his statue on the Calcutta Maidan with garlands.[24]

These early stages of the Boer War revealed that Great Britain had no striking force. Not even a complete battalion could be despatched from the home establishment without mobilising the reserve. Volunteer battalions sometimes proved more helpful to their opponents than to the British. An enemy soldier's diary, found after a battle, recorded that the Boers, often desperate for arms and ammunition, could get all they wanted when they came across a body of 'Gentle Annies'. As Salisbury commented, 'If we had had an army of Red Indians we should have been in many respects better off.'[25] More painful even than the revelation of inadequate forces and poor training were the evidences of incapacity among officers. Lack of a staff system, and the inadequacy of intelligence, produced the most ludicrous results. Within a few weeks of the outbreak, General Buller estimated the Boers to dispose of 145,000 men. The War Office curtly replied that the total Boer population amounted to 90,000.[26]

Early in 1900, the last British division had been mobilised. Curzon was informed that in case of war with Russia India could expect no reinforcements.[27] The Military Member had already reported India to be deficient in officers, in British troops and transport; the field army could not be mobilised with the proper complement of British soldiers; the transport organisation was inadequate, the native infantry armed with an inferior weapon. India, stated Collen, could not help England further. News had been received of the strengthening of Russian positions in the Caucasus and elsewhere. Though Roberts had said he would not move into Afghanistan unless assured of 30,000 men from home, they could hardly be expected while the South African war raged. Yet if Russia took Herat, which she could do at any time, her outposts would certainly appear on the Helmund before long.[28] Large reorganisation was needed; to which end Collen put forward proposals, some of which were admirable but which were collectively impossible. The Council, Curzon remarked, would be told that if they did not allow this or the other, they would bear responsibility for the future discomfiture of British arms:

The real weakness of a Military Department manned enitrely, as ours is here, by soldiers, lies in their total lack of perspective or proportion. Their plans, their proposals, their desiderata, vary every six months. But each, as it comes up, is pressed as absolutely vital to the salvation of the army.[29]

Re-equipment was set in train promptly, but Curzon refused, with the finances threatened by famine, to add to the Indian Army the numbers which would enable it to fight unaided against Russia in Afghanistan. Whatever committees might say, or the War Office decide, reinforcements from home must be sent.[30] In February, 1901, the Military Member and C-in-C formally warned their colleagues 'that the army of India is unprepared to embark in a considerable campaign, and that its efficiency for war cannot be placed beyond dispute without a very large expenditure'.

Collen, naturally enough, bewailed the lack of accurate intelligence and the absence of a staff system on the German model. Requests for reliable information from the Intelligence Division of the War Office elicited no response.[31] However, Curzon again damped down zeal for an increase of the establishment:

We have got along without nearly 30,000 men for a year, and without 8,000–9,000 for one and a half years. The country is poor. We are only just quit of a bad famine. We have had a series of lean years. An increase of the Army can only be paid for when our finances are more flourishing...Repair and reconstruct the present edifice before you build on a new wing to it...[32]

*   *   *   *

Shortly before Curzon left home in 1898, General Kitchener, fresh from his triumphs at Omdurman and Fashoda, said he would like to serve in India. During the spring of 1899, Brodrick told Curzon that Kitchener's methods had produced a very serious state of feeling in the Egyptian Army, of which he was then Sirdar.[33] Lord George, who had known Kitchener since he was a subaltern, saw something of him in that summer. He admitted that Kitchener was an 'extraordinary organiser', but he was also a hard and unpopular machine: 'He would no doubt brush up very much the organisation and transport of the Indian Army. On the other hand, I am sure, he would not be equally successful in dealing with the human beings under his control; and therefore I think we had, at any rate for the present, better dismiss the idea of employing him in a military capacity for India.'[34]

In the following month, August, 1899, Kitchener turned up unannounced at the India Office and said he was a candidate for the succession to Collen as Military Member. Lord George's view did not alter, though he wondered whether Kitchener might take the Punjab command. Curzon thought Kitchener might perhaps become C-in-C, but doubted his fitness for the Military Membership. For the moment, anyway, another seismic element in the placid pool of Indian administration might not be a good thing.[35] Reform, though desperately needed, could be successfully achieved only by a blend of experience, intelligence and conciliation: 'Kitchener is the man to drive through a campaign with relentless energy. You have only to go to Lord Cromer or to the Foreign Office to ascertain what is the effect he produces, when let loose in administration.'[36]

Rennell Rodd wrote from Cairo of Kitchener's many faults, his failure to inspire friendship or sympathy, his lack of charm and intolerance of other's failings, his unscrupulous methods largely attributable to the persistent opposition and jealousy of the War Office. Kitchener was, nevertheless, the ablest soldier he had met. 'I have a warm regard for him' Curzon replied. 'I do not think that, though I have, like you, a full conscious-ness of his foibles and of his somewhat unlovable temperament, he has got anywhere in India so firm a friend as myself.'[37]

By the time this letter reached Cairo, Kitchener had left, at the Cabinet's urgent request, to retrieve with Roberts the South African disasters. But for the Boer War, it is unlikely that he would have become C-in-C in India. Sir W. Lockhart, who assumed that post in November, 1898, showed signs of illness within a few months. By the end of 1899 he was absent from the Council. In this situation, Curzon found little help from Collen, and boggled to think what might happen to the Indian Army if it met a European enemy. Proposals from Army Headquarters came forward with a note advising acquiescence:

> The whole system is utterly vicious. These soldiers play into each other's hands: they connive at each other's irregularities: and there is neither check, nor supervision, nor responsibility, nor control.
>
> God forbid that we should ever have a war with such men at the head of affairs. I can see no hope until we clear them all off and get fresh brains to advise, and more virile energies to act...We want new blood. If Lockhart is invalided, or dies, we want a Kitchener to pull things together. If he is not available, I do not know whom to name...'[38]

With this poor opinion of military talent Hamilton associated himself. The soldiers at home all seemed to be exercising their industry in getting papers to save themselves when the conduct of the war was investigated. Lord George looked through the Army List, both Indian and British, and could find only one man in any way fit to succeed Lockhart, Mansfield Clarke. He was a sensible good man of business, but nothing more. Yet Lansdowne said he was the only man at the War Office at that moment upon whom he could rely. 'A good figure, a tight waistband and a certain physical proficiency,' Hamilton wrote, 'are supposed to be sufficient equipment for any post or office.'[39]

The revolution in warfare displayed in South Africa deeply impressed the Secretary of State. Old tactics had been put out of date by the accuracy and length of fire of the new rifles. Plans for the defence of India must be recast. Lockhart's death made immediate a question which had previously seemed academic, and Hamilton wondered whether Kitchener's obvious disqualifications for the post of C-in-C would not be counteracted by his experience of the most modern practice of war? Curzon, convinced that the machine had become clogged with tradition, wanted a virile reformer.[40]

Roberts favoured Kitchener, provided the Military Member were a strong man. Lansdowne, at the War Office, thought Kitchener unsafe without previous apprenticeship in India.[41] Queen Victoria wished to see her son, the Duke of Connaught, C-in-C at home. He, however, said he would like to go to India. Salisbury and Lansdowne suggested that he replace Lockhart for two years and then return to London, but Lord George objected, largely on the ground that the Duke was 'not the man to initiate the reforms and changes required...' He had now veered round against Kitchener, whose harshness, he thought, had a good deal to do with an attempted mutiny at Omdurman.[42]

There the matter rested for some time. Collen told Curzon that the whole Indian Army was against Kitchener's appointment because he knew nothing of the country and 'would offend everybody and turn everything upside down'. But the candidates were not strong. Lockhart had held a poor opinion of Sir Power Palmer, who was now acting as C-in-C. Curzon thought he would be acceptable but not very able, and Mansfield Clarke too old; while the Duke of Connaught could hardly be expected to relish either the peculiar position of the Viceroy or the frequent inter-vention of Curzon in military matters, from the need for which he hoped to be freed.[43]

In July, 1900, Roberts, impressed with his performance in South Africa, again recommended Kitchener. This advice carried much weight with Curzon, who enquired who might succeed Collen: 'For my part, fearless and capable Military Member ... even more important than energetic Commander-in-Chief; but in public interest it is desirable the two should not quarrel.'[44]

Kitchener was thereupon selected: 'I look with some apprehension' wrote Hamilton, 'upon this appointment, as I fear the effect of his rough and unsympathetic manner and strong economic hand upon the Native Army. You will have carefully to watch him, but he has rare organising skill and determination...'

Curzon admitted that it was a big risk. 'But I will do whatever I can to make it successful;' and to Clinton Dawkins he commented: 'Anything to get military matters here out of the old and frozen rut.'[45]

Curzon wrote a letter of warm congratulations to Kitchener, assuring him of support. As Viceroy, and knowing the frontier, he intended to take much interest in military affairs. The army needed reform, for which he relied on Kitchener's energy and experience:

> I see absurd and uncontrolled expenditure; I observe a lack of method and system; I detect slackness and jobbery; and in some respects I lament a want of fibre and tone. Upon all these matters I shall have many opportunities of speaking to you, and of suggesting abundant openings for your industry and force. On the other hand, in point of organisation, equipment, rapidity of mobilisation and fighting capacity, I believe that our army would take a high place, even among continental forces. India still remains the finest nursery of soldiers in the British Empire.[46]

Luckily, this was not posted at once; for within a few hours followed another letter from Hamilton, saying that the Cabinet had now reversed its decision of the week before, believing that Kitchener was the man to initiate the drastic reforms required at the War Office.[47] The Queen swore that nothing should induce her to consent to Kitchener's becoming C-in-C in India. His manners were too ferocious. This, said Salisbury, was her riposte for his refusal to allow the Duke of Connaught to exclude Roberts from the post of C-in-C at home.[48]

The new Secretary for War, Brodrick, like the Queen desired Kitchener at the War Office. Kitchener himself, convinced that under the existing system he would fail hopelessly, refused point-blank: 'I would sooner sweep a crossing ... I have no intention of going to the War Office in any capacity ... If I am not fit for India I am not fit for anything else...'[49]

At the end of 1900, he took over the South African command from Roberts. It was then proposed that Sir P. Palmer might be appointed to March, 1903, when Kitchener would succeed him, but Curzon, despite warnings about 'Kitchener of chaos', appealed to the authorities not to detain him until the last year of the Viceroyalty. March, 1902, was agreed upon. Brodrick later claimed that he had done everything in his power to prevent Kitchener from going to India till Curzon had left. If this is true, he had by now given way:

> George – [he wrote] I tore my vitals out for you about Kitchener. It will probably go far to wrecking my period of office. Roberts is glorious but he wobbles...It would be everything to have Kitchener to appeal to...But as you know I think the Empire is a whole and your need is greater than mine. So I gave in and told the Cabinet the reason. I had want[ed] to make him Chief of the Staff. You have helped us so much you deserve anything.[50]

When Lady Curzon saw him later that year, Brodrick talked long of the 'huge sacrifice' he was making in giving up Kitchener; 'only friendship and love for you had induced the sacrifice. If he (Brodrick) hadn't been where he was you would never have got him.'[51] This, in view of Kitchener's absolute refusal to go to the War Office, seems disingenuous. Anyhow, the question was now settled, although the Boers made no hurry to surrender. Curzon thanked Brodrick, took out his unposted letter to Kitchener of the previous August, and added a covering note. Indian military administration, he commented, was entangled in interminable writing and undue centralisation, which he had been trying to reduce. The panjandrums indulged in mild jobbery 'against which I have set my face like a flint', and liked to shrug off unpopular decisions on to the masterful Viceroy. Curzon looked forward to their co-operation as the cure for these ills. 'I will serve you loyally' replied Kitchener from Pretoria. 'I have no fear regarding the personal feelings of officers, which, owing to my want of experience of India, I can well understand. I am not so black as I am painted...'[52]

Observing keenly its performance in South Africa, Curzon judged that the British Army must have scientific, in place of ramshackle, military education, and a broader base of entry, so that the officers' ranks were not reserved for the stupider members of good families. Brodrick, he remarked, was a resolute man, with much strength of character and rectitude of purpose. Perhaps he would do more than most expected.[53]

Salisbury's quip about the drawbacks of the War Office was soon shown to be apt. The new Secretary of State determined to bring forward large changes without awaiting the end of the war or an investigation. He ran a serious risk thereby, calculating no doubt that if he did not press hard while the fruits of the old system were so universally admitted to be rotten, he would never get the money. The army estimates had risen under Lord Lansdowne by a third, to £24,000,000. Having been Secretary of State for a few weeks only, Brodrick carried, on pain of resignation, a scheme for six Army Corps, at an extra cost in the first year of £6,000,000. Salisbury and

Beach protested sternly but in vain.[54] At this time the desire for a larger
force sprang in part from a conviction that the heart of the Empire was
vulnerable. 'Invasion' said Brodrick, 'may be an off-chance, but you
cannot run an Empire of this size on off-chances.'[55] His doctrine was not
well received by the Admiralty or by Parliament. One of its more persistent
opponents was Mr Churchill, who said pithily that if Britain had command
of the sea she needed fewer soldiers; if she had not, she needed more ships.
That she might need more of both does not seem to have crossed his mind.
Brodrick soon realised that although the government had just been returned
with a large majority, there was good reason to fear Parliamentary opinion.
Many on the government side would rather vote for reduction than for
increase.[56]

During the China crisis of 1900, known as the Boxer rebellion, India's
importance as a reservoir of trained troops was demonstrated again.
Curzon and Palmer took immense pains to select a force which would
impress the European contingents also making for China. Though the
Queen felt anxious at sending away yet more soldiers, Curzon assured her
that there was no danger of external attack for the moment. Since it had
not been permissible to use Indian combatants in South Africa, this opportunity was welcome and would help to restore the approved ratio of European and native troops in India. The Cabinet upheld his view that the
balance should not be tilted further.[57] Yet by the early part of 1901, nearly
a half of the 70,000 British troops normally stationed there were either
absent or about to leave. This was by far the lowest figure reached at any
time since the Mutiny.

In the autumn of that year, Kitchener telegraphed that the Boers were
fighting with even greater determination. The only suitable reinforcements
were four battalions of infantry and two regiments of cavalry from India,
to be sent forthwith and replaced later. Hamilton protested warmly at the
Cabinet, but found himself alone. When it transpired that the force available at home hardly amounted to an infantry regiment, Lord George felt
he must agree. He confessed, as well he might, that these investigations had
filled him with very considerable apprehensions for the future. A regiment
or two might come from the colonies, and a few hundred men now and
again from the yeomanry; otherwise Great Britain had 'literally no
resources in reserve'. The situation in South Africa, he informed the
Viceroy, was an unhappy one, and the composition of the Cabinet did not
lend itself to bold or thorough measures:

> There are one or two older men in it, occupying very important posts, whom
> I need not name, and who are completely played out; and yet, so long as they

form part of the Government, it is not possible for anybody to assume or undertake the duties they ought to discharge. The younger men are doing well; but in a critical time such as we have before us, we want a stronger lead than we now get.[58]

Curzon responded at once. In all, India sent to the Boer War 13,200 British soldiers and over 9,000 Indians, mainly followers; and to China some 1,300 British troops, 20,000 Indians and 17,500 followers. She produced also for those campaigns 21 million rounds of ammunition, 114,000 shells, nearly a million items of clothing, and huge quantities of saddlery, helmets, blankets and boots.[59] 'It did me good' wrote Brodrick, 'to get your telegrams and to feel your loyal and self-sacrificing support in South Africa. Of one thing you may be sure, that if you have a scare I will send you troops from there at all hazards... '[60]

At that time some 225,000 British troops were locked up on South Africa. Hamilton had already calculated that when the war ended, there would be less than 50,000 in India, amidst a population of nearly 300 million. Brodrick said that if India could not support an increase in their pay and a change in the terms of enlistment, her establishment could not be maintained 'as I literally have not the men'.[61] Feeling the deficiency so acutely that he mused on resignation, he proposed to enlist every man initially for three years with nine years in the reserve and higher pay for service abroad, so that 'even with European complications we could afford to stoke up India'.[62] This plan was approved by a small majority against the opinion of Salisbury, 'after an appeal such as he never made to the Cabinet in his life, and we all thought he would go'.[63]

Since a large proportion of the British Army spent part of its time in India, the increase of pay seriously affected her revenues. Curzon had indicated that he expected India to be consulted and had understood from Hamilton that his view was shared at the India Office. In February 1902, he learned with astonishment that the final decision had been taken. Clearly, he telegraphed, the change was dictated by factors unconnected with India, for the existing system had supplied her wants. If men opted to enter the reserve at home, instead of receiving extra pay abroad, the flow of troops to India must dry up. If not, the British Army there at a given time would be on a higher scale of pay than that at home. Curzon refused to heed the plea that the creation of a large reserve at home would benefit India to any great extent, for the despatch of reinforcements would depend upon command of the sea, unaffected by the new scheme. The political result in India could scarcely be happy.[64]

Believing that British needs could be met only by some form of

conscription, Curzon thought the decision unfair. The cost to India would
rise swiftly to £786,000 per annum, an increase of fifty per cent. The
government of India asked that the British Treasury should meet half of the
cost. The case for such payment, they remarked, would be the stronger if
the home government continued to ask India to send troops abroad. In his
private letters Curzon did not trouble to hide his indignation at unimagina-
tive and ungrateful treatment of India. The new scheme could provide
troops for overseas garrisons only if a large proportion of recruits elected
to stay on beyond their three years. Brodrick felt sure that they would. 'I
do not share your confidence', Curzon replied.[65]

In the event, the proportion of men re-enlisting, estimated at seventy-five
per cent, was by the end of 1903 less than twenty per cent. Of a draft of one
hundred men leaving for India, ninety-seven were shown to be on the
three years' engagement, which meant that most would serve there but a
few months. That dénoument, which helped to wreck Brodrick's career,
lay in the future. For the moment, he refused the request for financial help,
despite a plea from Curzon that the loss of £¾ million must reduce India's
capacity to do what was really needed in her military organisation.[66] In
view of the developments of 1904 and 1905, this was a matter of crucial
importance. No one was amazed when the Lord Chancellor ruled that
India must pay the whole sum; nor can Curzon have been much surprised
to learn from Godley that in his view the government of India had no
right to be consulted on such a matter.[67]

Discussions about the right size of the Indian Army continued to flourish.
The authorities in India refused to accept that reinforcements would not
arrive for nine or twelve months. Nor did they believe that Russia could
make a sudden advance in force towards India so menacing as to call for a
reply by a very large army. Probably the Russians would be well occupied
once they had moved forward, in absorbing the Herat province, Afghan
Turkestan and Badakshan.[68] The eighteen battalions suggested from home
as an addition to the Indian Army were refused. India, said the despatch, was
already bearing a sufficiently heavy burden and could not be expected to do
more. If Imperial interests were at stake, the Empire must pay; and if the
Indian Army grew larger, it would be indented upon the more freely.
Anyway, after the pay increase of the same year, it simply could not be
done. An appeal by Brodrick at the Colonial Conference of 1902, that each
colony should provide a reserve liable for service abroad, fell upon deaf
ears.[69]

*   *   *   *

On the afternoon of 9 April, 1902, the 9th Lancers arrived at Sialkot. A general carouse followed. That night Atu, an Indian cook, was beaten outside their barracks. In hospital he deposed that it was men of the 9th Lancers who had assaulted him. The Commanding Officer, informed at once, did nothing. A week later Atu died. A court of enquiry, composed entirely of officers of the regiment, declared itself unable to discover the culprits. Further enquiries were ordered by a higher authority. Meanwhile, a coolie had died of a ruptured spleen after an assault by a trooper of the 9th Lancers. The facts came to the notice of the C-in-C, Palmer, and of Curzon. He minuted:

> The not unpopular theory that these offences ought to be whitewashed for fear of the scandal that they may cause, is one that it is impossible for the Government of India to maintain. If it be said 'don't wash your dirty linen in public,' I reply 'don't have dirty linen to wash.' These dreadful cases will never be stopped by concealment, or evasion, or excuses. They will only be stopped by punishment of the offenders. It is disagreeable to all of us to see a brave and famous British regiment guilty of these atrocities. But it is much more than disagreeable, it is dangerous, to pass them by with impunity. If a third disaster occurred in another two months, how should we all feel?

Another investigation was ordered. The reports, as it seemed to Curzon, reflected a spirit not of careful enquiry but of desire to exculpate. General Blood ruled in the case of Atu that 'disciplinary action is quite out of the question'. The Viceroy dissected his report mercilessly, pointing out that while the Rangoon case was more serious, in that almost every officer involved had tried to suppress the case, the 9th Lancers' outrages must be punished; that collisions between Europeans and Indians were occurring more and more frequently; that 84 Indians had been thus killed in the previous twenty years; and that only two Europeans had been hanged for the murder of Indians since the Mutiny:

> I know that as long as Europeans, and particularly a haughty race like the English, rule Asiatic people like the Indians, incidents of *hubris* and violence will occur, and that the white men will tend to side with the white skin against the dark. But I also know, and have acted throughout on the belief, that it is the duty of statesmanship to arrest these dangerous symptoms and to prevent them from attaining dimensions that might even threaten the existence of our rule in the future...I have observed the growing temper of the native. The new wine is beginning to ferment within him, and he is attaining to a consciousness of equality and freedom...looking to the future, as every ruler of this country that is worthy of the name must incessantly do, I recognise that unless this movement [towards violent collisions] is kept in check—and check is only

possible, not by crushing the aspirations of the native, which are destined to grow, but by controlling the temper of the European — it may, nay it must, reach a pitch when it will boil over in mutiny and rebellion, and when the English may be in danger of losing their command of India, because they have not learned to command themselves.

On the efforts to discredit Atu's story, Curzon noted 'It is this sort of attitude on the part of so many of the officers concerned that makes one burn with a sense of injustice and shame.'[70]

Palmer and Elles recommended that all officers and men of the 9th Lancers on leave in India should be recalled and that no more leave be granted to officers for six months. This applied to the winter and did not affect the migration to the hills. The regiment was to be addressed, privately, in unmistakable terms. The C-in-C and Military Member also proposed the exclusion of the regiment from the Durbar soon to be held at Delhi. From this disgrace Curzon intervened to save them. Nothing was announced in public. That would have ended the matter but for the exceptional circumstances which give this squalid story its significance. For the 9th Lancers was one of the most select and smart regiments, with innumerable social and parliamentary connections. Curzon, realising that fact only too well, did not know whether the higher standard he had enforced would endure. Much, he recognised, would depend on Kitchener. In three and a half years, Curzon had not so far met a single soldier in India who was on his side. Most denounced him freely at table and in the mess or clubhouse. Such tales, as he knew well, circulated in India and at home and were used to influence 'persons in high station' in England. Nonetheless, there would be no flinching.[71]

In the early autumn, the agitation and gossip in London began. It was said that Atu had not been assaulted by any soldier of the regiment, that the Viceroy had personally ordered the punishments over the heads of the military authorities, that the penalties were unduly severe. The pressure reached such a pitch that on Hamilton's advice a public statement, sparing individual officers, was issued. By this time, the CO of the 9th Lancers had told his superiors that the identity of one of the assailants was almost certain, though the case could not be proved at law.[72] It was still being asserted that officers and men on leave in England had been punished. The King protested to Hamilton, who replied that His Majesty was misinformed, praised Curzon's stand and said he intended to support it. This he did faithfully, hating the favouritism so openly shown by 'certain authorities' to 'so-called smart regiments'.[73]

Though the Viceroy and Secretary of State were at this moment in conflict upon another issue, they were agreed that in this matter there could be no going back. If, wrote Curzon, it were known that they would stand up 'even against the crack regiment of the British Army—packed though it be with Dukes' sons, Earls' sons, and so on—then a most salutary lesson will be taught to the Army. If we yield to military and aristocratic clamour, no Viceroy will dare go on with the work that I have begun.'[74]

His position at the Durbar must be a most trying one, for there would be 40,000 soldiers present and Curzon realised how heartily he was detested. But acts of brutality must stop:

> I will not be a party to any of the scandalous hushing up of bad cases of which there is too much in this country, or to the theory that a white man may kick or batter a black man to death with impunity because he is only a 'd----d nigger'. There is too much of that spirit abroad; and I have sacrificed ease and popularity to combat it.[75]

Curzon refused Roberts' appeal that he should announce at the Durbar remission of the punishments. 'Crack' regiments, he replied, had no right to preferential treatment; collisions must be checked; suppression of evidence and perjury stamped out. 'I have set my face like a flint against this iniquity...The argument seems to be that a native's life does not count; and that any crime ought to be concealed and almost even condoned sooner than bring discredit upon the army...'[76]

Roberts understood and supported this argument, for he had just had to deal with serious bullying in the Life Guards and to suppress a vicious system of illicit courts-martial, run by subalterns and enforced by floggings, in the Grenadier Guards. Both cases had been troublesome, on account of these regiments' 'tremendous social influence'. He was now satisfied that the 9th Lancers had deserved their punishment. The King agreed once he realised the facts. The regiment had, he said, if anything been treated with leniency.[77]

The policy was upheld with the support of Hamilton, who took pleasure in repulsing agitation supported by social connections. 'A stiff back and a hard hand is sorely wanted at the War Office in putting down this kind of influence...' Curzon's courage called forth his unstinted admiration.[78] No aspect of the Viceroyalty reflects more credit upon both.

✳   ✳   ✳   ✳

Complaints of the army's inefficiency and jobbery occupy a less prominent place in Curzon's letters after the first year or two. In certain respects the situation had changed. The institution of a new administration, and of a more coherent policy, on the frontier reduced the opportunities for expeditions. Occasionally, however, Curzon would allow a foray. A tribe called the Bebejiya Mishmis were alleged to be ferocious cannibals, whose activities must be curbed. A large force was assembled. Then it was found that most of it could not get through to the Mishmi country. The tribe turned out to be well-behaved and inoffensive, but their villages had been burned before this fact was discovered. After ten weeks of campaigning the force returned with a bag of two captives, three children and one gun. Curzon's minute is a classic.[79]

A little later a place called Khrum was reported to be 'a warlike and blood-thirsty village', the existence of which, near the Burmese border, constituted 'a standing menace to peace'. An expedition was sent. The villagers showed no sign of hostility and bore no arms. They were given, by signs, an hour's grace.

> Poor wretches! [Curzon minuted] they probably had not an idea of what was meant. Then issued a scuffle, the result, as I should think, of great mismanagement, in the course of which some men were killed. Meanwhile everyone else had bolted. The next step was to burn the village and destroy the live-stock and grain. The local officers seem to think all this very grand. To my mind it is very pitiable.
>
> Finally another scuffle ensues and another man is killed, or rather dies of the injuries received, and the climax is set to the whole thing by the Hospital Assistant, evidently a wag, who 'could not say what was the cause of death'. I shall write privately to the Lieutenant Governor about the case.[80]

Such incidents, however, were rare in the extreme. Frontier expeditions virtually ceased. Curzon's attention to detail, and the frequency and range of his tours, probably had the same enlivening effect upon army authorities as upon the civilians.[81] Estimates would be more scrupulously watched and irregularities suppressed. Some features of the system seem to have been proof against reform. Though Hamilton and Curzon were united in regarding the elaborate reports upon individual officers as a farce,[82] they did not succeed in altering it much. The Viceroy did his best, by recording sharp minutes, to curb the more extravagant productions. When a report disclosed that the officers of the 30th Beluch Infantry fell into no less than nine categories of excellence, he noted 'It is very strange that all these subtle variations of ability should be confined to this single regiment. I cannot find them anywhere else.' Sir Power Palmer' assessment of a General—'an officer of some character'—was admired for its masterly ambiguity. Usually, however, superlatives robbed the reports of value:

> The number of officers who are reported as very smart, very able, very good, very keen, very promising, very clever, very satisfactory, very pushing (and even in one case 'very unsophisticated') is such as to make one wonder whether there can be any ability left over outside of these commands.[83]

The military system, or lack of it, had driven the Finance Member almost to distraction. Sir E. Law, the Viceroy noted, could barely articulate on the subject.[84] This was in February, 1901, when Collen was about to vacate his office. Army HQ and the Military Department, Curzon also observed, had been working 'in close and suspicious harmony' and had thrown at their colleagues a mass of undigested proposals.[85] Sir P. Palmer, though conciliatory, was not likely to reform the Army, and was really run by his Adjutant-General, Sir E. Elles. Curzon thought highly of Elles' common sense and dignity, though they had not always agreed, and secured his appointment to the Military Department.[86]

Thereafter the administration seems to have functioned better. The worst financial effects of the famine over, the pace of re-equipment accelerated. Elles worked well with Palmer, and interfered less with Army HQ than Collen had done. This at least was Curzon's firm belief, and he rarely misjudged such matters of fact. It is said that Palmer resented somewhat cavalier treatment at the Viceroy's hands,[87] and that may well be so. Those who lacked parliamentary training, and were accustomed to the disciplined respect of army life, often failed to relish his unvarnished criticisms. At the time, however, Sir P. Palmer thanked Curzon for the patience with which reforms had been thrashed out and the energy with which they were put through 'which has been such an advance on the policy of previous years when the Commander-in-Chief was looked upon as an ex-officio blood-sucker!'[88]

Long before Kitchener set foot in India, the government of India under Curzon had rearmed cavalry, infantry and artillery, revitalised the Madras Army, reorganised the system of transport, built frontier railways. Still more important, they had deliberately embarked on a programme of self-sufficiency for India in armaments and ammunition. Large measures of decentralisation had been passed, the Staff Corps increased, the reserves of the Native Army doubled. The number of communications passing between Army HQ and the Military Department had been reduced, with Curzon's encouragement. The proposal to increase India's field force by reducing provincial garrisons, which Kitchener was later to expand, had already been recommended to the home government.

In 1902, the senior Staff Officer, General Smith-Dorrien, put forward a plan for improving the military knowledge of Indian officers. It was defeated by the Military Department. He consented to withdraw his resignation only when allowed to go home and tell Kitchener the tale of disputed cases.[89] It was probably with this information in mind that Kitchener spoke earnestly with Lord George Hamilton, asking to what degree he would be the first military officer in India. Hamilton replied that whichever of the two officers, C-in-C and Military Member, had the stronger personality obtained most power, but he had never known any competent C-in-C who could not hold more than his own. According to his later recollection, Kitchener said 'I ought to be Military Member'.[90] The new C-in-C told Walter Lawrence, who was in England that summer, that he was interested only in questions of transport and supply, not in the concerns of the Adjutant-General, and assured Godley that he intended to keep quiet until he had been long enough in India to form his own opinion. 'You must not be surprised if you hear nothing of me for a very long time.' They talked of the War Office. 'You should go there to reform it' said Godley, 'when you return from India.' Kitchener replied that he hoped he would never be asked to do anything of the kind.[91]

For the moment all seemed to be set fair. Brodrick found Kitchener a changed man, full of schemes and enthusiasm for his Indian work, 'still vehement and vigorous— but he has developed a reserve (in action) and consideration which make him a very different investment for India to the Egyptian K. He will I know serve you well.'[92]

Curzon wrote to tell Kitchener how much he looked forward to co-operation with the foremost soldier of the British Army. A great work was to be done. Many stables must be cleansed. The Viceroy would smooth the way.[93] This was the spirit in which Curzon approached their work. Kitchener was at that moment basking in the adulation of his countrymen. His fame eclipsed that of other celebrated Generals, Wolseley, Buller and Roberts. By the time of his death in 1916, indeed, many half-believed Kitchener to be immortal. Even at this stage, in 1902, he realised well enough the extent to which hero-worship placed the levers in his hands. He was being sent to India to examine urgently the problem of defending that sub-continent against the threat from Russia which caused such lively apprehensions to the new Prime Minister. That fact alone lent special force to his wishes. Curzon could hardly foresee the methods which the new C-in-C would adopt, though he found out quite soon. But one serious note

of warning was sounded by Clinton Dawkins, who had been seeing a good
deal of his friend Kitchener

> able, energetic, domineering, very little troubled by scruples. All these qualities
> have been intensified. He is going out to India with one idea and one idea only,
> that of running 'the whole show'. He tells me frankly that he has got a year
> with you which he will need to look round, and he won't collide with you.
> After that, he will use the whole of his popularity and prestige to dominate
> the next Viceroy.

The fancied candidates for the succession to Curzon were Selborne and
Brodrick. Kitchener was busily advancing many good reasons against
both, his own candidates being Eddy Stanley, later Lord Derby, who had
been his subordinate in Africa, or Lord Cranborne, an intimate friend.
Impressed by his determination to be supreme, Salisbury said characteristically that the best way was for Kitchener himself to become Viceroy.
Dawkins, who had worked with Kitchener in Egypt, had glimpsed the
inwardness of the situation. In this prophetic letter he told Curzon he
would find that Kitchener

> who is spoken of as a great organiser, and with justice, is a great organiser in
> the sense that he can hold 100 threads in his hands and 1,000 details in his head,
> but that he is a great centraliser, and has very little appreciation of the proper
> organisation of a great administration. He will obliterate the distinction
> between the Commander-in-Chief and the Military Member, and insist on
> doing the Military Member's work himself.[94]

★   ★   ★   ★

The Boer War, expected by most to last a few weeks, did not end until the
summer of 1902. Lord Salisbury, in rapid physical decline, clung to the
Premiership until its close, and then left political life for ever. 'Poor old
man!' exclaimed Schomberg McDonnell, '... all work has become a
burden to him and he longs for rest.'[95] Brodrick reported more brutally
that Salisbury had to go: 'We had taken to ignoring him at committees.'
Beach insisted on leaving the Treasury, which averted the resignation of
Selborne. He was glad to have to fight his father-in-law, Salisbury, who
had generally been the Chancellor's only kindred spirit in the Cabinet on
naval and defence questions.[96]

For the new Prime Minister Curzon felt genuine, but watchful, affection.
He had long realised and perforce accepted the inconveniences which arose
from Balfour's slackness in attending to correspondence and from his idle

weekends and prolonged holidays. He had realised too that Balfour's
outward charm was bestowed upon many but his inner affection upon very
few: 'You will have had your talk with Arthur' Curzon wrote to Mary,
'long, long ago, and I have no doubt you will have found him as gentle
and as attractive as ever—sitting down at once to write the letter that is
never penned, and pouring out the appreciation that fades away so quickly
in absence.'[97]

Some facets of Balfour's character and methods of doing business will
emerge in this story. He had displayed much courage during the Boer
War. Verbal felicity and nimbleness of mind gave him a pre-eminent
Parliamentary position among ministers, much accentuated after the
Cabinet reconstructions of 1902 and 1903. In discussion with him, wrote
Edgar Vincent, one was reminded of a fort surrounded by barbed wire,
with reserve troops ready to succour any threatened point.[98] Balfour
remained all his life a master of the well-conceived retort. Asked by Lady
Brooke why he had written *A Defence of Philosophic Doubt* he replied,
'Because I could not be bothered to make up my mind about the great
problems that worry the learned professors.' Many years later, she was still
asking herself whether he had really meant it.[99] Curzon, who had been on
close terms for nearly twenty years with Balfour, wrote on his succession:

> He has all the intellectual powers and moral character of a great Prime
> Minister. If only he could purge himself of his intellectual nonchalance and
> philosophical indifference to the mundane aspects of political life, he may
> become so.[100]

Curzon sent a letter of warm congratulation and support, adding, no
doubt with tongue in cheek, that he hoped Balfour might assert a real
control over the Cabinet.[101] This Balfour was no more likely to do, except
at fitful intervals, than his uncle. Here was a real weakness, of which the
effects became glaringly apparent in the next three years. Into some areas
of the government's work, and especially in education and defence,
Balfour brought much needed order and decision, notwithstanding a strong
tendency to theorise on an exiguous basis of knowledge; but with the
wearisome grind of co-ordination, keeping the ministers in line, setting
down explicit directions promptly on paper, dealing with a dozen different
subjects each day, Balfour could not or would not cope. Moreover, a Prime
Minister of those times had not the machinery for the efficient discharge of
his task. There was nothing comparable with the Private Office of the later
twentieth century. Balfour employed a private secretary, Jack Sandars, who
on certain occasions behaved, and was treated, as the equal of a minister.
No proper facilities existed for the planning of the parliamentary timetable

and the drafting and expert scrutiny of bills. In this government, which passed much constructive legislation, an undue burden fell upon a Prime Minister who had to shoulder much of the parliamentary work, half of whose Cabinet colleagues were in the Lords, and whose administration never recovered from the resignations of 1903.

With these features of the system were coupled the characteristics of a man prone to frequent bouts of influenza and other illness, tired after many years in high office and temperamentally averse from rows, unpleasantness and self-assertion. It was said with truth that he could 'never bring himself to dip his hands into dirty and troubled waters'. Balfour hesitated to interfere with his colleagues' work, or even to indicate that they were going astray. Inscrutability was carried to the point where he would leave an interlocutor under the false impression that they were agreed.[102] Colleagues were driven almost to distraction by the problems of inducing him to retain detailed information. 'By the time the debate comes on' wrote Arnold-Foster sadly, 'all the facts which I took so much trouble to explain will have faded away from A. J. B.'s memory, and nothing will remain but the purely fancy picture which he has evolved out of his own consciousness, and from a variety of tags of conversation, scraps of speeches and mis-applied general propositions, which are the materials with which he works.'[103]

The Cabinet appointments of 1902 were unremarkable. Beach's place was filled by C. T. Ritchie. Austen Chamberlain and George Wyndham came in, while Gerald Balfour moved, with no apparent qualification, to the Board of Trade. The 'Hotel Cecil Unlimited' appeared to be thriving and upon it Curzon exercised his fondness for doggerel:

> In Trade's keen lists, no alien herald
> His trumpet blows but brother Gerald;
> Foreign Affairs have Cousin Cranborne
> To hint that ne'er was greater man born;
> While Cousin Selborne rules the Fleet,
> Even the sea is 'Arthur's Seat'.[104]

He commented acutely that shifts in the ministries, designed for parliamentary approbation, would not move the people in the least, and predicted a gradual widening of the gap between public and House of Commons opinion:

> Arthur continues to manage and placate the latter while the former is drifting from him.
>
> I do not say that this is his fault or that of the Government. But the country is getting tired of the same men for 7 years. It is after all only human.[105]

At the moment of the old Prime Minister's departure, Curzon, feeling his greatness with renewed force, sent a charming letter of thanks for his influence and example. Salisbury's reply breathes a premonition of gathering perils, of some great change in public affairs

in which the forces which contend for the mastery among us will be differently ranged and balanced. If so it is certainly expedient that younger men should be employed to shape the policy which will no longer depend upon the judgments formed by the experience of past times...The large aggregations of human forces which lie around our Empire seem to draw more closely together, and to assume almost unconsciously a more and more aggressive aspect. Their junction, in menacing and dangerous manner, may be deferred for many years—or may be precipitated with little notice at any moment. It is fortunate for us that the satraps of the Empire were never more conspicuous for intelligence and force than they are now—yourself, Cromer, Milner, Kitchener. I earnestly hope that your tenure of power will continue in the path of success in which it has begun. I have watched your administrative career with deep sympathy and admiration: and have fully recognised the promise of a brilliant future...[106]

NINE

Reforms

BELIEVING THAT the great questions had been shirked for twenty years and more, and determined upon a reappraisal of India's needs, Curzon soon decided that the machine itself must first be scrutinised. The vastness of the country, the changes of personnel, the complexities of caste and custom, the volume of complicated subjects, all made accurate records essential. But by the end of the nineteenth century, it seemed that the tyranny of the pen had triumphed over the enterprise and originality which Curzon and Hamilton wished to foster. Everywhere, tranquil procrastination prevailed. Some members of the Viceroy's council, it transpired, hardly set foot in their offices, but conducted the business from home by written minutes. The Foreign Department occupied a building which resembled a dilapidated villa in a run-down London suburb. 'In the Public Library I found pigeons flying about and dropping their dirt on the table and chairs, because no one would think of arresting so well-established and consecrated a habit.'[1]

One who knew him said 'Curzon will hustle you Secretaries'. 'Oh no,' replied an official, 'he will be paper-logged in three months.'[2] Though the new Viceroy asked for details and grappled with subjects long dormant, his rapid return of files became a by-word. But what files! Often the stack of papers on a single subject would be a foot high, and one matter which soon came up had been under consideration for sixty years. It was, Curzon reported, like living in a kind of literary bedlam, in which all the gentlemen stated 'their worthless views at equal length'. Explicit instructions were issued, transgressions of the rules queried, orders wired hither and thither: 'I am prodding up the animal with most vigorous and unexpected digs, and it gambols plaintively under the novel spur. Nothing has been done hitherto under six months. When I suggest six weeks, the attitude is one of pained surprise; if six days, one of pathetic protest; if six hours, one of stupefied resignation.'[3]

The first task, and no light one, was to make officials feel that their work would be carefully overseen. Curzon's decisions were accompanied by an explanation, and often by a joke, a protest against sloth or a commendation of zeal. A few examples, taken from dozens, will illustrate the technique and the problem. The question whether turret-ships and floating defences at Bombay should be considered permanent had been most earnestly debated for two years when Curzon minuted:

> I regard the whole case as one of a storm in a tea-cup, which has raged with an intensity proportionate to its minute dimensions and confined surroundings. I have read through the past notes. Everybody seems to have said the same thing —over and over again—very well—for nearly two years. There does not seem to be any cause why I should repeat it. The turret-ships are there. It is unlikely that they would be taken away in an emergency. If it seemed probable, the Viceroy could veto the removal. In these circumstances they clearly should be regarded as a part of the permanent defences of Bombay.[4]

And on another file:

> It is difficult for me to form an opinion as to the value of this branch. The only evidence that I see of its activity is a weekly publication, which appears to me to be chiefly concerned with reporting the movements of Mr *** and other obscure persons, who are always being shadowed, but who, as far as I can make out, never do anything.[5]

When an enormous heap of papers arrived, the Viceroy noted that it reminded him of the music-hall song:

> Waltz me round once again, Willie,
> Waltz me around and around,
> Waltz me round once again, Willie,
> Don't let my feet touch the ground.

To the representation that critical notes, seen by Indian clerks, offended and lowered the standing of British officials, Curzon merely replied 'Good heavens, they should have seen the way Lord Salisbury used to cut my work to pieces.' He does not seem to have taken much notice. After a proposed reduction of telegraph rates had failed to materialise, the department found on the file, in the Viceregal red ink, a long list of suggestions prefaced by a minute: 'As it is more than 2¾ years since I first took up this matter, and as we are all getting old and would probably like to do something before we die, I propose... '[6]

The bureaucracy had indeed invented not only a procedure but a language of its own. An index became a 'précis docket', notes 'keep-withs'. 'Flat system', 'keyword', 'major head' and other recondite terms were freely bandied about and decisions issued in a manner which provoked a celebrated protest: 'Must we really adhere to these antedeluvian absurdities of 'Observation', 'Resolution', 'Order?' One might as well describe a guest at a State Ball as 'Coat, Waistcoat, Trousers'.[7]

Most official telegrams or despatches would be accompanied by demi-official or private letters enforcing the views of the originator. By Curzon's time, when junior officials had taken to noting at length, these commentaries often exceeded the documents in volume by three or four to one. District Officers all over the continent produced thousands of pages of statistics and reports. No system excelled this for the marshalling of accurate facts or for the repression of independent thought. It resembled, Curzon thought, a gigantic quagmire 'into which every question that comes along either sinks or is sucked down; and, unless you stick a peg with a label over the spot at which it disappeared, and, from time to time, go round and dig out the relics, you will never see anything of them again'.[8]

Exceptionally for a politician, Curzon felt a deep and detailed interest in the mechanics of office-work. Already possessing a detailed knowledge of the Foreign Office's methods, he sent to other departments for information. Within six months of arrival he was ready to criticise every aspect of the Indian system. A classic minute of 24 May, 1899, drew attention to its pervasive influence, which had taken so sure a grip on the faculties of the victims that reforms had been abandoned. The last effort had been made five years earlier, when the growing files on the need to reduce the size of files had ambled peaceably around the departments for a twelvemonth. Curzon dismissed the notion that juniors must show their mettle by inditing note upon note. As Under-Secretary to Lord Salisbury, he had often read in a day fifty or a hundred despatches: 'Had each paper carried upon its back, like a snail, its entire official history and tenement, a regiment of porters would have been required to carry ... the preposterous burden.'

He protested against superfluous minuting, whereby the original point became overlaid and then, unless disturbed, lay mummified until stumbled across by some later generation. When departments differed, they would act as if each inhabited a separate planet, firing off its missives to another world, although a few minutes' talk would settle the issue. The promotion of a Colonel, debated for fifteen months in the bureaux, had amassed no less than fifty-three pages of printed notes by the time it reached the Viceroy:

> When once the Departments have, so to speak, got their flannels on, and the game has begun, they appear to lose sight of all other considerations but that of keeping up the ball or the shuttlecock (and as a rule, the latter is the fairer parellel) over the net, while the faithful official marker calls out the strokes, and records them (in print) for the admiration of later ages. I had a case the other

day, in which the Secretary of State had, in June, 1897, invited the Government
of India to express an opinion as to a change in the marking of their confidential
maps. From that date until May, 1899, the rally was heroically sustained, and
might, but for an accident, have gone on till the crack of doom. Can we not in
our departments abandon this idiotic system, and treat each other as if we were
human beings?[9]

Curzon instituted the needful reforms in the Foreign Department, and
invited his colleagues to do likewise in their offices. After three months'
trial, he sent to each for files. The bulk of printed and written material had
decreased markedly. An expurgated copy of his minute, with the new
rules, then went to the local administrations; all replied favourably except
the government of Madras, which avowed that the proposed reforms were
unnecessary there, 'as the evils which they are intended to remove do not
exist'. This statement, Curzon remarked, would anyway have strained his
credulity; even had the Governor not admitted in private that the minute
had put a finger on some sore spots, it would be hard to believe 'that there
should be found in Madras or anywhere else one Aristides in a sinful
generation'.

When Havelock could recommend only patience and time, he met the
retort that Viceroys and Governors were too short-lived to adopt such
remedies with much hope of success.[10] Curzon knew that in this matter
argument from the general to the particular meant nothing. After examination of every incoming paper, those found useless were abolished at once.
The rest were to be curtailed in length. The 18,000 pages of reports printed
each year came down to 8,600, and statistics from 35,000 to 20,000.

* * * *

Between the political border with Afghanistan and the frontier up to which
the regular system of Indian government prevailed lay a region of nearly
25,000 square miles. This mountainous territory, inhabited by perhaps a
million and a half tribesmen, extending in a crescent from Beluchistan to
the Pamirs, was penetrated by fingers and tentacles of British power in the
vital passes and valleys: the Khyber, Kurram, Tochi and Gomal. The
North-West frontier had simmered and overboiled ever since the Company
had first annexed the Punjab and the areas west of the Indus, peopled largely
by Beluchis and Pathans. John and Henry Lawrence made frontier administration their life-work and selected officials of daring and steadfast character,
who were encouraged to travel widely and mingle freely with the tribesmen. Slowly the work of such officers became overlaid with that welter of

reports, meetings, memoranda and despatches endemic in every bureaucracy. Knowledge of the frontier and its languages became a less weighty qualification than it once had been. Between 1894 and 1898 there had been thirteen changes, involving four officers, in the tenure of the key post of Commissioner of Peshawar.[11]

In 1897-8, after the outbreak of fanaticism and pillage all along the border, as widespread as it was apparently unexpected, bitter charges of neglect and inefficiency had been levelled at the government of the Punjab, through which the frontier was administered. In Beluchistan, a hierarchical system made relations with the tribes comparatively straightforward. The *maliks*, headmen, held real influence over their fellow tribesmen. Nothing so convenient prevailed amongst the Pathans. Criminals were not surrendered, fines went unpaid and outrages unpunished. The independent doings of Sir Robert Sandeman in Beluchistan had frequently caused heartburnings at Lahore and Simla; but as Curzon remarked, it is of no use to have a Warden of the Marches unless you give him a free hand. Sandeman's policy had been one 'not of spasmodic and retributive interference, but of steady and unfaltering conciliation ... *parcere subjectis pacisque imponere morem*, far more than *debellare superbos*, was his motto'.[12]

That had been the line which Curzon recommended to the House in February, 1898. Just before then, while the frontier was still ablaze, Lord George Hamilton had ordered that unnecessary interference with the tribes must be eschewed. He told the Prime Minister of his ripening conviction that the Punjab government was 'quite unsuited to the conduct of frontier policy' and had taken Khyber affairs out of their hands.[13] In the latter part of July, he was preparing a despatch for the Cabinet's approval. Parts were recast after consultation with Curzon. Hamilton proposed a dual responsibility for the Commissioner of Peshawar, who would be appointed by and answerable to the central government for frontier affairs, but to the Punjab on other matters.

The Cabinet too favoured a transfer of responsibility, so as to avoid what Salisbury termed 'the red tape and paper administration' of the Punjab. Detailed arrangements would be left to the new Viceroy, who promised an early visit to the frontier.[14] This was certain to be no mean task. The tribes, the most wayward and inflammable in the world, had bought or stolen many modern weapons and enjoyed enviable opportunities for plunder and smart retreat to the hills. All the same, Curzon, in his wanderings along the frontier, had come to appreciate their light-hearted temperament, manliness, passion for independence and love of a well-delivered joke.

At root, the question resolved itself to this: could a system be devised

8

which, while preventing a recurrence of the recent outbreak, would allow
the maintenance of an administrative border well behind the political? Or
would it be necessary, in order to remove a liability which might prove
fatal during a military advance through these areas into Afghanistan, to
attempt annexation? Salisbury, writing just before the explosion of 1897,
seemed to think the case hopeless:

> ... mountaineer neighbours force you to fight them: and you will get tired of
> the annoyance in the long run and strike a strong blow to have done with it.
> It is quite right to avoid a forward policy if you can, but you cannot. If we could
> only take our line and stick to it. But our policy is Jingo and penitence in altern-
> ate doses. Unluckily the penitence usually coincides with a period of exhaustion
> on the part of our opponents; so that we miss our chance of settling the trouble
> once for all.[15]

Elgin's government had more or less committed themselves to the
construction of fortifications and the maintenance of garrisons beyond the
administrative border. On taking over, Curzon was confronted with
copious files, endowed with contradictory opinions; but in this matter he
had the advantage of arguing with the experts on even terms. A garrison of
regulars at the upper end of the Khyber, he ruled at once, would provide a
provocation to the Amir and the tribes. A railway through the pass would
present them with a hostage. To keep regular troops in such territory must
entail increased interference.[16] After a tour on the frontier, and prolonged
conferences with the officers, Curzon laid it down that garrisons must not
be locked up in costly forts far from base 'where the troops themselves are
practically lost to the offensive strength of India, and in time of emergency,
would probably require additional forces to be detached from the Indian
army to their assistance.'[17]

Along the marches, the method varying with the locality and nature of
the tribal organisation, forces were raised from the tribes as levies, militia or
police. By this means the government not only enhanced its own troops'
tactical mobility, but also escaped the reproach or odium of reverses.
Moreover, the tribesmen would become attached to the authority that paid
them. At safe bases on or near the administrative frontier columns were to
be kept ready. These proposals were quickly agreed in London.[18] Curzon
realised that had he been unfamiliar with the ground, he could not have
resisted his military advisers, whose elaborate frontier schemes seemed to
him extravagant and unsound. With some justice, Clinton Dawkins told
Salisbury during the Boer War that Curzon's swiftness and decision had
saved the Empire the additional strain of frontier troubles which would
have followed if the policy had not been recast.[19]

In the spring of 1900 Curzon visited the frontier again. At Quetta the Beluch Sirdars attended a durbar. As the name of each was called, he rose, touched his breast with a huge carved sword and extended it to be touched by the Queen-Emperor's representative, uttering a loud 'salaam'. Curzon vouchsafed appropriate words of praise or warning. All along the border such ceremonies were held. In his element, he exulted to Brodrick:

> I am never so happy as when on the Frontier. I know these men and how to handle them. They are brave as lions, wild as cats, docile as children. You have to be very frank, very conciliatory, very firm, very generous, very fearless.
>
> It is with a sense of pride that one receives the honest homage of these magnificent Samsons, gigantic, bearded, instinct with loyalty, often stained with crime.[20]

The next stage was to determine through which agency the frontier policy should be executed. Each of the officers interviewed in 1899 preferred, to Curzon's surprise, a province separate from the Punjab. He too had no doubt that the administration must come directly under the government of India. The existing system was 'like handing over the custody of the National Gallery—on the score of propinquity—to the householders of Trafalgar Square'.

This confirmed the opinion at which the Cabinet had arrived two years before; but could hardly be welcome to the Lieut-Governor of the Punjab, Sir Mackworth Young. Curzon had long since been told by Elgin that any decision would be loyally accepted by the Punjab government.[21] Though frontier questions formed the constant preoccupation of the Foreign Department, the Viceroy could not issue an order except through the Punjab government or make most of the appointments. The Chief Secretary, principal adviser of the Lieut-Governor, was selected without reference to the Viceroy.

Walter Lawrence, who knew the Punjab, urged that the indictment should be sufficient only to settle the issue convincingly, but Curzon replied that a statesman ought never to omit an argument.[22] In a long minute, he denied the suspicion entertained in London that a separate province would mean a more aggressive policy,[23] pointing to the forty frontier expeditions mounted in fifty years of control from Lahore. Nor would it lead to greater centralisation, for the old system represented 'centralisation in a most aggravated and pernicious form. What more mischievous evidence of centralisation could be afforded than the ladder of compulsory and dilatory reference ... whose foot is across the frontier but whose head is at Simla or Lahore?' And again: 'Labour without responsibility is the experience of the Local Government; responsibility without control is that of the Government of India.'

Curzon proposed a new frontier province, the officers being given a larger measure of authority. Questions which had to be decided at a higher level would go directly to the Foreign Department.[24] Curzon asked whether he should now consult Sir M. Young, with the certain risk of a rejoinder. Hamilton advised against it, for members of the India Council would otherwise begin to receive letters from India. They could be over-ridden in this matter by the Cabinet, but must not be unduly irritated, or they might later refuse funds for increased outgoings.[25] At his request, Curzon had been supplying almost weekly fresh examples of the Punjab's inability to manage the frontier:

> My dear George, [runs one of these letters] I cannot work a Government under this system. I cannot spend hours in wordy argument with my Lieu-tenant-Governors as to the exact meaning, purport, scope, object, character, possible limitations, conceivable results of each petty aspect of my frontier policy. If they deliberately refuse to understand it, and haggle and boggle about carrying it out, I must get some fairly intelligent officer who will understand what I mean and do what I say.[26]

The decision was promptly pushed through by Hamilton. Curzon wrote to Sir M. Young and received an acknowledgment of his courtesy. Arrangements for the transfer of power began, the Punjab officers, from the Lieut-Governor downwards, feeling sore at the strong criticism of their methods. One member resigned in a flourish of publicity. In the spring of 1901, when both were at Simla, Curzon hoped after a friendly talk with Sir Mackworth that the wound was now healed. But shortly afterwards the Governor made a tart public speech. He then sent a handsome apology, which Curzon accepted, and an offer to publish it, which was refused. Having heard that Lady Young was speaking about him with much bitterness, and fearing hasty words and embarrassment, the Viceroy decided that it would be better not to meet socially in Simla. At one stage, Sir M. Young spoke of an action for libel, but it came to nothing. Presently he retired.[27]

Since the outbreaks of 1897–8, the frontier had remained peaceable, except for the activities of an especially contumacious tribe, the Mahsud Waziris. Having no confidence in ponderous, full-dress expeditions, Curzon resorted to a blockade; but the Mahsuds, who had secured by one means or another a large supply of rifles, made no haste to yield. The first important act of the newly-appointed Chief Commissioner of the Frontier Province was to recommend more vigorous methods. Curzon agreed in part. The blockade was maintained while flying columns of five hundred or less pushed forward to penetrate the heart of the Mahsuds' country. Soon they surrendered, paid the balance of the fine, gave up the rifles, and acknowledged tribal responsibility for future transgressions.

With this good augury, Curzon visited the new province in the spring of 1902. At Peshawar, for the first time, a Viceroy addressed the notables of the frontier with ceremony, simplicity and brutal frankness: 'You are the keepers of your own house. We are ready enough to leave you in possession. But if you dart out from behind the shelter of the door to harass and pillage and slay, then you must not be surprised if we return quickly and batter the door in.'

This was an occasion after Curzon's heart, one of those personal conferences to which he attached such value, with

> three thousand of the most unmitigated blackguards in the world—bearded faces, wild eyes, dirty clothes—all squatting on the ground in a semi-circle, absolutely silent and motionless, save when at intervals one or another rose from his place, retired from the ring to perform his evening prayer and then returned and seated himself again.[28]

As a mark of confidence in the new arrangements, Curzon and his wife traversed the Khyber and slept at Lundi Kotal, guarded exclusively by the Afridi militia, surrounded by men of whom every other one was a cut-throat or villain, in territory so lately the scene of violent revolt. The first Chief Commissioner of the North-West Frontier Province was that Colonel Deane who, said Mr Churchill, was unpopular with the soldiers because he managed to prevent skirmishes.[29] Of the 38,000 square miles in his territory, only 13,000 lay within the administrative line. Some outstanding young officers, whose careers Curzon followed with intense interest, made good use of the latitude they were now allowed in their relations with the tribes. Among them Major Roos-Keppel, who compiled the standard manual of the Pushtu language, became a by-word for straightforward and direct dealing.

Though the success of this policy was later denied, and though Deane himself charged that Curzon gave insufficient support when the frontier was troubled,[30] the facts speak for themselves. That the Afridis and others would pursue their blood-feuds with undiminished ferocity was expected by everyone, and so they did; but the new administration brought a greater degree of peace, a continuous reduction in violent crime and marked progress in public works, revenue and irrigation. Curzon, who fought a long and largely successful battle against plans for large fortifications, strategic railways and the annexation of land across the administrative border, was the first Viceroy for a quarter of a century who did not have to authorise a major expedition. The number of regulars beyond that border fell from 10,200 to 5,000, and the total cost of military movements on the North West frontier from £4,584,000 in 1894–8 to £248,000 in the seven years 1899–1905.

★ ★ ★ ★

No country suffers more cruel extremes of climate than India. In one year, a rainfall of 905 inches was recorded at Cherrapunji, where Kitchener insisted on building a huge and useless barracks. The average there was about 460 inches; in upper Sind, about 3 inches. In addition to the hazards of nature, plague, brought by rats from Hongkong in 1896, is thought to have killed by 1905 some 8,000,000 Indians. Rigorous remedies were attempted, but not for long in face of indifference or religious objection. This scourge was not lifted in Curzon's time, though moderately effective vaccines were developed.

The famine of 1897 overshadowed the last years of Elgin's Viceroyalty. Luckily, a commission had reported promptly; and in another respect, India was the better endowed with every passing year, for the extension of railways provided the means to bring succour speedily. However, when the rains failed in the summer of 1899 the Central Provinces, some parts of Rajputana, central India and the south-east Punjab had not recovered from the earlier visitation. This second drought extended even into the garden of India, Gujerat and Kathiawar, where abundance had been so long enjoyed that the people were unprepared and the government poorly equipped. After mid-June, no rain fell in an area of 600,000 square miles. The grass, the flowers, the crops withered away.

In order to see all the arrangements for himself and to encourage the people and officers, Curzon toured the relief works and camps. His wife, at Simla, read the newspapers with dread. 'I have been absolutely miserable over the accounts of your doings in hospitals, and Colonel Fenn [the Viceroy's doctor] shares my horror and anxiety. As you listen to no human voice of reason I must turn into a fatalist.'[31]

By the end of that year, 1899, three and a half million souls were receiving relief, more than double any figure yet recorded in the history of British rule. In the following months a continuous stream of heart-rending reports of destitution, emaciation and starvation flowed in. A fund was opened. The Queen, telegraphing frequently for the latest news, sent £1,000. The

Viceroy increased his own contribution to the same figure, in order to stimulate Indian generosity; for many of the people were subsisting upon berries, fruit and bark, while the desperate devoured charred human remains from pyres.

Curzon's dissatisfaction with the performance of the Bombay Government has already been noticed. In one district, the death-rate rose steadily from 1·75 per thousand in September, 1899, to 24·0 in May, 1900. Over the desolated areas in general, the death-rate had more than doubled; pleas of the local authorities in Gujerat for early remission of land revenues had been overridden. The Viceroy enjoined liberality. By the latter part of July, 1900, when the monsoon seemed to have failed again, the situation had become critical. India could hardly expect to cope from her own resources and Curzon thought that he would probably have to ask for large help from the Treasury. The responses of the Cabinet did not excite enthusiasm: 'India is for the most part governed by sentiment; and all Balfour's assurances that in the last resort Great Britain would come to our aid have availed little in contrast with the patent fact that so far she has done nothing.'[32]

In that parching summer, the surviving people and animals were walking skeletons. Corpses lay in the streets and fields. At Lawrence's suggestion, Curzon decided to visit the regions most horribly afflicted. All the usual accompaniments of ceremonies, ADCs and Viceregal paraphernalia were dispensed with. Certain deficiencies stood out at once. Many of the hospital assistants could not manage their work. One hospital, with 262 patients, was found to be in the charge of a single Indian. 'I have not a doubt about it' Curzon wrote, 'that scores of the inmates perished daily because of his inability to pay any attention to them.' Often the relief works, hurriedly set up, proved valueless. The Indian municipal authorities, with honourable exceptions, stood by with a passive and depressing indifference. Hindus, kind in many ways 'such as saving the lives of pigeons, and peacocks, and monkeys', were frequently callous about human suffering, upon which they looked with resignation. At another hospital, Lawrence began to talk with a patient. An astonished English official exclaimed, 'This is my gardener.' The gardener said that although enjoying excellent health, he was occupying the bed to oblige the City Fathers.[33]

By some miraculous chance, much remarked in the Indian press, the tour coincided with the belated breaking of the monsoon. As the sun had risen and set, day after day, in the hot and copper sky, every man's gaze had turned longingly to the horizon for a sight of the cloud that would presage the monsoon. At the moment of promise and refreshment, the people rushed out, soaked in an instant by the torrent but thankful for it. After that the downpour fell regularly. By night, thunderstorms raged and the purple lightning crackled. Salvation had come.

Curzon's visits, Lawrence noted privately, had an excellent effect, 'but he will notice trifling defects and his remarks perturb and confuse the overworked officials'.[34] No doubt this was true, and regrettable, but Curzon did not fail to pay public tribute a few weeks later to the officers of the ICS and Army. He pressed on the Governors the need to be lenient with revenue assessments and applauded the generosity with which North-cote, out of his own pocket, helped to save the magnificent breed of Gujerat cattle from extinction.

The breaking of the monsoon did not mean the end of these troubles, but only the end of the beginning. Those who had been fed during the winter and spring had to be got back to their homes and set up again. In the wake of famine stalked cholera, dysentery and fever, and then, after the rains, malaria, mowing down those who had barely scraped through. It had been a crop failure, followed by a dearth of fodder and therefore by the death of cattle in millions. The whole working capital of many cultivators had gone. At one time in that summer of 1900, some six million Indians were receiving relief. No state anywhere had ever shouldered such a burden. The wheat crop fell by a half, the cotton crop by more and the oilseed crop by more still. The direct loss to cultivators in the Bombay Presidency alone totalled £30m. and elsewhere another £20m. In relief and remitted revenue, the government of India spent some £10m. The area most directly hit contained a population of sixty millions, more than half of whom lived in Native States. Yet in British India alone, where the administrations were generally better equipped, three quarters of a million had died.

Curzon accepted the duty to enquire conscientiously into charges that excessive taxes contributed largely to such disasters; but although the general movement of revenue assessments had been downwards, the incidence of famine had increased. In the latest visitation, the most highly assessed regions, with the exception of Gujerat, had not been the most grievously afflicted. In relation to the fickleness of the climate, land revenue became a relatively minor factor. In the Central Provinces, the agricultural classes had lost between 1894 and 1900 produce worth £26m., equal to the land revenue for fifty years. Since 1896, the state itself had spent there, on famine relief alone, the equivalent of seven years' land revenue. Even though the abolition of that tax, which brought in a quarter of the budget, would not prevent famine, there were evidently some important lessons to be learned. After a commission had criticised unwillingness to remit land revenue during the famine, a new code, allowing district officers to suspend its collection, and embodying numerous other improvements, was passed.

The grant for irrigation had already been increased by thirty per cent since 1898 and once the worst of the famine was over, Curzon determined that a swift survey of the whole sub-continent must be made. He secured as president Sir Colin Scott-Moncrieff, who knew and loved India, sympathised with the poor and had a fine record as an engineer. In their conversations, the Viceroy asked that purely financial considerations should not dominate. After all, famine cost India dearly, in loss of production, works of relief, death and disease. The criterion should be the extent of protection, not the return on capital. The report, completed in 1903, proposed a programme for every province that could benefit from irrigation in the next twenty years. It would cost some £30m, provide work for a labour-force of 300,000 during the better part of each year, and irrigate another 6,500,000 acres. 'More interesting than a novel' said Curzon. In that shadowy realm of financially unprofitable works, to which he had paid much attention in framing the terms of reference, the Commission's best work was done. Especially in the Central Provinces, United Provinces and the Deccan, work began on projects which could not pay their way.[35]

No feature of British rule appealed more forcibly to Curzon's imagination than this alleviation of suffering by the transformation of the land. In 1899, when he saw the newly-built Chenab Canal in the Punjab, it irrigated a million acres. By 1905, that area had been doubled, at a cost of only £500,000. What had been a forsaken waste had become a granary supporting a million cultivators. The Jhelum Canal was extended to irrigate 750,000 acres, and the great group of works known as the Upper Chenab, Upper Jhelum and Lower Bari Doab canals was authorised before Curzon left, at a cost of £5m., to add two million acres of irrigated land and produce a return of no less than ten per cent. The Scott–Moncrieff report proved to be the springboard for a vast extension of irrigation in every part of India. Within a few years capital spending on this essential element of economic strength had doubled.

An efficient railway system was of importance to India for several reasons: as the best guard against famine, since the difficulty arose in most instances not from a general dearth of food but from inability to place it at the point of shortage in sufficient quantities; as the means of concentrating and supplying the armies for frontier campaigns and, perhaps, for war in Afghanistan; as the only means of rapid transit over huge distances; and, most important of all, as the precondition of economic development. Indian railways had been built up by a mixture of agencies, sometimes by private enterprise, sometimes through State control and construction.

The hand of India's dual system of government lay heavy on railway development. Substantial obstacles had to be surmounted in India, for the Public Works Department appeared to fight out the rival claims of railway companies as if they were theological dogmas.[36] Yet building was still going forward, and if the government could put its own house in order, and then prevail upon the India Office to be reasonable, there was still a hope of coherence. The railways were beginning to show a general return on capital of five per cent or even more.

As a broad aim, Curzon wished to replace the prevailing patchwork by complete state control, the working of the lines being left to private companies. Before large loans could be raised, a plan for the whole continent must be mapped out, to prepare which he asked Lord George for a really good railway manager from home.[37] The choice fell upon Mr Thomas Robertson, who duly arrived and began to travel. After a few talks, the Viceroy realised that Robertson could neither understand the Indian constitution nor express himself on paper. Eventually he submitted a collection of bald and chiefly uncorroborated dicta, followed by a 'report', which looked little better, or longer, than the notes.

To the sweeping condemnation of Indian railway management Curzon took no objection. But there was little to show in the report for nearly eighteen months' investigation and £11,500 of India's money. Pausing only to cancel Robertson's passage home, he refused to accept the report and insisted on something fuller. There was an able man in the Public Works Department. The Viceroy provided a long table of criticisms and introduced him to Robertson. Their revised version bore a remarkable resemblance to certain minutes already recorded by the Public Works man. 'The voice is the voice of Jacob,' Curzon noted, 'but Esau's hands protrude.' This report was generally accepted as a convincing indictment, a conclusion naturally resented in India but which he thought must be accepted: 'You cannot send for a doctor to prescribe for you from a distance of 6,000 miles, pay him an unprecedented fee, and then, when he has stethoscoped you from head to foot and said that you are utterly rotten, altogether reject his advice. Moreover, there is a great deal in this advice that is very shrewd and sound... '[38]

The central proposal of the report, a Railway Board detached from the Public Works Department, Curzon heartily approved. He asked Brodrick, just installed at the India Office, to permit some surrender of power in

London. It was never easy to persuade British investors to put money into India, least of all into railways. As Godley had often confessed, that fact owed a good deal to the methods of the Railway authorities at the India Office. 'Were ... anyone,' Curzon wrote to the Secretary of State, 'who desires to apply science to business, to seek an illustration of a form of railway enterprise calculated to impede enterprise at every turn, he could hardly find a better example than that over which we jointly preside.'[39]

This situation was a good deal eased by the acceptance of Robertson's report. It provided the opportunity for Curzon to do as he had long wished and reallocate work among the members of his minuscule Council. A new Department of Industry and Commerce was set up, under which a Board of three superintended the railway system of India. The extent of the network increased from 22,040 miles in 1899 to more than 28,000 by 1905.

★ ★ ★ ★

Even in the early years of the Viceroyalty, many friends spoke of the Foreign Office, and of 10 Downing Street to follow, in terms of certain anticipation. However, Lord Lansdowne seemed to be well established, and Balfour made no offers. Anxious to root his reforms deeply, Curzon had no desire to leave, despite a good deal of criticism from an impulsive Indian press. He refused a safe seat in 1902. In that summer, when he complained so severely of the India Council's attitude, there was indeed a prospect of his resignation. Lawrence, then at home, detected among the politicians envy of Curzon and a desire that he should not come back to London.[40] The uncertain future of the government also clouded the issue, as did the tiresome legal difficulty that a Viceroy or C-in-C could not leave India, for however short a period, and retain his office. There could be no personal consultation, although the journey from Bombay to London took but seventeen days. 'Communicating with you through a Secretary of State' said George Wyndham justly, 'is like talking through a stack of mattresses.'[41]

As early as 1901, Curzon had begun to think of an extension;[42] and in February, 1903, he explained to the Prime Minister that if the Cabinet desired he would be willing to stay on and see through more reforms, especially in irrigation, the police, railways and universities. A new Viceroy, knowing nothing of India, could not carry all this. Whereas at home Parliamentary elections turned upon promises and programmes and the House clamoured for new ventures, in India there existed no a priori appetite for reform. Many interests and individuals might almost be said to be banded together to prevent it. 'It requires an initiative, a control and almost an autocracy at the top, to drive anything through.' If reappointed, he would want four or five months' leave in 1904.[43]

Hamilton and Balfour agreed that there were strong reasons for an extension, provided Curzon would fall in with the Cabinet's Asian policy.[44] The King and various ministers did not want so long an interval in 1904. Balfour, conveying this, paid a graceful tribute to Curzon's work and wrote of 'your plan' and 'your suggestion'. 'I only offered,' Curzon replied, 'in what I conceived to be the public interest, to stay on, should the government desire me to do so. Otherwise I would strongly prefer to consult my own health and interests by returning home.' He refused point-blank to accept six or eight weeks' holiday after five and a half years' continuous toil in the Indian climate. Such an offer, he commented to Hamilton, was 'like handing a glass of Kummel to a thirsty miner fresh from the mouth of the pit'.[45]

Brodrick did his best to smooth matters, remarking that Balfour did not realise the strain which Curzon had borne. 'He thinks you and I and G. Wyndham and everyone else could delegate much more than we do, and he thinks we disturb ourselves unduly ... I find but one opinion among our colleagues, viz. of admiration for your work and a desire that you should remain in India as long as you think it necessary to complete it.'

Curzon had explained to King Edward how ill the Indian climate suited his wife. If he returned for a second spell, she and the children must remain for most of that time at home. Balfour, to whom Brodrick had injudiciously passed one of Curzon's private letters, called his behaviour extraordinary and his letters 'still more extraordinary'; and Curzon learned that Brodrick himself, told that the Viceroy needed a good holiday, had banged his fist on the table, crying that nobody was indispensable.[46] However, the difficulties were eventually overcome, Balfour entering a friendly protest against Curzon's last letter. He replied that Balfour had seemed to imply that the Cabinet were doing him a great favour. He did not feel seriously offended when his advice was not taken on foreign affairs. Ambassadors and governors should be a little ahead of their governments, whose tendency was to go slow, 'sometimes unnecessarily slow'. There had been but two occasions when he had felt deeply the attitude of the Cabinet, but he had never contested their right to overrule. On other instances—for instance, the Persian Gulf and Kuwait—the Cabinet had come into line with him: 'Apart from these small differences, my dear Arthur, which are the incidents of public life, I have never been indifferent to the support which has on many occasions been given to me by the Government, and which I am confident that, within reason, I may always be hopeful of receiving from yourself.'[47]

Curzon believed that apart from completing the reforms, he might settle India's relations with Afghanistan and Tibet, and even, perhaps, rescue Southern Persia; for it would be more difficult, so he imagined, to ignore his advice in the fifth year of the Viceroyalty. In health and reputation he would suffer.[48] The extension would mean the loss of Walter Lawrence's encouragement, tact and wisdom. Those Indians who looked for political concessions would be bitterly angry when they realised their failure. The Bengali papers would like his departure, for further reform and redress of grievances would weaken their case:

all my policy and my acts tend to rivet the British rule more firmly on to India and to postpone the longed-for day of emancipation. I am an Imperialist, and Imperialism is fatal to all their hopes. I hold the scales with exasperatingly even hand, but this is the last thing that they desire . . . I have had a period of peace, and this deprives them of their most fertile source of grumbling. One by one I am . . . laying down lines of policy upon all the vexed questions of the day . . . those lines are not their lines . . . for they do not wish for settlement or solution. They prefer the open sore which can always be kept angry by a twist of the goad. . .[49]

In general, Curzon's relations with the Congress party had so far been comparatively friendly. He refused, however, requests for official recognition, believing that the Congress could hardly desire patronage by the government and that its attempt to guide the counsels of 'the respectable reforming party' and simultaneously to keep in with extremists who wanted something very different, must eventually break down.[50] Yet he recognised that Europeans in India were becoming a white caste, with social intercourse in decline and moral and intellectual aloofness more marked. The young officer of the ICS knew and saw less of Indians than before, to the loss of both. The Viceroy himself, working with British officials from day to day, had little to do with prominent Indians except in the Legislative Council and the native states. Ampthill, Viceroy for seven and a half months in 1904, noted that he had not come into personal contact with more than a dozen Indians.[51]

It is not hard to understand how jealously the tiny European community of India scrutinised any measure or pronouncement which might prejudice the standing of the white races and therefore, in the long run, their jobs or even their lives. Curzon's insistence that assaults by Europeans must be punished produced amidst the European community a reaction comparable with that of the soldiers. Especially from Assam, reports of violence and brutality came in growing numbers. European juries almost always refused to convict, while even in the most flagrant cases magistrates there applied standards so flexible that justice became a mockery. 'It is an interesting, though not, I think, an agreeable thing,' Curzon minuted, 'to contrast these sentences upon coolies, who merely threatened an Englishman ... with those recently inflicted upon Englishmen who have thrashed coolies almost to the peril of their lives. The coolies are imprisoned rigorously for one year. The Englishmen are fined R.50 and R.150.'[52]

Miscarriages of justice so gross and obvious, he believed, were not only incompatible with the true character of British rule but also, if unchecked, a serious practical danger, left quite untouched by his predecessors and now, therefore, all the harder to tackle. Curzon realised quickly enough that he would get no help on the spot

> because all Englishmen in India are banded together in a conspiracy to gloze over whatever an Englishman does: and I have no doubt they bitterly resent my attitude. But I see very clearly that we can only continue to hold this country by fairness and justice; and if I am given sufficient health, I vow that when I leave I will, without having abated one jot of our necessary authority or prestige, have placed the relations between the two races on a better basis.[53]

1903 produced a rash of bad cases which, Curzon wrote, 'make my blood boil. But they pass without a murmur from the English Press and with a smile and shrug of the shoulders from nineteen out of twenty Europeans in the country.'[54]

He judged that if the native press (so-called to distinguish it from papers published in India but directed by Europeans) printed with the obvious comments these instances of assault, the British position could be made almost untenable within a few years. Among merchants, planters and business men these racial prejudices seemed to be strongest. On this issue, as on many another, Lord George lent staunch support, holding the same opinion of the European community and having learned that even the most fairminded were not keen to bring their compatriots to justice. He feared that too many young Englishmen used their hands and feet in dealing with Indians, not from malice or sadism, but because it was the fashion: 'it is our business to break the fashion'.[55]

During that last long talk at Hatfield, a few weeks before his death, Salisbury asked how Curzon was faring? Hamilton spoke of the collisions and miscarriages of justice. Salisbury then said, in his most emphatic manner, 'this cannot be allowed to go on: if it is not stopped, it will ultimately upset our rule in India'.[56] When Lord George resigned the India

Office, Curzon asked him to bespeak his successor's support for a just attitude. If it were not given, another Viceroy must be found.[57] But by then the battle was largely won. Before the end of Curzon's term, assaults by Europeans on Indians had become rare.

★ ★ ★ ★

Outside British India, the princes remained responsible for their own administrative methods. Many provided assistance in war—contingents of Imperial Service Troops, hospital ships, donations—besides contributing handsomely to famine relief and good works. Curzon took immense pains to enjoin upon them high standards of duty to their people. The Chiefs' Colleges, at which future rulers were trained, he caused to be remodelled. In the Army, of course, the problems of race and caste were of special importance: a man of one creed could not easily command those of another; a man of low birth must not give orders to a higher-born; a man of high caste must not associate with those of a lower. These were questions which an alien government hardly dared trench upon.

Curzon felt, however, that some embarrassing difficulties must be tackled. In 1897, the Maharajah of Cooch Behar had asked whether his son might compete for Sandhurst and a commission. The regulations said that only European candidates might enter. Both Salisbury and Hamilton spoke at the Cabinet in favour of a change, but the War Office was hostile, and the government of India only lukewarm. The other Ministers believed that British soldiers would not obey Indian officers in a crisis.[58]

On the outbreak of the Boer War, many chiefs asked to join the army in any capacity. Some told the Viceroy of their anxiety that a suitable occupation be found for their sons. In recent years a policy of increasing confidence in native regiments had been adopted. They were being armed with the latest rifles, and it seemed to him contradictory to say that the British could not afford to place additional confidence

> in the one class in this country who are bound to us by every tie of self-interest, if not of loyalty ... I would myself fearlessly lay down the proposition that India cannot be held without the aid (and that the spontaneous aid) of her own sons: that great as is the heroism, and indispensable as is the power of lead of the British officer in battle, these sources of strength will receive reinforcement by no means to be despised in the military comradeship of Indian gentlemen of the highest birth and position, not merely serving themselves, but exercising, as they can hardly fail to exercise, a personal influence upon the Native troops with whom they are associated.

He recommended, as a tentative beginning, a corps of twenty or thirty young men, drawn from the chiefs' colleges, who after attachment to the Viceroy's court would become officers in the Imperial Service Troops or of the Indian Army.[59] This issue had already come before the Cabinet twice in 1900. Again Hamilton and Salisbury had been the only avowed supporters. Godley and the India Council, with one exception, were hostile. 'Why raise this difficult racial controversy? We have got on well enough without any such concession.' At a crucial moment in Cabinet, when Hamilton hoped he had carried his point, the First Lord established a mental connexion between commissions for Indians and the employment of lascars on men-of-war.[60]

'We shall never be really liked in India' wrote the Queen, 'if we keep up this racial feeling, and some day real danger may result from it.' Lord George again proposed that Indians should be allowed to enter Sandhurst, but found all his colleagues, except the old Prime Minister, so hostile that he could not proceed.[61] This posture of superiority, commented Salisbury, 'the damned nigger attitude', was not merely offensive; it was already a political peril, and would become a much more serious one. 'It belongs to that phase of British temper which has led detachment after detachment of British troops into the most obvious ambuscades—mere arrogance.' He lamented the failure to secure military honours and rank for the princes. This was the fashion in which Turkey treated her Christian subjects: 'But we in India are a good deal less numerous than the Turks: and the Indian populations are infinitely more numerous than the Rajahs. It is painful to see the dominant race deliberately going over the abyss.'[62]

Nothing if not pertinacious, Curzon tried again. He argued, with the additional evidence of the princes' contributions to the China force, that the government was accepting in growing measure the military support of the chiefs. 'We have no right to train up a young Indian noble to be an English gentleman up to the age of 18, and then to shut to him all the doors which are open to an Englishman of the same age. We must find him some occupation, some career, suitable to his rank, congenial to his tastes, and free from danger to our own military and political system.'

He proposed that Indians should be able to hold commissions, not in the ranks of the army—'for that would or might involve a black man commanding a white man, which no one will look at'[63]—but on the staffs of General Officers. Britain simply could not go on taking help in men, animals, ships and guns while returning nothing but gratitude and a star. 'India is very tranquil, and is longing for some recognition, other than mere verbal thanks, of her loyalty.'[64]

With evident reluctance, the King assented to a trial of Curzon's plan. Hamilton remarked on the great difference between his views and those of the Queen in this question of colour. The King's sympathy with the princes would not induce him to concede changes which the 'average military man' would dislike.[65] After further haggling, the Imperial Cadet Corps was constituted. The most Curzon could secure at the time was that those who passed the examination should hold a special kind of commission. Kitchener, as C-in-C and subsequently, was absolutely opposed to commissions for Indians;[66] and it was not until 1917 that Curzon, by then a leading figure in the War Cabinet, was able to secure that Indians in future hold their commissions on the same terms as Englishmen, from the sovereign.

★   ★   ★   ★

In the development of India's economic sinews, Curzon and his colleagues had the advantage of a stable currency. The closure of the silver mints to free coinage by Lord Lansdowne produced a slow rise in the value of the rupee. By 1899 it was worth 1s. 4d., the intended figure, at which level it remained. Curzon had realised that some day India would be a great industrial and manufacturing country. One of his first acts was to assist J. N. Tata in the foundation of the steel industry;[67] but India had only five cities with a population of more than 250,000, while two hundred million depended directly upon agriculture and cattle. It would not be difficult to fill a chapter with an account of the work for agriculture begun or expanded between 1899 and 1905. Most significant was the development of scientific research into the improvement of crops and livestock and the prevention of disease. This, like many another aspect of India's development, reduced itself largely to the availability of money and expertise. 'I believe' Curzon wrote in his last year, 'that an enormous future lies before agricultural research, experiment, demonstration, and education in India. Could we start straight away, with institutions and officers, which of course we cannot do, ten times the sum per annum would not be wasted. As it is, let us make a beginning and our seed will one day grow into a mighty tree...'[68]

The rôle of India's government was about to expand, a tendency which could not be resisted but might be guided. For the new world of agricultural and industrial progress, the government, 'which in this country is nearly everything, must be ready with the appliances...'[69] That was possible, but to an extent limited always by resources and often by the alien nature of the government at its highest level. It could and did give more efficient encouragement to business, develop commercial intelligence, raise loans, improve educational opportunity; but it was less easy for a white administration to overcome extreme conservatism or fragmentation of the land into uneconomic units, and impossible to launch a determined attack upon other customs—for instance, the subordination of women, or the Hindus' veneration of the cow, which virtually ruled out good pastoral farming— sanctified by religion.

That the Indian state must intervene in the economic life of the people Curzon did not doubt. He refused to believe either that matters would work out well if left to themselves, or that reform would be so hard that it would be better untouched. 'If successive British Governments' he said when recommending a bill to prevent land from being steadily swallowed up by usurers, 'had contentedly accepted the proposition that social and agrarian evils are not to be rectified by legislation, where I wonder, would the boasted advance of the nineteenth century have been? How would the men in our coal mines, the women and children in our factories, ever have secured the full protection which they now enjoy? Would labour have emancipated itself from the all-powerful control of capital?'[70]

In 1896–7 the deficit had been rather over £1m., rising to £3½m. in the following year. But in 1898–9 a surplus of £2,640,000 appeared; in the next financial year the surplus was much the same, in 1900–1 nearly £1¾m; in 1901–2 very nearly £5m., in 1902–3 just over £3m., in 1903–4 almost £3m. On this modest basis the reforms were grounded and taxes reduced. When we recall that the Finance Member, Sir E. Law, thought the government should not borrow more than £1½m. in India in a good year, we begin to realise the magnitude of the problem facing any Viceroy. Loans in sterling could be raised only with Parliament's sanction. Indian investment was not popular in London, although, as Law ruefully remarked, any amount of capital was forthcoming for railways in Argentina or Mexico. Nevertheless, India's financial position was a sound one. In 1903, her commercial indebtedness amounted to some £320m., her assets at a conservative estimate to £295m.[71] The gross charge on the debt came to only 8d. per head, less than a sixth of that carried by the citizens of any other civilised state; but in relation to a population of 300,000,000 the cash resources were pitifully small. Against that background three other reforms —of the police, of education and of the official attitude towards archaeology —must be set.

A marked rise in crime had been recorded since 1890. Co-operation between the various police forces was often poor. By no means all the officers, and few of the constables, were literate. Low pay brought obvious temptations. That the police did not possess public confidence was only too apparent from the innumerable criticisms of the native press. The prevalent disease of interminable writing had spread. 'I am keeping my eyes and ears open' Curzon wrote in 1899, 'about this great question, the real base of the administrative system on which our none too stable system rests—and I may require to take it up seriously and on a wide scale before long.'[72]

This he did in 1902, by the usual method of a small commission. Believing that the Indian public liked to be consulted, and that valuable information would be gained from public hearings, Curzon resisted Hamilton's pressure to hold the proceedings in secret. The report contained an unvarnished account of the corruption, inefficiency and sloth which characterised much of the police's work. When Lord George refused to allow immediate publication, the Viceroy reminded him that the fears of embarrassment, and of failure to obtain evidence, by public hearings had proved groundless. The police had not become disorganised, nor had the administration broken down. 'I should be most reluctant' Hamilton had then written, 'to attempt to over-rule you and your Council upon any purely Indian question upon which you were unanimous.'[73]

It would be tedious to recount the details of the subsequent controversy. The result of the process was a tightening-up all round; the creation of a directorate of Criminal Intelligence for the whole country; improvements in pay and training; and the creation of a national force, from which the senior provincial posts would be filled, comparable in status with the covenanted service of the ICS.

The promotion of Indian education, the Court of Directors had ruled, must be regarded as a duty of the state. The purpose was to be a diffusion of knowledge of the arts, science and philosophy of Europe. Macaulay had believed that after a few generations nothing would distinguish Indians from Englishmen but the colour of their skins, whereas Curzon thought that object undesirable and the actual state of Indian education deplorable. Decentralisation had been carried to the point where the provinces' work was hardly known to the central authority, or the latter's policy to the provinces. Four in five villages lacked a school; only one Indian boy in four, and one girl in forty, received any education. Of the existing schools, the majority were ill-equipped in personnel and buildings; the vernacular languages and literature were neglected for the pursuit of English; and at the higher levels, the exaggerated value placed upon feats of memory seemed to make a mockery of university education. In 1900, the central and local governments spent on education £1,140,000; fees and endowments provided £1,360,000.

Curzon did his best to inject some order. He minuted severely in 1899 about the contradictory and chaotic tendencies of provincial systems, the tyranny of the universities, the inadequacy of training colleges, the poor system of inspection and especially the slow progress in primary education: 'What on earth can be the good of filling our Colleges and manufacturing B.A's unless we attack, permeate and elevate the vast amorphous, unlettered substratum of the population?'[74]

Somehow the priorities must be altered. Curzon objected to the prevailing fashion of opening technical institutes without the necessary infrastructure. 'To start with Polytechnics, and so on, is like presenting a naked man with a top-hat when what he wants is a pair of trousers.' All the directors of Public Instruction, with the Vice-Chancellors of Calcutta, Madras and Bombay universities, foregathered under Curzon's chairmanship at Simla in September 1901 for a fortnight.[75] He never gave a better exhibition of his methods, powers and failings. The one hundred and fifty resolutions passed by this conference, all drafted by the Viceroy, inaugurated a systematic attempt to repair the results of neglect. Primary education became a leading charge on provincial revenues; decent schools were built, training colleges expanded, teachers' salaries raised; and the coping-stone, the universities, reformed. India then possessed five, modelled on the London University of 1854, examining bodies without tutorial staff or halls of residence. Nearly two hundred colleges, far and wide, were affiliated.

A universities commission reported in 1902 that the education given in many private colleges was cheap and nasty; that examination standards were often absurdly low; and that quality had been sacrificed to quantity. The obstacles to reform showed up plainly, and Curzon realised that violent changes might so frighten the public as to be self-defeating. 'The Bengalis are denouncing me like fury because the Universities Commission has reported in a sense that they dislike. They seem to think that I both dominated the enquiry and wrote the reports! What a strange people. They take the heart out of one.'[76]

Yet in 1900 the pass-rate at the B.A. examination of Calcutta University was nineteen per cent. Only one student out of every nine beginning a university course successfully proceeded to the first degree. Lord George too, lamented the day when the cold breath of Macaulay's rhetoric had passed across Indian education. Anything, he remarked gloomily, would be better than expansion of purely literary education, joy of the Babu and anglicised Brahmin. 'It produces a wholesale mass of discontented individuals who, if they cannot get Government employment, spend their time in abusing the Government which has educated them.'[77]

No measure of Curzon's Viceroyalty until the partition of Bengal aroused more criticism than the Universities Bill of 1903. It was described then, and is often described now, as an attempt to make the universities appendages of the government. Though the size of the swollen senates was reduced, more rigid conditions for affiliation and for the recognition of schools laid down and the examination system revised, the suspicion does not do Curzon justice. 'Higher education' he said, 'ought not to be run either by politicians or by amateurs.'[78] The professionals must play a fuller part; and the powers possessed for fifty years to appoint inspectors and frame regulations were brought into use.

From childhood Curzon had interested himself in buildings, in their architecture, history and decoration. Though Persia boasted some of the finest in Asia, nothing could compare, in his eyes, with the monuments of India. He could never forget that first glimpse of the Taj Mahal 'designed like a palace and finished like a jewel—a snow-white emanation starting from a bed of cypresses and backed by a turquoise sky, pure, perfect and unutterably lovely. One feels the same sensation as in gazing at a beautiful woman, one who has that mixture of loveliness and sadness which is essential to the highest beauty.'

The swelling dome and sharp-pointed minarets, the exquisite symmetry and form, held him entranced 'the singular loveliness of it pouring in waves over my soul and flooding my inner consciousness till the cup of satiety was full, and I had to shut my eyes and pause and think'.[79]

During this and the three other visits preceding his Viceroyalty, Curzon saw many of the mosques, temples, palaces and ruins of India. Some had already crumbled away beyond recovery; others were swiftly succumbing. He brushed aside the argument that a Christian administration had no duty to preserve pagan monuments or the sanctuaries of other faiths:

> Art and beauty, and the reverence that is owing to all that has evoked human genius or has inspired human faith, are independent of creeds, and, in so far as they touch the sphere of religion, are embraced by the common religion of all mankind. Viewed from this standpoint, the rock temple of the Brahmans stands on precisely the same footing as the Buddhist Vihara, and the Mohammedan Musjid as the Christian Cathedral ... What is beautiful, what is historic, what tears the mask off the face of the past, and helps us to read its riddles, and to look it in the eyes—these, and not the dogmas of a combative theology, are the principal criteria to which we must look.[80]

Thus was conceived that feature of the Viceroyalty for which Curzon is most gratefully remembered. The marble fount of Shah Jehan at Agra; the

Pearl Mosque in the Fort at Lahore; Akbar's city of Fatehpur Sikri, abandoned when the water-supply failed; the Palace at Mandalay; the ruins of Bijapur, where had been perpetrated 'feats of vandalism of which only the British people could have been capable'; the Taj Mahal; all these and many another historic building were restored according to an intelligent plan. To the post of Director-General of Archaeology, unfilled since 1889, was appointed Mr John Marshall, still in his twenties and a distinguished scholar of Cambridge, whose enthusiasm transformed the outlook. The beginning was necessarily a slow one. When, in 1902, Curzon pointed out that certain work should be undertaken in Madras, it turned out that the government there had never heard of their own official archaeologist.

By 1905, the expenditure of £120,000 had rescued the most notable remains, nearly half the money being spent at Agra and Fatehpur Sikri. Instead of a scruffy bazaar and dusty courts, a park now stood before the Taj. The mosques, tombs, arcades and lawns had been restored to the state in which they had been left by the masons of Shah Jehan. The discovery of old plans, showing where the water-channels once ran and the flowers bloomed, enabled the gardens to be laid out as they had been. The annual budget for archaeology had risen more than sixfold.

> I call to mind [wrote Marshall], a day spent with him in the Fort at Agra. It was a broiling hot day at the end of April. We had been to the Taj at daybreak and after breakfast went on to the Fort; and there we stayed until sunset, toiling backwards and forwards ... examining plans and estimates, and taking down directions for the further progress of the work.[81]

✶　　✶　　✶　　✶

Labour on this scale necessarily threw a severe strain upon the whole machine. Walter Lawrence, who took a less despairing view of customs long sanctified in India, records Curzon to have been fretful at the delays and red tape. 'Unless the next Viceroy is *ejusdem generis*,' Lawrence observed, 'I think the Departments will win.'[82] A few months later, Lawrence found his master 'worrying about little things ... over-anxious and unsettled.' Curzon complained of too much work, saying that he sometimes felt as if he were going mad. Asked to leave some of it, he replied that he could not trust the departments. His output, Lawrence noted, had distinctly fallen off in volume. This period of depression had been induced by the uncovering of two fine examples of departmental delay.[83] When, a little later, he discovered that an assortment of Secretaries had been adjusting provincial boundaries on paper, Curzon was moved to minute:

Departmentalism is not a moral delinquency. It is an intellectual hiatus – the complete absence of thought or apprehension of anything outside the purely departmental aspects of the matter. For 14 months it never occurred to a single human being in the Departments to mention the matter, or to suggest that it should be mentioned. Round and round, like the diurnal revolution of the earth, went the file, stately, solemn, sure, and slow: and now, in due season, it has completed its orbit, and I am invited to register the concluding stage.[84]

Sometimes Curzon despaired. Lawrence replied that India 'worked all right at half-speed.' The frictions might well have been reduced, though not eliminated, had Curzon exercised his charm more consistently. By the summer of 1901, the conviction had become widespread that he trampled on others' feelings.[85] Nevertheless, the machine carried the strain of a most notable series of reforms. A volume would not convey Curzon's mastery of facts and files, the unsparing attention to detail and the careful watch over the progress of each reform. He did not make the mistake of starting too many hares at once, or of aiming at too small a target. The government of India was infinitely too vast a business, as he remarked, to be run by one man; but it could be, and was, supervised by one man, 'which is the very best form of government, presuming the man to be competent'.[86] Whatever may be thought of that doctrine, which as a practical proposition soon ceased to be feasible in India, Curzon's method of drive from the top, expert enquiry and prompt action justified itself, even though the results were not always proportionate to the effort.

The excessive centralisation of which the India Council so often complained was in part a myth. Curzon always denied the charge that he wished to concentrate authority needlessly at Simla or Calcutta, but insisted that India must have, in such vital matters as education, irrigation, the police, railways and famine, a policy laid down at the centre, the only alternative being fitful effort by local authorities and misuse of meagre resources. When authority could profitably be devolved, there was no hesitation. The greater latitude allowed to frontier officers, the railway commission and the substitution of permanent allocations of money to local governments in place of quinquennial reviews were all important acts of decentralisation. The general intent of these reforms was to emphasise the binding elements in a country where, as he used to say, one region tended to be cut off from another by water-tight bulkheads. No one could escape the significance of regional differences, marked as they were by variations of language, custom, religion and history. Nonetheless, the object of Curzon's work was not to rule by dividing but rather to provide the means of making a policy effective the continent over. Hence the experts – the Chief Inspector of Mines, the Director of Criminal Intelligence, the Sanitary Commissioner, the Directors-General of Archaeology, Education, Irrigation, Commercial Intelligence—whose powers of overseeing introduced some coherence. Hamilton pointed out that even Curzon's phenomenal powers of work were taxed to the utmost; if business continued to increase no successor could sustain the burden. He would reply that once each department had a sensible and feasible programme, the work at the top would become manageable. Admittedly, supervision at the centre had been much tightened, but 'that is not grabbing fresh authority. It is making existing authority a reality'.[87]

Though deeply interested in the smooth working of bureaucracy, Curzon cared more for the excellence of the men. If he provided impulse from the centre, he sought initiative at the periphery. The officials whose work he most warmly approved—Lawrence, H. W. Orange, Sir Denzil Ibbetson, Percy Cox, Deane, Roos-Keppel, Sir Antony MacDonnell, Sir Hugh Barnes—were not nonentities. On the contrary, they were distinguished for independence and mental capacity. 'Pick out the best men; run them to the front; give them their chance. That is the whole secret of administration.' 'I am in favour of sweeping out every gutter, whatever the stink that it causes.' 'Make your face like flint—and never give way merely to avoid a row.' 'State the case fairly: never extenuate: don't hush up or gloze over: take the public into your confidence: and make them feel interested in your success.'[88]

The distinguishing marks of Curzon's contribution were a consciousness of continuity and history; an insistence that undue simplification of complicated problems would produce bad administration; a willingness to override official advice and take the responsibility of standing up to the Cabinet; an orderly system dependent upon the accurate recording of decisions in writing. It did not lie within his nature to know placid contentment, though he often knew happiness and sometimes ecstasy. He was an artist, striving always for the attainable best and demanding in double measure from himself those standards of devotion and excellence which he demanded from others. A member of the ICS, who saw his work at first hand, called Curzon 'the greatest Indian Viceroy of our times—possibly of all times—fearless, creative, ardent, human ... his were great days, and to us who knew and served under him they are a treasured memory'.[89]

TEN

The Durbar

THE CORONATION of King Edward was arranged for the summer of 1902. As in 1887 and 1897, representatives of the British Empire were invited, but in this instance the peculiar circumstances led to a curious arrangement. As there had been no coronation for sixty-five years, no direct precedent existed. So embarrassed was the Treasury by the cost of the Boer War that Hamilton asked India to pay the expenses of her representatives and troops, though the cost would in ordinary times fall upon the British exchequer.[1] Knowing that the war was costing £6m. per month, the Viceroy's Council agreed to pay the passages, and part of the entertainment, of the fifteen representatives of the provinces, five chiefs and one thousand troops whom India was sending to London. There the matter rested until June, 1902, when news arrived that the India Council, without any consultation, had decided that India must also pay for the cost of a great pageant at the India Office and for the entertainment of Indian guests throughout their stay in England.

This was too much. The Boer War had ended on 31 May. It was learned that no guests from other countries were to be treated in the same manner. Curzon minuted that a mischievous precedent would be set if India made no protest.[2] He had already told Hamilton by private letter that now the peace of Vereeniging had removed the cause of his Council's assent, India should not be made to pay. This incident arose only a few weeks after the decision about extra pay for British soldiers, and Godley told Curzon privately that he was glad a protest had been made against burdens laid upon India. To him, some of the things that had been done appeared quite indefensible. The cost of the entertainment at the India Office (£7,000) was out of all proportion to India's interest in the English celebration of the coronation.[3] India was already pledged to her own magnificent festivities. At this stage Curzon had received no hint that the India Office would ask, or receive, any concession from the Treasury. A strong official letter of protest was accordingly sent on 10 July, 1902. The Indian press had not forgotten the famous ball given many years before, at India's expense, to the Sultan of Turkey, against which the government of India had not complained. Curzon tried to impress upon the new Prime Minister, Balfour, how a renewed gesture of shabbiness would rankle in India, which had served Great Britain right well during the last three years. She had accommodated nine thousand Boer prisoners, had sent tens of thousands of troops abroad, had remained absolutely quiet. For all this Lord Salisbury had never, in public or in private, uttered a single word of thanks. 'Let his successor make amends by this simple act of generosity and consideration.'[4]

The Indian newspapers could not be expected to take any line but one. Curzon, sympathising entirely with them but debarred from saying so, asked in amazement why the British wanted to outrage these people for the sake of a paltry fifty or seventy thousand pounds? 'We look to India for everything—soldiers to fight the battles of the Empire, officers, stores, subscriptions, loyalty—and yet we drive bargains with her (or rather, they are not bargains, for she is not an equal party to the contract) that would shame the combined ingenuity of the usurer and the attorney.'[5]

Though Curzon did not yet know it, Hamilton had already approached the Treasury, without expecting to get the whole sum refunded. When, a few days later, the protest of the government of India reached him, Hamilton was angry. He called it ridiculous and improper, vowing to write very plainly to Curzon: 'It is the best way of dealing with him. He is a fine fellow, with immense capabilities, but lacking proportion or the sense of what is due to others.'[6]

He telegraphed at once, asking for withdrawal of the letter, which would, if passed on, exasperate India Council and the Treasury and diminish the chance of receiving liberal help. Moreover, it must seriously strain relations between the Secretary of State in Council 'whom it implicitly censures', and the government of India. Hamilton refused to press the argument that the end of the war made all the difference, preferring a claim on general grounds of equity. As for the India Office ceremony, Curzon was told to remember

> that the Secretary of State in Council, who has, by law, exclusive control of Indian revenues, decided, after full consideration of the circumstances, to incur this charge ... in my judgment the expenditure on the Delhi Durbar and the cost of the India Office ceremony stand or fall together. The greater cannot be justified by impugning the lesser. I have sanctioned both and am ready to defend both.

If Curzon would not cancel his letter, the India Council must write a strong minute of dissent. Just before sending this telegram, Hamilton had

an interview with the Duke of Connaught, after which he was compelled
to add that unless the whole of the Duke's expenses, including those of the
Duchess and their suite, were paid for by India he could not go to the
Durbar. Only that morning he had told Curzon that he assumed there
would be no charge to Indian revenues.[7] Curzon minuted that he could not
see why the Indian Government's letter should exasperate the Treasury,
to which it contained nothing derogatory. Nor could the Viceroy's Council,
for obvious reasons, censure the India Council. That they might be offended
was likely enough:

> ... the moment we write anything that the Secretary of State does not like, he
> threatens us with strained relations with his Council. But there is no question of
> strained relations when his Council, as they frequently do, overrule and interfere
> with us. Then we have to swallow our feelings without a murmur.

There did not seem to be any reason why the argument about the end of
the war should be 'fatal'. It was the whole explanation. As for the India
Office party, the principle mattered. A protest must be made in order that
succeeding governments might have a firm position. Curzon said he did not
mind in the least if Hamilton dissociated himself from the letter. Each
member of the Council agreed that the protest, whether successful or not,
should remain on record.[8] The government of India therefore refused to
withdraw their letter, arguing again that it was on account of the Boer
War that they had agreed to bear the cost: 'There was no reluctance to ask
our help while war was proceeding; and we feel ourselves entitled to
generosity at its close.'

It was not the prerogative of the Secretary of State in Council that was
in question, but rather the equity and prudence of making India pay.
Hamilton's analogy between the India Office party and the Delhi Durbar
they rejected; the former was part of England's entertainment of her Indian
guests, and guests were not normally asked to pay for their entertainment.
The Durbar was India's own celebration. All the expenses of the Duke and
Duchess of Connaught would be paid. The contrast could not fail to be
noticed in India.

To the Prime Minister, who had sent a telegram containing a broad
hint of a compromise, Curzon replied that the Cabinet's refusal to pay
would have a deplorable effect upon Indian public opinion: 'How can you
possibly make us pay for the Connaughts' visit in addition to our Durbar
unless you assume the whole English expenditure?'[9]

Lord George confessed that he felt deeply wounded at the language and
purport of the Indian Government's letter. Godley wrote that it would be
useless and would merely annoy the Treasury, India Council and Lord

George, a most loyal supporter who had spoken of Curzon in terms of affection. It was most unfortunate, Sir Arthur protested, that the Viceroy should have written, for publication evidently, a letter which would be thought to have been sent in order to show up the Secretary of State and put him in the wrong.[10]

In advising his colleagues, Hamilton recognised rather ruefully that if the matter came into the open, the sympathies of public, press and parliament would be largely on India's side. Indeed, the whole sum (£62,000) must be paid unless the Cabinet were 'prepared to face a certain defeat upon a sordid issue, repugnant to the feelings of the great mass of our supporters... '[11]

Before this came to the Cabinet on 7 August, another of Curzon's weekly letters had reached Hamilton. Since it was full of kindly expressions, he realised that there had been no intention to provoke a quarrel. He responded with equal generosity, but wrote that the letter of 10 July had ' ... met in the Cabinet with an absolute universal chorus of disapprobation, and everybody who read it put on it exactly the interpretation I did in my last letter, and some of the language used by my colleagues was exceedingly strong'.

Hamilton loyally represented to the colleagues that he was sure that interpretation was a wrong one, but what most impressed his colleagues, particularly Beach, was that the letter repudiated an engagement. There was a perfect right to ask for a large concession but no right to go further. Curzon had told Hamilton that there was a strong and growing feeling about the meanness of placing such charges upon Indian revenues. Hamilton agreed that if this were so it was advisable so to arrange these matters in future that India was on exactly the same footing as other parts of the British Empire; and that it was not worthwhile even for £55,000 to confirm the idea that in financial bargains Britain used her dominant position to impose unfair charges upon India. 'I own' wrote Hamilton, 'that this incident has grieved me greatly.' Characteristically, Godley pressed that no specific allotment of money be made by the Treasury for the India Office entertainment, which had been spontaneously offered by the India Council. To retreat under Curzon's pressure would look like a censure on them and would seriously weaken the position of the Secretary of State in Council in his relations with the Viceroy.[12] However, there was nothing for it; on the merits, India, which had responded nobly throughout the war, could not be made to pay, alone. The case was not defensible; and Curzon was soon told that on consideration the authorities had decided that every penny should be paid by the home government. He was delighted to have won this success for Indian interests and wrote to Hamilton in a way which closed, for the moment, some two months of unwonted disharmony.

Lord George had a method of approaching these matters which only a heart of stone could have resisted. He told Curzon that he had known, before 1899, of his exceptional powers of work and facility in speech and writing; but he had not been prepared

> ... for the remarkable exhibition of untiring industry, and of close laborious attention to masses of detail, or for the remarkable constructive and administrative ability that you have shown in every branch of government. No man has in India, since the time of Lord Dalhousie, achieved anything approaching to the amount of reforms and improvements which you have effected ... what I specially admire ... is that you have, by your personal attitude and example, raised the standard of duty and of administrative effort right throughout the whole civil and military services. And you have brought home to both those bodies a sense of responsibility, as regards the behaviour of Europeans towards Natives and their treatment, which no Viceroy of recent years has attempted to achieve.

Godley had passed on to the Secretary of State Curzon's last letter, containing a declaration of his determination to discharge his duty, at no matter what loss of popularity, in punishing white soldiers who disgraced their race and profession by brutal maltreatment of Indians. This resolve Hamilton applauded heartily, saying how sorry he would be if any serious difficulty arose between them and became public knowledge. He looked forward, if Curzon could keep his health, to his becoming Prime Minister. If he achieved that position, it would be due to his extraordinary powers of absorption and concentration: ' ... but that great power sometimes leads to an insufficient appreciation of another colleague's difficulties, or how a cogent argument and a rigid attitude, which aids the one, may embarrass the other'.[13]

Lord George had still not rid himself entirely of a belief that Curzon was trying to hedge against attacks on the Durbar by assailing the home government. Godley thought otherwise and was almost immediately shown to be right. The King, who had taken Curzon's part, wrote robustly that the attempt to make India pay had been 'really a scandal'.[14] 'Lord George' commented Godley, 'is the last person in the world to bear a grudge; but I cannot help fearing that, with him and other Members of the Government, certain traces will be left which one would be glad to dispense with.'[15]

Ostensibly, that was the end of the episode. However, it may well have influenced attitudes taken up in London a little later during the year, attitudes which nearly resulted in Curzon's resignation.

★   ★   ★   ★

Indian rulers, on succeeding to a throne or title, habitually held a great ceremony in order to symbolise the community of interest and goodwill between themselves and their people. It was under British dominion that all India had for the first time acknowledged one Sovereign, loyalty to whom spanned many divisions. Shortly after King Edward's accession, Curzon proposed that a Durbar be held at Delhi as a demonstration to India of her unity and to the world of her vitality. The weak spot of India, as he remarked, was the 'watertight compartment system. Each province, each Native State, is more or less shut off by solid bulkheads even from its neighbour...' It could not fail to benefit the princes and chiefs to meet others from different parts of the continent. Among the administrators and soldiers, many a man in Madras had never seen the Punjab. They would meet and exchange their ideas at Delhi. Nevertheless, it would be a public, rather than official, celebration.[16] The Viceroy tried hard to persuade the King to come, but he did not take the idea seriously, mentioning it to Hamilton as an illustration of Curzon's vagaries.[17] Eventually, the Duke of Connaught's visit was arranged. In the meantime, elaborate plans for a fortnight's celebration had been set in train.

By the latter part of 1901, the worst effects of the famine, which had crippled Indian finances during Curzon's first two years, were diminishing. In December, he advised Hamilton that the salt tax should be reduced, but later:

> I must have something up my sleeve to give to the people at the great Coronation Durbar in January 1903. Eastern peoples associate successions and coronations with the grant of privileges and the removal of disabilities ... India, in view of its many sacrifices and contributions to Imperial interests in recent years, will, on this occasion, expect something more. Now, what have we got to give them? I know of no extension of political privileges that may be prudently or safely made. We do not want to expand representative institutions or to add to the power or number of the Legislative Councils, or to appoint leading Natives to any higher places than they at present enjoy.[18]

A remission of taxation would doubtless give satisfaction, Lord George responded; but should it not be made when the King was crowned in England, since it was that act which made him Emperor of India? Curzon said that the people of India would expect concessions at the Durbar, rather than at the Coronation.[19] The argument was not pressed further for the time being. Curzon assumed that the Secretary of State saw no constituentional objection. The good monsoon of 1902 meant that reductions were financially feasible. Some criticism of the supposed cost of the

Durbar, and hopes of political concessions, had begun to appear in the Indian press. Having again alerted Godley and Hamilton to his desire to announce a cut in taxes, Curzon told the King that this would be popular throughout India, whereas the time for political concessions had not yet come. 'Politically the Indian people, even the most advanced, are still in the nursery, and no worse fate could befall them than to be mistaken for grown-up men.'[20]

On 24 September, Hamilton replied that while he favoured a reduction of the salt tax, he did not think that it could be coupled with the accession of the sovereign, for a most awkward precedent would be established. A similar benefit would be expected at the beginning of every reign and unpopularity caused if it were not given. He suggested a general statement about an intention to remit some taxes, with a detailed exposition when the budget was discussed in March.[21]

Curzon did not take these apprehensions too much to heart. He was not holding himself bound by the precedents set by Lord Lytton's Durbar of 1877, though on Hamilton's argument the concessions made then should now be repeated. Indians would fail to understand a Durbar which merely consisted of pageant and a plausible speech. Its value would depend upon a definite act of goodwill, which would be remembered with gratitude.[22] Each member of the Viceroy's Council backed Curzon strongly; and a despatch of 23 October proposed officially a reduction of the salt tax, a raising of the level at which income tax became payable and a refund of loans made to native states for fighting the famine.

Before this despatch had reached London, Godley, the Finance Committee at the India Office, the Chancellor and the Prime Minister had advised that it would be impossible to do as Curzon wished. Hamilton had, for the moment, forgotten that he had been forewarned in 1901. Though a remission would doubtless accord with Eastern practice, he argued, the personality of the King of England could not be introduced into such matters; and nothing would induce the India Council to agree. He realised that Curzon, working always at high pressure, must be annoyed or depressed at seemingly pedantic objections. Though the surpluses were enormous, Godley said simply that no remission was justified, either in January or March, 1903. He felt much more strongly about that aspect than about the occasion of announcement, and did not believe that the success of the Durbar would be seriously impaired by the absence of a remission.[23]

Curzon's colleagues had already authorised him to make a strong protest should Hamilton reply unfavourably. A telegram was accordingly sent to London on 12 November:

Do not put me in invidious position of holding a Durbar to which all India is looking forward with happy expectation, but which I solemnly warn you that your decision, if adhered to, will convert into disastrous failure. In my view rather than condemn Durbar to such a fate, it would be better not to hold it at all.

Hamilton replied that feeling in the India Office was unanimous. He repeated that 'until a few weeks ago' they had no knowledge that any such proposal would be made. The Cabinet would be consulted.[24] There followed a fortnight of frantic telegraphing to and fro. The arguments used on either side, apart from additions of detail, did not vary, but the dispute raised questions of constitutional significance, threatened at one stage to cause Curzon's resignation and affected the remainder of his Indian career. A few days before the Cabinet met, he represented to the King's Secretary that the decision to allow no reduction of taxation would check sentiments of loyalty in India and would be 'an act not merely of political folly, but almost of political danger'. He asked for the King's support in this effort to save the Durbar 'from regrettable and gratuitous failure'. The flourishing state of the exchequer was well known. Financial relief was everywhere expected.[25]

Hamilton had by now conceded that the proposal had been put to him nearly twelve months earlier, when he had said he did not think the salt tax could be touched that year, assuming that his comment disposed of remissions at the Durbar.[26] Curzon blinked a little at this, for he had never intended to touch the salt tax during 1902, and the Secretary of State had himself suggested a remission to coincide with the King's coronation in England. The Viceroy wired that his plan did not upset accepted principles, for the only question was whether the announcement should be made in January or in March. This was a matter of political expediency and India sorely needed the relief. 'Upon such an issue, which is not one of financial control by the India Council, but of Indian statesmanship, I have been sent here to advise His Majesty's Government, and I shall be glad to learn that I still retain their confidence.'[27]

The Cabinet met on 19 November. Brodrick had weighed in with a memorandum observing that insufficient allowance had been made for larger military expenses in the Indian budgetary calculations.[28] Several members expressed warm appreciation of Curzon's services but all agreed that his proposal would mean a dangerous innovation. The telegrams sent by him to Knollys excited strong comment. Ministers felt that this was not a subject on which an appeal should have been made, for the King must be influenced by Curzon's representation that the popularity of the Sovereign would increase or diminish according to the decision.

Immediately after the Cabinet, Brodrick telegraphed privately in terms which showed that the Viceroy's resignation would in the last resort be accepted:

> I regret to say that their opinion was unanimously unfavourable . . . I would urge you not to push the question to extremities as it would avail nothing. You can understand our personal regret. Selborne and Wyndham agree.[29]

The general view of the Cabinet, Hamilton told Knollys, was that Curzon could not resign before the Durbar 'and that it would be an act of gross discourtesy on his part, if he were so to behave upon a refusal to comply with a novel and quite unprecedented request'.[30] Hamilton also took exception to statements in the telegrams implying that he had acted in bad faith. 'After the manner in which I have been treated by you during the last week' he wrote sorrowfully, 'I think it is better that I should freely express to you the sense of the unfairness and injustice of the allegations you have made.'[31]

Curzon, having received only Brodrick's telegram, which contained no indication of the grounds on which the Cabinet decided, talked of resigning. He wrote at once to the Prime Minister, insisting that the Durbar was an issue different from normal political questions; there the Viceroy would act as the King's representative and at his command, to celebrate his coronation. Success or failure would depend largely upon what the Viceroy, not as the King's representative but as head of the Government, was able to announce. If he uttered nothing but a few empty platitudes, the Durbar must be a failure and the prestige and position of the Sovereign affected. As for the India Council, Curzon found it hard to credit that they were inspired solely by motives of constitutional and financial orthodoxy. He told Balfour that since 1899 and especially in the past twelve months, he had suffered greatly from 'their perpetual and nagging interference'. The question of Indian guests at the coronation had caused great tension, and while Walter Lawrence had been on leave in England that summer a member of the Council had hinted that it was in their power to take it out of Curzon over the Delhi Durbar. He protested that he deserved better, after four years of effort, than to have thrust upon him the duty of announcing a great disappointment to the Indian people.

> Is this fair? Is it generous? Is it just? You have never served your country in foreign parts. For your own sake I hope you never may. English governments have always had the reputation of breaking the hearts of their proconsuls from

9

Warren Hastings to Bartle Frere. Do you wish to repeat the performance? If the government are fixed in their views I feel disposed to say that it will be fairer upon me and fairer upon yourselves that you should get someone else to carry them out. Do not make me the instrument of this great failure. I am ready to put myself out of court and even face political ruin ... sooner than share the responsibility for such a result ... [32]

Lawrence, who was freely consulted during these days, sympathised entirely and thought his master's willingness to resign a noble act.

It is the wretched India Council revenging itself for their humiliation over the Coronation guests. It is not a State or departmental matter. It is a question affecting the King. Statesmanship, generosity and requitement of loyalty alike demand some boon to the Indian people. I feel convinced that the V. will announce at Delhi a remission of taxation, malgré Brodrick, Selborne, Wyndham and the other lions who roar for England. [33]

The official reply of the home government, carefully drafted so that it might be published if Curzon resigned, did not advance new arguments. However, it did reveal the significant fact that no one in London had understood what was proposed. The India Council, the Secretary of State and the Cabinet, so it appears, all imagined that the announcement was to be linked directly with the sovereign's name. [34] Curzon then explained that he would play two separate rôles at the Durbar; first, to read out, as the King's representative, his message; second, as head of the Government of India, to tell the people how it was proposed to commemorate the occasion. He had never wished to proclaim in the King's name a reduction of taxation, or to tell the people that the King was remitting taxation, or to associate the King with administrative changes. If, however, the Cabinet remained adamant, then Curzon asked to make a general statement indicating that financial relief should soon be possible. Less than this he could not say: 'The people of India have suffered cruelly and endured patiently for four years, and now that the tide has turned, they expect their reward. It is impossible to go on any longer withholding it.' [35]

This telegram indicated that Curzon, despite Brodrick's message, desired to resign unless the home government went some way to meet him; and it was so intended. [36] By 25 November the Cabinet, the King and the India Council had agreed that a general announcement of intention to reduce taxes should be made. This was the compromise which Brodrick and others had put forward, unsuccessfully, at the Cabinet six days before. It brought the immediate crisis to an end. [37] A couple of weeks later, Curzon received an account of what had transpired at the Cabinet on 19 November.

There was no doubt, Brodrick admitted, that Hamilton had at one time encouraged the plan, but he had stiffened, and had his Council's support 'while you pay the penalty of greatness and force—your Council are your slaves or are so regarded'.

The case as it came to the Cabinet was simply one of timing and precedent. Curzon's telegraphing to the King had left a very bad impression. Ministers, suffering from H.M.'s 'untimely interferences' were keen to keep the constitutional position straight. Lord George's tribute to Curzon had been warmly received but the colleagues

> were all determined that if you elected to go on such an issue we must face it ... I don't know what it costs me to have been however humbly a participator in such an action if you go. I have thought and dreamed of your work and sacrifices and high courage and broad ideas till they personify all that is best of achievement, to which we all looked forward for you.

Brodrick hoped that by the time this letter reached Curzon, the crisis would have passed with no more than a protest from him. 'If not it will be a tragedy. Everyone is so nice about you.'[38]

Though Curzon could regard the general announcement only as a second-best, he thought it would prevent the Durbar from being a political fiasco. The King sent assurances of his complete confidence in the Viceroy's zeal, judgment and ability[39] while Balfour wrote a charming letter, contesting Curzon's view that he had been entitled to deal direct with the King:

> You seem to think you are injured whenever you do not get exactly your own way! But which of us gets exactly his own way? Certainly not the Prime Minister; certainly not any of his Cabinet colleagues. We all suffer the common lot of those who, having to work with others, are sometimes over-ruled by them ... do not let any of us forget that there cannot be a greater mistake committed by a British statesman than to interpret any difference of opinion as a personal slight, or as indicating any want of confidence among colleagues.
>
> Dear George, I do assure you that no one has marked with greater pride or greater pleasure your triumphant progress, and the admirable courage, energy and sagacity with which you have grappled with the immense difficulties of your task, than your old friend and colleague. I have differed from you on this or that point. I may have (who knows?) to differ from you on others. But nothing will for a moment diminish either the warmth of my friendship or the enthusiasm of my admiration ... [40]

This was the first letter Balfour had sent in four years to Curzon, who replied that the picture of the imperious colleague, never happy unless he got his own way, had drawn from him more than a smile. Yet he had managed to get on with a Council, none of whom was bound to the Viceroy by personal or party links. Close relations between colleagues were easy and natural when they could meet and talk. The defeated party at least knew that he had been fully heard:

> I daresay if, having framed your Budget, or decided upon your Education Bill, and obtained the unanimous support of your Cabinet, you then knew that your decision was to be submitted, first to a small committee of old Chancellors of the Exchequer or Education Ministers, living in retirement in Toronto, and afterwards to another and larger body of authorities in Quebec, the immense majority of whom had never been in England at all, you might feel that there was something a little wanting in the full sense of colleague-ship, and a little difficult in the spirit of unquestioning acquiescence which such a situation ought (according to your theory) to develop.

As for the duty of surrender, it had long since been learned from India's relations with the Foreign Office, but Curzon recognised that the Foreign Secretary, deciding upon a much wider purview, must have the final say:

> And now, dear Arthur, having acquitted myself of my mild apologia let me in conclusion thank you for your warm and affectionate words and congratulate you upon the brilliant Parliamentary statesmanship—unequalled I believe during the last half-century—which has enabled you to place your Education Bill upon the Statute Book.[41]

Others, Curzon surmised, would imagine him to be looking forward with pride and elation to the great show, every detail of which he had supervised. Yet he started out for the ceremonies with no feeling of pleasurable anticipation. Beyond a desire that the Durbar should pass off well, his heart and mind were 'an absolute blank', largely because of the disappointment imposed by the Cabinet. And there could be no pleasure in being at the centre of a military society, where three quarters of the people around him would be cursing him for having dared to do his duty. After four years of extremely hard work, the moment of reaction seemed to have come.[42]

However, his spirits soon revived. Among the honours announced on 1 January, 1903, was a knighthood conferred on Walter Lawrence at Curzon's request: 'You will know', he wrote to Lady Lawrence in the early hours of that morning, 'that this little symbol expresses sincere gratitude for the devoted and sympathetic assistance of your husband which has helped to carry me through many hours of trial—trials from which I know that you too have not been exempt but which in his interest, and therefore indirectly in mine, you have so patiently borne.'[43]

The Duke and Duchess of Connaught, having visited Egypt to open the Aswan Dam, duly arrived and were welcomed by the Viceroy and some of the leading princes. The huge procession—one hundred men of the bodyguard, heralds and trumpeters, the Imperial Cadet Corps on their black chargers, the great personages on their elephants—moved slowly through the streets, decorated with innumerable pictures of the King and Queen, thronged by nearly a million people. In the amphitheatre were gathered nearly thirty thousand, amongst them one hundred ruling chiefs; all the great Indian fendatories, Arab sheikhs from Aden, representatives from Muscat, the Trucial states and the Gulf; the rulers of the marches of India, from Dir, Chitral, Hunza, Sikkim, Manipur and Nepal to the borders of Burma. The sweep of the territories they represented extended over 55 degrees of longitude.

Curzon read the King's message and said on behalf of the government of India that those who had suffered much deserved much. It was difficult to give the princes more than they already enjoyed, but to others he hoped soon to announce relief:

> In the midst of a financial year it is not always expedient to make announce-ments, or easy to frame calculations. If, however, the present conditions continue, and if, as we have good reason to believe, we have entered upon a period of prosperity in Indian finance, then I trust that these early years of His Majesty's reign may not pass by without the Government of India being able to demonstrate their feelings of sympathy and regard for the Indian population by measures of financial relief. . .

This was the announcement which the Cabinet had been induced to allow. In the last part of his speech, Curzon looked ahead with confidence to India's development. All the problems—population, food, education—were within the power of statesmanship to solve. If peace on the borders and unity within them could be maintained,

> the India of the future will, under Providence, not be an India of diminishing plenty, of empty prospect, or of justifiable discontent; but one of expanding industry, of awakened faculties, of increasing prosperity, and of more widely distributed comfort and wealth. I have faith in the conscience and purpose of my own country, and I believe in the almost illimitable capacities of this. But under no other conditions can this future be realised than the unchallenged supremacy of the paramount power, and under no other controlling authority is this capable of being maintained than that of the British Crown.[44]

The Ruling Chiefs came forward to greet the Duke of Connaught and present to the Viceroy their homage to the remote King–Emperor. When the Native Retinues were reviewed it was as though eighteenth-century India had awoken revivified from a sleep. Hindus, Mohammedans, Mahrattas and Sikhs in traditional costumes, accompanied by forces in suits of mail and many-coloured coats, mounted on elephants, camels and horses, even on stilts, 'carriages, litters, musicians, dancers, men fighting, men in masks, giants, dwarfs, hunting hawks and hounds. It was alternately splendid and comic—the familiar contrast of the East…'

The celebrations lasted for two weeks. As his friend Selborne remarked, Curzon had a gift of taking himself seriously at a function which was equally un-British and invaluable.[45] Each event was accounted a triumph of organising skill and efficiency. One reaction proved less welcome, though most revealing. When Palmer and Elles had proposed the exclusion of the 9th Lancers from the Durbar, Curzon had refused to go so far. He reasoned that it would be better for the regiment to take part in the cere-monies than for the officers to turn up there on leave. Lawrence disagreed, but it was so arranged. As the regiment passed by in the review, intense cheering and applause burst out from the Europeans, including Curzon's own guests, to entertain whom he had spent some £3,000 out of his own pocket. Kitchener, at the saluting point, scowled and muttered curses.[46] Before such a crowd, the Viceroy told Hamilton, nothing better could be expected, for every European in India was on the soldiers' side:

> But as I sat alone and unmoved on my horse, conscious of the implication of the cheers, I could not help being struck by the irony of the situation. There rode before me a long line of men, in whose ranks were most certainly two murderers. It fell to the Viceroy, who is credited by the public with the sole responsibility for their punishment, to receive their salute. I do not suppose that anybody in that vast crowd was less disturbed by the demonstration than myself. On the contrary, I felt a certain gloomy pride in having dared to do the right. But I also felt that if it could truthfully be claimed for me that 'I have (in these cases) loved righteousness and hated iniquity'—no one could add that in return I have been anointed with the oil of gladness above my fellows.[47]

Although he affected indifference to this demonstration, Curzon felt upset and wounded. He blamed Sir Bindon Blood for much of the damage, noticing frostily that among the General's guests at the Durbar was Mr Pearson of the *Daily Express*, who daily despatched lying and inflammatory telegrams. Sir B. Blood, writing at the age of ninety, could not conceal his fury at the punishment of the 9th Lancers (who, according to him, had nothing to do with the death of Atu) or his satisfaction that Curzon should have been shown what was thought of his conduct 'by the best men and women among his compatriots in India'.[48]

Nevertheless, this incident did not obscure the general success of the Durbar. All India had been scoured for the finest examples of art and craftsmanship, everything European being rigorously excluded. The result was an unsurpassed exhibition of delicate work in precious metals, enamels, carving, pottery, carpets, silk and brocade, side by side with the best work of the past. It made a net profit of 100 per cent. Some three hundred and fifty veterans of the Mutiny, now nearly fifty years past, paraded in the amphitheatre. The Viceroy was a good deal criticised for refreshing these memories, but held that he had been justified in paying a public tribute to those last survivors, almost all Indians, of the forces by which British power had been upheld. They presented Curzon with an address of thanks. He almost broke down in replying, treasured it and placed it in a position of honour at Kedleston.[49]

Curzon always regretted that the Durbar was associated at the time only with expense. It had, of course, greatly increased the profits of the railways, posts and telegraphs, all of which accrued to the government, and had given employment to the armies of builders, gardeners and craftsmen who had laid many miles of new roads, water mains and cables in a camp with a circumference of twenty-four miles. The net cost of the whole affair worked out at some £200,000, about one sixth of a penny per head. Though much disappointment was aroused by the failure to announce definite concessions, Curzon reported that the royal message had been 'universally acclaimed and a sense of partnership in a vast and powerful and benevolent system, under the shelter of the British Crown, has most certainly been diffused ... positive strength has accrued to the Empire and the Throne'.[50]

Hamilton, who had feared that Curzon might collapse from overwork, told the King that the Durbar had shown India second to none 'in the spontaneity and depth of her loyalty'.[51] Lord Crewe, though of another party and of cool, sceptical mind, took as sanguine a view as Curzon of the Durbar's value. His conversations indicated that the Viceroy had made a marked impression on the official mind of India:

> His extraordinary industry and power of grasping facts (when they found he asked for details the departments tried to smother him with them but failed completely) are everybody's admiration, as is his independence, though they think the latter somewhat excessive. He can't be called popular with the official world, as they evidently think him curt and arbitrary; but they do full justice

to his very remarkable qualities. He seems also to have impressed the native chiefs to a special extent.[52]

Another visitor of a month of two later, Sir M. Hicks Beach, observed that the natural effect of his position had been to exaggerate Curzon's 'superior person' manner, resented by those who had lived all their lives in India. 'But I never came across such "crabbing" as seems to me to go on all over India of everything and everybody in power. The official women are awful at it. I think that even his enemies would admit that in point of ability and hard work he is far above his predecessors.'[53]

The Durbar, as Lord George generously acknowledged to the King, reflected the highest credit on Curzon's powers of organisation and forethought. In Curzon's eyes, the whole thing served to prove again his long-held conviction of the value of 'middle-class method'. One directing will must plan, scheme, superintend: 'I say that if you want a thing done in a certain way, the manner in which to be sure that it is so done is to do it yourself.' Sir Schomberg McDonnell told him that by universal consent nothing had ever been so wonderfully carried through; Asquith wrote of 'complete unanimity as to the splendour of your hospitalities and your unfailing tact and judgment'.[54]

The Prime Minister's reaction was somewhat less enthusiastic. 'Our friends are now beginning to return from the Durbar' he wrote to his friend Lady Elcho. 'They seem unanimous on two things (1) that the show was the best show that ever was shown, (2) that George is the most unpopular Viceroy ever seen. Whether this is because his reforms are too good or his manners too bad seems doubtful.'[55]

At Delhi, the Duke of Connaught presented the Viceroy with a handsome silver flagon, bearing a suitable inscription. He expressed warm thanks, suppressing his own amusement, in which the Duke probably joined, at the reflection that India was paying for it. The Duke then set off on a shooting tour, also at India's expense. Considerations of etiquette had to be most scrupulously weighed. The Maharajah Holkar of Indore, whose offer to vacate his throne Curzon had joyfully accepted, had long been notorious for uncertain temper. He had once harnessed the moneylenders, whose profession he had good reason to detest, to the State coach, which he had then driven personally round Indore. The British Residents at his court were naturally unwelcome. One, said the Maharajah, gave him 'the sensation of a rat in his pyjamas'. As the Duke of Connaught alighted at a railway station, the Maharajah leapt forward to greet him. Francis Younghusband, the Resident, realised that deep offence would be given if Holkar greeted the Queen's son before senior chiefs had shaken hands. He swiftly seized the Maharajah's coat-tails, made of the finest silk. They took the strain. Crisis was averted.[56]

The rule that the Viceroy must take precedence over everyone but the reigning Sovereign was imperfectly understood and gave rise to the complaint that the whole affair had been arranged for his own glorification. Curzon too thought it rather absurd that he should have to appear everywhere as the central figure in the presence of the King's brother. He tried to emphasize the Duke's rôle whenever he could, but felt the incongruity. At the review of nearly 40,000 troops, the Viceroy, a civilian, far from beloved of the soldiers, was called upon to ride first and receive the salute. Behind him rode a Royal Field Marshal, a soldier by profession, beloved of the Army.[57]

Amongst those who complained most vehemently was Lord Ampthill, Governor of Madras. Hamilton, whose father had been Viceroy in Ireland, understood the issue and warmly supported the view that no precedence should be allowed, even for a short period, to the Duke of Connaught. No such precedence had been permitted in Ireland to any member of the Royal Family. Once sanctioned in India, it would encourage appeals to them against decisions of the government. Ampthill averred, with copious illustration, that Curzon had deliberately intended to slight the royal visitors and the Governors of Madras and Bombay, a suggestion promptly and fully repudiated by Hamilton. The Duke said nothing of the kind and indeed eulogised Curzon for his powers of organisation. The King pronounced himself thoroughly satisfied. To Curzon's satisfaction, the Connaughts' tour produced vast demonstrations of devotion to the throne. 'It is no mere lip-service' he wrote to the Duke, 'but an intense and deep-rooted sentiment. . .'[58]

★ ★ ★ ★

Brodrick's account of the Cabinet's proceedings, and of their willingness to accept Curzon's resignation, hurt him deeply. That the Cabinet, including his most intimate personal friends, should have been willing to break his Viceroyalty and career 'on a point, as it seemed to me, of purely constitutional pedantry (based on a misunderstanding of what I had proposed)—or—if you will not accept this version—because I wanted to announce in specific terms on January 1 what I am to be allowed to announce in specific terms on March 18, and what I was after all authorised to announce in general terms at the earlier date—is a thing that I can never forget as long as I live and that will affect me throughout my political career'.[59]

The bitterness, Curzon said, had passed. Brodrick wrote at once to say that he was distressed at this letter. The Cabinet, he thought, had wished to give Curzon 'a free hand' except on questions like Persia, where Lord Salisbury was immovable. Over the Durbar, Curzon seemed to exaggerate the bad effect that would be produced by the failure to announce a remission, and by wiring to the King had committed what 'we should all vis-à-vis each other regard as a capital crime'. Brodrick recalled how Salisbury, Chamberlain and he had been overruled in the Cabinet on serious issues without any threat of resignation. His private telegram had been pitched strong in order to prevent Curzon from telegraphing something irrevocable:

> Try and forget this sad interlude in our unbroken friendship. Also remember that this Cabinet is not Lord Salisbury's Cabinet. Arthur takes up everything personally. It is thrashed out as nothing has been before. We are going step by step through all the schemes offensive and defensive for Afghanistan and Persia, as well as the near East. All opinions are being carefully sifted and our power to give effect to them. In all these your view is of course of the chief importance but Arthur himself takes a most powerful interest in all decisions.[60]

Curzon replied that he was delighted to hear it. The one danger was Balfour's tendency to apply to Imperial questions 'arguments of a purely academic description'. As for the other issue, there was all the difference between a Cabinet Minister asking on behalf of a department and a representation by the Viceroy on behalf of all his colleagues. A few months later, Brodrick told Curzon that he had no doubt that the quarrel about Indian guests' expenses at the coronation had something to do with the events of November. 'Large public Departments can always pay each other out ... '[61]

Curzon did not repent of the stand he had made, and Hamilton, though upset by the wrangle, again healed the breach in a handsome manner:

> My vocabulary never was exuberant; my feelings always were and are in excess of my power of expression; and the older I get, the greater becomes the gap between the two. But, although we may here and there have differed, I shall ever feel proud that I was associated with a Viceroy of such originality, of such courage, and of such a high standard of duty ... [62]

Notes

Chapter I: Apprenticeship

1. L. Mosley, *Curzon, The End of an Epoch*, p. 9. Hereafter cited as Mosley.
2. Sir Walter Lawrence's diary, 13 Feb., 1902, gives a good example. On Oscar Browning, see his *Memories of Sixty Years*; the article by G. Lowes Dickinson in *The Dictionary of National Biography*; and H. E. Wortham, *Oscar Browning*.
3. For Curzon's time at Eton, see the Earl of Ronaldshay, *The Life of Lord Curzon*, vol. I, pp. 21–36, hereafter cited as Ronaldshay; Mosley, pp. 13–21 and G. J. D. Coleridge, *Eton in the Seventies*.
4. Ronaldshay, vol. I, p. 37.
5. There is a copy of this speech in C.P.2, Box Z.
6. O. Browning, *Memories of Sixty Years*, p. 276; Sir Walter Lawrence's obituary notice of Curzon in *The Times*, 25 March, 1925; Sir J. A. R. Marriot, *Memories of Four Score Years*, p. 48.
7. W. S. Churchill, *Great Contemporaries*, p. 212.
8. Ronaldshay, vol. I, p. 54; Mosley, p. 24.
9. Curzon to Brodrick, 12 Nov., 1885, M.P. 50073. All further references to the Midleton papers in this chapter are taken from this volume.
10. Salisbury to Curzon, 3 Dec., 1885, C.P. 52.
11. Lady Oxford, *More Memories*, p. 165; *The Autobiography of Margot Asquith*, pp. 146–7; Curzon to Lord Rennell, 26 April, 1922, Rennell Papers.
12. Curzon to Brodrick, 24 April, 1886.
13. *The Autobiography of Margot Asquith*, pp. 162 and 167; Balfour to Curzon, 17 Jan., 1887, B.P.
14. *The Autobiography of Margot Asquith*, p. 139; Lord Balfour, *Chapters of Autobiography*, p. 232; Lord d'Abernon, *Portraits and Appreciations*, pp. 91–6; Lady V. Bonham Carter, 'The Souls' in *The Listener*, 30 Oct., 1947. For press cuttings about the Souls, see C.P. 127.
15. Lord d'Abernon, *Portraits and Appreciations*, p. 94.
16. Lord Vansittart, *The Mist Procession*, p. 90; Lady Warwick, *Life's Ebb and Flow*, p. 72.
17. Sir R. Rodd, *Social and Diplomatic Memories*, vol. III, pp. 393–4.
18. Ronaldshay, vol. I, pp. 106–7.
19. Quoted in Lord Scarsdale to Lord Salisbury, 20 Dec., 1887, S.P.
20. Memorandum of 1877 cited by G. H. Bolsover, 'Aspects of Russian Foreign Policy' in *Essays presented to Sir Lewis Namier*, p. 348.
21. Ronaldshay, vol. I, pp. 143–4.

22. On Anglo-Russian rivalry in Central Asia 1870–80, see B. H. Sumner, *Russia and the Balkans*, especially pp. 35–56; A. Meyendorff, *Correspondance Diplomatique de M. de Staal*, pp. 18, 26.

23. For Curzon's articles, and for reviews of *Russia in Central Asia*, see his volume of press cuttings marked 'Central Asia I'. See also Curzon's notes for his lecture to the British Association, C.P. 20.

24. Balfour to Curzon, 9 Sept., 1889, C.P. 58.

25. Sir A. Hardinge, *A Diplomatist in the East*, p. 262.

26. G. N. Curzon, *Persia and the Persian Question*, vol. I, pp. 401–2, 419.

27. Curzon to Brodrick, 13 Nov., 1889.

28. G. N. Curzon, *Persia*, vol. I, pp. x–xi.

29. Ronaldshay, vol. I, p. 188.

30. Salisbury to Curzon, 27 and 30 Nov., 1891, C.P.2, Box 70.

31. G. N. Curzon, *Persia*, vol. I, p. 4.

32. Ronaldshay, vol. I, p. 191.

33. G. N. Curzon, *Problems of the Far East*, pp. 155–6.

34. ibid., p. 39; for Curzon's letters to *The Times* and other relevant cuttings, see his cutting-book 'The Far East, vol. I'; *The History of The Times*, vol. III, pp. 186–8.

35. Ronaldshay, vol. I, pp. 202–3.

Chapter II: Viceroy

1. A. Meyendorff, *Correspondance Diplomatique de M. de Staal*, vol. II, pp. 154–6, 162–3.

2. ibid., pp. 181–2, 193–200, 222, 229.

3. See G. N. Curzon, *The Pamirs and the Source of the Oxus, passim*; Marquess Curzon of Kedleston, *Leaves from a Viceroy's Notebook*, p. 94 ff.

4. Sir M. Durand, 'The Amir Abdur Rahman Khan' in *Proceedings of the Central Asian Society*, 1907, p. 8.

5. ibid., p. 23.

6. Curzon to Salisbury, 4 Nov., 1888. S.P.

7. Lord Newton, *Lord Lansdowne*, pp. 106, 115; Sir M. Durand, *The Life of Field-Marshal Sir George White*, p. 419.

8. Marquess Curzon, *Tales of Travel*, pp. 231–6; Lord Sandhurst, *From Day to Day, 1916–1921*, pp. 75–6.

9. Minute by Curzon, 19 July, 1901. C.P. 399.

10. For Curzon's articles in *The Times* about the Amir and Afghanistan, see C.P. 57; *The St. James's Gazette*, 5 Jan., 1897, in C.P. 53; Sir M. E. Grant Duff, *Notes from a Diary, 1892–5*, vol. II, p. 165; Marquess Curzon, *Tales of Travel*, p. 52.

11. For Curzon's manuscript notes of his six conversations with the Amir, see C.P. 52; *The Life of Abdur Rahman*, vol. II, p. 141; G. N. Curzon, 'A Recent Journey in Afghanistan' in *The Journal of the Royal Institution of Great Britain*, 1895; Marquess Curzon, *Tales of Travel*, pp. 41–84.

12. Ronaldshay, vol. I, p. 170; G. N. Curzon, *Problems of the Far East*, p. 4; Balfour to Curzon, 2 Jan., 1893 (letter not sent) B.P.; *Lord Riddell's Intimate Diary of the Peace Conference and After*, pp. 184, 410–2.

13. Sir M. Darling, *Apprentice to Power*, p. 33; Curzon to Brodrick, early Dec., 1882, M.P. 50073; Lady Salisbury, *Hatfield 1887–1903*, p. 2; A. M. W. Stirling, *Victorian Sidelights*, p. 155.

14. Ronaldshay, vol. I, p. 222.
15. Lady Ravensdale, *In Many Rhythms*, p. 11.
16. Abdur Rahman to Curzon, 12 Aug., 1895, C.P. 51.
17. Salisbury to Curzon, 27 and 28 June, 1895, C.P.2, Box 70; Curzon to Salisbury, 27 June, 1895, S.P.
18. W. S. Churchill, *Great Contemporaries*, pp. 213–4. For cuttings about Curzon's Parliamentary activities and reputation, see C.P. 269 and the volume of press-cuttings marked 'Central Asia, vol. III'.
19. M. V. Brett (ed.), *Journals and Letters of Reginald, Viscount Esher*, vol. II, p. 55.
20. Lady Warwick, *Afterthoughts*, p. 51; A. L. Kennedy, *Salisbury*, p. 355; Lady G. Cecil, *Biographical Studies of the Life and Political Character of Robert, Marquis of Salisbury*, p. 55.
21. Curzon to Salisbury, 25 June, 1897, C.P.2, Box 70.
22. Salisbury to Curzon, 23 Dec., 1897, C.P.2, Box 70.
23. Lady G. Cecil, *Life of Robert, Marquis of Salisbury*, vol. II, p. 130; Salisbury to Curzon, 15 April, 1898, C.P.2, Box 70.
24. Earl Curzon, *Modern Parliamentary Eloquence*, pp. 35–6.
25. W. S. Churchill, *My Early Life*, p. 176; Lady V. Hicks Beach, *Life of Sir Michael Hicks Beach*, vol. II, pp. 359–63.
26. W. S. Churchill, *My Early Life*, p. 81.
27. Salisbury to Curzon, 23 March, 1896, C.P.2, Box 70.
28. Salisbury to Roberts, 6 July, 1885, R.P.
29. G. E. Buckle (ed.) *The Letters of Queen Victoria*, 3rd series, vol. III, pp. 22–3.
30. ibid., pp. 20–1, 39, 84–7; C. Whibley, *Lord John Manners and his Friends*, vol. II, pp. 278–9.
31. Salisbury to E. B. Iwan-Muller, 31 Aug., 1896, S.P.
32. Salisbury to Curzon, 2 Nov., 1897, C.P.2, Box 70.
33. Cited by G. H. Bolsover, 'Aspects of Russian Foreign Policy, 1815–1914' in *Essays presented to Sir Lewis Namier*, p. 325.
34. Curzon to Salisbury, 8 Feb., 1898, S.P.
35. Draft minute, undated, Curzon to Salisbury; Salisbury to Curzon, 18 Feb., 1898, C.P.2, Box 70.
36. Lady G. Cecil, *Life of Robert, Marquis of Salisbury*, vol. V, p. 246. Unpublished MS. at Christ Church, Oxford.
37. Curzon to Salisbury, 29 Dec., 1897, S.P.; Lady G. Cecil, *Biographical Studies*, pp. 57–8.
38. G. P. Gooch and H. Temperley (eds), *British Documents on the Origins of the War*, vol. II, pp. 5–18.
39. Memorandum by Curzon, 'Advantages of a British Lease of Weihaiwei', 13 March, 1898; and Manuscript note by Curzon, undated but before Sept., 1898, (since signed 'G.N.C.') C.P.2, Box 70.
40. A. Meyendorff, op. cit., vol. II, pp. 375–7, 380.
41. ibid., pp. 382–3; Salisbury to Curzon, 15 April, 1898, C.P.2, Box 70; Curzon to Salisbury, 19 April, 1898, S.P.
42. See memorandum by Curzon, dated Nov.–Dec. 1922, C.P.2, Box 65.
43. Memorandum by Curzon entitled 'Chitral', 28 July, 1895; General Sir H. Brackenbury to Curzon, 30 June, 1895, S.P.; Marquess Curzon, *Leaves from a Viceroy's Notebook*, pp. 141–6; G. J. Alder, *British India's Northern Frontier*, pp. 263–99.
44. W. S. Churchill, *My Early Life*, p. 145.

45. On these frontier campaigns of 1897, see W. S. Churchill, *The Story of the Malakand Field Force* and *My Early Life*; Sir B. Blood, *Four Score Years and Ten*; Sir F. O'Connor, *On the Frontier and Beyond*.

46. See Curzon's letter, signed 'N', in *The Times*, 9 Sept., 1897.

47. Curzon to Salisbury, 26 Aug., 1897, S.P.

48. G. E. Buckle (ed.), *The Letters of Queen Victoria*, 3rd series, vol. III, pp. 201, 209–10.

49. Curzon to Salisbury, 5 Nov., 1897, S.P.

50. This speech is reported in *The Times*, 7 Dec., 1897, and corrected by Curzon in the cuttings-book marked 'Central Asia III', pp. 18–9.

51. T. H. Thornton, *Colonel Sir Robert Sandeman*, passim.

52. Speech in the debate on the Address, 15 Feb., 1898.

53. Salisbury to Curzon, 17 Oct., 1896, 9 April, 1897, C.P.2, Box 70.

54. Curzon to Salisbury, 18 April, 1897, S.P.

55. Salisbury to Curzon, 26 April, 1897, C.P.2, Box 70.

56. Curzon to Salisbury, 19 April, 1898, S.P.

57. *The Letters of Queen Victoria*, 3rd series, vol. III, pp. 225–6.

58. ibid., p. 251.

59. Lord George Hamilton to Salisbury, 4 June, 1898.

60. Salisbury to Curzon, 24 June, 1898. C.P.2, Box 70.

61. Curzon to Salisbury, 25 June, 1898.

62. *The Times*, 11 Aug., 1898; *Novoe Vremya*, 3–15 Sept., 1898. Translation enclosed in cutting-book 'India, vol. I', pp. 16–17, which volume see also for cuttings about Curzon's appointment.

63. Curzon to Lawrence, 26 June, 1895. Lawrence Papers.

64. Lady Warwick, *Afterthoughts*, p. 128.

65. ibid., p. 128.

66. J. Schumpeter, *The Sociology of Imperialisms*, p. 6.

67. Earl Curzon, *Subjects of The Day*, pp. 5–7.

68. Milner to Curzon, 9 March, 1898, C.P. 5.

69. Salisbury to Joseph Chamberlain, 3 June, 1898, J.C.P., JC 11/30/125.

70. Monson to Salisbury, 1 and 4 July, 1898; Salisbury to Hardinge, 15 July, 1898, S.P.

71. Monson to Salisbury, 28 and 30 Sept., 1898, S.P.

72. Salisbury to Queen Victoria, 10 Nov., 1898, RA A 75/33.

73. Salisbury to Queen Victoria, 29 Oct., 1898, S.P.

74. Joseph Chamberlain to Salisbury and reply, 29 April and 2 May, 1898, JC 11/30/117 and 119. On British commitments in 1898 see C.9088.

75. For the text of this speech, see C.P. 24.

76 Brodrick to Curzon, 14 Dec., 1898, C.P. 9.

Chapter III: The Government of India

1. Curzon to Brodrick, 14 Sept., 1904.

2. Curzon to Godley, 10 May, 1899.

3. Curzon to Brodrick, 7 June, 1899.

4. Lady Curzon to Brodrick, 12 April, 1899.

5. Curzon to Salisbury, 31 March, 1901.

6. Curzon to Queen Victoria, 3 Oct., 1900; on Holkar see the papers in H.P. 61.

7. Curzon to King Edward VII, 19 June, 1901.

8. Hamilton to Curzon, 8 Aug., 1900.

9. Curzon to Hamilton, 29 Aug., 1900.

10. Hamilton to Queen Victoria, 18 Sept., 1900, RA o8/53.

11. Hamilton to Godley, undated but c. 6 Oct., 1898, G.P. 6; Hamilton to Curzon, 17 Jan., and 5 April, 1899; Godley to Lawrence, 18 Jan., 1899.

12. Hamilton to Curzon, 6 Oct., 1899, C.P. 53.

13. See, e.g., Curzon to Sandhurst, 18 and 26 May, 1899.

14. Curzon to Hamilton, 7 June, 1899; Godley to Curzon, 22 June, 1899.

15. Hamilton to Curzon, 20 Oct., 1899; Curzon to Hamilton, 29 July and 26 Aug., 1903.

16. Curzon to Hamilton, 11 July, 1900.

17. Curzon to Hamilton, 29 Aug., 1900.

18. Hamilton to Curzon, undated but sent 23 Aug., 1900, with annotation by Godley, H.P.; Hamilton to Salisbury, 24 Aug., 1900, S.P.

19. Hamilton to Curzon, 4 Oct., 1900; Hamilton to Ampthill, 9 Jan., 1901, A.P. 4.

20. Curzon to Hamilton, 28 Aug., 3 Sept., 5 Dec., and 13 Dec., 1899.

21. Hamilton to Ampthill, 23 Oct., and 13 Dec., 1901, A.P. 4; c.f. Ampthill to Hamilton, 5 Sept., 1903, A.P. 7.

22. Hamilton to Ampthill, 12 Sept., 1901, A.P. 4.

23. Hamilton to Curzon, 1 May, 1902.

24. Curzon to Hamilton, 21 May, 1902.

25. Lawrence's diary, 1901, introduction, and 9 Jan., 1901, Lawrence Papers; Mr H. Cotton (Assam) to Curzon, 5 May, 1899, Cotton Papers.

26. Curzon to Hamilton, 18 Jan., 1900.

27. W. S. Churchill, *Great Contemporaries*, p. 215; R. S. Churchill, *Winston S. Churchill*, vol. I, p. 436; Marquess Curzon, *British Government in India*, vol. I, p. 117; Lord Mersey, *A Picture of Life*, pp. 132–3.

28. Lawrence's diary, 1901, introduction, and 10 March, 1902.

29. Curzon to Knollys, 11 Sept., 1901; Knollys to Curzon, 9 Jan., 1902; Hamilton to King Edward VII, 24 Aug., 1901, with the King's minute, H.P. 55.

30. Hamilton to Curzon, 22 Aug., 1901.

31. Curzon to Brodrick, 18 June, 1900; Curzon's minute of 30 Sept., 1902, enclosed with Government of India to Secretary of State, 5 Feb., 1903, C.P. 282.

32. Secretary of State to Government of India, 14 Aug., 1903, C.P. 282; Curzon to Hamilton, 2 Sept., 1903.

33. Curzon to Lansdowne, 20 June, 1903; Curzon to Dawkins, 2 July, 1902, original in Lawrence Papers; Curzon to Brodrick, 18 July, 1900.

34. Lawrence's diary, 1901, introduction p. 3; Curzon to Brodrick, 25 June, 1903.

35. Marquess Curzon, *Leaves from a Viceroy's Notebook*, pp. 18–24.

36. Curzon to Hamilton, 23 April, 1900; Curzon to Queen Victoria, 11 March, 1900.

37. Sir E. Maconochie, *Life in the Indian Civil Service*, p. 118.

38. Marquess Curzon, *Tales of Travel*, pp. 139–42.

39. Marquess Curzon, *Leaves from a Viceroy's Notebook*, pp. 31–8; Lawrence's diary, 3 Jan., 1901.

40. Curzon to Brodrick, 23 Feb., 1904; Marquess Curzon, *Leaves from a Viceroy's Notebook*, pp. 47–62.

41. Curzon to Brodrick, 20 Sept., 1899, cf. Curzon to G. T. Goschen, 5 June, 1900, C.P. 181; Hamilton to Curzon, 22 March and 2 April, 1901; Curzon to Hamilton, 22 April, 1901; Hamilton to Ampthill, 15 Aug., 1901, A.P. 4.

42. Curzon to Hamilton, 28 June, 1899, 11 March, 1900; cf. Curzon to Brodrick, 30 June, 1902.
43. Curzon to Hamilton, 15 May, 1901; Godley to Hamilton, 24 July, 1899, G.P. 6; Curzon to Hamilton, 25 July, 1900; Curzon to Ampthill, 19 July, 1904.
44. Curzon to Hamilton, 4 June, 1903.
45. Curzon to Brodrick, 20 Sept., 1899.
46. Lawrence's diary, 1901, introduction.
47. Lawrence's diary, 27 Jan., 19 March and 1 May, 1901.
48. Sir W. Lawrence, *The India We Served*, p. 221.
49. Lady Curzon to Brodrick, 17 July, 1902, M.P.; R. S. Churchill, *Winston S. Churchill*, vol. I, p. 436.
50. Lady Ravensdale, *In Many Rhythms*, p. 16.
51. Curzon to Rennell Rodd, 29 June, 1899, Rennell Papers.
52. Curzon to Hamilton, 22 Dec., 1900, 5 June, 1901.
53. Curzon to Balfour, 31 March, 1901.
54. Curzon to Hamilton, 11 Jan., 1900.

Chapter IV: The India Office

1. *The Reminiscences of Lord Kilbracken*, pp. 233–4.
2. Dawkins to Curzon, 30 Oct., 1901; Godley to Curzon, 24 Feb., 1899.
3. Curzon to Godley, 13 March, 1902.
4. Curzon to Godley, 5 Aug., 1903.
5. Hamilton to Godley, 23 Sept., 1900, 4 April, 1901.
6. Hamilton to Ampthill, 25 Sept., 1901.
7. Hamilton to Curzon, 31 Aug., 1899, 15 Aug., and 5 Jan., 1900.
8. Curzon to Hamilton, 22 Aug., 1900, Hamilton to Curzon 16 June, 1899.
9. Queen Victoria to Curzon, 12 April, 1900.
10. Queen Victoria to Curzon, 3 March, 1899.
11. McDonnell to Curzon, 26 Oct., 1901.
12. See, e.g. McDonnell to Curzon, 10 Oct., 1902.
13. Brodrick to Curzon, 28 July, 1899, 20 May, 1900.
14. Curzon to Rennell Rodd, 20 March, 1902, Rennell Papers.
15. Roberts to Minto, 17 May, 1907, Minto Papers.
16. See Salisbury's pamphlet of 1893, *The Case against Home Rule from an International Point of View*.
17. Curzon to Sir W. Wedderburn, 17 April, 1900.
18. Hamilton to Curzon, 2 March and 20 Oct., 1899.
19. Curzon to Wedderburn, 31 Oct., 1900.
20. Hamilton to Curzon, 13 Dec., 1900; Hamilton to Ampthill, 10 April, 1901, 10 April and 17 May, 1902, A.P. 4 and 5.
21. Hamilton to Curzon, 20 Oct., 1899.
22. Hamilton to Curzon, 6 Jan. 1903.
23. Hamilton to Ampthill, 2 April, 1902.
24. Curzon to Hamilton, 30 April, 1903.
25. G. N. Curzon, *Persia and the Persian Question*, vol. II, pp. 630–1.
26. Curzon to Godley, 9 April, 1901.
27. Curzon to Salisbury, 21 June, 1903.
28. Godley to Curzon, 29 March, 1904.

29. Godley to Brodrick, 8 Aug., 1904.
30. Hamilton to Curzon, 19 Dec., 1902; Lord George Hamilton, *Parliamentary Reminiscences and Reflections*, vol. II, p. 261; Hamilton to Godley, 20 Nov., 1898.
31. For a good example see *The Autobiography of Sir O'Moore Creagh*, pp. 252–3.
32. Curzon to Dawkins, 12 June, 1900.
33. Godley to Curzon, 19 Jan., 1900.
34. Curzon to Hamilton, 6 June and 20 Dec., 1900.
35. See, e.g., Hamilton to Curzon, 21 Feb., 1901, Godley to Curzon, 14 June, 1901; Curzon to Godley, 29 Oct., 1900.
36. Godley to Curzon, 22 Nov., 1900; Curzon to Dawkins, 12 June, 1901 (original in Lawrence Papers); Godley to Curzon, 3 Feb., 1899, 20 Feb., 1902.
37. Law to Curzon, 15 Aug., 1902.
38. Hamilton to Curzon, 14 Feb., 1901.
39. Curzon to Hamilton, 7 March, 1901.
40. Hamilton to Curzon, 24 April, 1902.
41. R. Ritchie to Curzon, 12 July, 1901, C.P. 160.
42. Lawrence to Curzon, 16 and 29 May, 1902, C.P.2, folder marked c/32/3.
43. Lawrence's diary, 13 June, 1902; Lawrence to Curzon, 10 and 20 June, 1902.
44. Curzon to Hamilton, 28 May, 1902.
45. Curzon to Hamilton, 28 May, 1902; Curzon to Dawkins, 2 July, 1902 (original in Lawrence Papers.)
46. Lady Curzon to Hamilton, 28 May, 1902, H.P. 62.
47. Curzon to Hamilton, 4 June, 1902; Hamilton to Godley, 16 June, 1902, G.P. 6B.
48. Hamilton to Curzon, 19 June, 1902.
49. Curzon to Hamilton, 9 July, 1902.
50. Godley to Curzon, 11 Jan., 1901.
51. Godley to Curzon, 20 June, 1902.
52. Godley to Curzon, 19 Sept., 1901; Godley to Richards 1 Aug., 1904, Richards Papers 3a; Hamilton to Curzon, 9 Jan., and 28 March, 1901.
53. Curzon to Godley, 17 Dec., 1903.
54. Curzon to Lansdowne, 20 June, 1903.
55. Curzon to Col. Sir H. E. McCallum, 5 June, 1902, copy in C.P. 280.
56. Selborne to Curzon, 24 April, 1903.
57. Curzon to Buckle, 10 April, 1903.
58. Lawrence's diary, 8 July and 2 Sept., 1901.
59. Curzon to Hamilton, 15 Aug., 1900.
60. Mosley, pp. 88–9.
61. Curzon to Hamilton, 19 March, 1903.
62. Godley to Ampthill, 29 March, 1904.
63. Curzon to Balfour, 31 March, 1901.
64. Curzon to Lord Northbrook, 12 Aug., 1903.

Chapter V: The Advance of the Glacier

1. G. N. Curzon, *Persia*, vol. I, p. 391.
2. Memorandum by Durand, 27 Sept., 1895. This and other official papers on Persia cited in this chapter for the period 1895–98 are to be found in C.P. 69.

3. Memorandum by Curzon, 17 April, 1896, C.P. 69.

4. G. P. Gooch and H. Temperley (eds.), *British Documents on the Origins of the War*, vol. IV, p. 375.

5. Salisbury to Curzon, 14 Oct., 1897. C.P.2, file 70; Bertie to Hardinge, 7 Nov., 1897, Hardinge to Sanderson, 18 Nov., 1897, Hardinge Papers 2.

6. Durand to Salisbury, 1 June, 1898.

7. Durand to Salisbury, 30 June and 15 Aug., 1898.

8. Salisbury to Balfour, 31 Aug., 1898.

9. Salisbury to Durand, 14 Sept., 1898.

10. Durand to Salisbury, 12 Feb., 1899, C.P.2, Foreign Affairs file II.

11. See Curzon's memorandum of 19 Nov., 1898, in C.P. 69.

12. Godley to Curzon, c. 6 Jan., 1899, C.P. 181; cf. Curzon to Hardinge, 15 June, 1901.

13. Hamilton to Curzon, 6 Jan., 1899.

14. Hamilton to Curzon, 24 Jan. and 10 March, 1899; Col. Meade to W. R. Lawrence 24 March, 1899, C.P. 199; Curzon to Hamilton, 9 Jan., 1899; see for an exhaustive account J. B. Kelly, 'Salisbury, Curzon and the Kuwait Agreement of 1899' in K. Bourne and D. C. Watt, (eds.) *Studies in International History*, pp. 249–90, and B. C. Busch, *Britain and the Persian Gulf*.

15. On Muscat, see papers in C.P. 399.

16. Fagan to Secretary, Foreign Department, Calcutta, 18 Jan., 1899.

17. Hamilton to Curzon, 25 Jan., 1899.

18. Curzon to Hamilton, 2 Feb., 1899.

19. Cf. Rear-Admiral Douglas to Curzon, 10 March, 1899, C.P. 199.

20. Despatch of government of India to Secretary of State, 2 March, 1899, C.P. 242.

21. Hamilton to Curzon, 16 Feb., 1899; Curzon to Hamilton 9 March, 1899; Hamilton to Curzon, 28 March, 1899.

22. Hamilton to Curzon, 24 Feb., 1899; Hamilton to Salisbury, 27 Feb., 1899, S.P.; Salisbury to Hamilton, same date.

23. Godley to Curzon, 3 March, 1899.

24. Curzon to Hamilton, 2 March, 1899.

25. Hamilton to Curzon, 10 March, 1899.

26. Curzon to Hamilton, 23 March, 1899; Godley to Curzon, 24 Feb., 1899; Curzon to Godley, 23 March, 1899.

27. Curzon to Salisbury, 16 March, 1899.

28. Salisbury to Curzon, 21 April, 1899.

29. Curzon to Salisbury, 18 May, 1899. Staal was the Russian Ambassador in London.

30. Hamilton to Salisbury, 2 June, 1899; Hamilton to Curzon and Godley to Curzon, 2 June, 1899.

31. Col. Meade to W. R. Lawrence, 24 March, 1899, C.P. 199; Rear-Admiral Douglas to Curzon, 10 March, 1899.

32. Curzon to Hamilton, 19 Sept., 1899.

33. Hamilton to Curzon, 5 July and 17 Aug., 1899; Lord George Hamilton, *Parliamentary Reminiscences and Reflections*, vol. II, pp. 192–3.

34. Brodrick to Curzon, 28 Sept., 1899; Wyndham to Curzon, 8 Sept., 1899.

35. Lord Newton, *Lord Lansdowne*, p. 157.

36. Hamilton to Curzon, 28 Sept., 1899.

37. Hamilton to Curzon, 14 Sept., 1899. On Wolseley's unfitness, see also Brodrick to Roberts, 20 Dec., 1900, R.P.

38. Salisbury to Roberts, 11 Oct., 1888.

39. Sanderson to Curzon, 30 July, 1912, C.P.2, Box 13.

40. G. N. Curzon, *Persia and the Persian Question*, vol. II, pp. 590–600; Curzon's memorandum for Balfour, 'The effects of Russian ascendency in Persia upon the Indian Empire', 30 May, 1892.

41. Godley to Curzon, 15 March, 1899.

42. Curzon to Godley, 12 April, 1899; cf. Curzon to Godley, 24 May, 1899.

43. Hamilton to Curzon, 14 April, 1899; Hamilton to Salisbury, 18 April, 1899.

44. Godley to Curzon, 3 May, 1899; Godley to Curzon, 16 June, 1899.

45. Brodrick to Curzon, 26 May, 1899.

46. Brodrick to Curzon, 14 and 21 July, 1899.

47. Brodrick to Curzon, 28 Sept., 1899; Salisbury to Queen Victoria, 16 Aug., 1899, *The Letters of Queen Victoria*, 3rd series, vol. III, p. 392.

48. Salisbury to Durand and reply, 14 and 17 July, 1899, Cab. 37/50/44 and 45; Curzon to Hamilton, 19 July, 1899.

49. Salisbury to Durand, 8 Aug., 1899; Durand to Salisbury, 19 Sept., 1899, S.P.

50. S. Gwynn, *Letters and Friendships of Sir Cecil Spring-Rice*, vol. I. pp. 284–5.

51. The more important parts of this despatch are printed in G. P. Gooch and H. Temperley (eds.), *British Documents on the Origins of the War*, vol. IV, pp. 356–63; for spheres of influence, see Brodrick to Curzon, 14 July, 1899; for Curzon's private commentaries, see Curzon to Brodrick, 24 Aug. and 20 Sept., 1899; Curzon to Hamilton, 19 Sept., 1899; Curzon to Durand, 20 Sept., 1899.

52. Hamilton to Curzon, 2 Nov., 1899.

53. Hamilton to Curzon, 9 Nov., 1899; Hamilton to Balfour, 2 Dec., 1899, Hamilton to Curzon, 23 Nov., 1899.

54. Curzon to Hamilton, 22 Nov., 1899.

55. Brodrick to Curzon, 10 Nov., 1899.

56. Selborne to Balfour, 14 Dec., 1899.

57. Parl. Deb., House of Lords, 4th ser., vol. 78, cols. 32–3.

58. Curzon to Brodrick, 1 Feb., 1900.

59. Brodrick to Curzon, 9 Feb., 1900.

60. *The Letters of Queen Victoria*, 3rd ser., vol. III, pp. 533–43; Salisbury to Balfour, 19 April, 1900.

61. Brodrick to Curzon, 18 April, 1900.

62. Brodrick to Curzon, 3 Nov., 1899.

63. Hamilton to Curzon, 2 Nov., 1899.

64. Scott to Salisbury, 17 and 18 Dec., 1899, Cab. 37/51/98, Cab. 37/52/1; Hamilton to Curzon, 21 Dec., 1899.

65. Balfour to Salisbury, 16 Dec., 1899, copy in Joseph Chamberlain papers, JC 7/2/2A/36.

66. A. Meyendorff, *Correspondance Diplomatique de M. de Staal*, vol. II, pp. 445–51; Sir S. Lee, *King Edward VII*, vol. I, pp. 763–4; *Die Grosse Politik*, vol. XV, pp. 506, 576 ff. See Austrian archives, 124 P.A. VIII England 1900, Deym to Goluchewski No. 6, 2 Feb., 1900, for Salisbury's belief that France and Russia would not intervene.

67. *Krasnyi Arkhiv*, vol. XVIII, pp. 3–29; Lascelles to Salisbury and reply, 3 March, 1900, Cab. 37/52/33; Sir S. Lee, *King Edward VII*, vol. I, p. 769; *The Letters of Queen Victoria*, 3rd ser., vol. III, pp. 499–500, 502–3, 526–7.

68. Durand to Curzon, 16 Oct., 1899; A Hardinge to Lansdowne, 23 May and 19 July, 1904, L.P. 22.

69. Spring-Rice to W. R. Lawrence, 2 Dec., 1899, C.P.

70. Brodrick to Curzon, undated, but Dec. 1899 or Jan., 1900.

71. Hamilton to Curzon, 1 Feb., 1900.

72. Hamilton to Curzon, 1 March, 1900.

73. Durand to Curzon, 20 Jan., 1900; Spring-Rice to Sir E. Barrington, 2 May, 1900, S.P.

74. Curzon to Hamilton, 1 Feb., 1900; Curzon to Godley, 15 March, 1900.

75. Secretary of State to Government of India, 6 July, 1900, contains an account of some of these developments. There is a copy in C.P.2, Foreign Affairs file II.

76. *Krasnyi Arkhiv*, vol. XVIII, pp. 3–29; esp. pp. 14, 29; for a report that Mouravieff had urged on France a policy of active hostility to Britain in the Gulf, see J. A. S. Grenville, *Lord Salisbury and Foreign Policy*, pp. 270–1.

77. Hamilton to Curzon, 26 Jan, 1900.

78. Godley to Curzon, 16 Feb., 1902.

79. Godley to Curzon, 9 April, 1900.

80. Curzon to Brodrick, 22 Aug., 1900; Brodrick to Curzon, 14 Sept., 1900.

81. Curzon to Salisbury, 12 July, 1900; cf. Curzon to Salisbury, 7 June, 1900.

82. Secretary of State to Government of India, 6 July, 1900, C.P.2; Foreign Affairs file II; G. Gooch and Temperley, op. cit., pp. 363–5.

83. Godley to Curzon, 19 Jan., 1900.

84. See p. 15 of report on arms traffic to the North-West Frontier, 18 April, 1899, C.P. 315.

85. Dawkins to Curzon, 6 June, 1900.

86. Hamilton to Curzon, 29 June, 1900; Salisbury to Monson, 26 June, 1900; Sir A. Lyall to Hamilton, 3 July, 1900, H.P. 67.

87. Curzon to Salisbury, 12 July, 1900.

88. Curzon to Brodrick, 19 July, 1900.

89. Brodrick to Curzon, 8 Aug., 1900.

90. Curzon to Brodrick, 29 Aug., 1900.

91. P. Graves, *The Life of Sir Percy Cox*, pp. 69–70.

92. Hamilton to Curzon, 15 Aug., 1900.

93. Curzon to Hamilton, 5 Sept., 1900.

94. Salisbury to Curzon, undated but Aug., 1900, C.P. 222.

95. Curzon to Salisbury, 18 Sept., 1900.

96. Salisbury to Curzon, 17 Oct., 1900.

97. Government of India to Secretary of State, 6 Sept., 1900, C.P. 322; Curzon to Spring-Rice, 22 Sept., 1900.

Chapter VI: Persia and the Gulf

1. Hamilton to Curzon, 6 June, 1900.

2. Curzon to Brodrick, 18 June, 1900.

3. Brodrick to Curzon, 29 June and 6 July, 1900.

4. Hamilton to Curzon, 20 July, 1900.

5. Hamilton to Curzon, 27 July, 1900; cf. Brodrick to Curzon, 29 June, and 2 Aug., 1900.

6. Brodrick to Curzon, 14 Sept., 1900; Goschen to Curzon, 17 Sept., 1900.

7. Hamilton to Curzon, 12 Sept., 1900.

8. *The Letters of Queen Victoria*, 3rd series, vol.III, pp. 604–7, 611–12; Balfour to Akers-Douglas, 18 Oct., 1900, Akers-Douglas to Balfour, 19 and 20 Oct., 1900;

Lord Chilston, *Chief Whip*, pp. 286–92; Sir A. Bigge to the Prince of Wales, 18 Oct., 1900, RA A76/52; Duke of Connaught to Bigge, 20 Oct., 1902, and Queen Victoria's memorandum, RA A76/57 and 64; the Prince of Wales to Bigge, 21 Oct., 1900, RA A76/59; cf. V. Mallet (ed.), *Life with Queen Victoria*, pp. 210–14.

9. Lansdowne to Roberts, 1 Nov., 1900, R.P.; Balfour to Goschen, undated but c. Nov., 1900, B.P.

10. Lord Midleton, *Records and Reactions*, p. 121; Brodrick to Curzon, 9 Nov., 1900.

11. Balfour to Salisbury, 20 Oct., 1900; Brodrick to Curzon. 7 June, 1901.

12. Lady Milner, *My Portrait Gallery*, p. 221.

13. Brodrick to Curzon, 15 Feb. and 26 April, 1901.

14. A. Hardinge to Curzon, 6 and 8 Nov., 1901.

15. Curzon to Lansdowne, 7 Feb., 1901.

16. Curzon to Lansdowne, 5 April, 1901; cf. Walter Lawrence's diary, 15 March, 1901.

17. Lansdowne to Curzon, 5 May, 1901.

18. Hamilton to Curzon, 9 May, 1901.

19. Hamilton to Curzon, 28 June, 1901.

20. Salisbury to Curzon, 23 Sept., 1901.

21. H. Nicolson, *Sir Arthur Nicolson*, p. 242.

22. For Capt. F. C. Webb-Ware's reports for 1899–1900 and 1900–01, see C.P. 374, 375.

23. Curzon's minute on Seistan, 4 Sept., 1899, in C.P.2, Foreign Affairs file II; Lawrence to Spring-Rice, 26 Jan., 1900, C.P. 201.

24. Lord Ronaldshay (later Marquess of Zetland), *Sport and Politics under an Eastern Sky.* pp. 342–3, *Essayez*, pp. 25–6, 247–55.

25. A Hardinge to Lansdowne, 30 June and 20 Aug., 1901, Lansdowne to Hardinge, 9 July, 1901, C.P.2, Foreign Affairs file II; A Hardinge to Lansdowne, 29 May, 1901, L.P. 21.

26. See Curzon's minute of 7 Sept., 1901, in 'Persia (d) Customs Officers, Belgian', C.P.2, Foreign Affairs file II; other minutes in this file and minutes of 22 Aug. and 31 Dec., 1902 in Foreign Affairs file II.

27. Curzon to Hamilton, 24 July, 1901.

28. Curzon to Hamilton, 12 and 31 May, 1901.

29. A. Hardinge to Curzon, 9 Oct., 1901; A. Hardinge to Lansdowne, 12 Oct., 1901, cited Cab. 37/58/97.

30. F.O. memorandum, 24 Sept., 1901, Cab. 37/58/89; A. Hardinge to Lansdowne, 18 Sept., 1901, Cab 37/58/97.

31. Hamilton to Curzon, 30 Sept., 1901.

32. Curzon to Hamilton, 1 and 3 Oct., 1901.

33. Hamilton to Curzon, 8 and 9 Oct., 1901. L.P. 21 has a collection of telegrams, 28 Sept.–12 Oct., on this subject.

34. Curzon to Hamilton, 9 and 10 Oct., 1901.

35. A. Hardinge to Lansdowne, 12 Oct., 1901, cited Cab. 37/58/97. F.O. 60/645 has a large number of papers on the loan negotiations; and see also C.P.2, Foreign Affairs file II, folder marked 'Persia (e) Loan to'.

36. Lansdowne to Salisbury, 15 Oct., 1901, S.P.

37. Salisbury to Lansdowne, 18 Oct., 1901, L.P. 21.

38. Curzon to Hamilton, 16 Oct., 1901.

39. Hamilton to Curzon, 23 Oct., 1901.

40. Curzon to Hamilton, 23 Oct., 1901.

41. See his memoranda of 22 and 25 Oct., 1901, Cab. 37/58/101 and 105.

42. McDonnell to Curzon, 26 Oct., 1901.

43. Godley to Curzon, 8 Nov., 1901.

44. C. Hardinge to Bertie, 8 Nov., 1901, C. Hardinge to Sanderson, 28 Nov., 1901 Hardinge Papers 3.

45. A. Hardinge to Curzon, 14 Dec., 1901.

46. A. Hardinge to Curzon, 8 Feb., 1902.

47. Brodrick to Curzon, 25 Oct., 1901.

48. Godley to Curzon, 8 Nov., 1901.

49. Brodrick to Curzon, 15 and 22 Nov., 1901.

50. Curzon to Brodrick, 18 Dec., 1901.

51. Hamilton to Curzon, 23 June, 1899.

52. Curzon to Hamilton, 7 and 11 Jan., 1900; Hamilton to Curzon, 13 Jan., 1900.

53. Brodrick to Curzon, 19 Jan., and 9 Feb., 1900.

54. Brodrick to Curzon, undated but early 1900; Hamilton to Salisbury, 13 March, 1900, S.P; Brodrick to Curzon, 29 March, 1900.

55. Curzon to Brodrick, 8 Jan., and 29 March, 1900.

56. For an extended account, see R. Kumar, *India and the Persian Gulf Region*, pp. 150–7, and B. C. Busch, op. cit.

57. Hamilton to Curzon, 1 June, 1901, Curzon to Hamilton, 8 June, 1901, Hamilton to Curzon, 13 June, 1901; Gooch and Temperley, op. cit., vol. I, pp. 333–4; F.O. memo by R. V. Harcourt, 29 Oct., 1901, C.P. 358; R. Kumar, op. cit., pp. 94 ff.

58. Curzon to Hamilton, 3 July, 1901.

59. Curzon to Hamilton, 23 Oct., 1901.

60. N. F. Grant (ed.), *The Kaiser's Letters to the Tsar*, p. 83.

61. Memorandum of 21 March, 1902, cited R. Kumar, op. cit., p. 168.

62. Curzon to Hamilton, 6 Jan., 1902, quoting Col. Kemball to the Foreign Dept.; Hamilton to Curzon, 20 and 26 March, 1902.

63. Hamilton to Curzon, 23 May, 1901.

64. P. Graves, *The Life of Sir Percy Cox*, pp. 81–2.

65. Curzon to Godley, 18 June, 1902.

66. Minute by Curzon, 21 July, 1902, cf. Curzon to Hamilton, 3 and 13 June, 1902, Hamilton to Curzon, 9 and 17 June, 1902, C.P. 399; and C.P. 172 and 241 B for other Aden telegrams.

67. Curzon to Hamilton, 3 Aug., 1902.

68. Minute by Curzon, 29 Sept., 1902, C.P. 399; Curzon to Lansdowne, 1 Oct., 1902; Lansdowne to Curzon, 24 Oct., 1902.

69. Minute by Curzon, 23 Jan., 1903, C.P. 399.

70. Government of India to Secretary of State, 14 May 1903, C.P. 399.

71. Curzon to Selborne, 9 April, 1900.

72. Curzon to Hamilton, 10 April, 1900; Hamilton to Curzon, 27 April, 1900.

73. Goschen to Curzon, 17 Sept., 1900.

74. Curzon to Hamilton, 1 April, 1901.

75. Hamilton to Curzon, 25 April, 1901; cf. Hamilton to Curzon 25 Jan. and 17 Oct., 1901.

76. Curzon to Hamilton, 15 May, 1901.

77. Hamilton to Curzon, 6 June, 1901.

78. Curzon to Sir A. Lyall, 17 Nov., 1901; cf. Curzon to Hamilton, 25 Sept., 1901.
79. Memorandum by Selborne, 4 Sept., 1901, Cab. 37/58/81; see Z. Steiner, 'Great Britain and the Creation of the Anglo–Japanese Alliance' in *The Journal of Modern History*, vol. XXXI, pp. 27–36, and I. H. Nish, *The Anglo–Japanese Alliance*.
80. Lansdowne to C. Hardinge, 28 and 29 Oct., 1901, F.O. 65/1624.
81. G. P. Gooch and H. Temperley, op. cit., vol. II, pp. 99–100, 102–5; Salisbury to King Edward VII, 19 Dec., 1901, S.P.; Balfour's memorandum to Lansdowne, 12 Dec., 1901, B.P.; Lansdowne to Joseph Chamberlain, 31 Dec., 1901, J.C.P., JC 11/21/14.
82. J. A. S. Grenville, *Lord Salisbury and Foreign Policy*, p. 423; Lord Newton, *Lord Lansdowne*, p. 309.
83. Curzon to Lansdowne, 13 Feb., 1902; Lord Newton op. cit., p. 247.
84. Hamilton to Ampthill, 3 Jan., 1902, A.P. 5; G. Monger, *The End of Isolation*, pp. 12 and 82; Selborne to Balfour, 4 April, 1902.
85. Curzon's memorandum of 28 Oct., 1901 enclosed in Government of India to Secretary of State, 7 Nov., 1901, C.P.2, Foreign Affairs file II.
86. Godley to Curzon, 29 Nov., and 13 Dec., 1901.
87. Curzon to Hamilton, 16 Jan., 1902; cf. Curzon to Godley, 2 Jan., 1902.
88. Hamilton to Curzon 6 Feb., 1902; Godley to Curzon, 24 Jan., 1902.
89. Memorandum by Lord G. Hamilton, 27 Dec., 1901, H.P. 58; Lansdowne to A. Hardinge, 6 March, 1902, C.P.2, Foreign Affairs file II.
90. Lansdowne to A. Hardinge, 25 March, 1902, L.P. 21.
91. On Hardinge's influence, see D.D.F., ser. II, vol. II, pp. 311–14; Hamilton to Curzon, 8 and 15 May, 1902.
92. Rosebery to Queen Victoria, 28 June, 1895, Salisbury to Queen Victoria, 1 Sept., 1895, copies in Stamfordham to Curzon, 4 Nov., 1919, C.P.2, 65; A. Hardinge to Lansdowne, 5 March, 1902, Lansdowne to A. Hardinge, 5 April, 1902, L.P. 21; memorandum by A. Hardinge, 3 June, 1902, RA W42/84; Curzon to A. Hardinge, 30 July, 1902.
93. A. Hardinge to Curzon and reply, 5 and 30 July, 1902.
94. Lansdowne to des Graz, 18 and 21 Aug., 1902; Lansdowne to the Grand Vizier and reply, 22 and 30 Aug., 1902, Cab. 37/62/129 and 137. See also the papers in C.P. 360.
95. Selborne to Curzon, 31 Oct., 1919, C.P.2, Box 65.
96. Lansdowne to King Edward VII and reply, 23 and 24 Aug., 1902, RA W42/96/102–4; cf. Sir P. Magnus, *King Edward the Seventh, pp. 301–3*.
97. Note by Lansdowne, 4 Sept., 1902, on A. Hardinge to Lansdowne, 27 Aug., 1902; Balfour to Lansdowne, 6 Sept., 1902, RA W42/112a.
98. Curzon to Hamilton, 15 Oct., 1902.
99. A Hardinge to Curzon, 10 Oct., 1902.
100. A. Hardinge to Curzon, 12 Nov., 1902.
101. Balfour to Knollys and reply, 20 and 22 Oct., 1902, RA R22/125 and 126; Balfour to King Edward VII, 3 Nov., 1902, RA R23/8; Sir P. Magnus, *King Edward the Seventh.* pp. 304–5.
102. B. H. Summer, 'Tsardom and Imperialism, 1880–1914' in *Proceedings of the British Academy* vol. XXVII, 1941, pp. 50–1, footnote 1.
103. Godley to Curzon, 21 Nov. and 4 Dec., 1902.

Chapter VII: Afghanistan and Tibet

1. G. N. Curzon, *Russia in Central Asia*, pp. 314–31.
2. A. Meyendorff, *Correspondance Diplomatique de M. de Staal*, vol. I, p. 18.
3. Notes dictated by King Edward VII on his interview at Marienbad with M. Isvolsky, 7 Sept., 1907, Hardinge Papers 9.
4. R. L. Greaves, *Persia and the Defence of India*, pp. 75–6, 118.
5. A. Lamb, *The McMahon Line*, vol. I, p. 59.
6. Memorandum by Roberts, 22 Jan., 1891; see notes in Military file II, folder marked 'Defence of India', C.P.2.
7. See the papers preserved in C.P. 54; cf. D. P. Singhal, *India and Afghanistan*, p. 139.
8. Cab. 37/30/39.
9. D. J. Dallin, *The Rise of Russia in Asia*, p. 37.
10. Cab. 37/42/35; Meyendorff, op. cit., vol. II, p. 378.
11. Hamilton to Curzon, 14 Dec., 1899; O'Conor to Salisbury, 12 June, 1898, C.P. 28; cf. O'Conor to Curzon, 2 June, 1898, C.P. 116.
12. Abdur Rahman to Curzon, 9 Jan., 1899; Curzon to Abdur Rahman, 15 Feb., 1899. Curzon's correspondence with Abdur Rahman and Habibullah is printed in C.P. 213.
13. Curzon's notes of a talk with Sir S. Pyne, 14 May, 1898, C.P. 57.
14. Abdur Rahman to Curzon, 7 Feb., 1898, C.P. 51.
15. Hamilton to Curzon, 20 Sept., 1900.
16. Godley to Curzon, 27 Jan., 1899; Hamilton to Curzon, 2 Feb., 1899.
17. Curzon to Hamilton, 2 Feb., 1899; Abdur Rahman to Curzon, 18 April, 1899.
18. Curzon to Abdur Rahman, 15 Feb., 1899.
19. Abdur Rahman to Curzon, 4 April, 1899.
20. Curzon to Hamilton, 26 April, 1899.
21. Government of India to Secretary of State, 17 May, 1899, C.P. 399.
22. Minutes by Sir W. Lockhart and Curzon, 2 May, 1899, C.P. 399; Hamilton to Curzon, 23 June, 1899.
23. Curzon to Abdur Rahman, 27 July, 1899.
24. Abdur Rahman to Curzon, 27 Sept., 1899.
25. Curzon to Hamilton, 22 Nov., 1899.
26. Curzon to Hamilton, 12 June, 1899.
27. Hamilton to Curzon, 17 Aug., 1899.
28. Curzon to Hamilton, 6 Sept., 1899.
29. Salisbury to Joseph Chamberlain, 19 Feb., 1899, J.C.P., JC 11/30/155.
30. Conversation between Kuropatkin and Col. MacSwinney, enclosed in Scott to Salisbury, 12 July, 1899, RA H48/76.
31. Curzon to Hamilton, 21 Dec., 1899.
32. For a fine example see Abdur Rahman to Curzon, 22 Jan., 1900.
33. C. Hardinge to Sanderson, 8 Nov., 1899; Sanderson to Hardinge, 8 Nov., 1899, Hardinge Papers 3.
34. Curzon to Brodrick, 16 Nov., 1899; Hardinge to Sanderson, 16 Nov., 1899; Sanderson to Hardinge, 22 Nov., 1899.
35. Cited by B. H. Sumner, *Tsardom and Imperialism*, pp. 29–30.
36. D.D.F., ser. I., vol. XV, pp. 3–4, 85–90.
37. ibid., pp. 175, 269.
38. See *Krasnyi Arkhiv*, vol. 19, pp. 53–63.

39. Hamilton to Curzon, 11 Jan., 1900; Queen Victoria to Curzon, undated, but about March, 1900; Abdur Rahman to Curzon, 15 Jan., 1900.
40. Abdur Rahman to Curzon, 4 Feb., 1900; cf. D.D.F., ser. I, vol. XVI, p. 80.
41. Curzon to Hamilton, 1 Feb., 1900.
42. *Krasnyi Arkhiv*, vol. 18, pp. 15–18.
43. Brodrick to Curzon, 9 Feb., 1900; for a convenient summary of the negotiations about Russia's relationship to Afghanistan, see Lansdowne to Spring-Rice, 5 Nov., 1903, C.P. 296.
44. Curzon's minute, 7 Feb., 1900, in folder 'Officers, British, Numbers of', Military file II, C.P.2.
45. Minutes of conference of 23 Feb., 1900, in Military file II, C.P.2.
46. Curzon to Brodrick, 1 March, 1900; Curzon to Hamilton, 19 Feb., 1900 (telegram); Government of India to Secretary of State, Nos. 63 and 64, 17 May, 1900, C.P. 399; cf. Gooch and Temperley, op. cit., vol. I, p. 310.
47. ibid, vol. IV, p. 512; Curzon to Hamilton, 2 May, 1900.
48. Hamilton to Godley, 8 June, 1900, G.P. 6B; Hamilton to Curzon, 21 June, 1900; Godley to Foreign Office, 28 June, 1900; Sanderson to India Office, 5 July, 1900; Salisbury to Scott, 4 July, 1900, C.P. 399.
49. Government of India to Secretary of State, 26 April, 1900. Military file II, folder marked 'Defence of India', C.P.2; Hamilton to Curzon, 10 May, 1900.
50. Hamilton to Curzon, 29 Aug., 1900.
51. *Krasnyi Arkhiv*, vol. 19, pp. 53–63, cited by W. Walsh, 'The Imperial Russian General Staff and India' in *The Russian Review*, April, 1957.
52. Government of India to Secretary of State, 26 April, 1900; Secretary of State to Government of India, 13 July, 1900, Military file II, folder marked 'Defence of India', C.P.2.
53. Salisbury to Northcote, 8 June, 1900, cited by J. A. S. Grenville, op. cit., pp. 295–6.
54. Curzon to Hamilton, 17 Sept. and 28 Nov., 1900.
55. Hamilton to Curzon, 7 Nov., 1901.
56. Hardinge to Bertie, 17 October, 1901; see *Krasnyi Arkhiv*, vol. 19, pp. 53–63, especially Staal's reports, pp. 54–6.
57. Hamilton to Curzon, 17 and 23 Oct., 1901.
58. Hamilton to Curzon, letter and telegram, 24 Oct., 1901, with minute by King Edward VII, H.P. 52.
59. Curzon to King Edward VII, 21 Nov., 1901.
60. Curzon to Hamilton, 25 Sept., 1901; Curzon's memorandum of 28 Oct., 1901, enclosed in Government of India to Secretary of State, 7 Nov., 1901, Foreign Affairs file II, C.P.2.
61. Lansdowne to Curzon, 10 April, 1902.
62. Curzon to Godley, 14 May, 1902; Lansdowne to Hamilton, 16 May, 1902, H.P. 59; Hamilton to Curzon, 24 June, 1902; Sanderson to Hardinge, 12 March, 1902, Hardinge Papers 3.
63. Curzon to Habibullah, 7 Feb., 1902; Curzon to King Edward VII, 19 March, 1902.
64. Diary of the Kabul Agency for the week ending 12 Feb., 1902, C.P. 290.
65. Minute by Curzon, 19 July, 1901, C.P. 399.
66. Hamilton to Curzon, telegram, 30 May, 1902; note by Hamilton, endorsed by Salisbury, 23 May, 1902, H.P. 58; cf. Curzon's minute of 23 April, 1905, in C.P. 293.

67. Curzon to Habibullah, 6 June, 1902.
68. Calculation of about January, 1901, from notes on Military file II, folder marked 'Defence of India', C.P.2; Hamilton to Curzon, 27 June, 1901.
69. Note by Roberts, 29 April, 1901, on a memorandum by the Military Intelligence Division, *Russia's offensive strength in Central Asia*, F.O. 65/1635; Lansdowne to Salisbury, 7 July, 1901, S.P.
70. Hamilton to Curzon, 13 June, 1901.
71. Note by Sir Power Palmer, 29 April, 1901, Military file II, folder marked 'Defence of India', C.P.2; Secretary of State to Government of India, 4 Jan., 1901, ibid.
72. Government of India to Secretary of State, 13 June, 1901, ibid.
73. Secretary of State to Government of India, 7 Feb., 1902, ibid.
74. This account is generally based upon Lansdowne to Spring-Rice, 5 Nov., 1903; cf. Gooch and Temperley, vol. IV, pp. 512–19; Scott to Lansdowne 6 and 22 Jan., 1902, L.P. 24.
75. Curzon to Hamilton, 23 July, 1902.
76. Hardinge to Sanderson, 30 Oct., 1902, H.P. 3.
77. India Office to Foreign Office, 11 Dec., 1902, F.O. 539/85.
78. Curzon to Habibullah, 31 July, 3 Oct., 24 Nov., 1902; Habibullah to Curzon, 15 Oct., 9 Dec., 1902.
79. Curzon to Hamilton, 17 Nov., 1902.
80. Hamilton to Curzon, 25 Nov., 1902.
81. Hamilton to Knollys, 25 Nov., 1902; Hamilton to King Edward VII, 30 Nov., 1902, RA W1/55 and 61b.
82. Curzon to Hamilton, 27 Nov., 1902.
83. Hamilton to Curzon, 4 Dec., 1902.
84. Godley to Curzon, 5 Dec., 1902.
85. Hamilton to Curzon, 9, 11 and 19 Dec., 1902.
86. Balfour to King Edward VII, 9 Dec., 1902, RA R23/22a.
87. Memorandum by Balfour to Lansdowne, 12 Dec., 1901, B.P.
88. Memorandum by Balfour, 16 Dec., 1902, Cab. 37/63/167.
89. Hamilton to Curzon, 19 Dec., 1902.
90. Knollys to Curzon, 4 Dec., 1902; Curzon to Knollys, 25 Dec., 1902.
91. Hamilton to Curzon, 23 and 26 Dec., 1902.
92. Curzon's minute, 16 Feb., 1903, C.P. 399; Curzon to Hamilton, 28 March, 1903.
93. G. N. Curzon, *Russia in Central Asia*, p. 251.
94. Curzon's minutes of 23 Feb. and 17 May, 1899, Foreign Affairs file III, C.P.2.
95. Curzon to Hamilton, 24 May, 1899.
96. Curzon to Hamilton, 28 Dec., 1899.
97. Curzon to Hamilton, 18 Nov., 1900; cf. Curzon to Hamilton, 21 June, 1901.
98. Curzon to Hamilton, 11 June, 1901.
99. Hamilton to Curzon, 4 and 11 July, 1901.
100. Government of India to Secretary of State, 25 July, 1901.
101. Curzon to Hamilton, 16 July, 1901.
102. Curzon to Hamilton, 14 Aug., 1901.
103. Curzon to Hamilton, 29 Oct. and 3 and 5 Nov., 1901; memorandum by J. A. Bourdillon of a conversation with Captain Parr, Chinese Customs Officer at Yatung, with minute by Curzon, 7 July, 1903, C.P. 244; P. Mehra, 'Kazi U-gyen: "A Paid Tibetan Spy"?' in *Journal of the Royal Central Asian Society*, 1964.
104. Government of India to Secretary of State, 13 Feb., 1902, Foreign Affairs file III,

C.P.2; Hamilton to Curzon, 13 March, 1902; see C.P. 342 for the Nepalese agent's report and other papers on Russo-Tibetan contacts.
105. Hamilton to Curzon, 11 Aug., 1902.
106. Curzon to Hamilton, 20 and 26 Aug., 1902; Hamilton to Curzon, 6 Sept., 1902.
107. Hamilton to Curzon, 10 Sept., 1902; Satow to Lansdowne, 8 Sept., 1902, F.O. 539/85.
108. Sanderson to C. Hardinge, 27 Oct., 1902, Harding Papers 3.
109. Curzon to Hamilton, 9 Nov., 1902; Hamilton to Curzon, 16 Nov., 1902.
110. Curzon to Hamilton, 13 Nov., 1902.
111. Hamilton to Curzon, 26 Nov. 1902, enclosing Satow to Lansdowne, 19 Nov., 1902.
112. Minute by Curzon, 25 Dec., 1902, Foreign Affairs file III, C.P.2.

Chapter VIII: The Army

1. Curzon to Hamilton, 21 June, 1899.
2. Curzon to Hamilton, 28 June, 1899; on Collen, cf. Curzon to Joseph Chamberlain, 6 April, 1901.
3. Curzon to Brodrick, 27 July, 1899, M.P. 50073.
4. Curzon to Hamilton, 28 June, 1899.
5. Curzon to Godley, 12 July, 1899; cf. Curzon to Godley, 25 July, 1900.
6. Hamilton to Godley, 15 Aug., 1899; Hamilton to Curzon 20 Oct., 1899, 15 Aug., 1900, 13 March, 1903; cf. Hamilton to Ampthill, 22 May, 1903, A.P. 6.
7. Curzon to Hamilton, 26 July, 1899.
8. Curzon to Brodrick, 8 Jan., 1900, 16 March, 1902.
9. Hamilton to Curzon, 16 June, 1899.
10. Curzon to Hamilton, 18 Oct., 1899; Lockhart to Curzon, 12 Oct., 1899, minute by Curzon, 19 Oct., 1899, order of 20 Oct., 1899, Government of India to Lieut.-Governor of Burma, 24 Oct., 1899, C.P.2 Military file I.
11. Curzon to Hamilton, 25 Oct., 1899.
12. Knollys to Hamilton, and reply, 24 Nov., 1902, RA W1/49 and 50.
13. Minute by Curzon, 8 June, 1900, C.P.2 Military file I.
14. Curzon to Hamilton, 13 June, 1900.
15. Minutes by Curzon, 17 Aug., and 6 Sept., 1900, Government of India to Secretary of State, 25 Oct., 1900, C.P.2, Military file III; Curzon to Hamilton, 17 Sept., 1900.
16. Curzon to Dawkins, 24 Jan., 1901.
17. Curzon to Hamilton, 17 Sept., 1900.
18. See, for example, Gen. Sir H. Smith-Dorrien, *Memories of 48 Years' Service*, pp. 307–8.
19. Lawrence's diary, 1901 introduction, 12 July, 1901; Sir W. Lawrence, *The India We Served*, p. 243.
20. E. T. S. Dugdale (ed. and trans.) *German Diplomatic Documents*, vol. III, pp. 90–1.
21. Cited D. G. Gordon, *The Dominion Partnership in Imperial Defence*, pp. 60–1.
22. Hamilton to Curzon, 21 Dec., 1899.
23. Hamilton to Salisbury, 8 Feb., 1900.
24. *The Letters of Queen Victoria*, 3rd ser. vol. III, pp. 485–6, 495.
25. Arnold-Forster's diary, 7 Nov., 1905; Salisbury to Curzon, 23 Sept., 1901.
26. Lord Newton, *Lord Lansdowne*, p. 168.

27. Hamilton to Curzon, 16 Feb., 1900.

28. Collen to Curzon, 8 Jan., 1900.

29. Curzon to Hamilton, 1 Feb., 1900.

30. Curzon to Hamilton, 5 April, 1900; on re-equipment, see in C.P. 363 the article from *The Times*, 21 Aug., 1900, 'by an Indian officer', with Collen's minute of 22 Sept., 1900, admitting many of the charges to be true, and Curzon's original minutes, showing that many of the deficiencies were being remedied.

31. Memorandum by Collen, 23 Feb., 1901, C.P. 263; Collen's notes of 26 Feb. and 4 March, 1901, C.P.2, Military file II, 'Defence of India' folder.

32. Minute by Curzon, 1 May, 1901, ibid.

33. Brodrick to Curzon, 21 March, 1899.

34. Hamilton to Curzon, 14 July, 1899.

35. Hamilton to Curzon, 17 Aug., 1899; Curzon to Godley, 6 Sept., 1899.

36. Curzon to Hamilton, 6 Sept., 1899.

37. Rennell Rodd to Curzon, 12 Dec., 1899; Curzon to Rodd, 28 Dec., 1899, Rennell Papers.

38. Curzon to Hamilton, 15 Feb., 1900.

39. Hamilton to Curzon, 16 Feb., and 9 March, 1900.

40. Hamilton to Curzon, 23 Feb., 1900; Curzon to Queen Victoria, 22 March, 1900.

41. Hamilton to Curzon, 5 and 12 April, 1900; Lansdowne to Curzon, 20 April, 1900.

42. Hamilton to Curzon, 31 May, 1900.

43. Curzon to Hamilton, 9 May and 27 June, 1900.

44. Curzon to Hamilton, 21 July, 1900.

45. Hamilton to Curzon, 27 July, 1900; Curzon to Hamilton, 15 Aug., 1900; Curzon to Dawkins, 29 Aug., 1900.

46. Curzon to Kitchener, 21 Aug., 1900.

47. Hamilton to Curzon, 2 Aug., 1900.

48. Salisbury to Lansdowne, 22 Sept., 1900, L.P. 29; Lord Newton, *Lord Lansdowne*, p. 189; cf. Lansdowne to Salisbury, 11 Oct., 1900, S.P.

49. Sir G. Arthur, *Life of Lord Kitchener*, vol. II, p. 119.

50. Brodrick to Curzon, 22 March, 1901.

51. P. Fleming, *Bayonets to Lhasa*, p. 290.

52. Curzon to Kitchener, 31 March, 1901; Kitchener to Curzon, 8 May, 1901.

53. Curzon to Godley, 3 Jan., 1901.

54. Brodrick to Roberts, 10 May and 3 Sept., 1901.

55. Parl. Deb., H. of C., ser. IV, vol. XC, col. 1062.

56. Brodrick to Roberts, 10 May, 1901.

57. Queen Victoria to Curzon, 19 June, 1900; Curzon to Queen Victoria, 21 June, 1900; Salisbury to Queen Victoria, 4 Aug., 1900, RA A76/25.

58. Hamilton to Curzon, 7 Nov., 1901.

59. Curzon to Lord Northbrook, 12 Aug., 1903.

60. Brodrick to Curzon, 22 Nov., 1901.

61. Memorandum by Hamilton, 28 June, 1901, H.P. 47; Brodrick to Curzon, 26 Sept., 1901.

62. Brodrick to Joseph Chamberlain, 10 Sept., 1901, JC 11/1; Brodrick to Curzon 22 Nov. and 20 Dec., 1901.

63. Brodrick to Curzon, 15 March, 1903.

64. Hamilton to Curzon, 12, 17 and 26 Dec., 1901; Curzon to Hamilton, 16 Jan. and 12 Feb., 1902.

65. Curzon's minute of 6 March, 1902 'Pay of the British Army in India', C.P.2 Military file II; Curzon to Hamilton, 8 March, 1902; Curzon to Brodrick, 16 March, 1902.

66. M. Arnold-Forster, *The Rt. Hon. H. O. Arnold-Forster*, pp. 253–4; Curzon to Brodrick, 16 March, 1902.

67. Godley to Curzon, 14 Feb., 1902.

68. Report of a meeting at Simla, 6 June, 1902, C.P.2, Military file II, folder marked 'Defence of India'.

69. Government of India to Secretary of State, 21 Aug., 1902, Cab. 6/1 nos. 1 and 2; J. Amery, *The Life of Joseph Chamberlain*, vol. IV, pp. 426–8; W.O. 106/43.

70. See Curzon's minutes of 16 June and 26 July, 1902, and other papers on this subject, in C.P.2, Military file I.

71. Curzon to Godley, 30 July, 1902.

72. See the Government of India's press statement, enclosed with Curzon to Hamilton, 20 Nov., 1902.

73. Knollys to Hamilton, 24 Nov., 1902, H.P. 60; Hamilton to Knollys, same date, RA W1/50; Curzon to Hamilton, 21 Nov., 1902 and the King's minute, H.P. 52; Hamilton to Curzon, 27 Nov., 1902; Hamilton to Curzon, 6 Jan., 1903.

74. Curzon to Hamilton, 27 Nov., 1902.

75. Curzon to Kitchener, 14 Dec., 1902; cf. minute by Curzon 16 Dec., 1902, C.P.2, Military file I.

76. Curzon to Roberts, 28 Dec., 1902.

77. Roberts to Curzon, 23 Jan., 1903; Knollys to Curzon, 8 Jan., 1903.

78. Hamilton to Curzon, 6 Jan., 1903; Hamilton to Godley, 25 Jan., 1903. For some misleading accounts by soldiers of the 9th Lancers affair, see Gen. Sir G. de S. Barrow, *The Fire of Life*, p. 88; Maj.-Gen. Sir G. Younghusband, *Forty Years a Soldier*, pp. 233–4; Gen. Sir H. Smith-Dorrien, *Memories of Forty-eight Years' Service*, pp. 316–8, Gen. Sir B. Blood, *Four Score Years and Ten*, p. 347.

79. Curzon to Hamilton, 11 March and 23 May, 1900; Curzon's minute of 14 May, 1900, C.P. 240.

80. Curzon's minute of 28 May, 1901, C.P. 399, file marked 'Burma frontier'.

81. For an example, see the description of the affair of the fort at Manipur in Curzon to Hamilton, 21 Nov., 1901.

82. Curzon to Hamilton, 30 May, 1900; Hamilton to Curzon, 21 June, 1901.

83. Minutes by Curzon, 30 June and 4 July, 1902, 5 Feb. and 1 Sept., 1902, in C.P.2, Military file I.

84. Curzon to Hamilton, 21 Feb., 1901.

85. Curzon to Hamilton, 7 Feb., 1901.

86. Curzon to Hamilton, 14 Feb., 1901.

87. Gen. Sir H. Smith-Dorrien, op. cit., p. 313.

88. Palmer to Curzon, 26 Nov., 1902; cf. Palmer to Curzon, 5 Aug., 1903.

89. Gen. Sir H. Smith-Dorrien, op. cit. pp. 313–4; Smith-Dorrien to Kitchener, Feb., 1906, K.P. 31; Sir S. Reed, *The India I Knew*, pp. 49–50.

90. Hamilton to Curzon, 24 Dec., 1902 and 19 Feb., 1903; Lord G. Hamilton, *Parliamentary Reminiscences and Reflections*, vol. II, pp. 301–3.

91. Sir W. Lawrence, *The India We Served*, p. 247; Godley to Curzon, 4 June, 1903; *The Reminiscences of Lord Kilbracken*, p. 185.

92. Brodrick to Curzon, 25 July, 1902; cf. Lawrence to Curzon, 1 Aug., 1902.

93. Curzon to Kitchener, 13 Aug., 1902.

94. Dawkins to Curzon, 25 July, 1902.

95. McDonnell to Curzon, 3 July, 1902.
96. Brodrick to Curzon, 25 July, 1902; Selborne to Curzon, 17 July, 1902.
97. Mosley, p. 112; cf. Lady C. Asquith, *Diaries*, pp. 175–6.
98. Lord d'Abernon, *Portraits and Appreciations*, p. 43.
99. Lady Warwick, *Afterthoughts*, p. 125. On Balfour see also the biographies by B. E. C. Dugdale and K. Young; W. S. Churchill, *Great Contemporaries*; Lord Swinton, *Sixty Years of Power*; Lord Chilston, 'Balfour: The Philosopher at the Helm' in *Parliamentary Affairs*, vol. XIII, No. 4; *The Autobiography of Margot Asquith*; Hon. H. Asquith, *Moments of Memory*; Earl Curzon, *Modern Parliamentary Eloquence*, p. 44.
100. Curzon to Hamilton, 16 July, 1902.
101. Curzon to Balfour, 16 July 1902.
102. B. E. C. Dugdale, *Arthur James Balfour*, vol. I, p. 293; Sir Austen Chamberlain to Lord Midleton, 18 Feb., 1936, A.C.P.
103. Arnold-Forster's diary, 18 June, 1908.
104. Mosley, p. 92.
105. Curzon to Brodrick, 28 Aug., 1902.
106. Curzon to Salisbury, 16 July, 1902; Salisbury to Curzon, 9 Aug., 1902.

Chapter IX: Reforms

1. Curzon to Godley, 23 Feb., 1899.
2. Lawrence's diary, 10 Oct., 1901.
3. Ronaldshay, vol. II, p. 27.
4. Minute of 27 May, 1899, C.P.2, Military file I.
5. Minute of 25 May, 1902, C.P. 282.
6. Lawrence's diary, 16 May, 1901; E. J. Buck, *Simla Past and Present*, p. 56; Curzon's minute of 11 Sept., 1903, C.P. 282.
7. Minute, undated but about 26 Aug., 1902, C.P. 280.
8. Curzon to Hamilton, 3 May, 1899.
9. Minute of 24 May, 1899, C.P. 280; cf. C.P. 282 for papers on the reduction of the length of reports, and C.P. 239 for papers on noting and official routine.
10. Curzon to Godley, 18 Oct. and 22 Nov., 1899; Curzon to Sir A. Havelock, 23 Nov., 1899 and 15 Jan., 1900; cf. Curzon to Hamilton, 21 May, 1900.
11. See articles in *The Times*, 23 Aug., 13 and 27 Sept., 1898.
12. T. H. Thornton, *Colonel Sir Robert Sandeman*, pp. 294–5.
13. Secretary of State to Government of India, 28 Jan., 1898, Command paper 8714; Hamilton to Salisbury, 4 June, 1898, S.P.
14. Hamilton to Curzon and reply, 23 and 28 July, 1898, C.P. 112; Salisbury to Queen Victoria, 25 July, 1898, RA 05/187.
15. Salisbury to Curzon, 2 Sept., 1897, C.P.2, Box 70.
16. Curzon's note on the Khyber question, 30 Jan., 1899; cf. his minute of 6 Sept., 1900, C.P. 315.
17. Curzon's minute on the Tochi valley, 19 June, 1899, C.P. 307.
18. Government of India to Secretary of State and reply, 26 Oct., 1899 and 4 Jan., 1900, C.P. 312.
19. Dawkins to Curzon, 6 June, 1900.
20. Curzon to Brodrick, 17 April, 1900.

21. Curzon to Brodrick, 18 June, 1900; Elgin to Curzon, 10 Nov., 1898, Elgin Papers 33/b.

22. Sir W. Lawrence, *The India We Served*, p. 234.

23. Hamilton to Curzon, 28 April and 12 May, 1899.

24. Minute of 27 Aug., 1900, C.P. 212; Government of India to Secretary of State, 13 Sept., 1900, C.P. 310; for other minutes on the frontier, see C.P. 338.

25. Curzon to Hamilton, 15 Aug., 1900; Hamilton to Curzon, 8 Sept., and 17 Oct., 1900.

26. Curzon to Hamilton, 16 Nov., 1899; cf. Curzon to Hamilton 20 June and 24 Oct., 1900.

27. Lawrence's diary, 14 and 25 June, 24 Sept., 30 Oct., 1899; see C.P. 230 for letters and notes on this subject.

28. Sir T. Raleigh (ed.), *Lord Curzon in India*, vol. II, p. 148; Curzon to Hamilton, 30 April, 1902.

29. W. S. Churchill, *My Early Life*, p. 142.

30. Note by Col. H. A. Deane, 30 April, 1906, Minto Papers; see Sir M. O'Dwyer, *India as I Knew It*, pp. 103–34, on the new province.

31. Ronaldshay, vol. II, p. 84.

32. Curzon to Hamilton, 16, 23 and 30 May, 11 and 25 July, 2 Aug., 1900.

33. Curzon to Hamilton, 8 Aug., 1900; Lawrence, op. cit., p. 229.

34. Lawrence's diary, 1901, introduction.

35. M. A. Hollings, *The Life of Sir Colin Scott-Moncrieff*, pp. 298–314; see for papers on irrigation C.P. 281 and 667–70; cf. D. G. Harris, *Irrigation in India*, esp. chaps. IX and X.

36. Curzon to Hamilton, 24 Oct., 1900.

37. Curzon's minutes of 13 March and 31 May, 1901, C.P. 266b.

38. Curzon's minute, 3 Oct., 1903, C.P. 266c; for other railway papers see C.P. 266a and b, and for the report C.P. 647.

39. Curzon to Brodrick, 2 Oct., 1903.

40. Lawrence's diary, 20, 22 and 23 June, 24 July, 1902.

41. Wyndham to Curzon, 3 May, 1903.

42. Lawrence's diary, 3 May, 1901.

43. Curzon to Balfour, 5 Feb., 1903.

44. Hamilton to Knollys, 23 March, 1903, RA W2/17.

45. Curzon to Balfour, 30 April, 1903; Curzon to Hamilton, 28 May, 1903.

46. Knollys to Sandars, 26 May, 1903, Balfour to Knollys, 29 May, 1903, B.P., Ian Malcolm to Curzon, 12 June, 1903.

47. Curzon to Balfour, 8 July, 1903.

48. Curzon to Chirol, 13 May, 1903; Curzon to Hamilton, 17 June, 1903.

49. Curzon to Hamilton, 9 July, 1903.

50. Curzon to Sir W. Wedderburn, 15 Aug., 1902; cf. D. E. Wacha to W. R. Lawrence, 7 March, 1902, C.P., and Curzon to Godley, 9 April, 1901.

51. Ampthill to Godley, 21 Dec., 1904.

52. Minute of 10 Sept., 1900, C.P. 279; cf. Curzon to Dawkins, 24 Jan., 1901.

53. Curzon to Brodrick, 18 June, 1900.

54. Curzon to Godley, 4 June, 1903.

55. Curzon to Hamilton, 17 June, 1903; Hamilton to Ampthill, 27 Nov., 1902, 7 Jan., 1903.

56. Hamilton to Curzon, 2 Sept., 1903; cf. Hamilton to Curzon, 25 June, 1903.

57. Curzon to Hamilton, 23 Sept., 1903.

58. Memo. for the Cabinet by Hamilton and attached papers, 15 Nov., 1898, C.P. 253; Salisbury to Queen Victoria, 21 Nov., 1898, RA A 75/35.
59. Memorandum by Curzon, 4 June, 1900, Government of India to Secretary of State, 19 July, C.P. 253.
60. Hamilton to Curzon, 19 Jan., 14 and 26 Feb., 1900.
61. Queen Victoria to Curzon, 12 April, 1900; Hamilton to Queen Victoria, 5 June, 1900, RA 08/19.
62. Salisbury to Northcote, 8 June, 1900, cited J. A. S. Grenville, *Lord Salisbury and Foreign Policy*, p. 295.
63. Curzon to Dawkins, 24 Jan., 1901.
64. Curzon to Roberts, 10 Jan., 1901.
65. Hamilton to Curzon, 2 April, 1901.
66. M. Gilbert, *Servant of India*, p. 247.
67. Raleigh, op. cit., vol. I, p. 113; S. Harris, *J. N. Tata*, p. 156.
68. Curzon to Brodrick, 12 Jan., 1905.
69. Raleigh, op. cit., vol. II, p. 306.
70. ibid., vol. I, p. 187.
71. Sir T. Morison and G. T. Hutchinson, *The Life of Sir Edward FitzGerald Law*, pp. 282–3; cf. G. Paish, 'Great Britain's Capital Investments', in *Journal of the Royal Statistical Society*, vol. LXXIV, p. 186.
72. Curzon to Sir A. MacDonnell, 10 Aug., 1899; papers in C.P. 241(a) and C.P. 281.
73. Curzon to Hamilton, 29 July, 1903; Hamilton to Curzon, 10 July, 1902.
74. Minute of 23 Oct., 1899, C.P. 280.
75. Curzon to Ampthill, 21 Feb., 1901; for the proceedings of the conference see C.P. 248.
76. Curzon to Northbrook, 21 July, 1902; Curzon to Cotton, 31 Aug., 1902, Cotton Papers. For the report see C.P. 662.
77. Hamilton to Ampthill, 28 March, 1901; cf. Hamilton to Ampthill, 4 Sept., 1901, and Hamilton to Curzon, 13 Aug., 1902.
78. Raleigh, op. cit., vol. II, p. 74.
79. Curzon to Brodrick, 1 Jan., 1888, M.P.
80. Raleigh, op. cit., vol. I, p. 20.
81. D. G. Hogarth, 'Lord Curzon' in *Proceedings of the British Academy*, 1926.
82. Lawrence's diary, 8 Aug., 1901.
83. Lawrence's diary, 7, 10 and 15 March, 1902; Curzon to Godley, 19 March, 1902.
84. Curzon's minute of 24 May, 1902, C.P. 280, which see for a selection of Curzon's minutes on departmentalism.
85. Lawrence's diary, 11 Dec., 1902, 23 June, 1901.
86. Raleigh, op. cit., vol. II, pp. 317–8.
87. Hamilton to Curzon, 15 May, 1903; Curzon to Lamington, 27 Feb., 1904.
88. Curzon to Brodrick, 31 Jan., 1901, 27 Dec., 1900, 2 April, 1901.
89. Sir W. Lawrence, op. cit., p. 252, citing Sir E. Maconochie.

Chapter X: The Durbar

1. See, e.g., Hamilton to Curzon, 24 Sept., 1901.
2. Minute by Curzon, 24 June, 1902, C.P. 399.
3. Godley to Curzon, 6 June, 1902.
4. Curzon to Balfour, 16 July, 1902.

5. Curzon to Lord Northbrook, 21 July, 1902.
6. Hamilton to Curzon, 24 July, 1902; Hamilton to Godley, 29 July, 1902, G.P. 6B.
7. Hamilton to Curzon, 29 July, 1902.
8. Minutes by Curzon and others, 30 and 31 July, 1902, C.P. 399.
9. Curzon to Hamilton, 31 July, 1902; Balfour to Curzon, 31 July, 1902; Curzon to Balfour, 2 Aug., 1902.
10. Hamilton to Curzon, 31 July, 1902; Godley to Curzon, 1 Aug., 1902.
11. Hamilton's memorandum of 4 Aug., 1902, H.P. 60; see also drafts in H.P. 53.
12. Hamilton to Curzon, 7 Aug., 1902; Godley to Hamilton, 7 Aug., 1902, H.P. 53.
13. Hamilton to Curzon, 20 Aug., 1902.
14. Hamilton to Godley, 12 and 24 Aug., 1902, G.P. 6B; King Edward VII to Curzon, 2 Sept., 1902.
15. Godley to Curzon, 10 Sept., 1902.
16. Curzon's speech in the Legislative Council, 5 Sept., 1902; Curzon's minute, 11 May, 1902, C.P. 240.
17. Hamilton to Godley, 4 April, 1901, G.P. 6B.
18. Curzon to Hamilton, 16 Dec., 1901.
19. Hamilton to Curzon, 9 Jan., 1902; Curzon to Hamilton, 30 Jan., 1902.
20. Curzon to Godley, 27 Aug., 1902; Curzon to Hamilton, 3 Sept., 1902; Curzon to King Edward VII, 10 Sept., 1902.
21. Hamilton to Curzon, 24 Sept., 1902.
22. Curzon to Hamilton, 15 and 22 Oct., 1902.
23. Hamilton to Curzon, 6 Nov., 1902; Godley to Curzon, 12 Dec., 1902.
24. Curzon to Hamilton, 12 Nov., 1902; Hamilton to Curzon 13 Nov., 1902.
25. Curzon to Knollys, 15 and 17 Nov., 1902.
26. Hamilton to Curzon, 17 Nov., 1902.
27. Curzon to Hamilton, 17 Nov., 1902.
28. Memorandum by Brodrick, 18 Nov., 1902, Cab. 37/63/168
29. Brodrick to Curzon, 19 Nov., 1902, C.P. 172.
30. Hamilton to Knollys, 19 Nov., 1902, R.A. W1/47.
31. Hamilton to Curzon, 20 Nov., 1902.
32. Curzon to Balfour, 20 and 21 Nov., 1902.
33. Lawrence's diary, 19 and 20 Nov., 1902; cf. Lawrence to Curzon, 1 Aug., 1902, file C/32/3, C.P.2.
34. Balfour's draft and covering note, 20 Nov., 1902, H.P. 60.
35. Curzon to Hamilton, 23 Nov., 1902.
36. Lawrence's diary, 23 Nov., 1902.
37. Hamilton to Curzon, 26 Nov., 1902; Curzon to King Edward VII, 11 Dec., 1902.
38. Brodrick to Curzon, 21 Nov., 1902.
39. Curzon to Hamilton, 18 Dec., 1902; Knollys to Curzon, 19 Dec., 1902.
40. Balfour to Curzon, 12 Dec., 1902.
41. Curzon to Balfour, 29 Dec., 1902.
42. Curzon to Hamilton, 28 Dec., 1902.
43. Curzon to Lady Lawrence, 1 Jan., 1903, Lawrence Papers.
44. Sir T. Raleigh, op. cit., Vol. II, pp. 17-9.
45. Curzon to King Edward VII, 8 Jan., 1903; Selborne to Curzon, 4 Jan., 1903.
46. Lawrence's diary, 9 Nov., 1902; Sir B. Fuller, *Some Personal Experiences*, pp. 96-7.
47. Curzon to Hamilton, 8 Jan., 1903.

48. Sir G. de S. Barrow, *The Fire of Life*, p. 88; Curzon to the Duke of Connaught, 2 Feb., 1903; Sir B. Blood, *Four Score Years and Ten*, p. 347.
49. Marquess Curzon, *Leaves from a Viceroy's Notebook*, pp. 32–6.
50. Curzon to King Edward VII, 8 Jan., 1903.
51. Hamilton to Ampthill, 19 Dec., 1902, A.P. 5; Hamilton to King Edward VII, 3 Jan., 1903, RA W1/85.
52. Lord Crewe to Knollys, 8 Jan., 1903, RA W1/85.
53. Lady V. Hicks Beach, *Life of Sir Michael Hicks Beach*, vol. II, p. 184.
54. Hamilton to King Edward VII, 29 Jan., 1903, RA W2/1; Curzon to Hamilton, 13 Jan., 1903; McDonnell to Curzon, 29 April, 1903; Asquith to Curzon, 11 May, 1903.
55. Balfour to Lady Elcho, 13 Feb., 1903; on the Durbar see Consuelo Vanderbilt Balsan, *The Glitter and the Gold*, pp. 137–41.
56. G. Seaver, *Francis Younghusband*, pp. 198–9; Sir W. Lawrence, op. cit., p. 185.
57. Curzon to Hamilton, 8 Jan., 1903.
58. Hamilton to Ampthill, 7 Jan. and 5 Feb., 1903; Ampthill to Hamilton, 15 Jan., 1903, A.P. 6; Curzon to the Duke of Connaught, 5 March, 1903, RA Add A15/6440.
59. Curzon to Brodrick, 26 Feb., 1903.
60. Brodrick to Curzon, 15 March, 1903.
61. Curzon to Brodrick, 9 April, 1903; Brodrick to Curzon, 19 Aug., 1903.
62. Hamilton to Curzon, 19 Dec., 1902.

Index